THE WAR AGAINST LAW

In the UK, lawyers of the 'Judicial Power Project' – a group largely based at elite universities with close ties to far-right figures in the US and Europe – rail against 'judicial overreach'. In this groundbreaking book, David Dyzenhaus investigates the ideology of this group, contending that their true aim is to establish rule by an illiberal executive under the guise of benefitting the 'common good'. Dyzenhaus makes a powerful argument that this is a fundamentally illiberal ideology with roots in authoritarian thought from the 1930s, one which threatens to take a wrecking ball to the rule of law and democracy. *The War against Law* offers a fascinating examination of these lawyers' ideas against the backdrop of the 2024 Rwanda Act, which required rendering asylum seekers in the UK to Rwanda. The debates both before and after the Act make concrete profound questions about the nature of the rule of law and its role in a liberal democracy.

DAVID DYZENHAUS is University Professor of Law and Philosophy at the University of Toronto, Canada. He is the author of *Legality and Legitimacy: Carl Schmitt, Hans Kelsen, and Hermann Heller in Weimar* (1999), *The Constitution of Law: Legality in a Time of Emergency* (2006), and *The Long Arc of Legality: Hobbes, Kelsen, Hart* (2022).

THE WAR AGAINST LAW

What's Wrong with Common Good Constitutionalism

DAVID DYZENHAUS

University of Toronto

CAMBRIDGE
UNIVERSITY PRESS

CAMBRIDGE
UNIVERSITY PRESS

Shaftesbury Road, Cambridge CB2 8EA, United Kingdom

One Liberty Plaza, 20th Floor, New York, NY 10006, USA

477 Williamstown Road, Port Melbourne, VIC 3207, Australia

314–321, 3rd Floor, Plot 3, Splendor Forum, Jasola District Centre, New Delhi – 110025, India

Cambridge University Press is part of Cambridge University Press & Assessment, a department of the University of Cambridge.

We share the University's mission to contribute to society through the pursuit of education, learning and research at the highest international levels of excellence.

www.cambridge.org
Information on this title: www.cambridge.org/9781009864473

DOI: 10.1017/9781009864497

When citing this work, please include a reference to the DOI 10.1017/9781009864497

First published 2026

A catalogue record for this publication is available from the British Library

A Cataloging-in-Publication data record for this book is available from the Library of Congress

ISBN 978-1-009-86447-3 Hardback

For Alex and Ruby Misak on their ninetieth birthday:
In hope of the better world you did your part to build

CONTENTS

PREFACE

I wrote the first draft of this book during a year's research leave in Berlin in 2024/25. In early October 2024, I began work on the text of a public lecture I had agreed to give in early January 2025 on international law. I am not a specialist in international law, but I had an inkling that the debate in the UK about the Rwanda Act, a statute enacted by the UK Parliament earlier that year, would provide a good basis for a lecture on the relationship between international law and topics on which I do work, mainly the rule of law and its role in constitutional order. For the statute required that asylum seekers who arrived in the UK be summarily rendered to Rwanda and it stripped these seekers of the rights they would otherwise have under both UK and international law in order to make their forced 'relocation' unreviewable by judges.

I knew that a group of politically influential right-wing lawyers, led by Oxford law professors, had been instrumental in legitimizing the enactment of this cruel measure and that this episode was but part of their long campaign to undermine international law, the rule of law and constitutional government, all the while arguing that they were in the business of rescuing the constitutional order from its capture by 'liberal elites', mainly the judiciary and practising human rights lawyers. I also knew that these lawyers had close ties to like-minded sorts in the US and I had published some short essays about these ties and their theoretical inspiration in the work of German political and legal theorists from the 1930s who had sought to legitimize the rise of authoritarianism in prewar Europe.

I found that the Rwanda episode did provide the material for a rich case study of these phenomena, one that could help to expose these lawyers' arguments as not only bad in law, but also as leading to the establishment of an illiberal and undemocratic political order. But I soon realized that preparing a short text for the lecture would not suffice. I had to put in place a substantial draft of a book in order to begin to make my case.

That case is built on the work of the lawyers whose names will recur throughout, but the book is not so much about them as about the singularly powerful idea that drives their work, the idea of 'common good constitutionalism'. It is powerful because it would of course be foolish to oppose the idea that the rule of law, constitutional order, democracy and so on are worth having only if they aim at and achieve the common good of all. But it turns out that the common good in common good constitutionalism is the reactionary and illiberal ideology of an elite of lawyers and their allies, whose efforts will clear the way for the power of the state to be used to enforce that ideology. The law is at best an instrument to be used by the state as one tool of enforcing that ideology, and the way that it is used in fact gives the state a mode of operation that permits those at the highest reaches of government to rule by fiat, unchecked by the judiciary and the legislature. One gets, in short, executive rule.

The result in the world these lawyers will create is the appearance but not the substance of the rule of law, democracy and constitutionalism. Those subject to state power have rights only in virtue of the content of the common good as promulgated by their rulers, which means that you must be deemed fit for participation in the life of virtue stipulated by the elite in power if you are to enjoy the rights derived from the common good. Put differently, the common good here is achieved only when the pluralism associated with liberal democracies is eradicated. This ideology is naturally convenient to power-hungry politicians. They can harness the arguments of these lawyers and their allies in the academy to get to the position of power they need to be able to promulgate their own version of the common good, usually a crude nativism or nationalism that they think will have populist appeal and which has in common with this elite of lawyers a deep hostility to liberalism.

One of the reviewers for Cambridge University Press suggested that my title should be *Illiberal Constitutionalism: The War Against Law* rather than my *The War Against Law: What's Wrong with Common Good Constitutionalism* since the book's main theme is illiberal constitutionalism. I rejected this suggestion though it is most helpful. It prompted me to see that it is a mistake to dignify this idea of the common good with the thought that it is a kind of constitutionalism since its result will be the hollowing out of constitutional order and the reign of illiberal authoritarianism. Put differently, what's wrong with it is not only that it is illiberal, but also that it is unconstitutional.

Working on the book at a time when the world is becoming both more illiberal and more authoritarian has thus meant riding a roller coaster, with peaks of hope and dips of despair. In October 2024, the month I began work, a Labour government had been in power in the UK for three months, which meant that a period of renewal of respect for the rule of law and international law could begin after the raids on both by past Conservative governments, with the Rwanda Act one of the low points of disrespect. And one could still hope that Trump would not become President. However, under the hapless leadership of Keir Starmer, a former human rights lawyer, Labour has lurched ever rightwards in a vain bid to counter the threat of the Reform Party, led by the Trump acolyte Nigel Farage. Since Farage is both growing in popularity and becoming increasingly unabashed in his desire to recreate the galloping authoritarianism we have witnessed in the US since January 2025, there have been more dips than peaks along the way. By the time this book is published, it would not be all that surprising if Labour has moved so far to the right as to put Starmer's commitment to the rule of law in severe doubt. Indeed, he is likely to have become politically irrelevant, so precarious is his hold on his position.

Still I hope. I learned during my education in law and politics in apartheid South Africa that as long as governments pay lip service to the ideals of the rule of law and constitutional government, there will be resources to resist creeping or even galloping authoritarianism. A book-length exposure of the true nature of the arguments that will result in authoritarian rule is one small way of contributing to an appreciation of these resources. It also provides a rare opportunity to explore very concretely the rather elusive idea of the rule of law and its place in constitutional order.

I want to thank the Alexander von Humboldt Foundation for the award that made it possible for me to take my leave. Helmut Aust, Professor of International Law at the Freie Universität, Berlin, generously agreed to nominate me for the award and then to act as my academic host during my stay. Moreover, without his invitation to give the Thomas Franck Lecture, which commemorates the contribution of an eminent Berlin-born international lawyer, this book would not have been conceived. Helmut has been a constant source of help and advice throughout this process and I could not have asked for a better academic home than that provided by his colleagues and students at the Freie Universität, Berlin.

Another Berlin institution played a large role in preparing this draft. My wife Cheryl Misak was a fellow of the Wissenschaftskolleg zu Berlin during this period. As the spouse of a fellow, I enjoyed all of the privileges of the fellows and none of the duties. That afforded me the luxury of time to research and write in that most congenial context and the help of the altogether amazing library.

I presented parts of my work in progress at several institutions and I thank my hosts for the invitations and the audiences for very helpful discussions: Michał Krotoszyński and Marek Smolak, Faculty of Law, Adam Mickiewicz University, Poznań; Monica Garcia-Salmones Rovira, Faculty of Law, Maastricht University; Helmut Aust, Thomas Frank Lecture, Freie Universität, Berlin; Alexander Somek (Law) and Fabio Wolkenstein (Politics), Political Theory Seminar, University of Vienna; Amalia Amaya Navarro, Keynote Lecture, University of Edinburgh, Legal Theory Festival; the International Law Colloquium run by Helmut Aust and Heike Krieger at the Freie Universität, Berlin; a roundtable at Matrix Chambers, London; the workshop 'International Law and the Politics of Space', organized by Helmut Aust and myself at the Freie Universität, Berlin; finally, Pierluigi Chiassoni and Giovanni Battista Ratti, panel at the Faculty of Law, University of Genoa.

I want to give a special mention to one member of these audiences. In June 2025, I based my keynote lecture at the Edinburgh Legal Theory Festival on Chapter 6 of this book. The first hand up in the period devoted to discussion was Law Professor Conor Gearty's. Characteristically, he did not ask a question. Rather, he delivered an oration, at once humorous and hard-hitting, about the iniquities of the common good lawyers, mostly on the basis of what he regarded as their instrumentalization of a highly distorted version of Catholicism, a topic on which he as a knowledgeable Catholic could speak with authority. So incensed was he by the fact that these 'white men' were using their faith in the cause of imposing a reactionary ideology that he suggested that I should give the book the title 'These Bad Men'. Conor died later that year, a tragic loss for his family, his colleagues at the London School of Economics, but also for public debate in the UK on the themes of my book. I wish to record here both my own sense of loss at the death of this remarkable man and how much it meant to me that in his oration Conor spoke in his inimitable way of the importance he attached to my project.

As always, I am delighted to thank my home institution, the University of Toronto, and in particular the heads of my home units, Jutta Brunnée, Law, and Martin Pickavé, Philosophy, for continuing its tradition of facilitating the research of its scholars. I must also express my gratitude to the Social Sciences and Humanities Research Council of Canada for the research funding that accompanied the award to me in 2023 of its Gold Medal. This funding helped to make possible several of the events listed above, including the workshop 'International Law and the Politics of Space', as well as the services of two excellent research assistants, Anja Bossow and Megan Pfiffer, who helped me with both research and extensive comments on drafts. I also thank Cambridge University Press for agreeing to publish this book and in particular my editor Natasha Burton for her considerable help.

Several people generously devoted time to reading and giving me comments on all or parts of the manuscript and, while of course the responsibility remains entirely mine, they helped me to make many improvements: the two anonymous reviewers of the manuscript, Manula Adhihetty, Helmut Aust, Rueban Balasubramaniam, Geneviève Cartier, Raza Husain, Madhav Khosla, Coel Kirkby, Melissa Lane, Cheryl Misak, Jan-Werner Müller, Martha Shaffer, Wayne Sumner, Rayner Thwaites, Lars Vinx, Mark Walters and Ben Zolf.

Finally, my book owes most to my friend Murray Hunt, with whom I've been discussing the themes canvassed in it for more than thirty years.

Introduction

When President Trump calls for a federal judge to be impeached for issuing an order staying the deportation of some migrants, many are shocked and diagnose either a constitutional crisis happening in real time or at best on the horizon.[1] But such calls echo elsewhere, notably in 'Enemies of the People', an infamous *Daily Mail* headline about judges during the Brexit saga[2] and Oxford Law Professor Richard Ekins's call for judges who had interpreted a provision in a UK statute in a way he disapproved to be disciplined.[3] In issuing the call, Trump is supported by the work of legal scholars who have been arguing for the idea of the 'unitary executive', in effect that the President as the head of the government of the day is the 'guardian of the constitution' in that he gets to determine the limits of his own legitimate authority.

This idea has its roots in debates in late Weimar, in which the legal and political theorist Carl Schmitt argued that the President is the guardian so that the courts should bend to his will. Schmitt's political and legal theory has been adopted wholesale by Harvard Law Professor Adrian Vermeule, whose Tweet on this topic was reposted by Vice President J. D. Vance.[4] Vermeule is also a leading exponent of 'integralism', a highly controversial interpretation of Catholicism, vehemently opposed

[1] Chris Megerian, Lindsay Whitehurst, and Mark Sherman, 'Roberts Rejects Trump's Call for Impeaching Judge Who Ruled Against His Deportation Plans' (Mar 19 2025) online: *AP News* <https://apnews.com/article/donald-trump-federal-judges-impeachment-29da1153a9f82106748098a6606fec39>.

[2] Claire Phipps, 'British Newspapers React to Judges' Brexit Ruling: "Enemies of the People"' (Nov 4 2016) online: *The Guardian* <www.theguardian.com/politics/2016/nov/04/enemies-of-the-people-british-newspapers-react-judges-brexit-ruling>.

[3] Richard Ekins, 'Do Our Supreme Court Judges Have Too Much Power?' (May 14 2019) online: *The Spectator* <www.spectator.co.uk/article/do-our-supreme-court-judges-have-too-much-power->.

[4] Charlie Savage and Minho Kim, 'Vance Says "Judges Aren't Allowed to Control" Trump's "Legitimate Power"' (Feb 9 2025) online: *New York Times* <www.nytimes.com/2025/02/09/us/politics/vance-trump-federal-courts-executive-order.html>.

to liberalism, which requires the state to enforce religious doctrines on its citizens, and Vance has publicly embraced the same ideology. Vermeule combines this political ideology with a legal theory he calls 'common good constitutionalism'.[5]

A similar set of ideas has played an outsize role in the UK ever since the 'Judicial Power Project' was founded in 2015. Headed by professor Richard Ekins, the richly though secretly funded project has successfully sought to influence UK politics by using legal arguments to advance the political agenda of retired Oxford Law Professor John Finnis, one of the founders of 'new natural law theory', which amounts to integralism in all but name. Ekins and others in the UK have an alliance with Vermeule in another project, the 'Common Good Project', which seeks ominously to put in place a 'ruler' who will 'promulgate the common good'. There is one final commonality. The major political influence on Finnis is Eric Voegelin, another German authoritarian thinker from the Weimar period, who adopted Schmitt's legal theory in the 1930s, and, after emigrating to the US in 1938, became perhaps the most important intellectual inspiration for the right-wing ideology now ascendant there.

In this book, I focus on the UK to make a more general point about common good constitutionalism. As that label suggests, its theory of constitutional order is instrumental to achieving what it takes to be the common good. And, as the combination of integralism with common good constitutionalism suggests, the common good at which it aims is to be filled out by a highly controversial religious conception of the good which the state will impose on a political community. My focus on the UK manifestation of these ideas shows concretely how the political agenda of the Common Good Project drives the legal arguments of the Judicial Power Project with the help of powerful political allies, for example, Lord Wolfson, the Conservative Party's shadow Attorney General – a post in the cabinet of the official opposition party. I do this through an analysis of the heated debates about the rule of law and sovereignty which started in 2015 with the founding of the Judicial Power Project.

'The rule of law' is traditionally contrasted with 'the rule of men' to indicate that the first affords us the conditions of stable interaction with each other and with the state, while the second subjects us to the arbitrary

[5] Adrian Vermeule, *Common Good Constitutionalism* (Cambridge: Polity, 2022).

choices of individuals. But even under the rule of law, it is still flesh-and-blood people ruling us, just doing things differently from the way things are done under the rule of men. And the idea that a state to be such must be fully sovereign also somewhat obscures the fact that when the state acts, it is people making decisions, not some abstract entity. In naming one kind of rule 'the rule of law' and the acts of some group of people the 'acts of a sovereign state', or the laws of a 'sovereign parliament', we are shaping our world, often in controversial ways.

Ideas like the rule of law are fundamental, then, because the very shape of our political orders depends on which version of them we adopt. And of course there is controversy about which version is correct. If anything, sovereignty is more controversial than the rule of law, so much so that Hans Kelsen, the great Austrian philosopher of law, advised at the end of his 1920 book on the topic that the 'concept should be radically repressed', both because he thought that there is no theoretical need to rely on it and because it is politically pernicious, tied as it often is to nasty assertions of nationalism.[6] And in an influential paper in 2003, 'Sovereignty's Blight', UK human rights lawyer Murray Hunt argued that 'English lawyers' weakness for the alluring idea of "sovereignty" as a foundational concept' continued to 'blight contemporary public law and to prevent its evolution into a mature system regulating the exercise of power in a modern polity'.[7] In an important sense, both Kelsen and Hunt are right. A pernicious and nationalistic conception of sovereignty played an enormous role in the political debates around Brexit, as it continues to do in politics in the UK and elsewhere in the world. However, one can't get rid of the word, not least because it is such an essential tool in the kit of the political right, but also because there are good reasons to retain sovereignty as a foundational concept together with the rule of law.

The book's title is adapted from that of a paper published in 1988 in a South African law journal by two human rights lawyers analysing several decisions of the apex court of apartheid South Africa. They wrote it at a time when the apartheid government was using one declaration of a state of emergency after another, in a bid savagely to repress the growing internal opposition to apartheid that would ultimately bring that regime

[6] Hans Kelsen, *Das Problem der Souveränität und die Theorie des Völkerrechts: Beitrag zu Einer Reinen Rechtslehre* (Aalen: Scientia Verlag, 1981) at 320 (My translation).

[7] Murray Hunt, 'Sovereignty's Blight: Why Contemporary Public Law Needs the Concept of "Due Deference"' in Nicholas Bamforth and Peter Leyland, eds, *Public Law in a Multi-Layered Constitution* (Oxford: Hart Publishing, 2003) 337 at 339.

to an end. They charged the court with having 'reshaped our jurisprudence so as to grant the greatest possible latitude to the executive to act outside conventional legal controls'.[8] Their complaint was about judicial supineness in the interpretation by a majority of South Africa's highest court of a provision in a Public Safety Act which gave to the head of state extensive power to make regulations to deal with a perceived state of emergency.

The provision amounted to what gets called in South Africa and the UK an 'ouster clause' because if read literally it ousts judicial review of anything the executive does in the purported exercise of its powers. The executive is the branch of government that 'executes' or enforces the law. It can be used to refer to the people at the very top of government, for example Trump, but also to his cabinet, the senior officials directly answerable to them, and then all the way down to masked ICE agents picking people off the streets of US cities.

I will make these abstract issues entirely concrete in the UK context by focusing on a statute that removed the judges' authority to review the executive's implementation of a statute on the basis of the UK's legal commitments to international human rights law, commitments that had been firmly embedded in domestic law by Parliament in legislation. As I will show, this war against international law turned necessarily into a total one, not only against public or constitutional law in general, but even against the rule of law itself. And in metastasizing in this way, the war turned into one that can be fairly described as a war against law itself since it sought to change a political order in which government is by law into one where government is by unlimited executive power.

The statute in question is the Rwanda Act of 2024, a cruel law that required that asylum seekers who arrive in the UK be rendered to Rwanda, a country ruled by a regime notorious for its violations of human rights, to have their claims for refugee status processed. In order to be sent there, the statute enacted what I will call the

[8] Nicholas Haysom and Clive Plaskett, 'The War Against Law: Judicial Activism and the Appellate Division' (1988) 4 *South African Journal on Human Rights* 303. The section in the statute in question read that 'No interdict or other process shall issue for the staying or setting aside of any proclamation issued by the State President [under the Act] . . . and no court shall be competent to inquire into or give judgment on the validity of any such proclamation, notice or regulation'. And in reading the clause literally as precluding any judicial review of measures such as detaining people indefinitely, the judges gave the executive from top to bottom a free hand to do as it pleased in eliminating political opposition.

'deportation rule', a rule that required officials to deport asylum seekers without regard to the legally embedded human rights protections that would ordinarily apply, deemed Rwanda to be a 'safe' country for refugees in the face of a Supreme Court decision a year before which had found Rwanda to be 'unsafe', and ousted almost altogether the authority of judges to review the implementation of the statute.

The election of the Labour government later that year meant that the Act would not be implemented and it was repealed in early 2025. But a detailed analysis of this episode, in particular the debates that preceded it and which continue as I write more than a year later, can help us to understand one of the most important issues of our time – the role of judges in upholding the rule of law in a democratic political order. I can show in a very concrete fashion the stakes in claims that are commonly made about the rule of law, sovereignty and the role of judges in constitutional government. I thus hope to be able to explain this complex constellation of ideas to readers in a general audience who are interested in the relationship between law and politics, but have little acquaintance with the details of public law or knowledge of political and legal theory.

The book makes no pretence at presenting its themes from some 'neutral' perspective. Rather, I argue that no such perspective is available in this context and that the perspective of the group of the 'common good lawyers', as I will call Finnis, Ekins and their allies, is not only opposed to liberalism, but also to the rule of law. It is even opposed to democracy itself in that democratic government requires the rule of law. But while my focus is on the UK, we will see that a full analysis of these lawyers' arguments requires attention to important trends in political practice in Europe and the US as well as to profound issues in political and legal theory that bear on these trends. In addition, as I suggested, it requires attention to what I will show to be the political inspiration for these trends in the thought of major figures in the European turn to fascist rule in the 1920 and 1930s. My book is thus a case study of one country's part in the drift to authoritarian rule in Western democracies, a drift now accelerated with Donald Trump's return to the presidency of the US. It explains how it is possible to subvert the rule of law while claiming to serve its ideal.

Indeed, there may be no better way of understanding that ideal than through an account of its subversion from within. It is of course not unique to the UK, nor is it without historical precedent, especially in the rise of fascism in Europe in the 1930s. Then, as now, this war against law is claimed to be in the service not only of the rule of law, but also of the 'common good' of the political community. And in fighting under the banner of the common good, these Oxford lawyers forge a transatlantic alliance with similar sorts in the US and Europe. In short, my seemingly narrow focus illuminates deeply troubling geopolitical trends.

My book is not, however, a geopolitical account of these trends. Rather, it is an account of the interplay between law and politics, involving journeys into the legal landscape of the UK and into legal and political theory. The journeys are necessary because one cannot get a full grip on the concrete issues such as the Rwanda saga without a sense of the vitally important political principles that are at stake: the very survival of the rule of law and constitutional government. It is a journey for me as well as for my readers. When I began this project, I had a sense that my focus on the legal and political dimensions of this one episode in the UK would allow me to work through ideas with which I have been grappling during a long career as a scholar of the rule of law under stress. I hope to have at last succeeded.

As I enter into this controversy with a view to teasing out its most important legal and political implications, my book is at times hard-hitting. I will try to show why this is justified through a forensic analysis of the actual words used by the common good lawyers as well as the 'common advocates', as I will refer to the group which includes both these lawyers and those who are not lawyers but share their ideology. And I should make clear now the perspective from which my critique is launched.

In 2002, Suella Braverman, at that time Home Secretary in Boris Johnson's Conservative cabinet, described liberals concerned with human rights as '*Guardian*-reading, tofu-eating wokerati'.[9] While I reject the label 'woke' because it usually tells one nothing about the target of the abuse, but a lot about the kneejerk and obtuse mindset of the person who adopts it, and while I am no fan of tofu, I am sure that Braverman and others would suppose that I am part of this group. I am an avid *Guardian* reader because I share its liberal values – the commitment to the right of individuals to decide on how best to live their lives and to the view that the political order that best sustains and nurtures that right is a democracy firmly committed to government in accordance with the rule of law, a commitment which includes one to the rule of human rights and of international law. I also firmly believe that such

[9] Zoe Tidman, 'Home Secretary Suella Braverman Blames Protest Disruption on "Tofu-Eating Wokerati"' (Oct 19 2022) online: *Independent* <www.independent.co.uk/news/uk/politics/suella-braverman-just-stop-oil-tofu-b2205903.html>.

commitments are essential to a society which wants to be *awake* to injustices that might otherwise go unaddressed.

The journey I undertake here is not into completely uncharted territory. I was born and brought up in apartheid South Africa, where I completed degrees in political theory and law. I had no desire to practise law, as by the time I graduated I had become fascinated by the fact that while law can be used, as it was in apartheid South Africa, as an instrument of oppression and discrimination, it also provides a resource for resistance. That fascination took me to Oxford to work out through a doctoral thesis why and how it is that law provides this resource, the resource of the rule of law. My attempts to understand this phenomenon have involved explorations of the rule of law during the apartheid era,[10] in Germany's first experiment with democracy in the Weimar Republic and then in the destruction that followed Hitler's seizure of power in 1933,[11] in the surge of anti-terrorism measures that followed 9/11 in the US,[12] in the situation of fugitive slaves in the pre-Civil War US who had fled from the south to the north in an often vain bid to escape enslavement, and in Israel's Occupied Territories.[13] In the course of forty years of researching law's ambiguous role as both weapon and shield, I have often found that those who most share my sense of the rule of law's importance to sustaining a decent society have also grown up under some more or less authoritarian regime. That suggests that learning about the rule of law in political situations in which it is under severe stress may provide insights into its true nature.

It gives me no joy when such insights become relevant to the drift towards authoritarianism in the established liberal democracies of the West. Rather, it concerns me greatly to see lawyers at some of the great universities of the world not only enabling that drift, but also using their titles and the lustre of their university to legitimize it, all supposedly in

[10] David Dyzenhaus, *Hard Cases in Wicked Legal Systems: South African Law in the Perspective of Legal Philosophy* (Oxford: Clarendon Press, 1991); 2nd edition as *Hard Cases in Wicked Legal Systems: Pathologies of Legality* (Oxford: Oxford University Press, 2010); David Dyzenhaus, *Judging the Judges, Judging Ourselves: Truth, Reconciliation and the Apartheid Legal Order* (Oxford: Hart Publishing, 1998).

[11] David Dyzenhaus, *Legality and Legitimacy: Carl Schmitt, Hans Kelsen, and Hermann Heller in Weimar* (Oxford: Clarendon Press, 1997).

[12] David Dyzenhaus, *The Constitution of Law: Legality in a Time of Emergency* (Cambridge: Cambridge University Press, 2006).

[13] David Dyzenhaus, *The Long Arc of Legality: Hobbes, Kelsen, Hart* (Cambridge: Cambridge University Press, 2022).

the name of some vague idea of the 'common good'. This sense of deep concern is explicit in the book, as it was when I first began writing about this phenomenon during the pandemic in online journals, in particular *Aeon*,[14] and on blogs devoted to discussions of constitutionalism and the rule of law, such as the German site, *Verfassungsblog*.[15]

Responses on Twitter to these short essays have accused me of engaging in guilt by association, personal or *ad hominem* attacks, playing the man not the ball. But the charge of guilt by association is merited only when one tars someone with the same political or ideological brush of another merely because there is some personal tie between them. In contrast, whatever the personal relationships between the figures I criticize in this book, they are bound together by two things.

The first is their open adherence to the common tenets of an ideology that, whatever their own intentions, opens the door to authoritarianism. The second is their participation in joint projects that will result in hollowing out the preconditions for liberal democratic government, indeed, for democracy itself. As for personal attacks, the positions I criticize in these pages are of course positions articulated by particular individuals. An analysis of a war waged with words must focus on the words used by the principal actors, and criticizing the words of particular people does not on its own turn the critique into a personal attack. Rather, my aim is to engage and respond directly to the ideas they very clearly espouse.

Nor, I should mention, do I make any charge of conspiracy in this book. The association between the common good lawyers and their allies in politics and the media is in plain sight and my aim is only to make explicit the implications of their publicly held positions. I will frequently accuse them of making misleading or inaccurate claims. But in each case I will supply the evidence that backs the accusation.

I also want to mention that the fact that several of them are Catholics, and that I will severely criticize their views, is an attack neither on the Roman Catholic religion nor on religiosity in general. It is not even a

[14] David Dyzenhaus, 'Lawyer for the Strongman' (Jun 12 2020) online: *Aeon* <https://aeon.co/essays/carl-schmitts-legal-theory-legitimises-the-rule-of-the-strongman>; David Dyzenhaus, 'Democracy or Apocalypse' (Sep 20 2022) online: *Aeon* <https://aeon.co/essays/eric-voegelin-hans-kelsen-and-the-debate-over-nazism>.

[15] David Dyzenhaus, 'Schmitten in the USA' (Apr 20 2022) online: *Verfassungsblog* <https://verfassungsblog.de/schmitten-in-the-usa/>; David Dyzenhaus, 'The Snake Charmers' (Mar 7 2022) online: *Verfassungsblog* <https://verfassungsblog.de/os5-snake-charmers/>.

critique of theorizing based on faith-based values, only on their weaponization to attack the structure of liberal democracy in the guise of legal secular argument. Their views are deeply controversial within their own faith. But I will make no effort to enter into a contest about what the right interpretation of Catholicism is or how best to interpret important theological sources, most notably the work of Thomas Aquinas, an important figure in the Catholic natural law tradition.

Rather, I will focus on what the common good lawyers share in common with other enemies of liberal democracy: that their arguments will bring about what one of their number has called 'regime change'[16] – the replacement of liberal democracy with a form of authoritarianism in which a 'ruler' will dictate the common good of a political community composed of those whom the ruler deems authentic members. Thus, some base their ideological commitments on faiths other than Catholicism, notably Evangelical Christianity or Judaism, or put them on an entirely secular basis. In fact, despite these differences, theological and otherwise, it is easy for their alliances to form because of an important feature of the 'common good' as a political slogan. In and of itself, the idea of the common good is neutral on the question of content, so that a question presses here and elsewhere in this book: Who could be against the common good?

But, as we will see, answers about the content of the political vision of the common good lawyers are hard to come by. They are at best vague about it and for the most part define it negatively, against what one can broadly describe as liberalism. In past work on German legal and political thought of the 1920s and 1930s, I described Schmitt, the authoritarian theorist mentioned earlier, and hugely influential today, as a 'negatively prescriptive theorist'.[17] This label is cumbersome but I hope useful in that it conveys that Schmitt's ideology is for the most part an 'anything-but' one, in his case anything-but-liberalism.

Schmitt, as we will later learn in more detail, was a lawyer who enabled the Nazi rise to power, even though he was initially allied with a different political faction. Composed of aristocrats and military generals, this faction sought to destroy Germany's first experiment with parliamentary

[16] Patrick Deneen, *Regime Change: Towards a Postliberal Future* (New York: Sentinel, 2023).

[17] David Dyzenhaus, 'The Politics of the Question of Constituent Power' in Martin Loughlin and Neil Walker, eds, *The Paradox of Constitutionalism: Constituent Power and Constitutional Form* (Oxford: Oxford University Press, 2007) 129 at 130–34.

democracy in the Weimar Republic, and with it any political opposition, whether from Nazis, social democrats or liberals. But once the Nazis had won power, eradicated all political opposition, and set about establishing the 'substantive homogeneity' of the people – *Das Volk* – they fulfilled all the criteria for a legitimate regime on Schmitt's theory of political legitimacy. So while Schmitt had his own craven motives for ingratiating himself with the new regime, given the Nazis' success by his own criteria, he also had no principled basis for distinguishing himself from them.

Schmitt's example shows that to adopt a negatively prescriptive theory of anything-but-liberalism may force one to accept as legitimate whatever political force happens to fill the empty space of the common good. All such theorists have of course their own visions of how to fill that space, for example the vision of a state-imposed version of Catholicism that some among the common good lawyers espouse. But because they have to forge alliances with others who belong to different faiths, as well with yet others who have a secular basis for their right-wing ideology, what unites them is anything-but-liberalism, so whatever will happen to fill the space does the trick.[18]

In this regard, I should emphasize that my use of the labels 'right' and 'right-wing' to describe the lawyers, politicians, political theorists and other scholars who populate the pages of this book does not refer to people who are properly described as 'conservative'. Only a few years ago one could accurately refer to people on the right of the political spectrum that way. But in the age of Trump, Victor Orbán, Suella Braverman, Kemi Badenoch, and Nigel Farage, 'right' these days means that you are at a point on the spectrum in a cluster that goes from right to 'far right' and 'extreme right'. Where each common good lawyer is positioned on this spectrum is hard to determine because, as I just said, for the most part they are vague about the content of their political agenda. But such vagueness combined with hostility to liberalism is precisely what makes them negatively prescriptive theorists.

This is an important lesson for liberals. Yet it is even more important for those attracted to the common good slogan because they are rightly concerned about the high degree of inequality that has come to characterize the liberal democratic societies of the West. However, I hope that my book might make those who are critical of this development more

[18] On the topic of how to form such alliances, and to position oneself to give advice to the ruler, see Adrian Vermeule, 'A Christian Strategy' (Nov 1 2017) online: *First Things* <https://firstthings.com/a-christian-strategy/>.

wary of the 'common good' as a political slogan because of its appropriation by the right.

I will suggest that it is not happenstance that negatively prescriptive theory is a label that characterizes both European authoritarian thinkers of the 1930s and contemporary common good lawyers. For the major political influence on common good ideology is not, as the common good lawyers like to claim, the 'classical legal tradition', thus reaching for the mantle of the great Roman lawyers and of Catholic theologians, notably Aquinas. Rather, as I have already suggested, although they often appeal to a theological source or to Roman law, the roots of their *political* thought come directly from either Schmitt or Voegelin. I draw attention to this important point only because we live unfortunately in dramatic times, no less dramatic than the last years of the Weimar Republic.

Indeed, so dramatic are our times that both Schmitt and Voegelin have moved into mainstream thought. There has long been an Eric Voegelin Society in the US, which is very influential on the intellectual thought of the American right,[19] and for the last few years a Carl Schmitt Society has flourished in Germany, with an annual lecture in his honour, the latest given by Martin Loughlin, one of the UK's most eminent legal scholars.[20] Both societies are cultish in the way they portray their heroes, and of course leave out the really damning features of their thought, with the Schmitt Society even offering a guide to a tour of sites one can visit which Schmitt once frequented – a kind of pilgrimage.

Accompanying the sense of concern I mentioned is a sense of despair. Many of the politicians involved in the political movements which I will argue that these lawyers enable proudly claim the legacy in Italy of Mussolini's Fascist Party, or in Germany even of Hitler's Nazi Party. Nonetheless, the lawyers in this group will naturally and indignantly proclaim their distance from such movements. I do *not* doubt their sincerity if they make such proclamations. I do, however, think that such proclamations are both naive and blind to history. It is that blindness that leads to my despair.

In addition, my claim is not that, for example, the UK or the US today are exactly like Weimar in 1932, where the political choice seemed largely between an authoritarian regime dominated by aristocrats and generals or the Nazis with Hitler at their head. We have only a limited sense right

[19] 'About Us', online: *Voegelin View* <https://voegelinview.com/about-us/>.

[20] 'Welcome to the Carl Schmitt Gesellschaft e.V.', online: *Carl-Schmitt Gesellschaft e.V.* <www.carl-schmitt.de/en/>.

now of what kinds of political order are emerging and how they will emerge. But we should not downplay the common good lawyers' embrace of ideas that have once before proven destructive of a liberal democratic system, whatever their intentions are now, and whatever the nature of the political orders that will emerge if their arguments succeed.[21] If there is one thing I urge readers to take away from this book, it is that we live in perilous times, so that the analogy with the last years of the Weimar Republic is no exaggeration. The stakes are as high as they were in Germany in 1932 and, with Trump as president of the US and authoritarian populists winning elections almost everywhere, we are headed in the wrong direction. 'Headed', however, does not mean that we will reach the worst destination. Accompanying both anger and despair, there is in my book a deep sense of hope, a hope that we can course-correct.

Chapter 1 sets out the background for the book as a whole in more detail. Chapter 2 sketches the legal landscape into which the Rwanda Act was inserted, both the general characteristics of the UK constitutional order and the important post-war changes that are the background necessary for understanding the debates around the Rwanda Act. From there, in Chapter 3, I will build out to show how the different dots connect to form a picture in which it becomes clear why a war against law of this kind will target the rule of law and international law in particular. Chapters 4 and 5 explore the relationship between the rule of law, constitutional government, international law and democracy. Chapter 6 focuses on the political thought of John Finnis in order to set out a full account of the political stakes in the debate between the common good lawyers and those who wish to preserve the rule of law and its role in the constitutional order of democracy.

[21] See, for example, Serge Guriev and Daniel Treisman, *Spin Doctors: The Changing Face of Tyranny in the 21st Century* (Princeton, NJ: Princeton University Press, 2022). The authors carefully analyse the differences between the political orders that are emerging in our world and the totalitarian and fascist regimes of the twentieth century, at the same time as warning that the orders will be both illiberal and undemocratic.

1

The New Constitutional Lobbyists

1.1 The Judicial Power Project

In 2016 the UK's *Daily Mail* screamed out a shocking front-page headline: 'Enemies of the People', under which appeared a photo of three judges.[1] What had these judges done? They had decided that it was for Parliament not the government to issue the formal trigger to begin the process of exiting the European Union. The story I will tell in this book is equally shocking. It is the story of how the rule of law is under attack from within, but not from 'the People' – the audience whose rage the headline was designed to stoke by feeding trends of populist discontent with the 'deep state', often focused on elites such as judges and lawyers. Nor is my focus the media or politicians, though both play an important role in the story. Rather, it is on the prominent academic lawyers who have achieved outsize influence on politics and who are providing the arguments necessary for such trends to be translated into political and legal policy and practice.

What I will describe is happening in many Western democracies which have a long-standing commitment to the rule of law. For example, in February 2025, Vice President J. D. Vance, a Yale-trained lawyer, warned US courts that they 'aren't allowed to control the executive's legitimate power', as they reacted to Trump's slew of executive orders. What did Vance mean? Earlier that day he had shared a post by Harvard Law Professor Adrian Vermeule who had argued that the head of the executive gets to determine the legitimate limits of his constitutional power.[2] In July of the same year, Vermeule argued in the pages of the

[1] Claire Phipps, 'British Newspapers React to Judges' Brexit Ruling: "Enemies of the People"' (Nov 4 2016) online: *The Guardian* <www.theguardian.com/politics/2016/nov/04/enemies-of-the-people-british-newspapers-react-judges-brexit-ruling>.

[2] Charlie Savage and Minho Kim, 'Vance Says "Judges Aren't Allowed to Control" Trump's "Legitimate Power"' (Feb 9 2025) online: *New York Times* <www.nytimes.com/2025/02/09/us/politics/vance-trump-federal-courts-executive-order.html>.

New York Times that it wasn't Trump defying the Supreme Court as he increasingly used executive orders to override and sidestep legal and constitutional requirements, and as his officials defied the court orders that sought to impede their loyal implementation of illegality. Rather, the defiance came from the courts that were trying to maintain the rule of law.[3]

This is a view Vance and Vermeule clearly share with Trump as just a month or so later he called for one of the judges to be impeached, writing, in a kind of echo of the *Daily Mail*:

> HE DIDN'T WIN ANYTHING! I WON FOR MANY REASONS, IN AN OVERWHELMING MANDATE, BUT FIGHTING ILLEGAL IMMIGRATION MAY HAVE BEEN THE NUMBER ONE REASON FOR THIS HISTORIC VICTORY. I'm just doing what the VOTERS wanted me to do. This judge, like many of the Crooked Judges I am forced to appear before, should be IMPEACHED!!![4]

Vermeule is one of the leading American figures in the 'integralist' movement, which is animated by an ideology that seeks to make the state an instrument of a very conservative understanding of Catholicism, one that purports to be based in its 'natural law tradition'. He has also embraced fully the political and legal theory of the German authoritarian lawyer Carl Schmitt. His claim that the executive gets to determine the limits of its own legitimate power is a clear echo of Schmitt's claim in the 1930s that the President of the Weimar Republic was the true 'guardian of the constitution'.[5] In a way, that is the story of this book in a nutshell: an account of how this at first sight puzzling combination of natural law, religion and an extreme-right political and legal theory is helping to drive current political trends.

In order fully to understand the story, we need an account of the history and context in which such episodes take place, a story that can

[3] Adrian Vermeule, 'Someone Is Defying the Supreme Court, but It Isn't Trump' (Jul 31 2025) online: *New York Times* <www.nytimes.com/2025/07/31/opinion/supreme-court-trump-judges-defiance.html>. Sadly, Vermeule is right in one sense. The Supreme Court seems determined to let Trump get away with illegal executive rule.

[4] Chris Megerian, Lindsay Whitehurst, and Mark Sherman, 'Roberts Rejects Trump's Call for Impeaching Judge Who Ruled Against His Deportation Plans' (Mar 19 2025) online: *AP News* <https://apnews.com/article/donald-trump-federal-judges-impeachment-29da1153a9f82106748098a6606fec39>.

[5] Carl Schmitt, 'The Guardian of the Constitution' [1931] in Lars Vinx, *The Guardian of the Constitution: Hans Kelsen and Carl Schmitt on the Limits of Constitutional Law* (Cambridge: Cambridge University Press, 2015) 79.

help us to grasp some of the most important aspects of the process set in motion by Trump's return to power, but which actually began long before, and which has already radically changed the political and constitutional orders of some countries and is gathering steam in others. In particular, the book as a whole is designed to make a crucial point. The arguments of the eminent academic lawyers that are necessary for populist trends to be translated into political and legal policy and practice fail as *legal* arguments in two respects. First, they too often proceed on the basis of inaccurate or misleading claims about the law. Second, and much more significant, the result, if they are not resisted, is the destruction of the rule of law and of constitutional government. It is because the arguments are presented by lawyers trained at and teaching in elite law schools that they have the potential to reach this result – to destroy the rule of law from within.

In making this case, I will set out carefully the claim of the lawyers who figure most prominently in these pages that their arguments are designed to do the opposite – to save the rule of law and democracy from capture by various elites, mainly judges and human rights lawyers, a claim supported by the fact that they reason with copious reference to legal sources. That claim both makes it harder to demonstrate the point and even more important that this be done. It is more important because the point is not only one about bad legal arguments. I could describe my aim as showing that the arguments are not properly legal, but heavily disguised political arguments. That is accurate, but only to an extent. It is accurate only *if* one considers the legitimate terrain of political debate in a democracy to be populated by the kind of argument that seeks to preserve the secular and pluralistic orders governed in accordance with the rule of law that are claimed as the hallmark of Western democracies. Arguments on this terrain are both political and openly committed to preserving democracy, the rule of law and constitutional government. In contrast, the right-wing lawyers on whom I focus use the language of the rule of law and constitutional government, and occasionally of democracy, but without the substance.[6] The result, whatever their expressed intentions, is to take a wrecking ball to that kind of democracy

[6] Serge Guriev and Daniel Treisman, *Spin Doctors: The Changing Face of Tyranny in the 21st Century* (Princeton, NJ: Princeton University Press, 2022). For a remarkable example of such 'spin doctoring', see Richard Ekins, 'Political Polarization and the Rule of Law' (2025) 19 *Law & Ethics of Human Rights* 201, though clearly he does not understand his claim to be the saviour of the rule of law as spin.

through committing the state to the promotion of an illiberal ideology, thus radically undermining or even eliminating the pluralism of values that we associate with life in a democracy.

It is not only, then, the rule of law that is at stake but also democracy as we know it. If such lawyers succeed, we will find ourselves at best in the kind of political order described by political scientists Steven Levitsky and Lucan Way as 'competitive authoritarianism', a 'hybrid regime' that differs from the fascist regimes of the mid twentieth century mainly in that it combines features of democratic and authoritarian rule. The leading example is Victor Orbán's Hungary in which, in their summary, his government 'packed the Constitutional Court, limited opposition media access both by politicizing state-run media and by coopting much of the private media, and gerrymandered electoral districts to lock in the ruling party's control of parliament'.[7]

The great advantage such hybrid regimes have over their mid-twentieth-century predecessors in European fascism is that they garner the legitimacy that travels with preserving the institutions of democracy and the rule of law, what we can think of as 'constitutional government', while hollowing out these institutions. That process allows the regimes to maintain a virtually iron grip on power despite periodic elections. It also gives them the tools to repress political opposition and to control ideology to the extent they deem necessary. In March 2025, Levitsky deemed Trump's US to be not only well on the path to competitive authoritarianism, but also considered some of Trump's measures to go well beyond what Orbán and other would-be autocrats have attempted.[8]

However, while the US will figure from time to time in this book, my focus is on the UK and the role of academic lawyers there, again whatever their intentions, in putting that country on the path to being a hybrid regime and thus towards competitive authoritarianism. These are heavy charges. The only way I can make them stick is to analyse in some detail arguments that would result in turning one of the world's oldest democracies, regarded by many as the birthplace of the rule of law, into something quite different: a hybrid authoritarian regime. For only a

[7] Steven Levitsky and Lucan Way, 'The New Competitive Authoritarianism' (2020) 31 *Journal of Democracy* 51 at 54. For the book, see Steven Levitsky and Lucan Way, *Competitive Authoritarianism: Hybrid Regimes After the Cold War* (Cambridge: Cambridge University Press, 2012).

[8] Amanda Taub, '"This Is Worse": Trump's Judicial Defiance Veers Beyond the Autocrat Playbook' (Mar 20 2025) online: *New York Times* <www.nytimes.com/2025/03/20/world/europe/trump-courts-defiance-autocrats-playbook.html?searchResultPosition=1>.

detailed, often quite forensic analysis of the arguments can do the job of showing that, despite claims to the contrary, such arguments lead to the destruction of the rule of law and thus of the kind of constitutional government that is intrinsic to democracy.

The period which forms my main focus stretches from 2015 to 2025, a time when Conservative governments in the UK began an attack on the place of international law in the constitutional order that soon and necessarily became an attack on the rule of law. The high point of the attack was the passage of the Rwanda Act in April 2024, the law which required that all asylum seekers who arrive in the UK be deported to Rwanda, a country ruled by a regime notorious for its violations of human rights, to have their claims for refugee status processed. There they would remain whether their claims were accepted or rejected.

The debates around this Act can help us to understand one of the most important debates of our time, both about the role of judges in upholding the rule of law in a democratic political order and about what the rule of law *is*. We will do that by addressing one of the most contentious issues in this debate – the place of international law and human rights in our conception of the rule of law. This will show that the ambiguities, hesitations and tensions in the political positions of these academic lawyers are resolved by the destructive consequences of their legal arguments for the rule of law and the fundamental constitutional commitments of their political orders. It is only, that is, through a careful analysis of the legal dimension of their project that one can fully understand the political dimension.

Two Oxford law professors, John Finnis and his former student Richard Ekins, figure most prominently in this book because, over the past ten years or so, they have been largely responsible for providing these arguments. Finnis, who is retired from teaching, may be the most politically significant legal scholar of the post-war period. One of his former students is the US Supreme Court Justice Neil Gorsuch; another, Robert P. George – Professor of Jurisprudence at Princeton University – was described in *The New York Times Magazine* in 2009 as the 'most influential conservative Christian thinker' in the US.[9] Together, Finnis and George filed an amicus brief to the US Supreme Court urging it to overturn decades of precedent to abolish the right of women to abortion

[9] David D Kirkpatrick, 'Robert P George, The Conservative Christian Big Thinker' (Dec 16 2009) online: *New York Times* <www.nytimes.com/2009/12/20/magazine/20george-t.html>.

that had been established in *Roe v Wade*.[10] And in *Dobbs*, the decision which endorsed such arguments, Justice Samuel Alito for the majority cited an early article by Finnis in support of the claim that the scholarship on which *Roe v Wade* had relied had been 'discredited'.[11]

My concern here though is with Finnis's impact in the UK, where he has set the course over many years for dramatic changes in the UK's constitutional and political order. However, this focus provides important insights both into the wave of the right-wing ideology that seems to be overwhelming the liberal democracies of the West and into a curious alliance which has emerged between right-wing ideologues in the US and their counterparts in the UK, an alliance that extends to far-right figures in Poland and some elements of the British left.

Finnis has been able to play a central role in this network because he is a brilliant scholar, of great depth and range, and one of the founders of 'new natural law theory', a revival of Thomas Aquinas's political and legal theory. But the far-reaching implications of the political dimension of his theory are little appreciated, even by those who are more interested in his political philosophy than in his legal theory. Indeed, even the way in which that dimension is political is little appreciated. In addition, lawyers who seek to engage with his forays into legal debates seem often unaware of how these forays are animated by his ideological convictions. While disquieted by the way in which Finnis's legal arguments and the arguments of those who fall within his sphere of influence often depend on mischaracterizations of the UK legal tradition and constitutional order and inaccurate claims about the law, they find it hard to understand why it is that such arguments are being made since the politics behind them surfaces in rather oblique and mysterious ways. Moreover, even when one spends time on his political theory – my main task in the last chapter – one finds it is not that easy to make sense of its relationship to liberalism, since that relationship is both troubled and troubling.

My book will bring to light how Finnis's political project works in combination with his legal project, a combination which, while it is styled

[10] *Roe v Wade* 410 US 113 (1973). For the brief, see John Finnis and Robert P George, 'An Enhanced Amicus Brief in Dobbs' (Nov 3 2021) online: *SSRN* <https://papers.ssrn.com/sol3/papers.cfm?abstract_id=3955231>.

[11] *Dobbs v Jackson Women's Health Organization* 597 US 215 (2022) at 27, n 38 citing John Finnis, '"Shameless Acts" in Colorado: Abuse of Scholarship in Constitutional Cases' (1994) 7 *Academic Questions* 10. Alito did not mention that Finnis's argument in this article is premised on theological assumptions, nor that it is largely not about the right to abortion, since it is an attack on the idea of gay rights.

as a return to a 'traditional' mode of government and to the 'classical legal tradition', in fact it will bring about something like a revolution, one no less dramatic than that which seems to be unfolding in the US today, where talk is now common of a 'constitutional crisis' caused by Trump's executive orders and defiance of the courts. It is the implications of this combination of the political project with the legal project that starkly come to light when seen through the lens afforded by my focus in Chapter 3 on the debates about the rule of law and the Rwanda Act, an example of law-making that serves better than any I have encountered in a long career of trying to elucidate the content of the rule-of-law idea.

So important was Finnis in one significant episode, the executive's tussle with Parliament 'to get Brexit done', to take the UK out of the European Community, that Conservative Prime Minister Boris Johnson rewarded him in 2019 in the Queen's Birthday Honours, making him a 'Commander of the British Empire'. In 2023, Conservative Prime Minister Rishi Sunak made Ekins an Honorary King's Counsel, for his 'major contribution to the law of England and Wales', primarily for his leadership of the group of lawyers that provided the legal arguments to justify his government's policies, most significantly in respect of asylum seekers.

For the most part, these arguments appear on the website of Policy Exchange, which claims to be 'the UK's leading think tank', 'an educational charity … [whose] mission is to develop and promote new policy ideas which deliver better public services, a stronger society and a more dynamic economy'.[12] It is indeed the UK's leading think tank of the right and, judging by its appearance and the number of events and projects it hosts, it may be the best funded. But unusually for a 'charity', Policy Exchange does not disclose the sources of its ample funding. Such secrecy naturally leads to speculation about its sources of 'dark' money, though one has recently been revealed to be Sir Paul Marshall, a man with a fortune estimated at £875 million. He is also the owner of *GB News*, the UK's equivalent of *Fox*, and of the *Spectator* magazine, and he provided the funding for 'Ralston College' in the US, whose 'chancellor' is Jordan Peterson, one of the most influential figures on the conspiracy theory circuit.[13]

Among the projects Policy Exchange hosts is 'The Judicial Power Project', headed by Ekins, its founder.[14] He was approached by Dean Godson, the director of Policy Exchange, an influential figure in UK

[12] 'Policy Exchange' online: *Policy Exchange* <https://policyexchange.org.uk/>.

[13] See Peter Geoghegan, 'Making Media Great Again' (2025) 47 *London Review of Books* 25.

[14] 'Judicial Power Project' online: *Policy Exchange* <https://judicialpowerproject.org.uk/>.

Conservative politics, now Baron Godson of Thorney Island in the City of Westminster, to start the Project. It opened in 2015 with an introductory speech by Michael Gove, the Conservative politician with whom Marshall has been collaborating for some years, who is now editor of the *Spectator*. Gove, at that time Minister of Justice, said that he considered the project 'one of the most important pieces of work by any think tank and academic institution in Britain today'. In retrospect, it seems clear that Gove expressed this view because his government, Godson, Ekins and Finnis, who gave the keynote address at this event, saw the project as providing both the inspiration and the legal arguments for the campaign to come, of course helped by the lustre imparted by the Oxford professors driving the project.[15]

In November 2020, Godson awarded on behalf of Policy Exchange the inaugural 'Grotius Prize' to Scott Morrison, the Australian Prime Minister, 'in recognition of his work in support of the international rules based order', in a live online event, which included remarks by then Prime Minister Boris Johnson. Godson in his introductory remarks fully recognized that Hugo Grotius (1583–1645) is the Dutch humanist known principally as the father of modern international law.[16] In contrast, and not of course mentioned by Godson, Morrison was at that point already notorious for the harsh immigration policies he had introduced during a stint as Immigration Minister, policies which manipulated an already draconian migration regime that previous governments had established to give them the power to deal with migrants in an arbitrary fashion. So arbitrary, in fact, that two Australian immigration law experts gave an article about his efforts the title 'A Masterclass in Evading the Rule of Law'.[17]

This account of Policy Exchange's Grotius Award, last awarded to Giorgia Meloni, Prime Minister of Italy, and leader of the Brothers of Italy, an extreme right-wing party that has unabashed roots in fascism,[18]

[15] Maximilian Steinbeis, 'Right Wing Crits' (Nov 15 2019) online: *Verfassungsblog* <https://verfassungsblog.de/right-wing-crits/>.

[16] 'Inaugural Grotius Prize Presented to Hon Scott Morrisson MP' (Nov 20 2023) online: *Policy Exchange* <https://policyexchange.org.uk/events/inaugural-grotius-prize-presented-to-hon-scott-morrison-mp/>.

[17] Joyce Chia and Savitri Taylor, 'A Masterclass in Evading the Rule of Law: The Saga of Scott Morrison and Temporary Protection Visas' (2021) 44 *University of New South Wales Law Journal* 4.

[18] 'The Grotius Prize – Presented to Giorgia Meloni' (Apr 28 2023) online: *YouTube* <www.youtube.com/watch?v=qdFDhcMtOtY>.

is important background for my arguments to come for several reasons. First, one needs to keep in mind that the drift away from respect for international law is not the sole responsibility of conservative parties in the West, nor even of their current extreme right-wing manifestations. In the UK, it was after all Labour's Tony Blair who decided to join George Bush's war on Iraq, a decision which required his Attorney General Lord Peter Goldsmith to change his advice that it was illegal for the UK to do so, which he did after being subjected to considerable political pressure.[19]

Second, to the extent the drift away from the rule of international law has been accelerated by the right's rhetoric and policies on immigration, we must recall that the right often merely sharpens policies which were put in place by centrist governments – Labour in the UK or Democrat in the US – policies premised on the view that 'Migration is the mother of all political problems'.[20] This remark was made in 2018 by a member of Angela Merkel's cabinet, the government which had just three years before been applauded for restating Germany's commitment to admitting refugees.

It would therefore be a mistake to suppose that such policies appeal only to the far-right fringes in a country. Such views resonate widely, including in the UK today, where sociologist Gary Younge reports a poll after the anti-immigrant race riots there in the summer of 2024 showing that 'immigration is now considered the most important issue in the country with more than two thirds believing it to be too high'.[21] The big difference is that sharpening such policies renders them not only more cruel and inhumane, but undoubtedly crosses the threshold into violating the rule of law, including the country's obligations under international law.

Third, this account tells us much about the Rwanda saga. The Conservative government employed Alexander Downer, Australian

[19] Michael Savage, 'Goldsmith: Why I Changed My Mind on Iraq' (Jan 28 2010) online: *Independent* <www.independent.co.uk/news/uk/politics/goldsmith-why-i-changed-my-mind-on-iraq-1881329.html>; Richard Norton-Taylor, 'Chilcot Inquiry: Iraq Papers Show Lord Goldsmith's Warning to Tony Blair' (Jun 30 2010) online: *The Guardian* <www.theguardian.com/uk/2010/jun/30/chilcot-inquiry-lord-goldsmith-blair>; 'Iraq Inquiry Publishes Advice to Blair on War' (Jun 30 2010) online: *BBC* <www.bbc.com/news/10463844>.

[20] Melissa Eddy, '"Mother" of All Problems? Immigration Remark Reignites German Debate' (Sep 6 2018) online: *New York Times* <www.nytimes.com/2018/09/06/world/europe/immigration-germany-merkel.html>.

[21] Gary Younge, 'Scapegoating the Immigrant' (Oct 17 2024) online: *New York Review of Books* <www.nybooks.com/articles/2024/10/17/scapegoating-the-immigrant-gary-younge/> at 23.

Minister for Foreign Affairs from 1996 to 2007, to write the report on which the Rwanda Plan to deport asylum seekers was based. Downer was intimately involved with the Australian model for dealing with asylum seekers, a system first implemented in 2001 and designed to make would-be asylum claimants think twice before travelling to Australia by boat. Under this model, which combines offshore processing and settlement, Australia has relocated thousands of migrants to 'processing camps' in small Oceanic countries where they are detained until their claims are determined. Reports indicate that migrants have spent years in these camps, where the conditions combined with the experience of being in legal limbo were so inhumane that they prompted a pattern of detainee suicide, on several occasions by self-immolation.[22] Elaine Pearson, then director of the Australian Branch of Human Rights Watch, went so far as to say that the system made the nation 'a world leader in treating refugees with brazen cruelty'.[23]

Finally, on the basis of the account so far, one can already see emerging one of the central questions for this study – the question of rhetoric. In bestowing the Grotius Prize – an accolade for service to international law – on an Australian Prime Minister who had presided over an immigration regime that exhibited his contempt for the rule of law and international law, and which was to serve as a model for the UK Conservative government, and in quickly switching in his introductory remarks from talk of 'international law' to talk of an 'international rules based order', the director of Policy Exchange exemplified the kind of double-speak that the extreme right in both the UK and the US has honed and perfected. Godson was claiming the mantle of the rule of law and of international law for the efforts of the Conservative government to get away with flouting it, all the while preparing the ground for the Conservative government to put in place its version of the Australian model.

Another striking example of double-speak makes the Judicial Power Project's founding in 2015 even more significant. Prior to 2015, the 'Ministerial Code' – a document that sets out the obligations of the most senior members of the executive – contained a provision stating an

22 Austin Ramzy, 'Kept from Australia, Refugee at Nauru Center Sets Himself on Fire' (Apr 27 2016) online: *New York Times* <www.nytimes.com/2016/04/28/world/australia/nauru-iranian-refugee-self-immolation.html>.

23 Elaine Pearson, 'Seven Years of Suffering for Australia's Asylum Seekers, Refugees' (Jul 16 2020) online: *Human Rights Watch* <www.hrw.org/news/2020/07/16/seven-years-suffering-australias-asylum-seekers-refugees>.

'overarching duty on ministers to comply with the law including international law and treaty obligations and to protect the integrity of public life'. The Code is produced by the government and is amended from time to time. It is considered in the UK to lay out a set of 'constitutional conventions', principles that bind public officials but which are not legally binding, or, as lawyers put it, they are 'non-justiciable'. While non-justiciability precludes the courts from enforcing compliance, this does not mean that the principles are regarded as constitutionally or legally irrelevant. A breach of them often leads to serious consequences. If the 'Independent Adviser on Ministers' Interests' advises the Prime Minister that a serious breach has occurred, there is a public expectation, often vindicated, that the Prime Minister will demand the resignation of the offending minister.

In 2015, David Cameron's Conservative government quietly dropped from the Ministerial Code the phrase 'to comply with the law including international law and treaty obligations', leaving in place only 'an overarching duty on ministers to protect the integrity of public life'.[24] Cameron's amendment was greeted with consternation by senior lawyers. For example, Philippe Sands QC, a professor of international law at University College London, said the change was 'shocking. Another slap to the Magna Carta and the idea of the rule of law. A government that wants to ditch Europe and sever the connection with the European Convention on Human Rights now wishes to free itself from the constraints of international law and the judgments of international courts'. And Ken Macdonald QC, Baron Macdonald of River Glaven, the former Director of Public Prosecutions, said:

> It is difficult to believe that this change is inadvertent. If it's deliberate, it appears to advocate a conscious loosening of ministerial respect for the rule of law and the UK's international treaty obligations, including weakening responsibility for the quality of justice here at home. ... In a dangerous world, the government should be strengthening its support for the rule of law, not airbrushing it out of the ministerial code. On every level, this sends out a terrible signal.[25]

[24] Diane Taylor, 'Lawyers Express Concern Over Ministerial Code Rewrite' (Oct 22 2015) online: *The Guardian* <www.theguardian.com/law/2015/oct/22/lawyers-express-concern-over-ministerial-code-rewrite>.

[25] Ibid. King's Counsel – KC – status is awarded to barristers who have demonstrated excellence in advocacy in the highest courts of England and Wales. During Queen Elizabeth's reign, the award was Queen's Counsel or QC and barristers with that title switched to KC when Charles became the monarch.

Sharpening the shock was a sense of hypocrisy. On the same day that the revised code was published, Jeremy Wright QC, then Cameron's Attorney General, gave a speech to the government service legal department. In it, he said that '[i]nternational law binds the UK, both as a central tenet of our constitutional framework and as a distinct legal regime at the international level. The constitutional principle to respect the rule of law and comply with our international obligations is reflected in the ministerial code – which applies as much to me as to any other minister'. 'The code states that there is an overarching duty on ministers to comply with the law, including international law and treaty obligations to uphold the administration of justice and to protect the integrity of public life.'[26]

Faced with this flagrant example of double-speak, the Cabinet Office denied there was any intention to weaken international law and the administration of justice by omitting the phrases from the new code. The *Guardian* reported that a cabinet spokesman said: 'The code is very clear on the duty that it places on ministers to comply with the law. "Comply with the law" includes international law.' The spokesman further claimed that '[t]he wording was amended to bring the code more in line with the civil service code. The obligations remain unchanged by the simplified wording. The ministerial code is the prime minister's guidance to his ministers on how they should conduct themselves in public office'.[27]

However, the signal was clear. The Conservative government no longer deemed respect for international law to be part of the 'overarching duty on ministers to protect the integrity of public life'. The question, raised clearly by Macdonald, was whether the change also amounted to a 'conscious loosening of ministerial respect for the rule of law and the UK's international treaty obligations, including weakening responsibility for the quality of justice here at home'. In other words, is respect for international law and its rights protections intrinsic to respect for the rule of law at home such that diminishing such respect damages the 'integrity of public life'?

[26] Jeremy Wright, 'The Importance of International Law for Government Lawyers' (Oct 15 2015) online: <www.gov.uk/government/speeches/the-importance-of-international-law-for-government-lawyers>; Josh Halliday, 'Ministerial Code: No 10 "Showing Contempt for International Law"' (Oct 25 2015) online: *The Guardian* <www.theguardian.com/law/2015/oct/26/ministerial-code-no-10-showing-contempt-for-international-law>.

[27] Halliday, 'Ministerial Code'.

As we will see, this kind of double-speak offers an important insight into the Judicial Power Project. The courts are its main target, in particular the UK Supreme Court and its understanding of its state's human rights obligations and the European Court of Human Rights, the Court that oversees compliance with the European Convention of Human Rights, an international agreement ratified by the UK government and incorporated into its law by the UK Parliament. The manifesto of the Project identifies the judiciary as both the main threat to and guardian of the rule of law in the UK in that it claims that '[j]udicial overreach increasingly threatens the rule of law and effective, democratic government', and that 'the judicial power has a central, strategic place in any well-ordered constitutional arrangement: no state is well-governed without an independent judiciary, exercising legal and constitutional authority to adjudicate disputes, including disputes between citizens and officials, fairly and in accordance with settled positive law'. It also suggests that the 'British constitutional tradition has … long centred on a disciplined account of the proper scope of judicial authority, which has been held rightly subject to the legislature's final authority to choose the content of the law and not to undermine the executive's constitutional responsibility to choose how best to act within the scope of its lawful powers'.[28]

These statements are not in themselves inconsistent. It is of course possible that judges have strayed outside of their proper role. But the manifesto only hints at what it takes to be the limits of the judges' role in highlighting 'settled positive law'. Even more important is that in talking about 'strategy' and 'the judicial power', the manifesto rides roughshod over the tradition to which it constantly proclaims allegiance and in which judges are seen as the guardians of constitutional principle, not as players in a zero-sum strategic power game.

1.2 The Common Good Project

The Judicial Power Project is not, however, the expression of a political tendency confined to the UK. Its lawyers have much in common with another ideologue who occupies a similar role in the US, the Harvard Law Professor Adrian Vermeule. He and his Oxford counterparts are united in the 'Common Good Project', hosted on the Oxford Faculty of

[28] 'About the Judicial Power Project' online: *Policy Exchange* <https://judicialpowerproject.org.uk/about/>.

Law website.[29] They also gather at the Canterbury Institute in Oxford, which is not part of Oxford University, but is stocked with Oxford advocates of the common good who put on events featuring figures like Vermeule, but which are advertised only to a select group.[30]

In addition, the political tendency is not confined to a North Atlantic alliance. An increasingly important figure in the Judicial Power Project is Conor Casey, a legal academic based at the University of Surrey, specializing in public law and legal theory. He has made his mark in the UK as one of the main proponents of Vermeule's version of 'common good constitutionalism'.[31]

Casey's website at Surrey states that he is 'a Fellow of the Legal Chamber of the Copernican Academy, a Polish academic society made up of Polish and foreign fellows, who are appointed on the basis of academic accomplishment in their field by the President of the Republic of Poland at the request of the Minister of Education and Science'.[32]

Intended as a right-wing counterweight to the much older and more well-established Polish Academy of Sciences, the Copernican Academy was created in 2017 by Przemysław Czarnek, then Poland's Minister of Education and Science. Even at the height of Poland's drift to authoritarianism, Czarnek was notorious for being on the extreme end of the already far-right Law and Justice Party's political spectrum. Like Fidesz, the party of Victor Orbán, Law and Justice has found many admirers amongst the far right, including the common good lawyers, especially Vermeule, who is also a fellow of the Legal Chamber, and, as with Casey, was appointed for his service to common good constitutionalist thought. This is likely due to these parties' rapid and undeniable success at hollowing out the rule of law and democracy from within, thus creating the hybrid regimes of competitive authoritarianism, the descendants of the fascist regimes of the twentieth century.

Vermeule has openly expressed his admiration for Ryszard Legutko, a philosopher and driving intellectual force of Law and Justice as well as author of *The Demon in Democracy: Totalitarian Temptations in Free*

[29] 'The Common Good Project' online: *The University of Oxford* <www.law.ox.ac.uk/the-common-good-project/common-good-project>.

[30] 'Canterbury Institute' online: *Canterbury Institute* <www.canterbury.institute/>.

[31] Adrian Vermeule, *Common Good Constitutionalism* (Cambridge: Polity, 2022).

[32] 'Dr Conor Casey' online: *The University of Surrey* <www.surrey.ac.uk/people/conor-casey>. For the Academy, see 'About the Copernican Academy' online: *Copernican Academy* <https://akademiakopernikanska.gov.pl/o-akademii/>.

Societies,[33] a book that is popular with the right in the US.[34] It is a wildly implausible work since Legutko argues that liberalism is a more successful totalitarian ideology than communism, and so is the 'demon' within that must be destroyed if both democracy and freedom are to be preserved. However, like much else in politics these days, labels like 'wildly implausible' or 'unimaginable' may start to seem inappropriate, as the unimaginable becomes our reality and the wildly implausible becomes the stock-in-trade of mainstream politics and legal debate. For example, Kemi Badenoch, leader of the Conservative Party, on 9 December 2024 gave a speech in Washington that in effect restated Legutko's thesis.[35] Perhaps even more significant is that Lord Philip Sales, a judge of the UK Supreme Court, in a public lecture in November 2024 drew on Vermeule's idea of common good constitutionalism, I'm sure in complete unawareness of the lethal baggage with which that idea is freighted.[36]

However, and as already suggested, that baggage is no longer the possession of the right alone. For example, for some months in early 2025, another figure who has a prominent role in this book, human rights lawyer Richard Hermer, appointed in 2024 as UK Attorney General by the Labour government, was accused on a daily basis by right-wing lawyers, politicians and journalists of being a 'Marxist' who wants the UK to substitute the 'rule of lawyers' for the 'rule of politicians', all in a bid to 'capitulate' to international law. But his job, as described on the UK government website, is to occupy the role of 'chief legal adviser to the Crown' with a number 'of independent public interest functions', which include advising on 'questions of public law, international law, human rights' and 'promoting the rule of law at home and internationally'.[37] He was, that is, doing no more than what his job description required him to do.

Altogether astonishing is that Maurice Glasman, a *Labour* member of the House of Lords, added to the chorus of calls to the Labour Prime

[33] Ryszard Legutko, *The Demon in Democracy: Totalitarian Temptations in Free Societies* (New York: Encounter Books, 2016).

[34] Adrian Vermeule and Patrick Deneen, 'In Honor of Ryszard Legutko' (Jun 20 2022) online: *Postliberal Order* <www.postliberalorder.com/p/in-honor-of-ryszard-legutko>.

[35] Kemi Badenoch, 'Speech to the IDU in Washington' (Dec 9 2024) online: *Conservatives* <www.conservatives.com/news/kemis-idu-washington-speech>.

[36] Lord Sales, 'Purpose in Law and Interpretation' (Nov 19 2024) online: *UK Supreme Court* <https://supremecourt.uk/speeches/purpose-in-law-and-in-interpretation> at 18.

[37] 'Attorney General' online: *Gov.UK* <www.gov.uk/government/ministers/attorney-general>.

Minister Keir Starmer to fire Hermer on the ground that he imposes the rule of lawyers on politicians, accusing him of being a 'progressive arrogant fool'.[38] In January 2025 Glasman attended Trump's inauguration, apparently invited by his admirer Vice President J. D. Vance.[39] He is one of the political activists in 'Blue Labour', a movement within the Labour Party committed to a combination of left-wing economic policies and social and cultural conservatism.[40] He describes this combination as serving the 'common good', a goal for society that has been undermined by neoliberalism.[41] As in the manifesto of the Judicial Power Project, he suggests that achieving the common good in the UK requires restoring the 'Ancient Constitution', a balance which has been upset by the power that judges and lawyers have accrued[42] and, as in the Common Good Project, that this very British idea of the ancient constitution has philosophical roots in Catholic teachings on 'virtue ethics', in particular the 'natural law' theory of St Thomas Aquinas.[43] In addition, Adrian Pabst, described on the cover of one of his books as among the 'leading thinkers' of Blue Labour,[44] in a perhaps unwitting echo of the Polish far-right thinker Legutko, titled a prior work *The Demons of Liberal Democracy* and used phrases in it such as the 'tyrannical demon of liberal democracy'.[45]

What explains this alliance between the far right and some elements of the left, an alliance which, if it follows through on its goals, will leave us with only the shell of democracy, in substance little different from the fascist regimes of the mid twentieth century? The story of liberal democracies is one of success, but also of failure. The status of liberal democracy is regarded by many of its critics as tied inextricably to the way that it harnessed capitalism to exploit people and the natural environment. These critics suppose that liberalism is the political theory of the neoliberal international economic order of unchecked (and anti-democratic) corporate greed, that this system destroys the delicate balance that

[38] Eleni Courea, 'Labour Peer Calls for "Arrogant" Attorney General to Be Sacked' (Feb 10 2025) online: *The Guardian* <www.theguardian.com/politics/2025/feb/10/labour-peer-maurice-glasman-attorney-general-richard-hermer-sacked-labour>.

[39] Steerpike, 'Blue Labour Founder Jets Off to Trump Inauguration' (Jan 16 2025) online: *The Spectator* <www.spectator.co.uk/article/blue-labour-founder-jets-off-to-trump-inauguration/>.

[40] See Maurice Glasman, *Blue Labour* (Cambridge: Polity, 2022).

[41] Ibid at 38–40, 106–8.

[42] Ibid at 112–14.

[43] Ibid at 2.

[44] Adrian Pabst, *Postliberal Politics* (Cambridge: Polity, 2021).

[45] Adrian Pabst, *The Demons of Liberal Democracy* (Cambridge: Polity, 2019) at 146.

traditional societies had achieved with their natural environments over centuries, and that it is responsible for the obscene concentration of wealth in so few hands – in short, that liberalism is responsible for a world dominated by grotesque injustice.[46]

It is for such reasons that talk of the 'common good' is everywhere as people seek to find a political vision that moves beyond what they rightly perceive as the selfishness and excessive individualism of the last decades. Groups have thus emerged that adopt labels such as 'post-liberalism' to signal their desire to create a more just and more equal society out of the wreckage wrought by neoliberalism. I find this kind of critique of our world entirely convincing.[47] But it seems to me to be a grave mistake for those who make it to ally themselves with the figures in my book who also march under the banner of the common good. My book raises, though does not seek to answer, the question whether 'common good' talk can be rescued from its capture by the right. It arises through my demonstration that the Judicial Power Project's manifesto is a wolf in sheep's clothing, a vehicle for the Common Good Project whose illiberal agenda will be revealed through a careful account of the thought of John Finnis, its major intellectual figure in the UK.

For the moment, I want to note that the authors of the manifesto say, without offering further explanation, that 'some legal theorists find the term "common good" dubious in itself'.[48] But I will show that every *legal* theorist should find this project more than dubious because it will result in undermining the rule of law from within. Moreover, anyone who wishes to live in a society in which an authoritarian state does not get to dictate how one chooses to live one's life, including the most intimate choices as to personal relationships, religious affiliation, sexuality, child-rearing and indeed the very decision whether to have children and how many, should fear their version of the common good.

46 For an illuminating account, see Quinn Slobodian, *Hayek's Bastards: Race, Gold, IQ, and the Capitalism of the Far Right* (New York: Zone Books, 2025).

47 But in several months of subscription to the Substack 'American Postliberal' I did not find this critique. Rather, I found an echo chamber for the spectrum of elite intellectuals that goes from right to extreme right who manifest – in flights of sanctimonious rhetoric – fervent support for the worst excesses of Trump and Orbán. See Jan-Werner Müller, 'Caeser Wept' (Dec 4 2025) online: *London Review of Books* <www.lrb.co.uk/the-paper/v47/n22/jan-werner-muller/caesar-wept?utm_campaign=4001961_20251206ICYMI%20-%20subs&utm_medium=email&utm_source=LRB%20email&dm_i=7NIQ,2DRXL,3EIBBA,4QOO2,1>.

48 See 'The Common Good Project'.

I will refer, as indicated, to Finnis, Ekins, Casey and Vermeule as 'common good lawyers'. But since not all in their ideological camp are lawyers, I will refer, as also indicated, to those in the camp at large as 'common good advocates'. I need to be careful with these labels for three reasons. First, common good lawyers and advocates adopt the rhetoric of common good because it is so powerful. No one can be against the common good because in a sense all political argument is about what will best serve society as a whole, plausibly and often referred to as the common good.

Consider the classic statement of liberal individualism in John Stuart Mill's *On Liberty*, a frequent target for the common good advocates because they see it as the ultimate liberal statement that supports their critique. In the first chapter, Mill set out the 'Harm Principle': 'That the only purpose for which power can be rightfully exercised over any member of a civilised community, against his will, is to prevent harm to others'; that '[h]is own good, either physical or moral, is not a sufficient warrant'; and that '[t]he only part of the conduct of any one, for which he is amenable to society, is that which concerns others. In the part which merely concerns himself, his independence is, of right, absolute. Over himself, over his own body and mind, the individual is sovereign'.[49]

This liberal 'Harm Principle' requires that the state should be entirely 'neutral' – take no stand – on the question of what is best for the individual. It is, in other words, for the individual alone to decide what (if any) religion to practise, whether or not to bear children, what kind of intimate relations they engage in, including sexual relations, and so on. But Mill was also a leading 'utilitarian' thinker, who argued that society should be organized so as to maximize the happiness – the welfare – of all. So his argument is that such neutrality serves the common good of all in that it allows everyone to pursue their own vision of how to live their life.

That Mill's statement of liberalism claims to serve the common good permits the common good advocates to suggest that all political arguments boil down to competing conceptions of the common good.[50] What goes wrong for them in liberalism is that the good served is not truly

[49] John Stuart Mill, *On Liberty*, in *Collected Works*, JM Robson, ed (Toronto: University of Toronto Press, 1977) volume 18, at 223–24.

[50] For example, Michael Foran, 'Rights, Common Good, and the Separation of Powers' (2023) 86 *Modern Law Review* 599. Foran's strenuous efforts to show how an illiberal conception of the common good can be made consistent with the doctrine of the separation of powers unravel when he acknowledges at 606 that the common good of a community is not of the people who happen to be citizens of a democratic political order, but only for 'friends': 'This is because the good of an individual cannot be separate from

common. It is the good of an individual, not the good of a society. And such individualism, they claim, undermines the common good of the society, corroding the institutions that make possible the pursuit of a common good in which all may participate. In this claim we can see in a nutshell Legutko's thesis that liberalism is more totalitarian than communism since it requires that people not enforce their view of the good life on others, thus requiring them to confine their view to their own private sphere. And even within that sphere the liberal state may intervene, for example in seeking to protect what it regards as the interests of women and children.

There is, as I already acknowledged, substance to this critique of liberalism, which is why people on the left are sometimes attracted to it. But the group I call the common good advocates are very vague when it comes to filling out the content of the common good. Consider a recent 292-page book by another common good advocate, admirer of both Legutko and Vermeule, US political theorist Patrick Deneen's *Regime Change*.[51]

Deneen, both an admirer of and influential on the ideology of J. D. Vance, uses 'common good' a whopping sixty-nine times in his book, but only provides the vaguest of attempts at specification.[52] The 'rule of law' is entirely absent from the book, let alone considered part of the common good. 'Democracy' and 'democratic', meanwhile, occur frequently. However, these terms play a strange supporting role in an argument whose central thesis is that, as the title tells us with its ominous echo of 6 January 2021, what the US needs is *regime* change, a change already underway with Trump's re-election.

The second reason for care with my label flows from the first. Because the label 'common good' is so capacious, even vacuous, many adopt it not because they yearn for the kind of regime change that will usher in

the good of the community: my life is better when my friends' lives are better.' At this point, the Schmittian subtext of the article rises to the surface.

51 Patrick Deneen, *Regime Change: Towards a Postliberal Future* (New York: Sentinel, 2023). For his admiration of Legutko, see Vermeule and Deneen, 'In Honor of Ryszard Legutko'.

52 See Ian Ward, 'JD Vance Could Lead the Post-Liberal Elite – An Interview with Patrick Deneen' (Jul 18 2024) online: *Politico* <www.politico.com/news/magazine/2024/07/18/jd-vance-world-view-sources-00168984>; and Ian Ward, 'The Seven Thinkers and Groups That Have Shaped JD Vance's Unusual Worldview' (Jul 18 2024) online: *Politico* <www.politico.com/news/magazine/2024/07/18/jd-vance-world-view-sources-00168984>.

authoritarian rule, but only, as with the post-liberals and many attracted to Blue Labour, because they are deeply concerned about the rampant inequality in the democracies of the West as elites have grown wealthier and 'left behind' the majority of the people of their countries. Society should be organized, they rightly suppose, to serve the common good of all, not only the self-interest of Silicon Valley billionaires and their equivalents in the UK and elsewhere. Like the common good advocates, they often root their political beliefs in the tenets of their religion. But, they differ vastly from the common good advocates in that they are on the left side of the political spectrum, not the right. Their versions of the common good are far from the aim of achieving a homogeneous society. Rather, they are designed to serve the interests of a plurality of groups, in which individuals can pursue their own good in their own way, supplied by their society with the resources to do so which are to be secured by increasing democratic control over the institutions, companies and private individuals that wield power.[53]

Such post-liberals should surely be aware of the irony, indeed the naivety of those like Deneen who have urged the regime change now underway in the US. That change will centralize political power in the 'unitary executive' with Trump at its head, and reward the likes of Elon Musk while depriving the less well-off of what access they have to the kinds of social services that make life survivable.[54] But they do not seem fully aware that the labels of 'common good' and even 'post-liberal' have been hijacked to the point where it may be hard to see how they can be rescued from their capture by the far right. This brings me to the third and final reason for care.

There are naturally ideological divides within the ranks of the lawyers and political theorists who fall into my category of common good advocates. Vermeule, for example, like J. D. Vance, espouses the 'integralist' version of Catholicism mentioned earlier, one rejected by most Catholics, including the last Pope. It seeks to 'integrate' state and society by gaining control over state institutions to enable the use of law to

[53] For example, Pabst, *Postliberal Politics*. Pabst is described on the cover as a 'leading thinker in the "Blue Labour" movement'. In a perhaps unwitting echo of the Polish far-right thinker Legutko, Pabst titled a prior work *The Demons of Liberal Democracy* and uses phrases in it, at 146, such as the 'tyrannical demon of liberal democracy'.

[54] See Adrian Vermeule, 'The Head and Body of Leviathan: A Thought Experiment on Executive Power' (Jul 18 2024) online: *The New Digest* <https://thenewdigest.substack.com/p/the-head-and-body-of-leviathan?r=d9obe&utm_campaign=post&utm_medium=email&triedRedirect=true>.

enforce on citizens a set of 'moral virtues' so that they can 'flourish' in the 'community' organized around the preordained 'common good'.[55] As the manifesto of the Common Good Project reads:

> In relating law to the common good, the Project takes as its framing point a key criterion in Thomas Aquinas' definition of law as 'an ordinance of reason *for the common good*, promulgated by the one who is in charge of the community.' For Aquinas, a 'law must be directed to the common good to have the character of law'.[56]

However, it is a strange kind of integration since it seems to require that the state be made the instrument of one version of one faith. How that instrument should be used varies from integralist to integralist. It may require that the state enforce Catholicism on all those baptized into the faith, and that others not be permitted to do anything that would undermine its privileged place in the political order. But it can also be seen to require that infidels bend the knee to the faith, be demoted from full status in the political community, or driven out altogether in what the extreme right now imagines as 'remigration'[57] and which Finnis long ago advocated as a 'reversal of the inflow' of 'immigrant, non-citizen Muslims'.[58]

I will have more to say about integralism in my last chapter, but not a huge amount more, because the variation within the integralist ranks does not matter to my argument, nor indeed whether figures accept or reject the label of integralist. For example, as we will see, Finnis would not style himself as an integralist and often seems reluctant to ditch liberalism altogether. He is even regarded by figures further to the right as too liberal to count as a genuine member of their natural law

55 See, for example, Vermeule, 'A Christian Strategy'.

56 See 'The Common Good Project'. For an excellent analysis of the divides, see Laura K. Field, *Furious Minds: The Making of the MAGA New Right* (Princeton, NJ: Princeton University Press, 2025) and for an equally excellent account of the origins of their ideologies in the 1990s, see John Ganz, *When the Clock Broke: Con Men, Conspiracists, and How America Cracked Up in the Early 1990s* (New York: Farrar, Straus and Giroux, 2024).

57 Peter Hille, 'German "Remigration" Debate Fuels Push to Ban Far-Right AfD' (Jan 12 2024) online: *Deutsche Welle* <www.dw.com/en/german-remigration-debate-fuels-push-to-ban-far-right-afd/a-67965896>.

58 See John Finnis, 'Endorsing Discrimination between Faiths: A Case of Extreme Speech' in Ivan Hare and James Weinstein, eds, *Extreme Speech and Democracy* (Oxford: Oxford University Press, 2009) 430 at 440. For an illuminating account of such debates, see Kevin Vallier, *All the Kingdoms of the World – On Radical Religious Alternatives to Liberalism* (New York: Oxford University Press, 2023).

tradition.[59] But the variation does not matter because the important issue, as I will argue, is that there is no principled distinction between their positions.

In addition, the ranks of anti-liberals or illiberals are hardly confined to Catholic or other Christian adherents of a right-wing ideology, since the ticket of entry is a commitment to most of the political tenets of the ideology, not Catholicism. That is why the common good is often marketed under the vague label of the 'Judeo-Christian tradition', so as to include other ideologists of the right, for example the influential 'Judeo-nationalist' Yarom Hazony.[60] An American-Israeli philosopher, he is the founder of the National Conservatism Conference, an annual event since 2019 at which the likes of Victor Orbán, Tucker Carlson and Suella Braverman hold court.[61] It is also why the common good advocates so readily adopt the label 'post-liberalism'. It signals that whatever their differences, they are united in their common enemy: the liberal democratic state. This label permits one to enter the ranks despite the fact that one has no definite commitment to any of the religions that fit into the 'Judeo-Christian tradition'.

The ticket of entry is only a determination to harness state institutions and law in the service of a shared set of illiberal aims, mostly 'culture war' issues: anti-LGBTQ+, anti-abortion, anti-immigration and refugees, and 'pro-family', as long as it is a family within a formal marriage between a man and a woman with the woman relegated to the traditional role of mother and housekeeper. For these reasons, and for others explored in Chapter 6, I will term this set of beliefs a 'political theology', a term coined by Carl Schmitt.[62] It nicely conveys both the religious fervour of the belief system, and its fundamentally political ambition. Its religiosity is about depth of intensity of feeling, and so not necessarily found in people who root their ideology in a particular version of a particular religion.

It is already clear that terms like 'right-wing', 'authoritarian' and 'extreme (and far) right' are going to populate my arguments. There is a dual risk here. For one, with repetition such terms lose their force and, to the extent that I equate these terms, which I frequently do, one

[59] For example, Brian McCall, 'What Good Is John Finnis? Assessing the Personal and Common Good in *Natural Law and Natural Rights*' (2020) 83 *Persona y Derecho* 637.

[60] See Yarom Hazony, *The Virtue of Nationalism* (New York: Basic Books, 2018).

[61] See, for example, 'A Conference in Washington, DC' online: *National Conservatism* <https://nationalconservatism.org/natcon-4-2024/>.

[62] Carl Schmitt, *Political Theology: Four Chapters on the Concept of Sovereignty* (Chicago: University of Chicago Press, 2005).

collapses distinctions between authoritarian rule and fascism, or even between these two and totalitarianism of the Nazi variety. So it may seem that my attempt to take care has failed. But there is a different and even greater risk, which pertains to principle in the way I will now sketch.

1.3 The Weimar Backdrop

One must be careful not to underestimate the danger the Finnises, Ekins and Vermeules pose because one believes that such a highly educated and polite person, who has achieved one of the highest positions at one of the best universities in the (perhaps) still liberal democratic world, could never really be making arguments that will lead to authoritarianism. Indeed, they would indignantly deny that those are their intentions. And while in my last chapter I will quote at length some of the more shocking claims that Finnis is prone to making, these claims are still far distant from the level of the sewer in which unabashed racists like Tommy Robinson in the UK or Nick Fuentes in the US swim, or even some distance from the sewer of political operators such as Donald Trump or Nigel Farage.[63] Indeed, whether there is any distance from the sewer is now debatable in the wake of the furore about the podcast Tucker Carlson did with the neo-Nazi Nick Fuentes. The refusal of Trump and Vance to speak out against the entry of explicit antisemitism into mainstream Republican discourse is in effect an embrace of such views.[64]

But still I think it is a mistake to write off the likes of Finnis, Vermeule and Ekins as merely providing the rhetorical cover for a crude nativism or nationalism even if one fears, as I do, that crude nativism or nationalism will be the result of their success. Vermeule, for example, has argued that because in the short term it will not be possible to re-establish the equivalent of the Holy Roman Empire, a political entity ruled over by a Catholic monarch anointed by the Pope, nationalism is but a second-best

[63] My use of 'the sewer' in this context is inspired by the aptly titled review 'The Tower and the Sewer', by the historian of political thought Mark Lilla, of several books by common good advocates, including Deneen and Vermeule, in which at the end he warns young people drawn to this movement that the 'political waters surrounding their conservative … [enclaves] are starting to smell distinctly like a sewer'. See Mark Lilla, 'The Tower and the Sewer' (Jun 20 2024) online: *New York Review of Books* <www.nybooks.com/articles/2024/06/20/the-tower-and-the-sewer-why-liberalism-failed-deneen/>.

[64] Chris Cameron, 'Trump Defends Tucker Carlson After Nick Fuentes Interview' (Nov 16 2025) online: *New York Times* <www.nytimes.com/2025/11/16/us/politics/trump-tucker-carlson-nick-fuentes.html>.

step along the way.[65] And Robert George resigned from the Heritage Foundation because its head put out a video defending the Carlson podcast.[66]

But one needs to recall that the European universities in the late 1920s and early 1930s were full of like-minded gentlemen, eager to bring about ‘regime change’ but who did not have exactly the political agenda in mind that in fact unfolded in Europe after 1933. And it is in the lack of a principled difference between the gradations as one goes from what these days counts as right-wing to authoritarianism to fascism or worse that the principle at stake emerges. Once one crosses, as the common good advocates urge us to do, the threshold between the liberal democratic world and the world beyond, the ‘ruler’ that the Common Good Project and their allies wish to put in charge of us can not only ‘promulgate’ whatever he deems to be ‘good’, but can also implement that good through whatever means he considers appropriate.

My reference to the gentlemen in the European universities in the late 1920s and early 1930s is not casual. As Chapter 6 will explore, the intellectual origins of common good theory are not in classical natural law thought or in Catholic theology, as many of them claim. Rather, they are in German authoritarian political and legal thought of the 1920s and 1930s, in what I called in the Introduction the work of ‘negatively prescriptive theorists’, whose ideology boils down to anything-but-liberalism. For Finnis, the main inspiration is Eric Voegelin (1901–1985). Vermeule has embraced Carl Schmitt (1888–1985), but finds Voegelin an additional, sympathetic source. This is unsurprising since Voegelin adopted Schmitt’s legal theory wholesale in 1936 in a book in support of the authoritarian Austrian state established by Engelbert Dolfuss in 1934 in his bid to crush both the Nazi Party and the socialists of ‘Red Vienna’.[67]

It is important at the outset to emphasize that Voegelin and Schmitt were not Nazis, indeed they were deeply opposed to the Nazis, though

[65] Adrian Vermeule, ‘Universalism and Nationalism: Thesis and Hypothesis’ (Dec 20 2024) online: <https://papers.ssrn.com/sol3/papers.cfm?abstract_id=5059515>.

[66] David A Fahrenthold, ‘Heritage Foundation Board Member Resigns over Video Defending Carlson’ (Nov 17 2025) online: *New York Times* <www.nytimes.com/2025/11/17/us/politics/heritage-foundation-tucker-carlson-nick-fuentes.html>.

[67] Eric Voegelin, *The Authoritarian State: An Essay on the Problem of the Austrian State* [1936] (Columbia: University of Missouri Press, 1989) volume 4 of *Collected Works*. See David Dyzenhaus, ‘“Immanentizing the Eschaton”: Eric Voegelin, Hans Kelsen, and the Debate over Secular Religion’ in Sander Verhaegh, ed, *American Philosophy and the Intellectual Migration* (Berlin: De Gruyter, 2025) 279.

Schmitt is often referred to as a 'Nazi legal theorist' because he successfully curried favour for a few years with the Nazi Party after 1933. And Voegelin fled Austria after Hitler's 'Anschluss' in 1938 and made his way to the US, where he became after the war perhaps the main intellectual inspiration for the far-right ideology now ascendant. Indeed, in past work, including work on the common good lawyers, I have been at pains to point out, as I do here, that there is no accusation that Schmitt and Voegelin were Nazis and that, as a result, the link I assert between the common good lawyers and these figures also does not attract that accusation.[68]

Schmitt's involvement with the conservative aristocrats who dominated the cabinets in the last years of Weimar was designed to help them establish an authoritarian regime by getting rid of Germany's first experiment with parliamentary democracy, and crushing all opposition. This included both the extreme-right Nazis, aka 'National Socialists', and the extreme-left Communist Party, but also the social democrats because of their commitment to democracy and the rule of law that distinguished them from the socialism of both the left and right. The same is also true of Voegelin's involvement in 'Black Vienna' – the far-right and fascist factions in Austrian society in the 1920s and 1930s. They succeeded for a time in realizing the ambition of their German equivalents in that Dollfuss, after becoming head of a coalition government of right-wing parties in 1932, assumed emergency powers in a coup against the Austrian Parliament. He governed thereafter by decree, instituting in the words of a historian of this period, 'a form of authoritarian, quasi-fascist government . . . "Austro-fascism"'.[69]

Schmitt and Voegelin were not then Nazis. Rather, they supported an authoritarian state whose closest equivalent today is much admired by the common good advocates: Victor Orbán's Hungary, a state which has successfully hollowed-out the institutions of democracy and the rule of law. To create such a society, the ruler needs to enlist lawyers, including law professors, in order to create and then maintain the façades of these institutions.

Often, though, my efforts to emphasize the important distinction between authoritarian supporters of fascism like Schmitt, on the one

[68] For example, David Dyzenhaus, 'Lawyer for the Strongman' (Jun 12 2020) online: *Aeon* <https://aeon.co/essays/carl-schmitts-legal-theory-legitimises-the-rule-of-the-strongman>.

[69] Steven Beller, *A Concise History of Austria* (Cambridge: Cambridge University Press, 2006) at 222. For Voegelin, see Janek Wasserman, *Black Vienna: The Radical Right in the Red City, 1918–1938* (New York: Cornell University Press, 2014).

hand, and the Nazis, on the other, are in vain, as illustrated by the podcast 'Double Jeopardy: UK Law and Politics', in the episode 'Debating the Rule of Law in the UK: Hermer versus Wolfson'. The podcast is run by two senior human rights lawyers, Tim Owen KC and Ken Macdonald KC, whom we just met. They were interviewing Lord David Wolfson KC, the shadow Conservative Party Attorney General about a speech he gave for Policy Exchange. There, Wolfson continued an attack on his counterpart in government Attorney General Richard Hermer's articulation of an approach to the rule of law for being political in contrast to his allegedly apolitical approach.[70]

As we will see in later chapters, Wolfson has turned his role as shadow Attorney General into chief cheerleader for the common good lawyers. Because of his continuing enthusiastic endorsement of Ekins's positions, Owen asked Wolfson whether his definition of the rule of law is not as political as that advanced by Hermer. Macdonald added: 'Just to underline Tim's point, one very well-known Canadian legal academic has referred to Professor Richard Ekins, who's been on this podcast, as the Carl Schmitt of modern legal philosophy. Carl Schmitt, of course, was a Nazi philosopher. So not just political, but quite viciously political in some senses.' Wolfson responded: 'Yes, well, I mean, I don't think that sort of language is helpful. I'm reminded of Henry Kissinger's comment about why academic debates are so vicious, because often so little is at stake. But even if it gets vicious, that sort of language is not helpful.'[71]

Whether or not I'm 'very well-known', I am that Canadian academic.[72] But, as I just pointed out, I did not in fact claim that Schmitt was a Nazi, the claim that leads to the charge that my association of Ekins, Finnis and Vermeule with Schmitt and Voegelin is an attempt to smear them by association with the Nazis. Telling here is that a recent lecture by Hermer on the UK's commitment to international law occasioned fury in the Conservative Party and the right-wing media because he mentioned Schmitt as one of the founders of the scepticism about international law that is now rife in the Party, with Wolfson its main promoter.

[70] See Chapters 4 and 5.

[71] Ken Macdonald and Tim Owen, 'Double Jeopardy: The Law and Politics Podcast - Debating the Rule of Law in the UK – Hermer versus Wolfson' (May 14 2025) online: *Apple Podcasts* <https://podcasts.apple.com/de/podcast/episode-29-richard-ekins-judges-and-political-power/id1633485236?i=1000611450876&l=en-GB>.

[72] For example, Dyzenhaus, 'Lawyer for the Strongman'.

Hermer did not use the word 'Nazi' in his lecture,[73] but the mention of Schmitt attracted the charge that he had made this association.

Notably, in an article in the *Spectator*, preposterously titled 'Lord Hermer Is Preposterously Wrong about International Law', Ekins said:

> Carl Schmitt is not, mercifully, a household name in Britain but he does still feature in scholarly debate, often when an academic lawyer wishes to smear his or her opponents without evidence or argument. Tim Owen KC and Lord Macdonald KC, two liberal lawyers in good standing, rightly decry this tactic in their podcast, *Double Jeopardy*, in conversation with Lord Wolfson KC, the shadow Attorney General.[74]

But, as we have just seen, it was Wolfson who 'decried', not Owen and Macdonald, the 'liberal lawyers in good standing'. And, as we will see, this kind of misrepresentation is hardly untypical. But the important issue is not academic squabbles. Rather, as Ekins says, it is the 'evidence or argument'; and this book presents all the evidence and argument needed to show the dependence of the common good lawyers on Schmitt and Voegelin. In doing so, I also show why, contra Wolfson, the stakes are extremely high, not merely academic: nothing less than the survival of the rule of law, constitutional government and thus democracy as we know it.

The term 'post-liberal' does not then accurately describe those I term common good advocates or lawyers. They are 'pre-liberals' or, as Orbán infamously named their projects, 'illiberal', in that they do not so much wish to change the regime to something new, but to return the world to something old, the pre-modern era, not only pre-Enlightenment, but even pre-Reformation. Theirs is, as we will see most clearly in Chapter 6, a

[73] Richard Hermer, 'Attorney General's 2025 RUSI Annual Security Lecture' (May 29 2025) online: *UK.Gov* <www.gov.uk/government/speeches/attorney-generals-2025-rusi-annual-security-lecture>.

[74] Richard Ekins, 'Lord Hermer Is Preposterously Wrong about International Law' (May 30 2025) online: *The Spectator* <www.spectator.co.uk/article/lord-hermer-is-preposterously-wrong-about-international-law/>. For a complete debunking of Ekins's claims, see Mads Andenas and Eirik Bjorge, 'Carl Schmitt, International Law, and Constitutional Tradition in the United Kingdom' (Aug 6 2025) online: *Voelkerrechts* <https://voelkerrechtsblog.org/carl-schmitt-international-law-and-constitutional-tradition-in-the-united-kingdom/>.

For a similar attack on Hermer, see the leader of the Conservative Party's equally preposterous speech: 'Kemi Badenoch Exposes the Laws and Treaties Holding Britain Back' (Jun 6 2025) online: *Conservatives* <www.conservatives.com/news/kemi-badenoch-exposes-the-laws-and-treaties-holding-britain-back?utm_source=substack&utm_medium=email>.

revolt against modernity itself. However, it is a revolt that is fought using thoroughly modern weapons, most prominently the internet.

The issue is not then whether someone like me smears the common good lawyers by association with the extreme right, when in the present or in the past. The question is for them – how to disassociate themselves from positions much more extreme than their own, positions which they of course will utterly condemn. For while there are, as I will continue to acknowledge, distinctions within the ideologies of those in the common good camp and between it and figures further to the right, these abstract theoretical distinctions collapse in practice because there is no principled basis for them. Similarly, distinctions within integralism do not really matter from the perspective of the 'other'. To use Schmittian terminology, the 'other' is the one who must disappear in some way if the common good of the political community is to be preserved, with that 'other' being whomever the 'ruler' deems to be an 'enemy' or 'essentially different' from the 'substantively homogeneous people'.[75]

Let me make the point in another way. When Nazi lawyer Georg Dahm remarked that all of Schmitt's works were 'from the ground up trained on one target: the unmasking and destruction of the liberal, rule-of-law state and the conquest of the legislative state', he was delivering what he thought of as high praise.[76] Of course, this aim marks a big difference between Schmitt's position and that of the common good lawyers, who claim that the Judicial Power Project is all about protecting the rule of law from human rights lawyers and judges. But we have to ask whether this is a difference that makes a difference.

One could conclude on the basis of the evidence and arguments that we saw Ekins claim are necessary for a demonstration of a link to figures such as Schmitt, and which I provide at length in this book, that the difference is only that the common good lawyers have learned in the post-war period how to make arguments cloaked in the language of the rule of law and rights – the language we can think of as 'legal liberalism' – to achieve the same ends. But while such arguments are required to create and maintain the façades of democracy and the rule of law while

[75] See Carl Schmitt, *The Concept of the Political* (New Brunswick, NJ: Rutgers University Press, 1976).

[76] FA Hayek, *Law, Legislation and Liberty* (London: Routledge, 1990) volume I, at 161, quoting from a review by Georg Dahm, my translation. Dahm was a member of the 'Kiel school' of law, which had the reputation of being a 'shock troop university' for the construction of National Socialist law – see Michael Stolleis, *A History of Public Law in Germany: 1914–1945* (Oxford: Oxford University Press, 2004) at 291–95.

emptying them of substance, as exemplified in Orbán's Hungary, I leave it to my readers to decide for themselves whether these arguments amount to what András Sajó, discussing mainly tactics in Eastern and Central Europe, calls 'legal cheating'.[77]

All I can and want to demonstrate is that the common good lawyers' arguments are bad for at least two reasons. First, they result in the creation of a situation – a space – in which law is hardly present. For this reason, one prominent public lawyer suggested that the Judicial Power Project should be renamed the 'Executive Power Project'.[78] That is, the arguments have the result, as in the apartheid-era war against law, of reshaping 'our jurisprudence so as to grant the executive the greatest possible latitude to act outside conventional legal controls'.[79] Second, they are bad as legal arguments. During the Brexit saga, another prominent public lawyer described a particular iteration of such arguments put by Ekins and his allies as 'risible' – that is, so ludicrous that they provoke laughter.[80] They are risible because, as we will see, they often hardly pass muster as arguments, let alone arguments that take the law seriously.

Nevertheless, while they should not be taken seriously as arguments, they must be taken seriously as rhetoric, because of their influence not only in the academy, but also and much more importantly in politics. It is then a sick kind of laughter, the only alternative to the expressions of despair evoked as one watches the drift to authoritarianism in liberal democratic societies and the way in which lawyers at great universities are facilitating the drift. It is the kind of project that commentators on Hungary and Poland have labelled 'autocratic legalism'[81] and 'abusive constitutionalism',[82] both associated with 'democratic backsliding' – a process in which legal and constitutional tools are used to hollow out constitutional and democratic institutions from within. That the arguments are so bad is the result of the fact that, while the common good

[77] András Sajó, 'Militant Rule of Law and Not-so-Bad Law' (2024) 16 *Hague Journal on the Rule of Law* 525 at 538.

[78] Thomas Poole, 'The Executive Power Project' (Apr 2 2019) online: *London Review of Books* <www.lrb.co.uk/blog/2019/april/the-executive-power-project>.

[79] Nicholas Haysom and Clive Plaskett, 'The War Against Law: Judicial Activism and the Appellate Division' (1988) 4 *South African Journal on Human Rights* 303.

[80] See Mark Elliott, 'Utterly Risible' (Sep 10 2020) online: *X* <https://twitter.com/profmarkelliott/status/1304076133827309569>.

[81] Kim Lane Scheppele, 'Autocratic Legalism' (2018) 85 *University of Chicago Law Review* 545.

[82] David Landau, 'Abusive Constitutionalism' (2013) 47 *UC Davis Law Review* 189.

lawyers on the surface play the language game of the rule of law and democracy, whatever their intentions, their arguments result in installing a different game altogether, the game of rule by executive diktat, the kind of game that Trump has been playing since the start of 2025.

Chapter 2 now turns to the Rwanda Act and the legal context into which it was inserted, both the general characteristics of the UK constitutional order and the important post-war changes that are the background necessary for understanding the debates around it. In it we embark on a journey into law coming back fully to politics only in Chapter 6. It is important to keep in mind on this journey that the Judicial Power Project is the legal face of the political Common Good Project. As Chapters 2–5 show, its lawyers make their arguments in the language of the law, not in the language of politics. Indeed, they like to accuse their opponents of making political arguments because of their commitments to human rights and international law, to, as we will see, a 'thick' or 'substantive' conception of the rule of law. At the same time, they assert that their 'thin' conception of the rule of law represents a politically neutral consensus and that they are seeking merely to restore some ancient constitution.[83]

However, while the common good lawyers make their arguments in the language of the law, I will show that they have a troubled relationship with the law and the legal authorities they claim as the basis for these arguments. That trouble supports two important conclusions. First, it is evidence of the fact that the arguments are a veneer over these lawyers' political agenda. Second, that political agenda has itself a troubled relationship with the rule of law. Indeed, the 'ancient constitution' they often claim to be in the business of restoring is in reality a new kind of order, one with only a tenuous claim to be a constitutional order. So while discussion of the 'common good' is going largely to vanish until Chapter 6, the political agenda of the Common Good Project is always just below the surface of issues we confront as I set the context for and then analyse the arguments made by the lawyers of the Judicial Power Project. And the political agenda of the Common Good Project is to put in place a state that will enforce 'the natural law', understood as the moral virtues as portrayed in their illiberal distortion of the Roman Catholic 'classical' tradition.

[83] See Richard Ekins, 'Political Polarization and the Rule of Law' (2025) 19 *Law & Ethics of Human Rights* 201.

2

Parliamentary Sovereignty and the Rule of Law

2.1 Constitutional Heresies

> I . . . watched with a mixture of fury, disbelief and profound sadness as the previous government introduced the Safety of Rwanda Act. I will leave it to my colleagues to make the obvious points about the workability and costs of the scheme – what to my mind was even more significant were the constitutional heresies contained in the Act. The Act starts with the otiose and therefore crass assertion of parliamentary sovereignty; it moves to the express disapplication of fundamental international law obligations owed, including under the ECHR [European Convention on Human Rights] and the Refugee Convention, and even customary international law; and it ousted the role of the courts in determining relevant facts except where individual circumstances were in issue, indeed obliging them to accept as true facts that may well have been false – it felt, not so much as though we had fallen through the Looking Glass but rather dived head first into it.[1]

This expression of anger, sadness and incredulity is from a lecture – 'The Rule of Law in an Age of Populism' – by Richard Hermer, Attorney General of the United Kingdom, on 14 October 2024 to the Bingham Centre for the Rule of Law. Hermer had been, up until July 2024, a practising human rights lawyer, specializing in international law, at a leading barristers' chambers in London.[2] He had just taken office in the newly formed Labour government headed by Keir Starmer, who had himself been in practice as a human rights lawyer before becoming Director of Public Prosecutions in 2008 and subsequently entering politics as a Labour member of Parliament in 2015. The Safety of Rwanda

[1] Richard Hermer, 'The Rule of Law in an Age of Populism' (Oct 14 2024) online: *Bingham Centre for the Rule of Law* <www.biicl.org/documents/12532_bingham_lecture_2024.pdf> at 2.

[2] 'About Us' online: *Matrix Chambers* <www.matrixlaw.co.uk/about-us/>.

(Asylum and Immigration) Act had become law on 24 April 2024, just five months before Hermer gave the Bingham Lecture.

Public lectures by this sort of high office holder require clearance by other high office holders, including perhaps by the Prime Minister. Thus, writing in the *Guardian* in reaction to the lecture, Martin Kettle said that 'it is surely not reckless to believe that [Hermer] ... was also saying things with which Starmer would be fully in accord and to which he himself attaches special importance'. He went on to suggest that both Hermer's appointment and the lecture showed that 'Starmer believes in the rule of law. It is his red line. He absolutely does not wish to cross it if he can avoid doing so'.[3]

In what world, we must ask, would one think that the contrary could be true? That the Prime Minister of a country that prides itself on being the birthplace of the modern idea and ideal of the rule of law would make it clear that he no longer believes in its worth by sacrificing it to pander to the populist right? The answer, regretfully, is the looking glass world into which the UK government under the leadership of Rishi Sunak – the Conservative Party Prime Minister – dived when Parliament enacted the Rwanda Act. And while the UK is for the time being rather tentatively on the path back to a place in which the government walks the rule-of-law walk, Donald Trump's return to power promises something very different for the world at large. In addition, Hermer is continually subject to attack, often vicious, by the common good lawyers, in concert with the right-wing press and politicians, including in debates in the House of Lords where Hermer now has a place in order to serve as Attorney General.[4]

[3] Martin Kettle, 'Does Starmer Believe in Anything, People Ask, and Now We Know: His Credo Is the Rule of Law' (Oct 17 2024) online: *The Guardian* <www.theguardian.com/commentisfree/2024/oct/17/keir-starmer-beliefs-attorney-general-rule-of-law>.
As I suggested in my Preface, Starmer's record in office has proved rather dismal and there is now even reason to doubt his commitment to the rule of law. See Daniel Trilling, 'Starmer v Starmer: Why Is the Former Human Rights Lawyer so Cautious about Defending Human Rights?' (Jul 29 2025) online: *The Guardian* <www.theguardian.com/politics/2025/jul/29/keir-starmer-labour-party-human-rights-mixed-record-international-law>.

[4] Consider that in his speech at the Conservative Party Conference in 2025, Shadow Justice Minister Robert Jenrick compared Hermer to a lawyer in the pay of the Mafia and accused him of treason:

> Like one of those infamous mafia lawyers of yesteryear, Hermer always chose a particular type of client: Shamima Begum, Osama bin Laden's right-hand man, terrorists involved in 7/7. Since taking office, we're told Lord Hermer's

To accuse one's predecessors in office of having engaged in 'constitutional heresies' is a serious charge and politically most controversial, despite Hermer's claim in the lecture that he would not make 'any party political points in this speech' and that he was determined 'to make the promotion of the rule of law a project we can all sign up to irrespective of our political allegiance, or indeed any political allegiance'. Indeed, his Department clearly disagreed with him on this point since on its official website the transcript of the speech omits these passages, noting their absence with 'Redacted Political Content',[5] so that one has to go to the Bingham Centre's website to find his full text.

This book will vindicate Hermer's claim that he was not making party political points, as well as the claim that his predecessors were guilty of committing constitutional heresies. That it was politically controversial to make the points is perfectly consistent, we will see, with claiming that they are not 'party political', at least so long as all the main political players pay more than lip service to the rule of law. I can't of course know how precise Hermer intended the charge of heresy to be. But it is worth noting that a 'heretic' differs from an 'apostate', one who abandons the faith altogether. A heretic, by contrast, adheres to a doctrine contradictory to at least one single and central principle of the faith. And if we take the faith here to be faith in the rule of law, and, more broadly, in constitutional government, my task will be to show what exactly the Rwanda Act did that amounted to a doctrine contradictory to principles crucial to both the rule of law and constitutional government. And that will require unpacking carefully the idea and practice of the rule of law.

My focus is on the Act, an episode in a war waged in the UK against its main target – its domestically enshrined legal commitments to international law. I will show that the war against international law turned necessarily into a total one, not only against international law, but even against the rule of law itself. And with the rule of law subverted, one no

> advice to Starmer and his cronies has been to give away the Chagos Islands to an ally of China and to pay billions of pounds for the privilege. In each of these incidents, he's wasted no time establishing himself as a useful idiot for our enemies. His rise symbolises the central truth of Keir Starmer's government. Labour is just not on Britain's side.

Robert Jenrick, 'Ending Judicial Activism' (Oct 7 2025) online: <www.conservatives.com/news/ending-judicial-activism>.

5 Richard Hermer, 'Attorney General's 2024 Bingham Lecture on the Rule of Law' (Oct 15 2024) online: *UK.Gov* <www.gov.uk/government/speeches/attorney-generals-2024-bingham-lecture-on-the-rule-of-law>.

longer has government according to law, including the state's international law obligations.

The Rwanda Act required that asylum seekers who arrived in the UK be stripped of the legal protections they would ordinarily have had under UK law and be summarily rendered to Rwanda, a country that the UK Supreme Court had found in 2023 to be an 'unsafe' country. It thus enshrined in law the 'Rwanda Plan', which purported to deter asylum seekers from coming to the UK, especially those who would do so by attempting the risky journey across the Channel in small unseaworthy boats, by deporting them to Rwanda where their claims would be processed. As we will see, the main difference the Act made was that, in combination with the Treaty that preceded it, and which purported magically to make Rwanda 'safe', asylum seekers would get to stay in Rwanda as permanent residents even if their claims for asylum failed.

The attempt to implement that policy by executive order had been thwarted first by the European Court of Human Rights and then by the UK Supreme Court in 2023. This is because the international refugee system operates based on a distinction between asylum seekers and refugees.[6] Asylum seekers are those who are pursuing refugee status but do not yet have it. Once they obtain that status, international refugee law imposes obligations on the relevant state to support their welfare and not to relocate them outside the state's jurisdiction. The major legal concern surrounding the Plan was that it violated the principle of 'non-refoulement', a principle of international law found in the 1951 Refugee Convention and its 1967 Protocol which extended the protections put in place by the Convention. The principle requires that asylum seekers not be returned to a country where their life or freedom is threatened, or where they risk facing torture or inhumane treatment. The UK is a party to both of these instruments – that is, it has formally agreed to be bound by the obligations they set out. In addition, the principle is codified in the European Convention on Human Rights and is incorporated into UK domestic law by a statute of the UK Parliament, the Human Rights Act 1998. It was the Supreme Court's finding that Rwanda was not a 'safe country' because there was a danger that the government there would send asylum seekers to unsafe countries that attracted the ire of the Conservative government and set in motion the process that ended with the enactment of the statute.

[6] Rhys Drakeley, 'Loophole or Law-Breaking? Rwanda Plan's Inconsistency with International Refugee Law' (2023) 4 *York Law Review* 141 at 143.

The Act's passage through Parliament was guided by James Cleverly, the Home Secretary and thus the minister responsible for immigration policy, who in his previous incarnation as Foreign Secretary had been overheard describing the Rwanda Plan as 'batshit crazy'.[7] When pressed by journalists, Cleverley found it difficult to deny his words, in part because the Plan was in three respects clearly crazy.

First, the Plan was crazy from a purely practical perspective, as Hermer suggested. The costs of relocating people and then subsidizing their stay in Rwanda were utterly prohibitive and, even if the Plan were implemented, it would hardly make a dent in the numbers of people arriving to seek asylum in the UK. In addition, the Plan's main stated aim – to deter migrants from making that illegal crossing – was widely regarded as futile. People who had made the dangerous journey to France and then had just one more short though dangerous boat ride to get to the UK were not going to be deterred by the faint prospect of being sent to Rwanda. It was clear that the Plan amounted to what gets called in the UK 'red meat' – the kind of populist policy thrown to the supporters of one's ideology to keep them in the fold or to bring them back in, in this case those whose cultural anxieties focus on immigrants as the main cause of their economic and social woes.

Second, the Plan was morally crazy. It required that all who enter the UK illegally, which means almost every candidate for refugee status, be deported to Rwanda. Wherever they came from – Syria, Afghanistan, the Russian Federation, and of course parts of Africa – they would find themselves, in most cases after a dangerous and traumatic journey to the UK, doomed to life in a country with a notoriously bad human rights record, so bad that the UK had in fact granted refugee status to Rwandans who had fled President Paul Kagame's authoritarian regime.[8] Moreover, a similar scheme which had been set up between Israel and Rwanda had been aborted when it became clear that the individuals Israel had deported to Rwanda were given rough treatment on arrival and then sent across the border to Uganda at their own

7 Archie Mitchell and Kate Devlin, 'James Cleverly Refuses to Deny He Called Rishi Sunak's Rwanda Scheme "Batshit"' (Nov 16 2023) online: *The Independent* <www.independent.co.uk/news/uk/politics/james-cleverly-rwanda-scheme-batshit-sunak-b2448446.html>.

8 John Ungoed-Thomas and Antony Barnett, 'Revealed: UK Granted Asylum to Rwandan Refugees While Arguing Country Was Safe' (Jan 27 2024) online: *The Guardian* <www.theguardian.com/world/2024/jan/27/revealed-uk-granted-asylum-to-rwandan-refugees-while-arguing-country-was-safe>.

expense.[9] The UK and Rwandan governments claimed that things would be different because the UK would be monitoring the situation through 'a bespoke joint committee'. But given the Rwandan government's record, not only of human rights abuses but also of reneging on assurances and then lying, only those with a stake in being convinced were impressed.

Third, and the main point Hermer was making, the Plan was legally speaking crazy. The Rwanda Act deemed a country 'safe' that the highest Court in the land had found unsafe, thus putting in place by legislative fiat a set of 'alternative facts'.[10] In addition, it almost entirely ousted or prohibited judicial review of the statute or its implementation. In this way, the UK's treatment of asylum seekers was made lawless. As I will show, it was no longer governed by the rule of law, even on an austere or 'thin' definition of it, one which says that all the rule of law requires is that officials obey the rules laid down by the superior authority of Parliament. For even on this definition, one does not have the rule of law if the officials get to decide what to do unconstrained by the law of their legal order.

But, one needs to ask, and the big question my book will answer: 'Did the rule that required deportation of asylum seekers violate the rule of law even on the thin definition?' It will take this whole book to substantiate the charge that it did, and thus Hermer's claim that the Act contained 'constitutional heresies'. I adopt the thin definition until Chapter 4 because, while what the rule of law requires is a matter of some controversy in both politics and in legal and political theory, the definition captures one important point of consensus. All agree that whatever else it may entail, the rule of law requires that officials obey the law that applies to them. A simple but still useful definition of the rule of law contrasts its rule with 'the arbitrary rule of men'. In other words, the rule of law is the rule of rules that constrain what officials may lawfully do, while the rule of men permits individuals with power do whatever they want. On this definition, rules made in accordance with the rule of law enable me to predict with fair certainty what decisions officials will make, which allows law to fulfil its function of guiding the

[9] Daisy Walsh, 'What Happened When Israel Sent Its Refugees to Rwanda' (Jun 22 2022) online: *BBC* <www.bbc.com/news/world-61882542>.

[10] This is a term invented by Trump's senior advisor in a bid to deflect criticism of lies he told about the size of the crowd at his inauguration in 2016. See Eric Bradner, 'Conway: Trump White House Offered "Alternative Facts" on Crowd Size' (Jan 23 2017) online: *CNN* <https://edition.cnn.com/2017/01/22/politics/kellyanne-conway-alternative-facts/index.html>.

behaviour of those subject to it. The rule of men, in contrast, does not provide a basis for such prediction.

In his Bingham Lecture, Hermer suggested that he was operating with a very different, much 'thicker' or substantive definition of the rule of law, one that includes respect for both international law and human rights. The lecture and the Bingham Centre itself commemorate the life and work of Tom Bingham, Baron Bingham of Cornwall (1933–2010), who rose to the highest judicial office of the land, and whose death provided the occasion for many tributes. For example, Sir Louis Blom-Cooper QC said: 'It is no exaggeration to say that Tom Bingham was the greatest judge of our time – arguably the most significant judicial figure among the long line of notables in the history of the Anglo-Saxon legal systems.'[11]

Among the reasons Bingham was so venerated was his commitment to the rule of law, a commitment expressed both in his judgments and in his book *The Rule of Law*.[12] The Bingham Centre states that its 'vision is of a world in which every society is governed by the Rule of Law in the interests of good government and peace at home and in the world at large', a vision set out in Bingham's 'wonderfully accessible' book, *The Rule of Law*. There, he wrote: '[t]he rule of law is one of the greatest unifying factors, perhaps the greatest . . . It remains an ideal, but an ideal worth striving for'.[13]

The book is indeed wonderfully accessible. But the content of Bingham's vision is hardly uncontroversial and he is regarded most of the time by the common good lawyers as one of their arch-enemies. Notably, he rejected the thin definition of the rule of law which he rightly took to be implicit in this passage from one of the most influential essays on this topic of the last century, Oxford legal philosopher Joseph Raz's 'The Rule of Law and Its Virtue':

> A non-democratic legal system, based on the denial of human rights, on extensive poverty, on racial segregation, sexual inequalities, and religious persecution may, in principle, conform to the requirements of the rule of law better than any of the legal systems of the more enlightened Western

[11] Maev Kennedy, 'Tributes to Lord Bingham, "the Greatest Judge of Our Time"' (Sep 12 2010) online: *The Guardian* <www.theguardian.com/law/2010/sep/12/tributes-lord-bingham-judge-dies>.

[12] Tom Bingham, *The Rule of Law* (London: Allen Lane, 2010).

[13] 'Our Vision' online: *Bingham Centre for the Rule of Law* <https://binghamcentre.biicl.org/our-vision>.

> democracies. . . . . It will be an immeasurably worse legal system, but it will excel in one respect: in its conformity to the rule of law . . . The law may . . . institute slavery without violating the rule of law.[14]

Bingham's discussion occurs within chapter 7, 'Human Rights', in the section in which he set out the fifth of the eight principles he identified as giving us the content of the rule of law – 'The law must afford adequate protection of fundamental human rights'. But all he said in response to Raz was that 'while one can recognize the logical force of Professor Raz's contention, I would roundly reject it in favour of a "thick" definition, embracing the protection of human rights within its scope'.[15]

That's an inadequate response as it concedes 'logical force' to Raz without telling the reader why Raz, while 'logical', is wrong. Hermer did not help in this regard in his lecture since all he offered was a statement of belief. He said that the thin definition of the rule of law amounts to 'rule by law; a purely procedural and formal conception that populists and authoritarians can themselves so often use as a cloak of legitimacy'. He went on:

> One of Lord Bingham's great contributions was to promote a more substantive conception of the rule of law, including the idea that the law must afford adequate protection of fundamental human rights. I too believe that human rights – both at the level of principle, and in practice through how they are enforced – are an essential element of the rule of law and a stable democratic culture. As well as recognising and protecting the dignity of all, they guarantee the essential rights and freedoms which underpin our system.[16]

Hermer's lecture attracted much criticism in the House of Lords not long after he delivered it, and his efforts to put the UK back on the rule-of-law track have attracted a sustained attack in the right-wing media and even from within his own party. The attack, fuelled by the work of the common good lawyers within the Judicial Power Project, and fully endorsed by Lord Wolfson, the Conservative Party's Shadow Attorney General, claims that the thin definition both represents a politically neutral consensus about the rule of law, and is the one supported by the UK's constitutional tradition. I can and will show that a commitment to this 'thin' definition is to a politically contested thick definition, in

[14] Bingham, *The Rule of Law* at 66–67; Joseph Raz, 'The Rule of Law and Its Virtue' in *The Authority of Law: Essays on Law and Morality* (Oxford: Clarendon Press, 1983) 210 at 211.

[15] Bingham, *The Rule of Law*, at 67.

[16] Hermer, 'The Rule of Law in an Age of Populism' at 3.

contest, that is, with even thicker definitions, and that such thicker definitions are in fact supported by the UK's constitutional tradition. This demonstration is important legally, because it is precisely the issue of thin versus thick that is at stake in the lawyers' arguments about the legality of the Rwanda Act. It is just as important politically because the very survival of the rule of law in the UK was and remains at stake.

For the moment we can note that Raz was one of the main standard bearers of a philosophical tradition in Oxford, still dominant today, known as 'legal positivism'. Put at its simplest, such philosophers argue that all there is to law is the rules in fact made or 'posited' by those who have authority to do so. The rule of law is then the rule of such posited rules and whether it is a good or bad thing will depend largely on what content the rulers choose to give the rules, whether, as Raz suggests, they are democrats, liberals, racists, misogynists, enslavers, and so on. An important implication is the rules made in accordance with the rule of law can have any content, including content that we might morally condemn. So we can add to the thin definition of the rule of law that as long as the rules are clear, so that citizens can know in advance what the law is and can guide their actions by the law, the rule of law is in place *whatever the content of the rules.*

I will later confront the philosophical theory that says all there is to the rule of law is this thin definition because it undergirds both the political attacks on Hermer and the position of the common good lawyers, who in fact provide the basis for the attacks by politicians and in the media. As I will show, the dispute over the thin and thick definitions of the rule of law can be settled through my account of the Rwanda saga – an account of the practical implications of a commitment to the rule of law and of the political stakes when the commitment is undermined, even as those whose efforts undermine it sincerely claim to serve its ideal.

It is here that I will register some disagreement with both Hermer and Bingham in that I will argue that they were mistaken to the extent that they entered into a definitional game which they were destined to lose. This is a game in which one side insists that it is a conceptual mistake to confuse the rule of law with the rule of human rights or the rule of international law because that collapses the thin and useful definition into what one happens to prefer politically. We will see that the thin versus thick definition debate is a complete red herring. No one in fact adopts the thin definition as just sketched other than lawyers like the common good lawyers, who exploit it in a way that results in the undermining of the rule of law, constitutional government and democracy.

Once one sees this, one can also appreciate that the issue is not a contest of definitions, but one of more or less thick 'conceptions' of the rule of law. And with that insight in place, not only does it become clear that a conception that includes a commitment to human rights and international law is a plausible candidate, but, given facts about the UK constitutional order, it is the only plausible candidate for the UK. Indeed, it is the only plausible candidate for any political order that wants to think of itself as democratic. A commitment to even the thinnest conception commits one to the view that the rule of law requires respect for legally protected rights, which in the UK in the post-war period has come to mean respect for both human rights and international law. Moreover, since the aim of the Judicial Power Project is to make way for the enforcement of the ideology of the Common Good Project, and since that ideology is committed to an altogether substantive set of values as intrinsic to law – the values they take to be 'the natural law' – their embrace of a thin definition is of a mere vehicle for delivering the most substantive conception of the rule of law on offer. For them, the rule of law is the rule of 'the natural law'.

2.2 The Deportation Rule

The Rwanda Plan and the legislative form it was eventually given provide a highly productive context for just this kind of inquiry. This is largely the case because the rule of law problem the Rwanda Act posed may seem at first sight wholly different from that of being subject to the arbitrary rule of men, if one puts to one side the huge practical problems that would have attended any attempt fully to implement the legislation. For, on the assumption of full implementation, it might seem to be the case that you would have known with complete certainty what your fate would be once you arrived as an asylum seeker in the UK. You would be deported to Rwanda. The officials are then not able to do whatever they want under the Act. They are subject to a rigid rule which requires them, with some small exceptions, to deport any asylum seeker. That rule – 'the deportation rule' – can do its work because of a key change the Rwanda Act made to the legal landscape.

First, the Act not only declared Rwanda to be 'safe', but also explicitly disapplied the legal rights that asylum seekers previously had and that various officials, tribunals and courts would have had to interpret in deciding whether an asylum seeker would get the refugee status that would permit that person to stay in the UK. Second, it explicitly ousted or removed almost all the avenues that would ordinarily be available to seek judicial review of the implementation of the statute. In a real way, then, the deportation rule seems to make matters a lot more certain than the prior regime, which left the determination of an individual's eligibility for refugee status in the hands of officials, administrative tribunals and the courts. Any arbitrariness that may be at play in this situation therefore cannot stem from the inability to predict what decision will be made. Rather, it is the certainty that an immoral and inhumane decision will be made. It may thus seem arbitrary only in a substantive sense, where arbitrary means something like immoral.

We will later see that the deportation rule did not provide such certainty. But for the time being, I'll assume that it would. At this point, I want to note a feature of the situation that is starting to emerge and which will receive more elaborate treatment later. The deportation rule is on the surface in conflict with other valid rules that protected the rights of asylum seekers, as well as with rules that require that courts have the authority to determine that the officials are in fact working within the scope of the authority afforded them by whatever law they are charged with implementing. At one level, there was no conflict, since the statute explicitly disapplied nearly all the first set of rules – that is, deemed them legally irrelevant so that officials implementing the deportation rule could do so unimpeded by challenges in court. In addition, it almost altogether ousted the authority of the courts to review the implementation of the deportation rule. However, the rules that the Rwanda Act disapplied or ousted remained valid rules of the UK legal order. So at another level there was an inconsistency, even an incoherence. As we will later see, the Act permitted this incoherence to become a matter for judicial scrutiny, thus uniting the levels, which gave human rights lawyers a resource to argue that the moral arbitrariness was also legally arbitrary because a group subject to the state's authority has been deprived of legal rights that the law would otherwise afford them.

Moreover, the incoherence was not between rules at the same level. Suppose that the legislature enacts in the same statute a rule that people must drive on the left-hand side of the road and a rule that they must drive on the right-hand side. The practical conflict this statute creates is serious and is inconsistent with any definition of the rule of law. But it is a conflict between rules at the same level – the level where the law tells those subject to it how to act. In contrast, the conflict the Rwanda Act creates is not a practical one, at least not in the sense that the individuals subject to it are pulled in two directions by their legal obligations.

However, at least arguably, it is a conflict between the deportation rule – a practical rule that tells officials how to act – and more fundamental rules. The latter are rules about protected human rights and rules about the authority of judges to review the implementation of statutes in order to check that the officials are acting within the scope of the authority delegated to them by Parliament. It follows that the conflict is a constitutional one, between a practical rule and more fundamental or constitutional rules. That argument, which I will show to be sound, tells us that this is not a practical conflict, but something more serious. The deportation rule is in some sense unconstitutional. That's the point of saying that it introduced an incoherence into the UK constitutional order.

The problem here is most vividly one for judges and other officials involved in interpreting and implementing the law. How are they to make sense of the fact that, on the one hand, the law tells them that they have an obligation to respect constitutional principles as well as legally protected rights, including rights that have their source ultimately in international law, while on the other hand, the law also tells them that such principles and these rights have been put out of the picture by the statute that regulates the processing of asylum claims? This problem is made even more complex by the fact that the asylum seekers had been deprived of their rights, and the courts of their review authority, by valid law enacted by the UK Parliament, the supreme legal authority in a democratic country. So one can argue, as the common good lawyers and their allies do, that the Rwanda Act was legally speaking the opposite of arbitrary since certainty has been brought by law to an otherwise uncertain situation and what's more it was perfectly constitutional because a sovereign parliament may enact any law it pleases.

And if that's right, even the judgment of moral arbitrariness might seem incorrect because the elected government that by definition speaks for the majority of the people in a democratic country has come to a different judgment. The judgment of moral arbitrariness may, that is, seem the preserve of the '*Guardian*-reading, tofu-eating wokerati', as Home Secretary Suella Braverman in Parliament in 2022 described liberals concerned with human rights,[17] or the 'lefty lawyers', as former Prime Minister Rishi Sunak described the opposition to the Rwanda Plan in 2023. This was a clear dig at his successor, Keir Starmer, then leader of

[17] Zoe Tidman, 'Home Secretary Suella Braverman Blames Protest Disruption on "Tofu-Eating Wokerati"' (Oct 19 2022) online: *The Independent* <www.independent.co.uk/news/uk/politics/suella-braverman-just-stop-oil-tofu-b2205903.html>.

the opposition, and at, again in Braverman's words, 'an activist blob of leftwing lawyers, civil servants and the Labour party'.[18]

As Charles Falconer, a former barrister who served as Lord Chancellor and Justice Minister for Labour from 2003 to 2007, pointed out in a column in that offending newspaper the *Guardian*, these attacks on lawyers by the most senior office holders in the government were of a piece with branding judges 'enemies of the people', as the *Daily Mail* had done in 2016 during the saga which laid the foundation for the Rwanda saga: Brexit.[19] Baron Falconer of Thoroton was right to see these attacks as not aimed merely at a distinct group of lawyers, but at the rule of law itself. As he put it, 'This perversion of the rule of law subjugates it to contested views of what the public want'.[20] He was right though, not because of his grand title, but because the *argument* for Hermer's claim that constitutional heresies were being perpetrated is sound.

I labour this point to emphasize that it takes an argument to get to this conclusion, one that squarely confronts facts about the law and about the constitutional order in which the law was made – in the case of the Rwanda Plan, a valid law enacted by a Parliament in a democratic country supposedly in an effort to bring certainty in a political controversy. It must confront principally the arguments made by lawyers that both the Rwanda Plan and the Act were perfectly consistent with both the rule of law and international law, and who, far from holding Bingham in high esteem, regard him as the judge who did the most to usurp authority from Parliament.

It must also confront a problem intrinsic to any legal order in which Parliament is considered to be the supreme source of legal authority, the paradox of sovereignty. For, as we will see in the next section, in the UK constitutional set-up, what Parliament gives, Parliament can take away. Evoking the Book of Job – 'The Lord gave and the Lord has taken away;

[18] Jasmine Cameron-Chileshe, William Wallis and Delphine Strauss, 'Sunak Attacks "Lefty Lawyers" Amid Criticism of Small Boats Strategy' (Mar 8 2023) online: *Financial Times* <www.ft.com/content/246232b7-2f83-4698-a2bd-368e396913fe>.

[19] Charles Falconer, 'Lefty Lawyers, "Enemies of the People": How Upholding the Law Is a Crime in Some Eyes' (Aug 12 2023) online: *The Guardian* <www.theguardian.com/commentisfree/2023/aug/12/lefty-lawyers-enemies-of-people-upholding-law-a-crime>. And see from 2016, Rachael Pells, 'Daily Mail's "Enemies of the People" Front Page Receives more than 1,000 Complaints to IPSO' (Nov 10 2016) online: *The Independent* <www.independent.co.uk/news/media/daily-mail-nazi-propaganda-front-page-ipso-complaints-brexit-eu-enemies-of-the-people-a7409836.html>.

[20] See Falconer, 'Lefty Lawyers'.

may the name of the Lord be praised' – is instructive in this context. God in Jewish and Christian theologies is considered to be all-powerful, omnipotent. And the attribute of omnipotence raises difficult questions, which philosophers group under the title of 'the paradox of omnipotence'. For example, can God create a stone so heavy that he could not lift it? As the Oxford philosopher John Mackie pointed out in 'Evil and Omnipotence', a classic treatment of the paradox, the problem does not arise only for theists. Indeed, his own attempt at a solution to the paradox was based on what he called a 'parallel Paradox of Sovereignty': 'Can a legal sovereign make a law restricting its own future legislative power? For example, could the British parliament make a law forbidding any future parliament to socialise banking, and also forbidding the future repeal of the law itself?'[21]

I will set out Mackie's solution to the paradox at the end of Chapter 5. For the moment, I want to recall that we already encountered an attempt in the Introduction, in the recommendations by the philosopher of law Hans Kelsen and the human rights lawyer Murray Hunt that we should get rid of the problems intrinsic to the idea of sovereignty by ridding legal and constitutional theory altogether of the idea. I suggested that this solution does not work and will provide an argument that retains the idea of legal sovereignty based in part on Mackie's solution in Chapter 5. That argument must squarely confront facts about the law and about the legal and political order in which the law was made, in the case of the Rwanda Plan a valid law enacted by a Parliament in a democratic country supposedly in an effort to bring certainty in a political controversy. It must also confront the arguments made by the common good lawyers that both the Plan and the Act were perfectly consistent with both the rule of law and international law.

In the next section, I set the stage for this confrontation in Chapter 3 by describing at some length the legal landscape in which the Rwanda Act was enacted. I hope this will be helpful not only to those readers who may not be acquainted with public law in the UK, but also to those for whom what follows is mostly old hat, as I also make clear what features of the landscape I am taking for granted. And, following on from the last point, my claim is not that my description is wholly uncontroversial. As we will see, different values are at stake in the very descriptions of what we can think of as the constitutional fundamentals of the UK legal order.

[21] JL Mackie, 'Evil and Omnipotence' (1955) 64 *Mind* 200 at 211–12.

Put differently, and to use a term of art from the social sciences, our very descriptions are not 'value-neutral' but 'value-laden' and it is only one perspective that illuminates the complicating factor – that the deportation rule is legally speaking both arbitrary and valid. However, that perspective is not 'subjective' in that one will adopt it or not depending on which 'blob' one belongs to. It is the only perspective available if one wishes to make sense of the rule of law. This is not to say that mine is the only available *political* perspective; for example, there is the common good lawyers' perspective. But I will show that their perspective risks destroying the rule of law from within. And since I am going not only to vindicate Attorney General Hermer's charge that the Rwanda Act contained 'constitutional heresies', but also to show that the common good lawyers did not think it was heretical enough, there is no better place to start than with the closest thing to a constitutional bible in the UK, A. V. Dicey's *Introduction to the Study of Law of the Constitution*, first published in 1885.[22]

2.3 The Legal Landscape

2.3.1 Dicey and the Constitutional Fundamentals

Albert Venn Dicey (1835–1922) was a lawyer who became Vinerian Professor of English Law at the University of Oxford. In that position, he delivered lectures to the undergraduate law students on which he based his book. So influential is his 1885 *Introduction to the Study of the Law of the Constitution* that the *Encyclopaedia Britannica* says that 'it is considered part of the British constitution'.[23] It continues that the constitution is 'an amalgam of several written and unwritten authorities'. Here the entry draws our attention to the fact that this constitution is often said to be 'unwritten' in that it is not contained in any one written document as is the case with the Constitution of the US. Rather, it consists of principles found in a muddle of judgments and statutes rendered and enacted over the course of centuries. Because much of its content is gleaned from judgments in a 'common law system', in which

[22] I will use here the eighth edition, republished as AV Dicey, *Introduction to the Study of the Law of the Constitution* [1915] (Indianapolis: Liberty Fund, 1982).

[23] 'Albert Venn Dicey' (Jul 20 1998) online: *Encyclopedia Britannica* <www.britannica.com/biography/Albert-Venn-Dicey>. Dicey, as we will see, referred to the constitution as the 'English constitution'. I will generally use 'UK constitution', which may irritate some readers, but which I think works well in the context of my book.

judgments on a matter today stand as precedents or authoritative pronouncements binding on courts in the future, it is also often said to be a 'common law constitution'. It is worth noting these descriptions since they explain how a book can be thought of as 'part of the British constitution', though, given that you will not find it referred to when the common good lawyers extol their fidelity to 'tradition', they may well disagree.

Confronted with that muddle, the first major statement of how to make sense of it will have a major influence if, as was the case, the jurist is not only brilliant, but also well versed in legal and political history, comparative constitutional law, and philosophy.[24] It also helps that the book is closely based on lectures given to undergraduates since that gives rise to exceptionally clear treatments of complex problems. But, as we will find out, in at least one major respect it is far from easy to determine the implications of some of Dicey's positions. In particular, it is difficult to discern the implications of the intrinsic relationship he took to exist between two principles of the constitution he claimed as fundamental, and which are at issue in my book: the principle of parliamentary sovereignty and the principle of the rule of law.

Most precisely, what should one make of a situation when Parliament enacts a law that in explicit terms seeks to undermine aspects of the rule of law or even to do away with it or any other constitutional principle altogether? Dicey himself for the most part gave this problem short shrift and, insofar as he addressed it, offered answers that were either bad or elusive from the perspective of his own constitutional theory. That feature of his account of the constitution makes his theory problematic, but also offers an opportunity to do better by his own lights. Unfortunately, it also offers an opportunity to the common good lawyers to do worse. But, as I will also show, that they do worse by Dicey's own lights matters a great deal.

The first constitutional fundamental of the UK constitution is that Parliament is 'sovereign', defined by Dicey as 'the right [of the UK Parliament] to make or unmake any law whatever; and further, that no person or body is recognised by the law of England as having a right to override or set aside the legislation of Parliament'.[25]

[24] For the definitive account, see Mark Walters, *AV Dicey and the Common Law Constitutional Tradition: 'A Legal Turn of Mind'* (Cambridge: Cambridge University Press, 2020).

[25] Dicey, *Law of the Constitution*, at 3–4.

That definition entails a further claim about the relationship between the courts and Parliament which Dicey stated as follows:

> The principle then of Parliamentary sovereignty may, looked at from its positive side, be thus described; any Act of Parliament, or any part of an Act of Parliament, which makes a new law, or repeals or modifies an existing law, will be obeyed by the Courts. The same principle, looked at from its negative side, may be thus stated; there is no person or body of persons who can, under the English constitution, make rules which override or derogate from an Act of Parliament, or which (to express the same thing in other words) will be enforced by the Courts in contravention of an Act of Parliament.[26]

So now we have an important implication of the first constitutional fundamental in place. Judges do not have the authority to declare a statute that has been enacted in compliance with the formal criteria for enactment invalid because they object to its content. For example, the prohibition on judges invalidating a statute includes not doing so even when the statute overrides rights that the judges consider morally important. And that is the case even when such rights are embedded in other parts of the law, including both international law at large and those provisions of international law that Parliament has explicitly incorporated into UK law by statute. Of course, that leaves as a nagging question for both Dicey and for UK constitutional theory today the one I have just posed: Is the situation any different when it comes to the law of the constitution, that is, when the content of the statute is in some sense unconstitutional? It is that question that raises the paradox of sovereignty Mackie identified.

In regard to international law, Dicey was absolutely clear, saying of both morality and international law that a 'modern judge would never listen to a barrister who argued that an Act of Parliament was invalid because it was immoral' or because it violated the principles of international law.[27] Here he adopted the view of one of his major theoretical sources of influence, the great nineteenth-century legal-positivist philosopher John Austin, who stated that international law is no more than morality, so no more binding on judges than any other set of moral values. But we should also note that Austin had the same view of constitutional law.[28]And here Dicey parted from him in setting out a treatise

[26] Ibid at 4.

[27] Ibid at 20.

[28] John Austin, *Lectures on Jurisprudence or The Philosophy of Positive Law*, 5th edition (London: John Murray, 1885) volume 1 at 177, 204.

on 'the law of the constitution', since Austin would have regarded such a work as a book in moral philosophy.

I will come back to this tension between Dicey and Austin in Chapter 5. Whatever one makes of it, it is the case that the constitutional fundamental of parliamentary sovereignty together with its implication for judges gives rise to an important feature of the UK constitutional order's relationship with international law. Domestic constitutional orders are classified as either 'monist' or 'dualist'. Put simply, monist orders regard a significant part of international law, the obligations a state assumes by ratifying an international treaty, as directly binding within the internal space of the state. In contrast, dualist orders do not regard such obligations as binding until they have been incorporated into domestic law by the body with authority to do so. In the officially dualist UK order, the body with the authority to sign and ratify treaties is the executive, while the body with authority to incorporate them into domestic law is Parliament.

Dualism is part and parcel of the constitutional fundamental of parliamentary sovereignty. If Parliament is the supreme source of legal authority, it would be constitutionally improper to permit the executive to make law with direct legal effect within the UK by the mere fact of 'ratifying' a treaty. Ratification is a formal legal process which follows the government's signing of a treaty. Before 2010, the government would by convention 'lay' the treaty before Parliament for twenty-one days – that is, present it to Parliament for scrutiny, which in theory gave parliamentarians the opportunity to object to it. Once, as was invariably the case, there was no objection, the government would ratify the treaty, thus signalling to the international community that the state considered itself bound to observe the treaty.[29] The passage of the Constitutional Reform and Governance Act 2010 made what was previously a convention into a legal obligation in requiring that treaties be laid before Parliament for twenty-one sitting days. That gives the House of Commons the opportunity to pass a resolution that the treaty not be ratified, in which case another twenty-one-day delay is triggered.

Notice how even before 2010, this feature seems to build a kind of double-speak into the very structure of the UK constitutional order. The executive may commit the state to observe treaty obligations externally, as a matter between states, while internally those obligations have no

[29] The Right Honourable The Lord Templeman, 'Treaty-Making and the British Parliament' (1991) 67 *Chicago-Kent Law Review* 459.

effect, despite the fact that they have the appearance of tacit approval by Parliament. Of course, things are not so simple since treaties are not the only source of international law.

First, there is customary international law, the law based on consistent state practice such that one can infer the states' commitment to there being a binding rule of international law. Fortunately, we don't have to go into the difficult issue of when consistent state practice hardens into a binding legal rule. We just need to note that when it hardens, the rule is considered binding within the UK in that when judges review executive implementation of statutes they will, if the rule is relevant, ask whether the official acted in compliance with the rule. Judges ask the same question with respect to an official's compliance with a rule of English common law, which is itself a kind of customary law, if such a rule is relevant. One example is the rule that officials must avoid bias in making their decisions. (Again fortunately, we don't have to go into the difficult issue of when judicial custom hardens into a binding common law rule.)

In performing such a check, judges are not questioning whether the statute itself is valid since they assume its validity in line with the first constitutional fundamental. Rather, they are checking whether the officials' act or decision in discharging their duty under the statute is within the scope of the authority delegated to them by Parliament. As it is often put, the judges review whether the officials acted *intra vires* – within their powers – or *ultra vires* – outside of their powers. Yet another way of putting the point is to ask whether the officials acted in accordance with an overarching principle of legality. This is the principle that all official action must be according to law, which includes statutory and customary law, both relevant common law rules and relevant rules of customary international law.

A second source of international law is *jus cogens*, the principles of international law that are considered so fundamental that they bind states even if they have not consented to them. Examples include principles prohibiting enslavement, genocide, piracy, acts of aggression or the illegal use of force, though any such list tends to be controversial. While the exact legal effect of such principles, in particular their status within the internal space of a dualist state, is subject to debate, it is uncontroversial that judges will rely on them, as they do on ordinary customary international law, in interpreting the limits on executive authority.

Finally, in much the same manner, if the UK executive has gone to the length of ratifying a treaty, thus signalling to the world its formal commitment to the obligations it contains, that creates both an expectation that Parliament will follow suit by incorporating it, and permits judges to assume they may rely on the treaty in assessing the lawfulness of executive action within the state. And once they do that, or rely on a rule of customary international law, or a *jus cogens* principle, that reliance incorporates the rule or principle into the common law.

Why is such judicial incorporation consistent with parliamentary sovereignty? For the same reason that the common law, a kind of customary law whose principles are developed, changed and adapted by judges over time, is considered consistent. Put simply, Parliament, relying on its place in the constitutional order as the ultimate legal authority, may by using explicit wording, either in advance or retrospectively, override or overrule any common law rule. International law rules that do not need incorporating are similarly vulnerable to parliamentary diktat, with the possible exception of *jus cogens*, not an exception that need trouble us.

In sum, given the first constitutional fundamental of parliamentary sovereignty, one might wonder about the basis for the claim we encountered in Hermer's Bingham Lecture that the Rwanda Act contained 'constitutional heresies' and that its assertion of sovereignty was 'otiose and therefore crass'.[30] After all, it had been enacted in accordance with the rules of 'manner and form' that govern the making of parliamentary law – the formal criteria that have to be met for a statute to be recognized as valid. It might therefore seem to follow that judges are constitutionally bound to respect Parliament's deeming of Rwanda to be safe as well as its exclusions of the review authority they would otherwise have had to scrutinize the implementation by officials of the statute.

Here we should note that, in his chapter on parliamentary sovereignty, Dicey quoted with approval his philosopher cousin Leslie Stephen's claim that '[i]f a legislature decided that all blue-eyed babies should be murdered, the preservation of blue-eyed babies would be illegal'. Dicey added Stephen's qualification: 'but legislators must go mad before they could pass such a law, and subjects be idiotic before they could submit to it'.[31] The received view of this passage is that Dicey accepted that Parliament could adopt a law that is morally arbitrary – that is, cruel

[30] Hermer, 'The Rule of Law in an Age of Populism' at 2.

[31] Dicey, *Law of the Constitution*, at 33. Sir Leslie Stephen (1832–1904) was much more than an important philosopher, a political activist and father of both Virginia Woolf and Vanessa Bell. For a wonderful study of Dicey, Stephen and their set, see Stefan Collini, *Public Moralists: Political Thought and Intellectual Life in Britain 1850–1930* (Oxford: Clarendon Press, 2006).

or even evil – and moreover override protections in other laws against such cruelties, and yet the law would be perfectly valid. As a result, whatever judges think of the mental states of the legislators who enacted the law or of the subjects who submit to it, their constitutional duty is to apply it and not to listen to any lawyer who would argue otherwise.

I will argue that the received view of this passage is incorrect in Chapter 5. But even if we treat it as correct, what makes for a complicating factor is the rule of law. It is also the reason why the claim that judges are entitled to check whether officials acted in accordance with an overarching principle of legality is a somewhat controversial way of putting the uncontroversial point that judges are entitled to check whether officials acted within the scope of the powers delegated to them by statute. For, as I have indicated, there is much disagreement among UK lawyers about whether the correct definition of the rule of law is 'thin' or 'thick', where thin connotes simply that there is a formally valid rule that authorizes the official, whereas 'thick' suggests that there is more to the rule of law, for example compliance with human rights which have their ultimate source in international law. As we will now see, Dicey is in part responsible for the controversy despite his observation that a 'modern judge would never listen to a barrister who argued that an Act of Parliament was invalid because it was immoral' or because it violated the principles of international law.

Dicey started his book by explaining that '[t]he lectures were given and the book written with the sole object of explaining and illustrating three leading characteristics in the existing constitution of England; they are now generally designated as the Sovereignty of Parliament, the Rule of Law, and the Conventions of the Constitution'.[32] Recall that we already encountered the phenomenon of conventions in Chapter 1 in the Ministerial Code and in this chapter in the convention that required laying a treaty before Parliament prior to ratification. In this book, I deal only with the first two characteristics because Dicey himself indicated their centrality when he opened his discussion of the rule of law, saying: '[t]wo features' have 'at all times since the Norman Conquest characterised the political institutions of England'. The first is the 'omnipotence or undisputed supremacy throughout the whole country of the central government', while the second, 'closely connected with the first, is the rule or supremacy of law'.[33]

[32] Ibid at xxxv.
[33] Ibid at 107.

Notice the double occurrence of 'supremacy' in the last sentence and also the fact that with the first Dicey talks about the 'undisputed supremacy ... of the central government', not of Parliament. It suggests that parliamentary sovereignty is equated with the supremacy of law over all state action and there is a vision driving his picture of the UK constitutional order as one of government according to law. As the ultimate source of law, Parliament has the most important role in this constitutional structure. But the thing to emphasize is that it is a role *within* a structure, the *legal* structure of the UK constitutional order. And so difficult questions arise if Parliament does something that appears to damage the structure by enacting a law that undermines the constitution.

Dicey himself provided no good answer to such questions. For example, he asserted that 'Should the Dentists Act, 1878, unfortunately contravene the terms of the Act of Union, the Act of Union would be *pro tanto* repealed, but no judge would dream of maintaining that the Dentists Act, 1878, was thereby rendered invalid or unconstitutional'.[34] It is worth unpacking this example. The Act of Union was enacted in 1707 by the English and the Scottish Parliaments, at that time the legislative bodies of two independent kingdoms. It was this Act that led to the creation of the United Kingdom as a constitutional order, to be called 'Great Britain'.[35] So the implication that Dicey seemed to draw from his account of parliamentary sovereignty is that Parliament in a statute regulating the dentistry profession can include a provision repealing a founding document of the UK constitution.

Carl Schmitt, the authoritarian legal theorist, in his own major contribution to constitutional theory, mocked Dicey's answer, quipping that liberal constitutional theory cannot tell the difference between a statute regulating the dentistry profession and a statute that amounts to a revolution of the constitutional order.[36] Unfortunately, the quip may seem accurate given what Dicey for the most part said in his attempts to answer questions about the appropriate response to statutes that arguably disrupt or even rupture the constitutional order of which Parliament is a part. Fortunately, he had better answers available to him from his account of the rule of law. Even with this example,

[34] Ibid at 78.

[35] 'Act of Union 1707' online: *UK Parliament* <www.parliament.uk/about/living-heritage/evolutionofparliament/legislativescrutiny/act-of-union-1707/>.

[36] Carl Schmitt, *Constitutional Theory* (Durham, NC: Duke University Press, 2008) at 71–72.

unremarked by Schmitt and by many interpreters of Dicey, there is the unelaborated qualification that the Act of Union would be only '*pro tanto*' repealed, repealed only to the extent necessary to carry out the intention of the Dentists Act. So Dicey was not saying that the statute about dentists could sunder the UK into two parts. Rather, his view was that judges should interpret the statute by limiting its reach to the dental profession. However, even with that qualification, he leaves us in the dark when it comes to the implications of a statute that explicitly purported to bring about a wholesale revolution – for example, a statute that did explicitly state its intention to expel Scotland from the union.

As we now see, that issue becomes only murkier when we take into account the features Dicey identified of the rule of law, which he introduced by saying that '[w]hen we say that the supremacy of the rule of law is a characteristic of the English constitution, we generally include under one expression at least three distinct though kindred conceptions':[37]

> We mean, in the first place, that no man is punishable or can be lawfully made to suffer in body or goods except for a distinct breach of law established in the ordinary legal manner before the ordinary Courts of the land. In this sense the rule of law is contrasted with every system of government based on the exercise by persons in authority of wide, arbitrary, or discretionary powers of constraint.[38]

> We mean in the second place, when we speak of the 'rule of law' as a characteristic of our country, not only that with us no man is above the law, but (what is a different thing) that here every man, whatever be his rank or condition, is subject to the ordinary law of the realm and amenable to the jurisdiction of the ordinary tribunals. . . .

> There remains yet a third and a different sense in which the 'rule of law' or the predominance of the legal spirit may be described as a special attribute of English institutions. We may say that the Constitution is pervaded by the rule of law on the ground that the general principles of the Constitution (as for example the right to personal liberty, or the right of public meeting) are with us the result of judicial decisions determining the rights of private persons in particular cases brought before the Courts; whereas under many foreign constitutions the security (such as it is) given to the rights of individuals results, or appears to result, from the general principles of the constitution.[39]

[37] Dicey, *Law of the Constitution*, at 110.
[38] Ibid at 114.
[39] Ibid at 115.

In making the distinction between the UK constitution and 'foreign constitutions', Dicey was pointing to the difference between a constitution whose principles are to be found largely in judgments in which courts decide constitutional matters – that is, a common law constitution – and a written constitution which contains formal statements of principle. Now imagine a statute enacted in the UK context that makes people suffer without any 'distinct breach of law established in the ordinary legal manner before the ordinary Courts of the land', thus contravening Dicey's first feature. In addition, the officials who inflict the suffering are not 'subject to the ordinary law of the realm and amenable to the jurisdiction of the ordinary tribunals', since they are subject not to the 'ordinary law', but to an extraordinary rule that is immunized against the scrutiny of the courts, thus contravening the second feature. Finally, the combination of extraordinary rule with immunity from judicial scrutiny results in the people at the sharp end of the rule being deprived of the protection given by 'the general principles of the Constitution', themselves 'the result of judicial decisions determining the rights of private persons in particular cases brought before the Courts'. It follows that the statute puts in jeopardy all three features of Dicey's understanding of the rule of law.

To imagine such a statute in, say, the year 2000 would be a feat of imagination similar to Dicey's philosopher cousin's imagining the blue-eyed baby statute. At that point in time, one would have to conclude that it would never happen because the legislators would have to 'go mad before they could pass such a law, and subjects [would] be idiotic before they could submit to it'. But in 2024 we no longer had to use our imagination since we had the Rwanda Act, which also put in jeopardy all three features. It deemed Rwanda to be safe when the Supreme Court had found it to be in fact unsafe. It required of officials that they implement the deportation rule and not the human rights law that would ordinarily apply to asylum seekers. Finally, it deprived judges of the authority to apply the principles of the constitution in supervising the implementation of the statute. For we will shortly see that, according to Dicey's third feature, by 2024 – indeed, well before that date – the UK constitution included human rights protections for asylum seekers which were in part 'the result of judicial decisions determining the rights of private persons in particular cases brought before the Courts'.

Moreover, as we saw, James Cleverly, the minister who guided the statute through Parliament, had been overheard before he had that position, describing the statute's policy as 'batshit crazy'. So he seemed to agree with both Stephen and Dicey about the mental states of legislators who would enact such a statute. But since he and his fellow Conservatives went ahead and did it, the question is what to make of the statute from the perspective of the rule of law.

In particular, did the statute contain, as Hermer claimed, 'constitutional heresies'? Recall that a heretic differs from an apostate, one who abandons their faith altogether. A heretic, by contrast, adheres to a doctrine contradictory to at least one single and central principle of the faith. And if we take the faith here to be faith in the rule of law, and, more broadly, in constitutional government, my task will be to show what exactly the Act does that amounts to a doctrine contradictory to some principle crucial to both the rule of law and constitutional government.

That task is not easy. Indeed, this book as a whole is necessary to carry it out. As I will now explain, not only was the Rwanda Act the valid act of a sovereign parliament, but one must also take into account that in one important dimension the Act may seem better than the legal regime that governed prior to it from the perspective of Dicey's first feature. For as we have seen, Dicey followed 'no man is punishable or can be lawfully made to suffer in body or goods except for a distinct breach of law established in the ordinary legal manner before the ordinary Courts of the land' with: 'In this sense the rule of law is contrasted with every system of government based on the exercise by persons in authority of wide, arbitrary, or discretionary powers of constraint.'

Dicey's contrast here expressed his antipathy to administrative law – the law that governs the discretion public officials possess in exercising the authority delegated to them by statutes to implement the programmes and schemes established by the statutes. Administrative law is the law that most of us are likely to encounter in our daily lives given the growth of the administrative state in the twentieth century, the state that manages the delivery of welfare, education and health, and regulates building, the environment and much else besides. Not only did such a state barely exist in the UK when Dicey first wrote his lectures, but he was deeply opposed to it on the basis of what he thought he had observed in the development of such a state in France. For in France he saw not only the growth of public administration, but also a separate jurisdiction in that a specialized set of administrative tribunals, not the 'ordinary' courts, supervised the officials' exercise of discretion. That, he thought, made the French system one of discretion writ large – statutes that delegated wide discretionary authority to officials to implement statutes, with their decisions subject only to the wide discretionary authority of yet another set of officials.

In the leading work on Dicey's constitutional thought, Mark Walters gives his chapter on Dicey and administrative law the title 'Dicey's Administrative Law Blind Spot' and says that Dicey was 'the administrative lawyer's public enemy number one'.[40] But, as Walters also points out, Dicey greatly softened his hostility over time, as was reflected in changes he made to the introduction to his book. At the start, he had equated French administrative law with 'the despotism implicit within the claims made for an extraordinary "law of state" allowing the executive to set law aside whenever it wanted merely by invoking the *salus populi*' – the welfare of the people. But, says Walters, by the eighth edition of his book, 'Dicey was driven to concede that [such law] . . . was not that at all. It was a body of case law carefully constructed by tribunals that viewed the legality of administrative action through a lens that gave some weight to administrative experience and the public interest, but some weight to private rights and interests too'.[41]

Nonetheless, it remains true that in the regime that existed prior to the Rwanda Act an asylum seeker's fate depended on how the individual immigration official that was assigned their case chose to interpret and apply the law governing asylum to their particular circumstances. In other words, any asylum decision was to some extent an inherently personal and discretionary one. An applicant's success could thus turn less on the actual merit of their case as on their luck of the draw with respect to the official they were assigned to.

The point is beautifully made in John Lanchester's novel *Capital*, in which the reader is first drawn into a relationship with Quentina Mkfesi, a hard-working woman from Zimbabwe, who is working illegally while her claim for asylum is being processed. The reader is then introduced to two immigration officials, Alyson, a liberal-minded sort, who cares about the humanity of the people who come before her, and Peter, a conservative, intent on saving the tax payer's money. Lanchester writes that when Alyson's name 'was on the docket, the asylum seeker's barrister cheered up, and the Home Office's groaned, and reached for the Redbull'. After building up the tension as to what Quentina's fate will be, Lanchester ends the chapter with a conversation in which Peter and Alyson are about to start work one morning. Peter asks, 'So what's on?' 'Saudi dissident. You?', she replies. Peter's answer – 'Some Zimbabwean woman. Quentina something'.[42]

[40] Walters, *AV Dicey and the Common Law Constitutional Tradition*, at 300.

[41] Ibid at 326.

[42] John Lanchester, *Capital* (London: Faber and Faber, 2011) at 483–87.

But with the deportation rule in place, it no longer matters whether you as an asylum seeker get an adjudicator who simply tries their best to interpret the law, or Alyson who will try her best to grant your application, or Peter who will try to find a reason to deny your application. You will be rendered summarily to Rwanda, without the opportunity of appearing before an adjudicator. So if, as Dicey tells us, the 'rule of law is contrasted with every system of government based on the exercise by persons in authority of wide, arbitrary, or discretionary powers of constraint', the deportation rule may seem to contrast starkly and positively with the lottery Lanchester depicts. Its absolute certainty may even seem to render it preferable from the perspective of the rule of law.

So now we have a tension within the classic statement of the UK constitutional position on the rule of law. On the one hand, the rule of law is opposed to personal, discretionary decision-making and demands certainty. On the other, it requires reliance on principles, such as principles of human rights law, which require interpretation by officials and judges, and thus imports some discretion into the decision as to how to interpret or apply the law. That tension reaches its peak when one of the features that makes a rule certain is that it disapplies principles that are considered part of the constitution.

I will now explain why this kind of tension has been made more explicit by changes in the UK legal landscape since Dicey wrote. But, on my argument, the landscape has not changed in terms of his two constitutional fundamentals of parliamentary sovereignty and the rule of law. Rather, it has changed in respect of facts about the content of what are accepted as general principles of the constitution – in Dicey's words, the principles established by 'judicial decisions determining the rights of private persons in particular cases brought before the Courts'. The judicial decisions in those cases have been deeply affected by legislative change, most dramatically for our purposes by the statutes that have incorporated human rights protections from international law. The decisions have also been affected directly by international law in the manner indicated above, that is by judicial reliance on customary international law and on treaties that have been ratified, even if not incorporated.

However, as I have already emphasized, argument is central to this account. On another version of this story, the one told by common good lawyers and others, there has been a change in constitutional fundamentals brought about by the way that judges have arrogated power to themselves to determine the principles of the constitution. In so doing, the judges have changed their constitutional role in a way that subverts the sovereignty of Parliament. Moreover, we saw in the last chapter that the Judicial Power Project in its manifesto claims that the threat is not only to parliamentary sovereignty. It is also to the rule of law. 'Judicial overreach', as we saw they claim, 'increasingly threatens the rule of law and effective, democratic government.'[43]

2.3.2 *The European Convention on Human Rights*

Key to this supposed judicial power grab and subversion of the UK's constitutional fundamentals is one of the common good lawyers' favourite foes: the European Convention on Human Rights and the statute that incorporated its protections into the UK's domestic legal order, the Human Rights Act 1998. The Convention was based on the United Nations Universal Declaration of Human Rights of 1948, the document that responded to the horrors of the Second World War. It was drawn up by the Council of Europe, which consisted of forty-five governments dedicated to promoting democratic government in Western Europe and of which the UK was a founding member. It was drafted in 1950 under the leadership of the Conservative British MP and lawyer Sir David Maxwell-Fyfe, and ratified in 1951 by all member states.[44]

As Ann Lynn summarizes the Convention's philosophy in her *Constitutional History of the UK*, it responded to 'a fundamental need for the individual to be protected against potential abuses by his own state, and a sense that the state should not be able to justify repressive action against its citizens by arguments of necessity and the interests of the majority, as totalitarian governments had frequently sought to do'. Hence the Council of Europe 'agreed to create a framework of basic

[43] 'About the Judicial Power Project' online: *Judicial Power Project* <https://judicialpowerproject.org.uk/about/>.

[44] Alice Donald and Joelle Grogan, 'Explainer: The European Convention on Human Rights' (Jun 24 2022) online: *The UK in a Changing Europe* <https://ukandeu.ac.uk/explainers/the-european-convention-on-human-rights/>. The common good lawyers have recently become aware of how telling it is that Conservatives were prominent in the foundation of the European Convention, so they have begun efforts to rewrite history in an attempt to show that there is a clear pattern of hostility to the Convention from the start. See Conor Casey and Yuan Yi Zhu, 'Revisiting the British Origins of the European Convention on Human Rights' (May 20 2025) online: *Policy Exchange* <https://policyexchange.org.uk/publication/revisiting-the-british-origins-of-the-european-convention-on-human-rights/>.

rights applicable to all governments, and a structure by which these could be enforced against governments'.[45]

The enforcement mechanism is set out in Article 19 which provided for the creation of a European Court of Human Rights, also known as the 'Strasbourg Court' or by the acronym ECtHR, to adjudicate alleged breaches and a European Commission to decide on the admissibility of applications to the Court as well as to investigate allegations and report on them. The Court is made up of one judge from each member state who serves for a nine-year term. A judgment of the Court binds member states, but it is for the Committee of Ministers, a political organ composed of the member states' foreign ministers, to ensure compliance. While it is expected that member states will undertake steps to remedy a rights violation, it is up to them to decide how to do so. Member states can also decide not to comply with the judgments. However, the UK has historically had a very strong record of compliance with ECtHR judgments, which has continued to be the case even as the political attacks against the Court from the likes of the common good lawyers have intensified.

Particularly important in the debate over the Rwanda Act are, first, the Convention's provisions that enshrine the non-refoulement principle of international law. Recall that this principle requires that asylum seekers not be sent to a country where their life or freedom is threatened, or where they risk facing torture or inhumane treatment. One relevant provision is Article 2(1) of the Convention which sets out the 'right to life': 'Everyone's right to life shall be protected by law. No one shall be deprived of his life intentionally save in the execution of a sentence of a court following his conviction of a crime for which this penalty is provided by law.' Another is Article 3 which prohibits torture: 'No one shall be subjected to torture or to inhuman or degrading treatment or punishment'.

Second, there are the enforcement provisions. Article 13 pertains to enforcement within a member state in setting out the right to 'an effective remedy': 'Everyone whose rights and freedoms as set forth in this Convention are violated shall have an effective remedy before a national authority notwithstanding that the violation has been committed by persons acting in an official capacity.'

Article 32 sets out the jurisdiction of the Court: '1. The jurisdiction of the Court shall extend to all matters concerning the interpretation and

[45] Ann Lynn, *Constitutional History of the UK* (Abingdon: Routledge, 2016) at 494.

application of the Convention and the Protocols thereto ... 2. In the event of dispute as to whether the Court has jurisdiction, the Court shall decide.' In addition, Article 34 states: 'The Court may receive applications from any person, non-governmental organisation or group of individuals claiming to be the victim of a violation by one of the High Contracting Parties of the rights set forth in the Convention or the Protocols thereto. The High Contracting Parties undertake not to hinder in any way the effective exercise of this right.'

As a result, the UK agreed along with the other member states to submit to the Court's interpretation of its jurisdiction. And, since its lawyers were steeped in their own common law tradition, they would have known that judges would develop their understanding of such jurisdiction as novel situations were presented to the Court. It is important to keep this point in mind because, as we will see, the Court's practice in this regard draws particularly ferocious fire from the common good lawyers.

That it took so long to incorporate the Convention into UK law in the Human Rights Act 1998 requires some explanation, especially since, as I have indicated, the UK government and its lawyers had been most influential in the drafting process. In his magisterial book on 'Britain and the genesis of the European Convention', legal historian A. W. Brian Simpson reports that its adoption by the member states was 'seen as a feather in the cap of the Foreign Office, rather than as a weapon which might be directed against the United Kingdom'.[46] The impression one gets from Simpson's account is that the UK government thought of the Convention as containing rights for others, not for itself, as the UK considered itself already a rights-respecting country.

However, as Simpson explains, the very ratification of the Convention – indeed the UK was the first to ratify it – was momentous. Previously, the international law position had been understood as allowing that states 'could legitimately complain if their own nationals were ill used in other countries', but 'in general ... were thought free to deal with their own people and abuse them as they wished; this was an aspect of state sovereignty'. So the ratification raised a 'real puzzle'. 'How did it come about that Britain, and certain other European countries, voluntarily gave up some of their [sovereignty]?'[47]

[46] AW Brian Simpson, *Human Rights and the End of Empire: Britain and the Genesis of the European Convention* (Oxford: Oxford University Press, 2010) at 5.

[47] Ibid at 12. I have substituted 'sovereignty' for Simpson's 'autonomy' to preserve uniformity.

While it took Simpson 1,161 pages to solve this puzzle, the account is gripping because he was both a marvellous historian and wrote with great clarity and humour. But, as in his other work, he more tantalized with hints at a solution than ever explicitly stating one. My understanding of his solution starts with the obvious point we saw Lynn make that after the Second World War the UK and the other European countries felt under an obligation to provide a formal legal response to the human rights violations that had occurred on such a massive and horrific scale. That explains why they were willing to come up with what Simpson calls the 'pre-eminent system of international human rights protection which exists anywhere in the world'.[48] But as he suggests, the government and the Foreign Office may, at least initially, have seen this move as largely symbolic since they conceived the protection of human rights as 'primarily an aspect of foreign relations, rather than an aspect of domestic government'.[49] He also points out that at the time of ratification the UK accepted neither the right of individuals in the member states to bring petitions against it, nor the jurisdiction of the European Court of Human Rights over its internal affairs.[50]

In this way we get the kind of double-speak I have mentioned before in regard to dualism. The UK maintains its understanding of state sovereignty as an internal matter. Parliament may enact any law it pleases. As an external matter, however, the UK holds itself out to other states as committed to protecting the human rights in the Convention. So the solution to the puzzle is that as long as sovereignty as an internal matter is preserved, nothing is actually being given up by this external commitment. If that's the solution, Simpson shows that it failed dramatically. Not only did the UK find itself compelled to respond positively to rulings against it when challenges were brought by other member states, but by 1966 it had come to accept the right of individuals, not just states, to bring petitions to the ECtHR.

Moreover, the fact that it took until 1998 for the UK to incorporate the Convention by statute did not mean that it failed earlier to affect domestic law. As I already indicated, UK courts have always exercised control over public bodies, checking to ensure that officials were acting within the limits of their legal authority. In the 1960s, the courts began to develop a much more expansive and flexible approach to judicial review,

[48] Ibid at 3.
[49] Ibid at 39.
[50] Ibid at 4.

itself a response to the sense in the post-war period of the need for the state to act in rights-respecting ways. In this 'spirit', to use Dicey's term, the courts would interpret statutes on the basis of a presumption that Parliament did not intend to legislate in a manner incompatible with Convention rights. However, this presumption would be defeated if the wording of the statute explicitly and unambiguously showed that Parliament intended otherwise. In this way, as already suggested, parliamentary sovereignty was preserved at the same time as the stock was enriched of 'general principles of the constitution', established by 'judicial decisions determining the rights of private persons in particular cases brought before the Courts'.

In addition, as Murray Hunt showed in a powerful argument for incorporation published in 1997 – that is, the year before the enactment of the Human Rights Act 1998 – besides judicial incorporation, there was legislative incorporation. Parliament of its own volition, as it were, on occasion amended legislation to bring it into line with the Convention, as interpreted by the ECtHR, or in enacting new legislation would seek to ensure that it was consistent with the UK's international commitments. Finally, Hunt traced the way that the same commitments made their way into administrative practice, in the way that delegated legislation, administrative rules and policies were drafted.[51]

Hunt's argument for incorporation had much to do with his sense of the resistance to international human rights law in the mindset of politicians and lawyers, including the senior judiciary. Recall from the Introduction that he argued that 'English lawyers' weakness for the alluring idea of "sovereignty" as a foundational concept' continued to 'blight contemporary public law and to prevent its evolution into a mature system regulating the exercise of power in a modern polity'.[52] That was in a paper published five years after the enactment of the Human Rights Act 1998. In his book, Hunt traced in detail the influence of what he termed 'atavistic dualism', the stance inherited from Dicey's disdain for international law and consequent insistence that within the internal space of the UK state Parliament is free to do as it pleases. One result of that mindset is that judges were inclined to operate with a

[51] Murray Hunt, *Using Human Rights Law in English Courts* (Oxford: Hart Publishing, 1997) at 308–11.

[52] Murray Hunt, 'Sovereignty's Blight: Why Contemporary Public Law Needs the Concept of "Due Deference"' in Nicholas Bamforth and Peter Leyland, eds, *Public Law in a Multi-Layered Constitution* (Oxford: Hart Publishing, 2003) at 339.

'precondition of ambiguity' according to which the statute must be clearly ambiguous before they will interpret it in accordance with unincorporated international norms in place of the presumption that Parliament did not intend to legislate in a manner incompatible with Convention rights. The courts, Hunt said, 'reserved to themselves a discretion as to whether or not to refer to unincorporated international norms'.[53]

Put more concretely, the difference is between judges whose stance is 'I will interpret the statute in accordance with the presumption unless clear wording forces me to conclude otherwise' and judges who suppose that the statute must be ambiguous before they will ask whether the provision can be given a rights-compliant interpretation. Judges in the first group are more likely to reach a rights-compliant interpretation. In contrast, judges in the second group are more likely to decide that the 'plain meaning' of the statute is that Parliament intended otherwise. Alternatively, if they find that the statute is ambiguous in regard to the protection of rights, they will have to choose between a rights-compliant interpretation and one that overrides the right. And once they have faced themselves with that choice, the sovereigntist impulse that leads them in the first place down this path makes it more likely that they will choose the interpretation which finds that Parliament did not intend its statute to be rights-compliant.[54]

The resistance that Hunt charted throughout his book continues to this day. The common good lawyers' opposition to the Human Rights Act 1998 is also to the European Convention. With Simpson, they see the UK's ratification of the Convention as the start of something new, in their case a rot, a giving up of sovereignty. In one sense they are right. Once the UK had ratified the Convention with its list of rights and its enforcement mechanisms, the UK's formal legal commitment to the Convention became a standing rebuke to its failure internally to give effect to the rights. It introduced an incoherence in the constitutional order within the state which human rights lawyers could work with in order to try to bring domestic law into line with the UK's commitment to Convention rights. But the question remains whether this was a giving up of sovereignty, a chink in its armour. And the answer to that question will tell us whether Hermer was correct to accuse the Rwanda Act of perpetrating constitutional heresies.

53 Ibid at 25.
54 Ibid at 39.

2.3.3 *The Human Rights Act 1998*

The Human Rights Act 1998 served only to make that question starker. It begins with the statement that it is an 'Act to give *further* effect to rights and freedoms guaranteed under the European Convention on Human Rights'. I have emphasized 'further', first, because it suggests that those rights were already given effect within domestic law, a reference to the phenomenon just discussed of judicial interpretation of statutes on the basis of a presumption that Parliament did not intend to legislate in a manner incompatible with Convention rights. Second, it suggests that the rights will be given enhanced effect through incorporation. Both suggestions are then formalized in the statute, in particular in sections 3, 4, 10 and 19.

Section 3(1) says: 'So far as it is possible to do so, primary legislation and subordinate legislation must be read and given effect in a way which is compatible with the Convention rights.' The 'must' enjoins judges to try as hard as they can to avoid finding that a statutory provision authorizes violations by interpreting the provision in such a way that it does not. The idea here is not that judges should pretend that a provision that authorizes a violation does something different. Rather, if a provision can be interpreted to be compatible with Convention rights, section 3(1) requires judges to adopt such an interpretation even if the provision appears at first sight to authorize violations. In sum, the section firmly establishes the presumption that did not always prevail previously.

Section 4 reinforces section 3 by addressing situations in which it is not possible for judges to identify a rights-compliant interpretation. Section 4(2) states: 'If the court is satisfied that the provision is incompatible with a Convention right, it may make a declaration of that incompatibility.' But section 4(6) makes it clear that a declaration of incompatibility 'does not affect the validity, continuing operation or enforcement of the provision in respect of which it is given' and moreover 'is not binding on the parties to the proceedings in which it is made'.

Both sections 3 and 4 thus arguably, and on my account to come do, preserve parliamentary sovereignty at the same time as they embed human rights in the constitution, in the first place by requiring judges to presume that the purpose of a statute should be interpreted as intended to respect rights, in the second place by requiring judges to alert the institutions of government and the public if legislation cannot be interpreted this way. In the second case, the point of the alert is to have the problem publicly addressed even if the result is that the institutions leave the problem intact.

In both cases, parliamentary sovereignty is preserved. Section 3 does so by preserving Parliament's ability to override protected rights by using in advance very explicit language. Of course, that forces Parliament to be very frank if it intends to override rights that are protected in its own law. And in a sense that gives judges more power than they had had before. It is a power given to them by statute. Moreover, it requires Parliament, really the government of the day, to invite public criticism. But that's something the state, as it were, priced in first when the UK ratified the Convention, and, second, when Parliament incorporated it. That is, the UK took a decision to bear the cost of an explicit legal commitment to human rights.

In addition, section 4 preserves parliamentary sovereignty by emphasizing that a declaration of incompatibility does not affect the validity of the statute or even the rights of the parties in the situation that gave rise to the declaration. The only section that may seem to whittle away at parliamentary sovereignty is section 10, which gives a government minister the authority to respond to a declaration of incompatibility by making 'such amendments to the legislation as he considers necessary to remove the incompatibility'. But even with this section, ministers are acting under authority delegated to them by statute. The government may choose Parliament as the vehicle to make the change, and of course Parliament could always legislate after a ministerial amendment to put in place its preferred version.

The last section to which I need to draw attention is section 19. It requires that the minister

> in charge of a Bill in either House of Parliament must, before Second Reading of the Bill – (a) make a statement to the effect that in his view the provisions of the Bill are compatible with the Convention rights ('a statement of compatibility'); or (b) make a statement to the effect that although he is unable to make a statement of compatibility the government nevertheless wishes the House to proceed with the Bill.

This formal statement of incompatibility 'must be in writing and be published in such manner as the Minister making it considers appropriate'.

The section is significant, first, because it contains Parliament's instruction to the government of the day that it must prior to presenting a Bill to Parliament do an internal check for compatibility and, if it finds that what it intends to do is incompatible, but still wants to go ahead, it must publicly announce that it will be violating the legally enshrined rights of those subject to its power. As we will see, when Cleverly introduced the Rwanda Bill to Parliament, he found himself compelled to issue a formal statement of incompatibility.[55]

2.3.4 *Institutional Machinery*

Three institutional changes to the legal landscape are also important. First, in 2001 the same Labour government that had brought about the enactment of the Human Rights Act 1998 established the 'Joint Committee on Human Rights'. As its website states, it 'is a parliamentary committee consisting of 12 members appointed from both the House of Commons and the House of Lords' and its task is 'to examine human rights issues in the UK, by scrutinising draft legislation and considering its compatibility with human rights'.[56] Over the years, the Committee has taken an active role in writing reports on Bills before Parliament and on the executive implementation of statutes in an attempt to ensure rights-compliance.[57] In the same year, the government established the House of Lords Constitution Committee to 'keep under review the operation of the constitution'.[58]

The third change is the establishment of the UK Supreme Court by the Constitutional Reform Act 2005, again under a Labour government. Up until that point the apex court had been a judicial committee in the House of Lords, which created an anomaly in that the judges could debate legislation the meaning of which might through litigation become a matter for their determination. The Reform Act formally and physically established a separation of powers by moving the judges out of the House of Lords into a separate building.

[55] House of Lords Select Committee on the Constitution, 'Safety of Rwanda (Asylum and Immigration) Bill' (Feb 9 2024) online: *UK Parliament* <https://committees.parliament.uk/publications/43291/documents/215532/default/>.

[56] 'Human Rights (Joint Committee)', online: *UK Parliament* <https://committees.parliament.uk/committee/93/human-rights-joint-committee>.

[57] See, for example, David Feldman, 'Democracy, Law, and Human Rights: Politics as Challenge and Opportunity' in Murray Hunt, Hayler Hooper, and Paul Yowell, eds, *Parliaments and Human Rights: Redressing the Democratic Deficit* (Oxford: Hart Publishing, 2015) 95 at 112–13.

[58] 'Constitution Committee' online: *UK Parliament* <https://committees.parliament.uk/committee/172/constitution-committee/>. See J Caird, R Hazell, and D Oliver, 'The Constitutional Standards of the House of Lords Select Committee on the Constitution' (London: The Constitution Unit, 2015) online: <www.ucl.ac.uk/constitution-unit/sites/constitution-unit/files/constitutional-standards-third-edition.pdf>.

Martin Loughlin, a leading UK public lawyer at the London School of Economics, whom we met briefly in the Introduction, comments in a short book on the UK constitution that the formation of the Court 'supports the judiciary's venture of articulating their newly discovered principles of the constitution'. He notes that section 1 of the Constitutional Reform Act states that it 'does not adversely affect ... the existing constitutional principle of the rule of law'. But he clearly disagrees, for he says that the result is that this is 'the sort of principle whose meaning only the judiciary is equipped to determine. We are perhaps only a short step away from the American aphorism that "we are under a Constitution, but the Constitution is what the judges say it is"'.[59] In his view, the judges have been involved in an attempt to 're-order constitutional fundamentals', a 'bold undertaking involving a theoretical shift of revolutionary proportions'.[60] Such shifts are, he thinks, indicative of 'the general experience of modern constitutional democracies, in which the language of law comes to colonize the discourse of politics. Whether or not the ideal of "rule of law" is ever realized, we surely end up with the rule of lawyers'.[61]

On Loughlin's view, then, human rights lawyers like Hermer, in league with the senior judiciary, have been responsible for an attempt at a constitutional revolution and so are the ones that should be charged with committing constitutional heresies. Indeed, he seems to think that the revolution has been successful. Recall that Dicey said that in the UK 'the general principles of the constitution (as for example the right to personal liberty, or the right of public meeting) are with us the result of judicial decisions'. But, Loughlin claims, 'one thing seems certain: contrary to Dicey's contention, the law of the constitution is now the source rather than the consequence of our rights'.[62]

I have brought Loughlin in to illustrate my earlier point that it is not only the common good lawyers who believe that there has been a change in constitutional fundamentals, that parliamentary sovereignty has been lost and so must be won back. He clearly shares the common good lawyers' view that judges have arrogated power to themselves to determine the principles of the constitution and, in so doing, have changed

[59] Martin Loughlin, *The British Constitution: A Very Short Introduction* (Oxford: Oxford University Press, 2013) at 116.

[60] Ibid at 113.

[61] Ibid at 118.

[62] Ibid at 104.

their constitutional role in a way that subverts the sovereignty of Parliament. However, Loughlin is far from being on the extreme right of UK politics. Rather, he is somewhere on the left and was associated with the 'Lexiteers', the left-wing figures in the UK who supported Brexit because they believed, naively as people thought at the time, and in fact as things have turned out, that exiting the European Union would free the UK from the grip of its neoliberal capitalist order, thus opening up the possibility of a new socialist dawn.[63]

Aside from their opposing political ideologies, there is another important difference between the right-wing common good lawyers and left-wing critics like Loughlin that pertains to their use of talk of rights, the rule of law and constitutionalism, one I'll return to in Chapter 6. Loughlin belongs to what a leading public lawyer called 'a tradition of dissent', which had its main home at the London School of Economics, and consisted of 'left-leaning scholars ... deeply resentful of what they saw as conservative judges twisting the pliable rules of statutory interpretation to favour the existing order, privileging the rich and the powerful, and defeating the purposes of statutes intended to further the interests of the workers, the homeless, and the least well-off in society'.[64] As a result, they are hostile to talk of rights, the rule of law and constitutionalism since they regard such talk as an attempt to mask the use of law by elites as an instrument to maintain their power. There is no better summary of their views than in the lapidary title of Loughlin's recent book, *Against Constitutionalism*.[65]

My use of 'mask' is meant to evoke the founder of their tradition, Jeremy Bentham, who accused Sir William Blackstone, one of the great figures in the development of the common law, of having 'varnished' the 'mask' of 'fiction and formality' in which the law shows itself. Bentham, meanwhile, wanted to strip that mask away so that the instrument of law could be put in the service of the common good of all, not only of elites.[66]

[63] Martin Loughlin, 'Brexit and the English Constitution' (Nov 28 2023) online: *LSE Research Online* <http://eprints.lse.ac.uk/120882/1/Loughlin_Brexit_and_the_British_Constitution.pdf>. The leading work by a Lexiteer is Richard Tuck, *The Left Case for Brexit: Reflections on the Current Crisis* (Cambridge: Polity, 2020).

[64] Michael Taggart, 'Prolegomenon to an Intellectual History of Administrative Law in the Twentieth Century: The Case of John Willis and Canadian Administrative Law' (2005) 43 *Osgoode Hall Law Journal* 257.

[65] Martin Loughlin, *Against Constitutionalism* (Cambridge, MA: Harvard University Press, 2022).

[66] See HLA Hart, 'Bentham and the Demystification of the Law' (1973) 36 *Modern Law Review* 2. I rely on Hart's quotations at 3–4.

It is worth noting now that Bentham was also the founder of both the political philosophy of utilitarianism and of legal positivism. We encountered his main legal theory disciple John Austin in this chapter, through his influence on Dicey, while in Chapter 1 we met his main philosophical disciple John Stuart Mill and his claim that if society were organized in accordance with the 'Harm Principle', which requires that the state intervene coercively in people's lives only to prevent harm, the common good of all would be better served.

In contrast to scholars from the Benthamite tradition, the common good lawyers have attempted to harness talk of rights, the rule of law and constitutionalism in the service of their political goals. However, as the rest of my book will show, the way they invoke these terms empties them of their real substance or content. For they ultimately share the view of Loughlin and his tradition that law is no more than an instrument of a common good determined outside of law, in the political realm. That contrasts with the view I will defend: that the ideal of the rule of law informs a legal framework that permits the institutional contestation of different claims about the common good in the way that a commitment to democracy and constitutional government demands.

I now turn to my main example of such contestation, the arguments made by the common good lawyers about the Rwanda legislation.

3

A Tale of a Parallel Universe

3.1 Judges: Enemies of the People

This chapter will take us deep into the weeds of the debate about whether the Rwanda Act was consistent with the rule of law, perhaps deeper than some readers would like. But this depth is required if one is to make the arguments that we saw Richard Ekins, the Oxford law professor and founder of the Judicial Power Project, claimed to be missing when he said that critics like me invoke Carl Schmitt 'when an academic lawyer wishes to smear his or her opponents without evidence or argument'.[1] However, as I said in Chapter 1, my intention is not to smear anyone, only to display by argument both the poverty of their arguments and the troubling content of the ideology they wish to install. And that display requires this journey into the weeds.

I set the stage for my argument with an extract from the podcast we encountered in Chapter 1, *Double Jeopardy*, run by the two leading human rights lawyers, Tim Owen KC and Ken Macdonald KC – their interview in 2023 with Ekins. Owen and Macdonald specialize in an old-school, occasionally wry, and very English courtesy in interviewing their guests, mostly other eminent lawyers who have special expertise in the topic they have chosen, usually some controversial legal issue. Their interview with Ekins is rather different in tone. One gets the sense that they invited him onto their podcast because they were genuinely baffled by the claims he and the other common good lawyers had been making in their interventions published on the Policy Exchange site. As Ekins tried to answer their patient and always courteous questions, one also gets the sense that he managed only to increase their bafflement. The extract is taken from quite late in the podcast, the point where Owen gets as close to exasperation as he and Macdonald ever get.

[1] Richard Ekins, 'Lord Hermer Is Preposterously Wrong about International Law' (May 30 2025) online: *The Spectator* <www.spectator.co.uk/article/lord-hermer-is-preposterously-wrong-about-international-law/>.

> Can I just go back to something in the executive summary of your 2019 paper, 'Protecting the Constitution', and it relates to what we've just been talking about, because reading it, as well as other material, the things that you've said, it just strikes me that you and I have been living in a parallel universe. . . . So the beginning of the executive summary says, the rise of judicial power in the UK in recent years is a striking change in our constitutional arrangements in how we are governed. A change, this is what you say, that threatens good government, parliamentary democracy and the rule of law. Now that is a strong opening statement. . . . I've been litigating human rights cases in the courts since 1983. And the world that you describe of activist judges developing and going sort of rogue and making law left, right and centre and granting illegitimate victories to litigants based on what you would describe as fundamental departures from constitutional principle. It's just not the world that I've been living in. I've had some victories, of course, but my experience, and I think you'll find this about most human rights lawyers who are litigating convention cases, you know, you lose probably more than you win. And so you pick in your writings a few cases . . . And all I'm saying is, you concoct, or sorry, I don't know if it sounds too pejorative, you describe a vision of hell of these judges, judges having, you know, judicial power having really just run out of control and needing to be reined in.[2]

Owen's claim that Ekins and he are living in a parallel universe not only gave me the title of this chapter, but also a clue as to its argument. A parallel universe is a world akin to the one we live in, yet also distinct because it operates according to some different fundamental laws. The common good lawyers see things from the perspective of such a world. Their universe is one in which the content of familiar concepts like the rule of law, parliamentary sovereignty and constitutional tradition is fundamentally different from that of the world in which the judges of the UK Supreme Court and 'lefty lawyers' like Owen and Macdonald live. That is why, to use the title of a book cited in Chapter 1, the judges and lawyers are important parts of 'the demon in democracy', a demon which the Judicial Power Project was founded to exorcise, even at the cost of hollowing out democracy.[3]

Indeed, a bit later in the interview, Owen accused Ekins of allying himself with the infamous *Daily Mail* headline, 'Enemies of the People',

[2] Ken Macdonald and Tim Owen, 'Double Jeopardy: The Law and Politics Podcast - Episode 29: Richard Ekins – Judges and Political Power' (May 2 2023) online: *Apple Podcasts* <https://podcasts.apple.com/de/podcast/episode-29-richard-ekins-judges-and-political-power/id1633485236?i=1000611450876&l=en-GB>.

[3] Ryszard Legutko, *The Demon in Democracy: Totalitarian Temptations in Free Societies* (New York: Encounter Books, 2016).

because of the 'inflammatory' nature of his critiques of the judiciary. This was in large part because in 'Protecting the Constitution', Ekins had claimed that the UK Supreme Court in the decision known as *Miller 2* had engaged in 'nothing but a political evaluation', one that was 'highly contestable, and overstated' and providing 'no legal ground whatsoever for judicial action'.[4] In accusing the judiciary of making political not legal decisions, Ekins was being only a little more polite than the *Daily Mail* in his charge that the judges had thwarted the will of the British people. For as we will now see, his claim is that a political actor, the Prime Minister, the leader of the government, had the constitutional authority to make the decision at stake in this matter, and so the judges were usurping his function on spurious legal grounds.

The decisions known as *Miller 1* and *Miller 2* arose during the Brexit saga.[5] The constitutional issue in these cases was complicated because the government was acting under prerogative, not statutory powers – powers inherited from a time when the monarch was the political sovereign. For our purposes, we need trouble ourselves with only two. First, the power now exercised by ministers to conduct foreign policy and make treaties. Second, the power still exercised by the monarch to summon and 'prorogue' Parliament – that is, end the current parliamentary session. Note that this second power is triggered by the Prime Minister requesting that the monarch exercise it.

Miller 1, the decision which attracted the wrath of the *Daily Mail*, asked whether the government could notify the European Union of the UK's intention to withdraw from the European Union via the foreign relations prerogative. 'No', answered the majority of the Court in January 2017, because, on the agreed facts, the withdrawal would definitely change domestic law, and rights and duties under that law, which is Parliament's role, not the executive's, and prerogative doesn't allow you to do that. This was settled law since at least 1688 and thus not a very controversial conclusion.

The case known as *Miller 2* was prompted by an article John Finnis wrote, suggesting that Prime Minister Boris Johnson should exercise the

[4] Richard Ekins, 'Protecting the Constitution: How and Why Parliament Should Limit Judicial Power' (Dec 28 2019) online: *Policy Exchange* <https://policyexchange.org.uk/wp-content/uploads/2020/01/Protecting-the-Constitution.pdf> at 13.

[5] *R (on the application of Miller and another) v Secretary of State for Exiting the European Union* [2017] UKSC 5; *R (on the application of Miller) v The Prime Minister* [2019] UKSC 41.

prerogative to prorogue Parliament, thus shutting it out of deliberation during Brexit negotiations. Finnis argued that prorogation was necessary to preserve the 'centuries-old practices' of the constitution, 'perhaps our greatest contribution to civilised political life in many countries'. Brexit was necessary to protect the 'British people' from the threat of legal acts 'illegitimate in intent and chaotic in effect'.[6] However, the legal question posed by the case was quite different from this apocalyptic description. It was whether the exercise could be reviewed and, if it could, whether it was lawful. 'Yes' it could be reviewed, said a unanimous Court in September 2019, and this exercise of prerogative was unlawful because it had 'the effect of frustrating or preventing, without reasonable justification, the ability of parliament to carry out its constitutional functions as a legislature and as the body responsible for the supervision of the executive. In such a situation, the court will intervene if the effect is sufficiently serious to justify such an exceptional course'.[7]

Owen was not claiming that the answer to the question in *Miller 2* was obvious. All he was pointing out was that it was inflammatory to accuse the Court of deciding on political not legal grounds. Ekins responded by saying that his commentary 'has never been, and my view has not, and has not been, and is not now, that the majority of the Supreme Court and *Miller* No. 1 were opponents of Brexit, so were trying to flout it. And that's the utter absurdity of the *Daily Mail*, that they thought the judges were going to vote their politics and that accrued in a way'. He also said that he didn't

> mean that the judges aren't engaged with legal reasons or doing their best to adjudicate the case before them. Of course not. But I think that the choices, the decisions that have been made in both those cases, especially in the second, ... do involve legal reasoning and an approach to high profile, clearly as they were, constitutional controversies that is incompatible with long settled constitutional law and does encourage politicization of litigation and an undermining of the techniques of the political constitution, which the law has otherwise been pretty careful to protect.[8]

But note that in the same piece, though Owen did not quote this bit, Ekins said that the Court in *Miller 2* 'simply hands victory to one side of a

[6] John Finnis, 'Only One Option Remains with Brexit: Prorogue Parliament and Allow Us Out of the EU with No-Deal' (Apr 1 2019) online: *The Telegraph* <www.telegraph.co.uk/politics/2019/04/01/one-option-remains-brexit-prorogue-parliament-allow-us-eu/?WT.mc_id=tmg_share_tw>.

[7] Ibid at para 50.

[8] Macdonald and Owen, 'Double Jeopardy – Richard Ekins'.

political controversy, the proper forum for the resolution of which, in our tradition, has always been Parliament and the electorate'. So while he did not use the phrase 'enemies of the people', he was making the very same accusation that the judges were illegitimately thwarting the popular will that is conveyed by these words.[9] Moreover, he was making it while ignoring the fact that Finnis had prompted the prorogation in order to sideline Parliament, thus freeing up the government to do as it pleased. That Ekins is more temperate in responding to a very senior lawyer in a podcast that is not directed at his usual audience is unsurprising, though, as we will see, he reverts to such rhetoric as soon as he is back on familiar ground.

I will come back to this exchange in Chapter 5 and in Chapter 6 to Ekins's rather opaque reference to 'the techniques of the political constitution, which the law has otherwise been pretty careful to protect'. As we will see, most elaborately in Chapter 6, the 'political constitution' is the constitution of the common good parallel universe.

3.2 The Rwanda Saga

The Rwanda saga began in April 2022, when, under the leadership of Prime Minister Boris Johnson, the governments of the United Kingdom and Rwanda entered into a 'Migration and Economic Development Partnership' which permitted the transfer of asylum seekers who had arrived in the UK to Rwanda.[10] Once they arrived, their asylum claims would be determined by Rwandan authorities, and if their claims succeeded they would remain in Rwanda. The 'Rwanda Plan' was highly controversial. It was a political agreement, not a binding treaty, and so its legal status was unclear; indeed, it was unclear whether it had any such status.

The major concern surrounding the Plan was that it violated the principle of 'non-refoulement', which in terms of the 1951 Convention on the Status of Refugees and other legal instruments by which the UK is

[9] Ekins, 'Protecting the Constitution' at 13.

[10] Melanie Gower, Patrick Butchard, and CJ McKinney, 'Research Briefing: The UK-Rwanda Migration and Economic Development Partnership' (2024) online: *House of Commons Library* <https://commonslibrary.parliament.uk/research-briefings/cbp-9568/> at 6. For an excellent summary of the saga, see Peter William Walsh, 'Q&A: The UK's Former Policy to Send Asylum Seekers to Rwanda' (Jul 25 2024) online: *The Migration Observatory* <https://migrationobservatory.ox.ac.uk/resources/commentaries/qa-the-uks-policy-to-send-asylum-seekers-to-rwanda/>.

bound, requires that asylum seekers not be returned to a country where their life or freedom is threatened or they risk facing torture or inhumane treatment. Codified both in the European Convention on Human Rights and the Refugee Convention, the principle is also incorporated into UK domestic law via the Human Rights Act 1998.

Within international law, the non-refoulement principle is the only meaningful substantive limit on the state's authority to exclude individuals from its territory. It does not require that the state process asylum claims within its territory. But it does require that asylum seekers not be sent to a state that will abuse their fundamental rights. This is because the international refugee system operates based on a distinction between asylum seekers and refugees that is usually elided in public discourse on migration.[11] Asylum seekers are those who are pursuing refugee status but do not yet have it. Once they obtain that status, international refugee law imposes obligations on the relevant state to support their welfare and not to relocate them outside the state's jurisdiction. In order to escape those obligations, and against the spirit of the Refugee Convention, states, including the UK, have found ways to avoid processing asylum seekers who arrive within their jurisdiction.

For example, the UK 'Immigration Rules' established under the Immigration Act 1971, permit the Home Secretary to hold that asylum seekers' claims are inadmissible if they had the opportunity to apply for asylum in a 'Safe Third Country' but failed to do so. Likewise, the Nationality and Borders Act 2022 permits asylum seekers who entered the UK via 'irregular' means to be sent to an alternative third country as long as it is considered 'safe' for this purpose. Finally, the Illegal Migration Act 2023 placed a legal duty on the Home Secretary to remove anyone who did not come directly from their home country to the UK, and who arrived 'irregularly', to either their home country or a 'safe, third country'. It had the effect that anyone crossing the channel in small boats or by other 'irregular' means and who came via a 'safe third country', for example, France, would find their asylum claims declared 'inadmissible'. Their claims would not then be considered under the UK's asylum system and the Home Office would not process their claims.[12] The

[11] Rhys Drakeley, 'Loophole or Law-Breaking? The Rwanda Plan's Inconsistency with International Refugee Law' (2023) 4 *York Law Review* 141 at 143.

[12] The statute was repealed by the Border Security, Asylum and Immigration Bill 2025, but this Act did little to improve the UK's statutory regime and in some respects made it more draconian.

Rwanda Plan was thus designed to put a cap on this legislation by exporting asylum seekers during their application process to Rwanda.

The Plan was highly controversial, both within the UK and outside. The legal challenges to it began with an application by an Iraqi national who had arrived in the UK by boat from France in May 2022. He claimed asylum on arrival, but had been served with a 'Notice of Intent' on 24 May, indicating that the authorities were considering deeming his asylum claim inadmissible and relocating him to Rwanda. A few days later a medical doctor in the Immigration Removal Centre issued a report indicating that he may have been the victim of torture. On 6 June, he was notified that his claim had been deemed inadmissible and that he was to be removed to Rwanda on 14 June. He applied to the High Court unsuccessfully for 'interim relief', an order that would have put his removal on hold until there could be a full judicial determination of his claim.

He then applied to the European Court of Human Rights under Rule 39 of the Rules of Court, which the Court uses to indicate 'interim measures' to any State Party to the European Convention on Human Rights. Such requests are granted only on an exceptional basis, when the applicants would otherwise face a real risk of irreversible harm. The Court's decision does not determine the merits of the applicant's claim. It merely decides that the applicant has made out a sufficient case for it to issue an injunction – a temporary stop – against the state proceeding against that person until such time as a domestic court has had the full opportunity to determine whether the officials have the authority to act as they want. The Court granted the remedy on the same day.[13]

The ruling barred removals only until the UK courts had given a final determination of the Plan's legality. It took seventeen months for the process to go from the Divisional Court, which deemed the policy lawful, through the Court of Appeal, where a majority found that it was unlawful, to the Supreme Court, which in November 2023 unanimously confirmed the Court of Appeal's holding in *R on the application of AAA (Syria) and Others*.[14] It agreed as a matter of fact, in part on the basis of

[13] 'Press Release: The European Court Grants Urgent Interim Measure in Case Concerning Asylum-Seeker's Imminent Removal from the UK to Rwanda' (Jun 14 2022) online: *European Court of Human Rights* <https://hudoc.echr.coe.int/app/conversion/pdf/?library=ECHR&id=003-7359967-10054452&filename=Interim+measure+granted+in+case+concerning+asylum-seeker%E2%80%99s+imminent+removal+from+the+UK+to+Rwanda.pdf>. See Alice Donald and Joelle Grogan, 'Defeat in the Supreme Court' (Nov 17 2023) online: *Verfassungsblog* <https://verfassungsblog.de/defeat-in-the-supreme-court/>.

[14] [2023] UKSC 42.

evidence proffered by the United Nations High Commissioner for Refugees, that there were clear grounds to believe that asylum seekers would face a real risk of refoulement if they were removed to Rwanda. As Adam Tucker put it, the Court's view was that 'Rwanda currently lacks the institutional and political-cultural capacities and commitment necessary to operate an asylum system which does not involve a risk of refoulement'.[15]

In the meantime, the Conservative governing party was in turmoil. In the seventeen months between the initial proceedings in May 2022 and the judgment on 15 November 2023, Boris Johnson was forced out of office by his own party after having been found by a Parliamentary Committee guilty of lying to Parliament during the pandemic. His successor, Liz Truss, managed to crash the UK economy on arrival in office by announcing financial policies that sent the markets into a panic. She was Prime Minister for only forty-five days before resigning, famously failing to outlast a lettuce that a newspaper had placed in competition with her in a bid to see whether it would rot before she did. She was succeeded by Rishi Sunak, someone with the reputation of being a wooden but competent manager. In addition, four Home Secretaries – the ministers in charge of immigration policy – had come and gone, with James Cleverly replacing Suella Braverman, whom Sunak had been forced to fire just three days after the Supreme Court's judgment after a series of events in which she had shown that her right-wing inclinations could not be confined with the limits of party discipline.

Despite Cleverly's reputation for being one of the centrists in the Conservative Party and the fact that he had previously described the Rwanda Plan as 'batshit crazy',[16] and despite Sunak's reputation for competent management, they chose to make the Plan the central pillar of their Party's platform up until their resounding defeat in the election of 2024. They likely did so in part because it was the only tool left in the depleted box of a government that had earned a reputation for economic incompetence, dishonesty and corruption. But in large part the Rwanda

15 Adam Tucker, 'The Rwanda Policy, Legal Fictions, and Parliament's Legislative Authority' (Nov 22 2023) online: *UK Constitutional Law Blog* <https://ukconstitutionallaw.org/2023/11/22/adam-tucker-the-rwanda-policy-legal-fictions-and-parliaments-legislative-authority/>.

16 Archie Mitchell and Kate Devlin, 'James Cleverly Refuses to Deny He Called Rishi Sunak's Rwanda Scheme "Batshit"' (Nov 16 2023) online: *The Independent* <www.independent.co.uk/news/uk/politics/james-cleverly-rwanda-scheme-batshit-sunak-b2448446.html>.

Act and the desperate attempt to deport at least one asylum seeker to Rwanda before the election was their unsuccessful bid to staunch the bleeding of support to the far-right Reform Party and its leader Nigel Farage, who seemed to dominate UK politics although he did not at the time hold elected office. So desperate were the Conservatives that they paid one asylum seeker to go 'voluntarily' to Rwanda in the vain hope that it would look like the Plan was being implemented.

To circumvent the Supreme Court's decision, the government entered into a formal treaty, a binding international agreement, with Rwanda, in which Rwanda provided assurances that it would not breach the principle of non-refoulement.[17] The government then introduced to Parliament the Bill which deemed Rwanda a 'Safe Third Country' and all but prohibited judges from reviewing its implementation. It was enacted into law as the Safety of Rwanda (Asylum and Immigration) Act on 24 April 2024.

3.3 Debating the Rwanda Bill

To make my case that the common good lawyers' argument led to the destruction of the rule of law, whatever their intentions, I will focus closely on one paper, 'Safety of Rwanda (Asylum and Migration) Bill',[18] authored by 'Richard Ekins KC (Hon), Sir Stephen Laws KCB, KC (Hon), Dr. Conor Casey'. Laws, a former senior government lawyer, is now a senior research fellow with the Judicial Power Project. We encountered Casey in Chapter 1 as the Irish constitutional lawyer who has made his mark in the UK as one of the main proponents of Harvard Law Professor Adrian Vermeule's version of common good constitutionalism.

Their paper comes with a Foreword by 'Hon Alexander Downer AC, Former Minister for Foreign Affairs and Australian High Commissioner to the UK; author of the recent Independent Review of the UK Border Force', so another acquaintance from Chapter 1. He wrote, as they advertise, for the Conservative government the report on which the Rwanda Plan was based, and had, as Australian Minister for Foreign

[17] 'UK–Rwanda Treaty: Provision of an Asylum Partnership' (Dec 5 2023) online: *Gov.UK* <www.gov.uk/government/publications/uk-rwanda-treaty-provision-of-an-asylum-partnership/uk-rwanda-treaty-provision-of-an-asylum-partnership-accessible>.

[18] Richard Ekins, Stephen Laws, and Conor Casey, 'Safety of Rwanda (Asylum and Migration) Bill' (Dec 11 2023) online: *Policy Exchange* <https://policyexchange.org.uk/publication/safety-of-rwanda-asylum-and-migration-bill/>.

Affairs from 1996 to 2007, been one of the architects of his country's immigration regime on which the Plan was based.

These titles are supposed to legitimize what follows. The papers Ekins and his co-authors produce often come equipped with a Foreword or Preface by some prominent person, usually an eminent member of the UK legal establishment, a senior lawyer or a retired senior judge. The short introductions congratulate Ekins and, if he has written the paper with others, his co-authors, on their brilliance and legal acumen which goes a long way to legitimizing the positions taken. After all, if Lord Hoffmann and Lord Sumption, two retired judges of the Supreme Court, bless Ekins and his argument from the lofty heights of the office they once held, surely the argument must provide the correct legal conclusion.[19]

In some cases, it allows for a self-reinforcing pattern of political legitimation. For example, during the period in which the Rwanda Bill was before Parliament, Ekins delivered a public lecture – the Atkin Lecture – with the title 'Human Rights and the Rule of Law', subsequently published on Policy Exchange.[20] The lecture was just one in a series of attacks by Ekins and others on the European Court of Human Rights and its practice of issuing 'interim measures' under Rule 39, the kind of judicial injunction which puts a temporary stop to the implementation of a policy until its legality can properly be adjudicated. As we saw, it was just such an injunction that first halted the implementation of the Rwanda Plan, which is why the common good lawyers have directed so much fire on Rule 39, as in the paper blessed by Hoffmann and Sumption.[21]

When published, 'Human Rights and the Rule of Law' came with a Foreword by 'Lord (David) Wolfson of Tredegar KC, former Justice Minister'. A senior banking and commercial lawyer, he had served in Boris Johnson's Conservative government, but had resigned over the 'Partygate' scandal in which Johnson was found to have broken his own government's pandemic rules. We will meet him again in Chapter 4 in his new role as Conservative Shadow Attorney General; and from which he led the onslaught in the House of Lords on Richard

[19] Richard Ekins, 'Rule 39 and the Rule of Law' (May 17 2023) online: *Policy Exchange* <https://policyexchange.org.uk/wp-content/uploads/Rule-39-and-the-Rule-of-Law.pdf>.

[20] Richard Ekins, 'Human Rights and the Rule of Law' (Apr 17 2024) online: *Policy Exchange* <https://policyexchange.org.uk/wp-content/uploads/Human-Rights-and-the-Rule-of-Law.pdf>.

[21] Ekins, 'Rule 39 and the Rule of Law'.

Hermer for endorsing a thick definition of the rule of law in his Bingham Lecture.

In his Foreword, Wolfson claimed that Ekins had shown that the problem with Bingham's account of the rule of law 'is that it runs together two separate ideals, the rule of law and human rights, and, more controversially, takes human rights to be almost indistinguishable from European human rights law'. Moreover, he continued, on the correct understanding of the rule of law, 'we rightly expect the rules in question to be clear, stable and prospective. But when it comes to human rights law, too many lawyers are less concerned about clarity, stability or predictability. Human rights law has a rule of law problem, as Professor Ekins vividly puts it'.[22]

Wolfson went on:

> It was for this reason that I raised the lecture in the House of Lords in the Second Reading debate on the Safety of Rwanda Bill, and his critique of the Court's practice, which I find compelling, was much debated in the Committee Stage of the Bill. The support that the argument received from distinguished legal peers, including notably Lord Hoffmann, another towering common law judge, shows that, putting the point at its lowest, there is a respectable argument that the UK is not obliged as a matter of international law to comply with Rule 39 interim measures. As and when the Bill comes into force, there will likely be an attempt to derail its implementation by way of an application to the Strasbourg Court for a Rule 39 measure. It will then be important for His Majesty's Government not to be intimidated by the persistence with which some commentators assert that Rule 39 measures are binding simply because the Court says they are.[23]

Since the paper which Lord Hoffmann and Lord Sumption blessed contained Ekins's most sustained assault on international law through his critique of Rule 39 and of the European Court of Human Rights, Wolfson's compliment to Hoffmann continues the circle of self-congratulation that is the mark of this echo chamber. In his Atkin Lecture, Ekins helped the circle along its way by mentioning that his earlier paper on Rule 39 'was commended by Lord Sumption and Lord Hoffmann and raised in Parliament'.[24]

Notice that Wolfson's claim in his Foreword that human rights lawyers – the commentators to whom he refers – 'intimidate' the other

[22] Lord Wolfson, 'Foreword' to Ekins, 'Human Rights and the Rule of Law' at 5.
[23] Ibid at 6.
[24] Ibid at 22.

side is hard to fathom unless making careful arguments based on the law amounts to intimidation. These lawyers do not 'assert that Rule 39 measures are binding simply because the Court says they are'. Rather, they base their arguments on the text of the European Convention on Human Rights, on consistent state practice by member states including the UK, and on the reasoned interpretation and development of that law by both the European Court of Human Rights *and* the Court of which Lord Hoffmann and Lord Sumption were members.

More important is that Ekins and Wolfson evade confronting the argument they claim to be missing. As Murray Hunt, at that time the director of the Bingham Centre for the Rule of Law, pointed out, they overlook 'the significance of a central provision in the Convention' relating to the place of the European Court of Human Rights which presides over the European Convention on Human Rights:

> The Court was established by the State Parties under Article 19 ECHR 'to ensure observance of the engagements undertaken by the High Contracting Parties in the Convention and the Protocols thereto'. Article 32(1) provides that the jurisdiction of the Court shall extend to all matters concerning the interpretation and application of the Convention and its Protocols. Article 32(2) provides that 'in the event of dispute as to whether the Court has jurisdiction, the Court shall decide'. . . . The Court's jurisdiction therefore expressly covers 'all matters concerning the interpretation and application of the Convention and the Protocols thereto'.[25]

As Hunt also argues,

> Binding interim measures are a necessary and inherent part of any adjudicative process, an integral part of an international court created by States to ensure the observance by them of their obligations under the Convention. A failure by a State to comply with interim measures would undermine the effectiveness of the right of individual application guaranteed under Article 34 and the State's undertaking in Article 1 to protect Convention rights. It amounts to a breach of the State's undertaking in the

[25] Murray Hunt, 'Clause 54 of the Illegal Migration Bill: A Rule of Law Analysis for House of Lords Report Stage' (Jul 23 2023) online: *Bingham Centre* <https://binghamcentre.biicl.org/publications/clause-54-of-the-illegal-migration-bill-a-rule-of-law-analysis-for-house-of-lords-report-stage> at 10. Hunt relied on a report by the Joint Committee on Human Rights, the committee we encountered in the last chapter, composed of members of both Houses of Parliament to monitor the UK's compliance with its human rights commitments. See Joint Committee on Human Rights, 'Legislative Scrutiny: Illegal Migration Bill' (Jun 11 2023) online: *UK Parliament* <https://publications.parliament.uk/pa/jt5803/jtselect/jtrights/1241/report.html>.

> second sentence of Article 34 'not to hinder in any way the effective exercise of this right'.[26]

In sum, and as we saw in the last chapter, in consenting to the jurisdiction of the European Court of Human Rights, the UK also consented to the provision that acknowledges the authority of the Court to interpret and thus develop the scope of its jurisdiction. Further, the practice of courts issuing injunctions on an urgent basis so that the legality of a matter can be properly adjudicated is considered an inherent part of any court's jurisdiction. So it was hardly surprising that Rule 39 came to be interpreted as permitting such injunctions and that state practice, including that of the UK, manifested acceptance of this interpretation.

Where Wolfson is partly right is that there is a 'rule of law problem'. But, as I will now argue, it is not a problem with 'human rights law'. Rather, it is a problem for his position and for that of the common good lawyers, which Wolfson wholeheartedly endorsed by saying that Ekins's lecture was a 'tour de force, illuminating both the idea of human rights and also the ideal of the rule of law, and helping to showcase the continuing appeal of the common law constitutional tradition to which Lord Atkin himself was firmly committed'.[27] It takes an argument to do this – to show that Ekins's position is rather a tour of a parallel universe – because, as we have seen, the deportation rule to which asylum seekers are subject provides, if fully implemented, a certain fate for nearly all asylum seekers. They will be removed or, as it is more accurate to say, rendered to Rwanda for processing. And recall that on the thin definition of the rule of law with which I am provisionally working, it requires no more than that officials obey the rules laid down by the superior authority of Parliament.

The question is whether the greater certainty allegedly brought about by the rules that prohibited judicial review and disapplied the principled commitments embedded in the law is consistent with the rule of law. As I have conceded more than once, the fact of the constitutional fundamental of parliamentary sovereignty in the UK legal order suggests that any such principled commitments are at the mercy of Parliament. So, if Parliament chooses, as it did in the Rwanda Act, first to disapply such commitments and replace them with the deportation rule, and

[26] Hunt, 'Clause 54 of the Illegal Migration Bill' at 10.
[27] Wolfson, 'Foreword' at 5.

second, explicitly to strip judges of their review authority over such commitments, that is arguably consistent with the rule of law, especially when the deportation rule delivers such certainty.

In addition, that these commitments are ultimately sourced in international law does not, so the common good lawyers think, get in the way of the argument. Recall that international law recognizes two kinds of constitutional order. First, 'monist' orders where obligations that stem from international agreements have direct effect within the order as soon as the state ratifies the agreement. Second, 'dualist' orders, like that of the UK, in which obligations that stem from international agreements have direct effect within the order only after Parliament has incorporated them into law by statute. Since within a dualist order the obligations have their immediate source in a statute, they can be overruled or disapplied by statute. Hence, the common good lawyers suggest, the Act is also consistent with international law.

My counter-argument will show that the deportation rule is inconsistent with both the rule of law domestically and with international law. The Rwanda Act thus introduced a dangerous incoherence into the UK constitutional order. It undermined the constitutional fundamental of parliamentary sovereignty by authorizing the executive to break free of Parliament, and it undermined the constitutional fundamental of the rule of law by ousting the jurisdiction of the ordinary courts. Moreover, that was not all that was wrong constitutionally speaking with the statute. Some commentators have suggested that the statute was so fundamentally flawed that judges would have been entitled to invalidate it.[28] Although I think that their arguments are sound, and so I'm open to their conclusion, it more than suffices for my purposes to show that the statute introduced an incoherence that threatened the integrity of the whole UK constitutional order.

I will focus mainly on the one paper by Ekins and two other common good lawyers because it so nicely illustrates my argument. But it is far from exceptional. Rather, its structure and content are typical of the papers that Ekins and his co-authors produce, as one can see from my

[28] Adam Tucker, 'The Rwanda Policy, Legal Fictions, and Parliament's Legislative Authority'; Mark Elliott, 'Could the Supreme Court Reject the Rwanda Bill as Unconstitutional?' (Dec 11 2023) online: *Public Law for Everyone* <https://publiclawforeveryone.com/2023/12/11/could-the-supreme-court-reject-the-rwanda-bill-as-unconstitutional>; Raffael Fasel, 'Ouster Clauses and the Silent Constitutional Crisis' (Feb 20 2024) online: *UK Constitutional Law Blog* <https://ukconstitutionallaw.org/2024/02/20/raffael-n-fasel-ouster-clauses-and-the-silent-constitutional-crisis/>.

briefer discussions of other documents authored by common good lawyers in this chapter and the next. Indeed, these lawyers constantly recycle the same content, using the same toolkit deployed elsewhere. For example, now that Brexit 'is done', their main targets are the European Convention on Human Rights, the European Court of Human Rights and the Human Rights Act 1998, which puts them in alliance with the ever more extreme Conservative Party and the far-right Reform Party.[29]

When I first introduced the problem faced by my argument that the Rwanda Act violated the rule of law, I offered as a foretaste of the argument that in part it would show that the deportation rule both introduced incoherence into the UK constitutional order and more uncertainty into the legal situation of asylum seekers than existed before various governments whittled away their rights under international law. We saw that the Conservative government responded to the Supreme Court's judgment, first, by entering into a treaty with Rwanda, second, by presenting the Rwanda Bill to Parliament for consideration and debate, and, finally, by enacting the Rwanda Act. Richard Hermer's charge that opened Chapter 2 was directed at the Act, which he said contained 'constitutional heresies'. Recall that he set out the heresies as follows:

> The Act starts with the otiose and therefore crass assertion of parliamentary sovereignty; it moves to the express disapplication of fundamental international law obligations owed, including under the ECHR and the Refugee Convention, and even customary international law; and it ousted the role of the courts in determining relevant facts except where individual circumstances were in issue, indeed obliging them to accept as true

[29] See, for example, Richard Ekins and Sir Stephen Laws, 'The Future of Human Rights Reform' (Oct 1 2025) online: *Policy Exchange* <https://policyexchange.org.uk/wp-content/uploads/The-Future-of-Human-Rights-Law-Reform_.pdf>.

See further Lord Wolfson's legal advice to the Conservative Party on withdrawal from the European Convention on Human Rights, 'Advice to the Leader of the Conservative Party', discussed with a link to the advice in Rosalind English, 'The UK Can, and Should, Leave the Human Rights Convention: Shadow AG's Advice Underlines Conservative Party's Policy' (Oct 7 2025) online: *UK Human Rights Blog* <https://ukhumanrightsblog.com/2025/10/07/the-uk-can-leave-the-human-rights-convention-shadow-ags-advice-underlines-conservative-partys-policy/>. This advice was the basis for Conservative Party leader Kemi Badenoch's announcement in her speech at the 2025 Conservative Party Conference that she would withdraw from the Convention as Prime Minister, thus aping yet further the policies of the far-right Reform Party. See Peter Walker, 'Badenoch Says Tories Open to Quitting More Treaties to Increase Deportations' (Oct 5 2025) online: *The Guardian* <www.theguardian.com/politics/2025/oct/05/badenoch-says-tories-could-quit-more-treaties-to-increase-deportations>.

> facts that may well have been false – it felt, not so much as though we had fallen through the Looking Glass but rather dived head first into it.[30]

The current chapter and the following two vindicate Hermer's charge. But, in doing so, they do far more than that. For in vindicating the charge, we can also gain insight into the nature of the rule of law, of constitutional government, and even of the political order of democracy. It is important to keep in mind as I take the reader though the at times intricate arguments, that I do so not through an analysis of the Act, but of a debate over the Bill initiated by Ekins and his co-authors' paper, 'Safety of Rwanda (Asylum and Migration) Bill'. However, all the clauses in this Bill that figured in this debate survived into the Act, so the debate is an excellent window into it. Even more important for the purposes of my argument are the changes the common good lawyers *wanted* Parliament to make to some of these clauses, but which Parliament did *not* make.

In his Foreword to the paper, Downer claimed that it makes 'a powerful argument that the Bill is a legitimate and effective response to the Supreme Court's recent judgment'. It showed that the Bill met the Supreme Court's concerns 'about the risk that Rwandan officials will make mistakes in processing asylum claims and may wrongly send a genuine refugee back to an unsafe country' and that the Bill went 'a long way towards making it lawful to promptly remove asylum-seekers to Rwanda in compliance with international law'. However, he also expressed concern that the Bill did 'not fully address the risk of further litigation, which may challenge the foundations of the Rwanda plan or may frustrate its operation in practice'. That led him to make the following prediction:

> If the Rwanda scheme continues to be frustrated by the courts and illegal migration continues, then this toxic political issue will continue to fuel public anxiety and concern. The consequences in Europe are there for all to see with the rise of extremist political movements. To avoid this plight, the UK needs to make sure that the Rwanda plan is legally watertight. This outstanding paper by three authors who are amongst the most qualified legal commentators in the country is a significant contribution to the debate about how to improve this most important of Bills.[31]

[30] Richard Hermer, 'The Rule of Law in an Age of Populism' (Oct 14 2024) online: *Bingham Centre for the Rule of Law* <www.biicl.org/documents/12532_bingham_lecture_2024.pdf> at 2.

[31] Alexander Downer, 'Foreword' to Ekins, Laws, and Casey, 'Safety of Rwanda (Asylum and Migration) Bill' at 3–4.

It is rather strange to suppose that the person whom the UK government had hired to set up the model for the Rwanda Plan is the appropriate person from whom to seek an endorsement. It is tantamount to Ekins and the other authors saying at the beginning of their paper: 'We, who are amongst the most qualified legal commentators in the country, offer you our outstanding paper – a significant contribution to the debate about how to improve this most important of Bills'. It is passing strange to suggest that a failure to remove the risk of further litigation would cause a rise in extremism given that the Rwanda Plan was all about pandering to extremist elements in the UK political scene. In what way does the Conservative Party hinder the rise of extremism by becoming itself more extreme and thus imparting its respectability to views considered some years ago beyond the pale?[32] Indeed, since Downer, the common good lawyers, and of course many politicians and 'influencers' had worked so hard to make the issue toxic, this claim took some gall.

I will, however, focus on Downer's main legal claim which sets the stage for the paper that followed that, while the Bill went 'a long way towards making it *lawful* to promptly remove asylum-seekers to Rwanda *in compliance with international law*', it did 'not fully address the risk of further litigation, which may challenge the foundations of the Rwanda plan or may frustrate its operation in practice'.[33] There are in fact two claims here – that the Bill is lawful as a matter of domestic law and it is lawful as a matter of international law.

In this chapter, I provide the argument that shows that these claims are groundless. Quite to the contrary, the Bill went a long way to ensuring that the removals would be *lawless* by stripping away the legal protections in both international law and domestic law that would otherwise apply to asylum seekers. To suggest that the only legal problem is that the Bill did not go far enough since it should have removed any vestige of legal protection is strange almost beyond belief. It is not, however, a strange suggestion in the parallel universe of the common good lawyers. Instead, it is a suggestion that is fully consistent with and in fact revealing of their

[32] Sadly, the question can equally be directed at the Labour Party today as it seeks to outflank Reform, especially the Home Office under the direction of Yvette Cooper, now under the direction of the even more conservative Shabana Mahmood, as Keir Starmer, the Prime Minister, dances ever more to Nigel Farage's tune on immigration.

[33] My emphasis.

broader project, the Judicial Power Project, which we may recall a UK public lawyer aptly renamed the 'Executive Power Project'.[34]

The aptness of the new name is fully supported by the changes we will now see Ekins and his co-authors proposed in order to 'fully address the risk of further litigation'. For they wanted almost all slivers of judicial review removed from the Bill so that the executive would have a completely free hand. It is this project that provides the basis for vindicating Hermer's charge of constitutional heresy because their true aim is to elevate the executive in the UK constitutional order. If successful, the project would displace both of the two constitutional fundamentals of parliamentary sovereignty and the rule of law that they proclaim to care so much about. Such displacement would represent the triumph of the 'political constitution' to which we saw Ekins refer in his response to Owen.

3.3.1 *Safe Because We Say So*

Recall that the Supreme Court unanimously found that there were clear grounds to believe that asylum seekers would face a real risk of refoulement if they were removed to Rwanda. Here is its full statement of the grounds:

> The matters which we have discussed are evidence of a culture within Rwanda of, at best, inadequate understanding of Rwanda's obligations under the Refugee Convention. The evidence also goes some way to support the suggestion of a dismissive attitude towards asylum seekers from the Middle East and Afghanistan. It is also apparent from the evidence that significant changes need to be made to Rwanda's asylum procedures, as they operate in practice, before there can be confidence that it will deal with asylum seekers sent to it by the United Kingdom in accordance with the principle of non-refoulement. The necessary changes may not be straightforward, as they require an appreciation that the current approach is inadequate, a change of attitudes, and effective training and monitoring.[35]
>
> As matters stand, the evidence establishes substantial grounds for believing that there is a real risk that asylum claims will not be determined properly, and that asylum seekers will in consequence be at risk of being returned directly or indirectly to their country of origin. In that event,

[34] Thomas Poole, 'The Executive Power Project' (Apr 2 2019) online: *London Review of Books* <www.lrb.co.uk/blog/2019/april/the-executive-power-project>.

[35] *R on the application of AAA (Syria) and Others* [2023] UKSC 42 at para 104.

> genuine refugees will face a real risk of ill-treatment in circumstances where they should not have been returned at all. The right of appeal to the High Court is completely untested, and there are grounds for concern as to its likely effectiveness. The detection of failures in the asylum system by means of monitoring, however effective it may be, will not prevent those failures from occurring in the first place. We accept the Secretary of State's submission that the capacity of the Rwandan system (in the sense of its ability to produce accurate and fair decisions) can and will be built up. Nevertheless, asking ourselves whether there were substantial grounds for believing that a real risk of refoulement existed at the relevant time, we have concluded that there were. The structural changes and capacity-building needed to eliminate that risk may be delivered in the future, but they were not shown to be in place at the time when the lawfulness of the policy had to be considered in these proceedings.[36]

In sum, the deportation rule greatly increased the uncertainty of the old regime in which your fate as an asylum seeker depended on how various officials interpreted the human rights law relevant to your claim. For it outsourced the uncertainty by rendering asylum seekers to a country where as a matter of fact their fate would be decided by a regime that did not have the institutional resources for processing such claims and, more important, had a record of human rights abuse, including the abuse of asylum seekers.

In response, the Conservative government entered into the Treaty with Rwanda which purported to deal with the problems identified by the Court.[37] The Treaty did so by stating that no 'relocated' person would be sent to any country except the UK, thereby removing the risk of refoulement. In addition, it provided that asylum seekers who were unsuccessful in their claims would be given permanent residence in Rwanda. These two provisions may seem in conflict as one might well ask why any persons would be removed from Rwanda given that all asylum seekers are guaranteed permanent residence there. The answer to the question is that removals to the UK would take place only if the UK government specifically requested that this happen, for example because the individual was needed to give evidence in a UK court. The Treaty also

[36] Ibid at para 105.

[37] 'Agreement between the Government of the United Kingdom and Great Britain and Northern Ireland and the Government of the Republic of Rwanda for the Provision of an Asylum Partnership to Strengthen Shared International Commitments on the Protection of Refugees and Immigrants' (Apr 30 2024) online: *Gov.UK* <www.gov.uk/government/publications/ukrwanda-agreement-for-the-provision-of-an-asylum-partnership-to-strengthen-shared-international-commitments-on-the-protection-of-refugees-and-migra>.

introduced new supposed safeguards. It expanded the powers of the Independent Monitoring Committee, which would report to a Joint Committee made up of senior officials from the Rwandan and UK governments, and required Rwanda to establish a new initial decision-making body and a new appeals court.

Now, *if* it were the case that the Rwandan government could be trusted to abide by the terms of the Treaty, there would be greater certainty for asylum seekers. We just saw that the Supreme Court said that it accepted the government's submission 'that the capacity of the Rwandan system (in the sense of its ability to produce accurate and fair decisions) can and will be built up'. That was rather too polite, not only because of the 'substantial grounds for believing' that Rwanda itself was unsafe, but also because of the record of a government that did not keep its promises. The Treaty thus purported to put a state notorious for its human rights violations, and in particular for its appalling treatment of refugees, into the magician's black hat and out popped a great respecter of human rights and international law.

But not only could the Treaty not perform the magic trick of transforming Rwanda into a safe country; it also provides its own evidence for this fact. The Treaty starts with proclamations about international law and human rights and the two governments' commitments to these, proclamations that were both pious and hypocritical given that the point was for the UK to evade its own international law obligations. Here are just two of five:

> **CONSIDERING** that the United Kingdom has a long proud history of providing protection to those who need it, in accordance with international obligations. As likeminded partners, the United Kingdom and Rwanda shall work together to promote a new, fair and humane approach to asylum, deter illegal migration and create safe and legal routes for those fleeing persecution,
>
> **HAVING** regard to the Parties' commitment to upholding fundamental human rights and freedoms without discrimination, as guaranteed by the Parties' national legislation, by their strong histories of implementing the 1951 Convention Relating to the Status of Refugees and the 1967 Protocol Relating to the Status of Refugees and by their other respective international legal obligations.[38]

[38] 'UK/Rwanda: Agreement for the Provision of an Asylum Partnership to Strengthen Shared International Commitments on the Protection of Refugees and Migrants' (Apr 30 2024) online: *Gov.UK* <https://assets.publishing.service.gov.uk/media/656f51d30f12ef07a53e0295/UK-Rwanda_MEDP_-_English_-_Formatted__5_Dec_23__-_UK_VERSION.pdf>.

Why care so much about international human rights law when the process one is putting in place makes such law irrelevant by turning the process into a meaningless charade? That is, you would get permanent residence whatever the bodies set up to process your claim decided. That made the outcome altogether certain. But the certainty it delivered was that you would be doomed to a life in the kind of place that mere words could not change into a safe country for refugees – indeed, a country from which citizens who sought asylum in the UK had been granted refugee status. The promised certainty was that if you made your way as an asylum seeker to the UK, you would be rendered in violation of the UK's international and domestic legal commitments to a place where you could be sure that your rights would be insecure. In effect, the law was intended as a sufficiently cruel punishment to deter those who had the effrontery to ask the UK to live up to its legal obligations, and the very threat that was supposed to induce deterrence made a nonsense of the statutory declaration that Rwanda was 'safe'.

The Bill further mocked the pious proclamations in the Treaty. It stated that to advance the purpose of the Act 'to prevent and deter unlawful migration', it gave 'effect to the judgement of Parliament that the Republic of Rwanda is a safe country'.[39] That 'judgement' was of course the judgment of a government determined for political reasons to render at least one plane-load of asylum seekers to Rwanda prior to a general election that it seemed destined otherwise to lose. For the judgment was based entirely on the Treaty, the only 'fact' that had changed in the year since the Supreme Court's decision. Under clause 2(1) of the Bill, '[e]very decision-maker must conclusively treat the Republic of Rwanda as a safe country'. Courts are 'decision-makers' for this purpose, meaning that the Bill would block legal challenges to the government's decision to remove an asylum seeker to Rwanda on the grounds that it is not in fact a safe country. The Bill thus ruled out any further judicial testing of the judgment that Rwanda was safe.

In 'Safety of Rwanda (Asylum and Migration) Bill', Ekins and his co-authors claim that the Treaty's 'guarantee against removal to an unsafe country entirely changes and supersedes the factual foundation for the Supreme Court's judgment'. It followed, they suggest, that

> In no way whatever does the Bill contradict, challenge or even put in question the Supreme Court's judgment. In enacting the Bill, Parliament

[39] Ibid.

> will give legislative effect to its own judgement that once the Treaty comes into force Rwanda is a safe country and that asylum-seekers may be removed there without placing them in danger and, in particular, without any real risk that they will be sent on to an unsafe third country.[40]

In a sense, though a very tenuous sense, they were correct. The Treaty was a change. But was it a change in the 'facts' or was it a botched attempt at a sleight of hand, the moment when all can see that the magician put the rabbit into the hat before he pulled it out with a flourish? It was of course the case that the combination of Treaty and Act could not change the real world in which human right abuses happen. Instead, it made it the case that such compliance with human rights was beside the point. For the real point was to deter asylum seekers and others from making the journey to the UK by the threat of being rendered to a country where their situation could be near indistinguishable from the one they had sought refuge from.[41]

In a way, Ekins and his co-authors, perhaps unwittingly, concede as much. They claim that 'the Government has acted precisely as if it agreed with the Supreme Court's conclusion. It has acted to *eliminate* the risk on which the Supreme Court passed judgment'. They then seek to make a virtue out of the startling fact that, even when asylum claims fail, asylum seekers 'will not be removed to an unsafe third country, including their country of origin' as that, they say, 'imposes an obligation on Rwanda that otherwise does not exist in international law, including under the terms of the Refugee Convention 1950, namely to refrain from removing *failed* asylum-seekers to any country other than the UK'. In emphasizing 'eliminate' and 'failed', they draw our attention to the fact that the Treaty made international law irrelevant through the guarantee that whatever the outcome of the legal process, asylum seekers were guaranteed permanent residence. They also acknowledge that the procedural protections in the Treaty are irrelevant both by noting their existence in one sentence in brackets – '(In addition, the Treaty provides for changes to the Rwandan system for processing asylum claims, which provide greater procedural protections and similar)' – and by pointing out that monitoring the obligation not to remove even failed asylum seekers 'is much

[40] Ekins, Laws, and Casey, 'Safety of Rwanda (Asylum and Migration) Bill' at 7.

[41] Moreover, we can recall that this threat existed only on the shaky assumption that the Act could be fully implemented. Cleverly's reason for calling it 'batshit crazy' was that it could not be implemented. The real political point was to shore up populist support for the Conservative Party, ahead of a general election that it seemed doomed to lose.

more straightforward than determining whether Rwandan officials were wrong to reject a particular asylum claim'.[42]

The Treaty did not then 'eliminate' the risk that asylum seekers would be vulnerable to human rights abuses. Rather, it increased the risk by permanently parking asylum seekers within the power of a rights-abusing regime. It is true that that they could not be 'refouled' from Rwanda – that is, sent to a third country which might be unsafe. But that risk was removed by the certainty that the only country in which they had the right to reside is, as the Supreme Court had found, an unsafe country for the purpose of refoulement.

In response to the clause that prohibited the courts from testing the claim that Rwanda was safe, Ekins and his co-authors say:

> The significance of the Bill is that it does not leave to the courts the function of determining whether the new Treaty is sufficient to make Rwanda a safe country. That is, it does not make the lawfulness of removals to Rwanda conditional on the outcome of future litigation in which the Supreme Court would be invited by claimants, with the support of interested parties such as the UNHCR,[43] to cast doubt on whether Rwanda will honour the Treaty. It is perfectly proper for Parliament to agree with the Government that there are good reasons to expect Rwanda to honour its treaty obligation (which will be monitored and supported by UK officials), so that persons sent to Rwanda will not be at any real risk of being removed to an unsafe third country. It would be inappropriate, in constitutional and practical terms, to continue to leave to the courts the ultimate responsibility for making the final and conclusive decision, in the course of judicial proceedings, about whether Rwanda is to be trusted or whether the Treaty is likely to prove to be a sufficient guarantee.[44]

They provide no details as to what the 'good reason' might be to expect Rwanda to honour its treaty obligations. Rather, they repeat several times that because Parliament said so, it is so, as if repetition is a good substitute for argument. They do put some energy into trying to undermine the Supreme Court's judgment that Rwanda was unsafe, principally by pointing to the judgment in the Divisional Court which had found Rwanda to be safe. But they omit to mention that the Supreme Court had

[42] Ekins, Laws, and Casey, 'Safety of Rwanda (Asylum and Migration) Bill' at 10. Their emphasis. Note that they get the date of the Convention wrong – it is 1951.

[43] In mentioning the UN Refugee Agency in this way, Ekins and his co-authors seem to suggest that it is pursuing some illicit 'special interest'. The agency of course does have a special interest – to monitor states' treatment of refugees.

[44] Ekins, Laws, and Casey, 'Safety of Rwanda (Asylum and Migration) Bill' at 10–11.

pointed out that the judges of the Divisional Court had not understood that it was for that Court to decide itself the factual question whether Rwanda was safe and had asked instead whether the government's assessment was 'tenable', a much weaker test.[45] Indeed, the real message of this part of their paper is that the courts should defer to the government's assertion of facts and if they don't, the government should use its majority in Parliament to exclude judges from even considering the facts. In this way, the government will ensure that judges will, as Ekins and his co-authors put it, never 'again speculate about the likelihood that another friendly state, and Commonwealth country, may not be capable of being trusted to honour its assurances, or about the independence of its judiciary'.[46]

3.3.2 Usurping the Judicial Function?

Ekins and his co-authors do acknowledge that many critics of the Bill considered this clause to amount to 'a legislative usurpation of the judicial function'. This point, they say, 'is a serious one in principle, but in relation to the present issue is entirely misconceived'.

> Parliamentary sovereignty entails that the King-in-Parliament may enact any law, but of course there are many laws that it should not enact, including for reasons of constitutional principle and/or comity to other institutions – or other states. However, Parliament is entitled to legislate based on its own understanding of the relevant facts and its evaluation of their significance and the legal effects which should flow from them.[47]

In a footnote to this claim, they state that it has 'long been accepted that it is an integral element of the doctrine of parliamentary sovereignty that the factual premise on which Parliament chooses to legislate should not be capable of being questioned in judicial proceedings; *British Railways Board v Pickin* [1974] AC 765'.[48] I draw attention to this rather technical point in a footnote because citing this decision as authority is telling. The factual premise in issue in this case was the ownership of land adjacent to an abandoned railway line. The statute in question had deemed the land to be as a matter of law owned by a railway board when in fact it had been acquired by Pickin. Pickin claimed that the

[45] *R on the application of AAA (Syria) and Others*, at para 39.
[46] Ekins, Laws, and Casey, 'Safety of Rwanda (Asylum and Migration) Bill' at 12.
[47] Ibid at 11.
[48] Ibid at note 10.

board had misled Parliament in promoting the enactment of the statute. The legal issue in the case was whether the courts could question the validity of the statute in light of evidence that the statute had been enacted on the basis of false facts.[49] To cite this decision in a discussion of the Rwanda Bill is to say: 'Yes, Rwanda is an unsafe country for processing asylum claims and to claim otherwise is false. But we should treat it as safe because Parliament has said it is safe.' And that is very different from the argument made by Ekins and his co-authors in their text that Rwanda had as a matter of fact been made safe by the Treaty.

Moreover, at a more fundamental – that is, constitutional – level, *British Railways Board v Pickin* is authority for the proposition that Parliament can use a statute to usurp the judicial function.[50] As Murray Hunt pointed out, '[e]nacting a conclusive deeming of Rwanda as a safe country is a legislative usurpation of the judicial function'.[51] This is because, as he argued, Articles 2 and 3 of the European Convention on Human Rights 'require a judicial determination of the question of safety where an individual claims that there is a substantial risk of refoulement by the country to which they are being sent. Safety is a factual question which cannot be conclusively determined in advance, for all cases, by the legislature'.[52]

Ekins and his co-authors wish to affirm that the Rwanda Bill had 'conclusively determined in advance' the 'factual question of safety', and, in so doing, they both deny the undeniable and avoid addressing the real legal issue raised by the Bill. As I have already suggested, the issue is not the technical validity of the statute. In this regard *British Railways Board v Pickin* is indeed authority for the proposition that the Rwanda Act would be valid *despite* its usurpation of the judicial function. The question is not even whether the Rwanda Act usurped judicial authority. On Hunt's explanation, it clearly did. Rather, the question raised by the Rwanda Act is the consequences for the rule of law and so for the constitutional order of the UK of such a usurpation, not whether one had taken place. We can already see that the consequences were dramatic

[49] See Peter Wallington, 'Sovereignty Regained' (1974) 37 *Modern Law Review* 686.

[50] Ibid.

[51] Murray Hunt, 'Safety of Rwanda (Asylum and Immigration) Bill: A Preliminary Rule of Law Analysis for House of Commons Second Reading' (Dec 11 2023) online: *Bingham Centre for the Rule of Law*. <https://binghamcentre.biicl.org/publications/safety-of-rwanda-asylum-and-immigration-bill-a-preliminary-rule-of-law-analysis-for-house-of-commons-second-reading> at 6. Emphasis removed.

[52] Ibid.

enough that, as I have mentioned, some commentators argued that the Supreme Court would for the first time in the history of the UK constitution be entitled to invalidate the Bill, when enacted.

3.3.3 *The Crack Where the Light Gets In*

My subsection title evokes the chorus of 'Anthem' – one of Leonard Cohen's most famous songs. 'Ring the bells that still can ring, Forget your perfect offering, There is a crack, a crack in everything, That's how the light gets in.' The crack in the Rwanda Bill was the slivers of judicial review that the Bill preserved, as did the Act that followed. The light is that shed by the rule of law and the commitments it entails. The 'perfect offering' desired by the common good lawyers was the perpetual darkness that would follow if judicial review were almost totally excluded, so that the executive could operate free of legal restraint in dealing with asylum seekers.

When the Bill was introduced to Parliament by James Cleverly, the minister responsible for guiding the Bill through its passage to enactment, he declared that: 'I am unable to make a statement that, in my view, the provisions of the Safety of Rwanda (Asylum and Immigration) Bill are compatible with the Convention rights, but the Government nevertheless wishes the House to proceed with the Bill'.[53] He thereby fulfilled the obligation imposed on ministers by section 19(1)(b) of the Human Rights Act 1998, to make a statement to Parliament, before the second reading of a bill for which he is responsible, on the proposed legislation's compatibility with Convention rights. We encountered Cleverly before as he had been overheard saying at a time when he had a different role in the Conservative government that the Rwanda Plan was 'batshit crazy'.

In Chapter 2, I suggested that Cleverly was correct because the Plan was crazy in three different senses. First, it was practically crazy as it could never be implemented to a sufficient degree to have the deterrent effect that was its official rationale. Second, it was morally crazy to render people who were seeking the protection of their legally enshrined human rights to a country that is a notorious abuser of human rights. Finally, it was legally crazy because of the damage it did to constitutional principles,

[53] House of Lords Select Committee on the Constitution, 'Safety of Rwanda (Asylum and Immigration) Bill' (Feb 9 2024) online: *UK Parliament* <https://committees.parliament.uk/publications/43291/documents/215532/default/> at para 39.

as section 19(1)(b) required Cleverley to announce. However, Ekins and his co-authors argue astonishingly not only that the Bill was compatible with Convention rights, but also that it could and should go much further than it did in undermining human rights and still remain compatible. Key to this argument were the Bill's very few remaining slivers of judicial review – avenues for judges to review the asylum-processing scheme it envisioned.

Clause 2(4) of the Bill barred a court or tribunal from considering whether Rwanda will or may remove a person to another state in contravention of any of its international obligations (including under the Refugee Convention); whether a person will not receive fair and proper consideration of an asylum or other similar claim in Rwanda; or whether Rwanda will not act in accordance with the Rwanda Treaty. Clause 2(5) of the Bill provided that the Act applied notwithstanding a range of provisions of domestic law, including parts of the Human Rights Act 1998, the common law and the UK's international law obligations. Specifically, the Bill disapplied section 3 of the Human Rights Act 1998, but not sections 4 and 10. In disapplying section 3, the Bill displaced the obligation on judges to interpret statutory provisions so as to make them human rights compliant. But in not mentioning section 4, it left intact the judges' authority to make a declaration of incompatibility in regard to provisions in the Bill when enacted; and in not mentioning section 10, it left intact ministerial authority to amend the statute to make it compatible after such a declaration.

In addition, section 4(1)(b) of the Bill allowed judges to review decisions on the basis 'that the Republic of Rwanda is not a safe country for the person in question, based on compelling evidence relating specifically to the person's particular individual circumstances (rather than on the grounds that the Republic of Rwanda is not a safe country in general)'. In other words, while the Bill declared Rwanda safe in general and precluded judges from reviewing this determination, it did allow them to review whether Rwanda was safe for an individual asylum seeker who could make a claim about 'particular individual circumstances'.[54]

[54] Section 4 amplified this qualification in brackets by stating that 'subsection (1) does not permit a decision-maker to consider any matter, claim or complaint to the extent that it relates to the issue of whether the Republic of Rwanda will or may remove or send the person in question to another State in contravention of any of its international obligations (including in particular its obligations under the Refugee Convention)'.

Ekins and his co-authors suggest that section 4 of the Human Rights Act 1998 had been 'left in play in order to soften the Bill's appearance – mollifying some parliamentarians who wrongly conflate the application of provisions of the HRA with respect for human rights and the rule of law, and providing a relatively harmless outlet for judicial opposition to (scepticism about) the Bill'.[55] In their view, that created 'a serious risk that opposition to the plan, and perhaps also to Parliament having chosen to legislate in response to the Supreme Court's judgment, will result in a very high-profile politically significant defeat for the Government'. The risk arose because the failure to rule out declarations of incompatibility would mean that 'the courts will be left entirely free to reconsider and contradict Parliament's judgement that Rwanda is safe, as well as the facts on which that judgement was made, and, on that basis, to denounce the Bill and other legislation providing for removals to Rwanda as incompatible with Convention rights'. This is not, they said, a 'minor point'.

> It is true and important that a declaration of incompatibility under section 4 of the HRA has no effect on the 'validity, continuing operation or enforcement' of the legislation that is declared to be incompatible with Convention rights. In theory, the Home Secretary and immigration officers would be able to continue to remove persons to Rwanda in reliance on the new legislation. But in practice, it would be very difficult to maintain the policy in the face of a declaration of incompatibility – especially one issued by the Supreme Court. In such a case, the Court will have had an opportunity to consider evidence, to question Parliament's judgement, and (if it disagrees) to hand down a judgment that declares Parliament to have been wrong.[56]

These quotations are only small samples from the pages of the paper that deal with this aspect of the common good lawyers' concern that the Bill did not go far enough. They make the same point over and over again in a way that conveys a sense of panic that the Bill did not disapply section 4. They also worry that a minister in some future government will use section 10 of the Human Rights Act 1998 to amend the statute so as to bring it into compliance with the Human Rights Act 1998 following a section 4 declaration of incompatibility.[57]

[55] Ekins, Laws, and Casey, 'Safety of Rwanda (Asylum and Migration) Bill' at 17.
[56] Ibid at 14–15.
[57] Ibid at 18.

Finally, they suggest that the explicit authorization to judges to review decisions on the basis 'that the Republic of Rwanda is not a safe country for the person in question' was not specific enough. They believe that the courts would continue to think

> that whatever Parliament may say Rwanda is not safe and that while this is not a conclusion they may reach in general, they are free (according to the statute) to reach it in individual cases. That is, the evidence raised about why Rwanda is not a safe country for this or that person might be received in the context of generalised suspicion about Rwanda's capacities and commitments, suspicion that the legislation may attempt to contradict, but fails to extinguish.

They thus suggest that clause 4 of the Bill 'should be tightened to specify that the particular individual circumstances in question must involve, or relate to, a pre-existing connection to Rwanda'.[58] Recall that the UK has accepted in the past claims by asylum seekers from Rwanda. So in effect what Ekins and his co-authors advocate here is that only individuals who are refugees from state oppression in Rwanda should be able to ask a court to stop their return to Rwanda.

In one respect, Ekins and his co-authors were entirely correct. The Conservative government did fear a revolt from within its own parliamentary party by the minority who still cared sufficiently about the rule of law and their country's reputation internationally. While deeply worried about the damage the Bill would do unless further amended to make it more compliant with the rule of law, they would hold their noses if these slivers were retained. These were the 'some parliamentarians' disparagingly referred to above, as if they were not sufficiently intelligent to understand that they had no reason for concern since all was well with the rule of law.

Ekins and the others were also correct that these remaining slivers of judicial review would lead inevitably to challenges by lawyers that would bring into question the legitimacy of the statute in light of the UK's own legal commitments, commitments that had been put in place by the very Parliament whose supreme place in the constitutional order Ekins and his allies claimed to be so anxious to preserve. Their panic mirrored that in a Conservative government still hoping to stave off defeat in the next general election by rendering at least one group of asylum seekers to Rwanda, a defeat which would put that 'lefty' human rights lawyer Keir Starmer in office as Prime Minister. The common good lawyers knew as

[58] Ibid at 21.

well as the government that such human rights lawyers would attempt to use these slivers to slow down the implementation of the statute until such time as it would die under a Labour government. Why, their paper asks their allies in the Conservative Party, do you not see that the statute could go much further and still remain compliant with the rule of law and international law, including international human rights law? I now turn to that question.

3.3.4 *The Rule of Law and International Law*

Ekins and his co-authors devote one section of 'Safety of Rwanda (Asylum and Migration) Bill' to the topic of the 'The rule of law and international law'. At the outset, it is important to note that it is quite difficult to work out the common good lawyers' stance on international law because they move between three different positions. First, they claim that it is fine for the UK to break its international law commitments because that is consistent with the constitutional status of international law in the UK, a dualist jurisdiction. It is also therefore consistent with the rule of law. Second, they claim that because the UK is a dualist jurisdiction, international law recognizes that its obligations bind within the jurisdiction only if Parliament has made that the case by enacting an incorporating statute. As a result, there is no departure from international law in breaking international law. Finally, they claim, and there is reason to suppose that this is their real claim, that there is nothing there to break because international law is not really law.

Their treatment of international law and the rule of law is so short that I quote it in full in three extracts in this section. These are in order of appearance and the footnotes within the quotations are in the original, though differently numbered here. Note that while short, the treatment is quite dense and to unpack fully it will require reference to another part of the paper, to another of their papers, and to an important earlier intervention by John Finnis on which they rely.

Here's the first extract, which states the premise of their argument.

> **Extract 1**
> Because a person's removal to Rwanda will not result in wrongful return to a refugee's country of origin – refoulement – the Government is on firm ground in saying that the Bill is compatible with international law, in particular with the Refugee Convention 1950.[59]

[59] Ibid at 13.

As we have seen, the ground was far from firm. Not only can one not make an unsafe country safe by mere say-so, but also the Treaty and the Bill made international law virtually irrelevant by requiring that Rwanda give asylum seekers permanent residence even if their claim to refugee status was denied. Most important of all, it is against international law to refoule asylum seekers by sending them to an unsafe country and, in declaring Rwanda safe for all purposes, the Bill precluded courts from performing their role of determining whether Rwanda itself was unsafe.

Now it is the case that if the premise of an argument is fatally flawed, the argument itself fails. But still it is important to examine the flaws in the argument itself in order to appreciate the way in which the common good lawyers play fast and loose with the law. This argument begins in the second extract

> **Extract 2**
> However, it is important to note that even if the Government did take the view that provisions of the Bill were clearly contrary to propositions of international law, including the ECHR, it would not follow that the legislation was for that reason alone illegitimate. There is no constitutional rule that the Government or Parliament must never act in ways that place the UK in breach of international law, or, relatedly, that the risks to the UK inherent in such breach or potential (or possible) breach must never be run. As we noted in a recent paper,[60] the constitutional and legal position in the UK, so far as international law is concerned, is quite clear. It has been repeatedly reaffirmed by our highest courts (previously the Appellate Committee of the House of Lords and more recently the Supreme Court),[61] and indeed is also reinforced by what is said in the Supreme Court's judgment in the Rwanda case itself.[62] The UK is a dualist state. Treaty obligations have effect in domestic law only so far as they are expressly incorporated into domestic law by or under an Act of Parliament; and, once incorporated, the relevant law is just as capable of being modified as any other domestic law, and in the same way.[63]

[60] Richard Ekins, Stephen Laws, and Conor Casey, 'Government Lawyers, the Civil Service Code, and the Rule of Law' (Dec 6 2023) online: *Policy Exchange* <https://policyexchange.org.uk/publication/government-lawyers-the-civil-service-code-and-the-rule-of-law/> paras 7 and 10.

[61] *JH Rayner (Mincing Lane) Ltd v Department of Trade and Industry*, [1990] 2 AC 418, 499; *R (Miller) v Secretary of State for Exiting the European Union (Birnie intervening)* [2017] UKSC 5, [2018] AC 61, paras 56, 78, 167 and 244.

[62] In *R on the application of AAA (Syria) and Others*, [2023] UKSC 42 paras 140–44 clearly reaffirm the supremacy of Parliament and its capacity, with clear and unambiguous words, to change the law.

[63] Ekins, Laws, and Casey, 'Safety of Rwanda (Asylum and Migration) Bill' at 13.

Ekins and the others are completely correct to assert in this passage that the constitutional position is that Parliament can legislate in a way that breaches international law, that because the UK is a dualist state, treaty obligations have direct effect only when incorporated by statute, and that Parliament can use a statute to modify what it has incorporated. The decisions they cite are all authority for that. But where they play fast and loose with the law is when they claim that: 'even if the Government did take the view that provisions of the Bill were clearly contrary to propositions of international law, including the ECHR, it would not follow that the legislation was for that reason alone illegitimate'.

Their claim here is misleading because the decisions Ekins and his co-authors cite are authority for the proposition that, unless a statute expressly and unambiguously excludes the application of relevant legal principles, including principles of international law, the scope of the authority of ministers and other state officials in implementing the statute is limited by those principles. For example, if a statute gives an official a wide authority to make decisions affecting people's important interests, the courts will hold that the decisions must be made in accordance with principles of fairness embedded in the common law, unless the statute very explicitly states that such principles should not govern.

That proposition – that unless a statute expressly and unambiguously provides otherwise, ministerial authority is limited by the law, including international law – is the real target of their short section on the rule of law and international law. Recall that ministers have a code of conduct that obliges them to follow the law in exercising their roles, and civil servants are also subject to such a codified duty. The concern driving Ekins and his co-authors is the possibility that if ministers or civil servants thought that 'the law' includes international law, they would find themselves in a conflict of legal duties if domestic law required otherwise, a conflict of duties that ministers or civil servants might resolve by choosing international law over domestic law. In addition, Ekins and his co-authors worry that the lawyers in the civil service who advise other officials about whether proposed conduct is unlawful would give their advice based on an understanding that the law that binds officials includes international law. One has to jump forward to another section of their paper to see this, where they say:

> The Bill anticipates the risk of interim measures being issued by judges of the Strasbourg Court. The Bill's answer, in common with section 55 of the Illegal Migration Act 2023, is to provide that the Minister, *acting personally*, has authority to decide whether the UK will or will not comply with an interim

> measure, a choice which will bind civil servants. Further, the legislation provides that no court or tribunal may have regard to such an interim measure in hearing an application or an appeal that relates to a decision to remove a person to Rwanda. (There remains a risk that the Minister's decision not to comply with a Rule 39 interim measure will be challenged by way of judicial review proceedings.) This is a welcome provision, so far as it goes, but parliamentarians should be well aware that the Rwanda plan is likely to collapse if the Government is unwilling in practice to remove asylum-seekers to Rwanda if or when Rule 39 interim measures have been made.[64]

I have emphasized 'acting personally' because, by talking in this way, the common good lawyers alert us to one respect in which the Bill most clearly violated the rule of law even on its thinnest definition. It did so by turning the obligation of officials to comply with the law into a matter for the personal choice of a minister. Indeed, a statutory provision that gives ministers this power creates a larger constitutional crisis than the one unfolding as I write in the US, where officials of the Trump administration are more or less openly but illegally defying court orders. For the provision authorizes the minister to order officials to act illegally, and thus both uses law to embed the crisis within the legal order and places the officials in an ethical conflict between two legal obligations. On the one hand, there is their general obligation to the law, stated in the Civil Service Code as the duty of civil servants to 'comply with the law and uphold the administration of justice'. On the other hand, there is the duty to the ministers to whom they are responsible, acting within the scope of their legislative authority. UK lawyers and judges like to quote Thomas Fuller's words from 1732: 'Be you ever so high, the law is above you.' But Ekins and his co-authors' support for this feature of the Bill further strengthens the claim that their Judicial Power Project is more aptly titled the Executive Power Project, one that seeks to elevate the executive above both Parliament and the judiciary in the constitutional order and, we can now add, above the law.

As Murray Hunt has pointed out, Article 13 of the European Convention on Human Rights grants applicants the right to an 'effective remedy'. One such remedy is an injunction issued by the European Court of Human Rights – an 'interim measure' under Rule 39. By making the effectiveness of this remedy depend on the personal say-so of a minister, the Bill made the human rights of asylum seekers depend on whim.[65]

[64] Ibid at 23.

[65] Hunt, 'Safety of Rwanda (Asylum and Immigration) Bill: A Preliminary Rule of Law Analysis for House of Commons Second Reading' at 3.

Ekins and his co-authors avoid confronting this rule-of-law problem by referring to it only obliquely in the part of their paper which purports to discuss the rule of law and international law. One has to trawl through their footnotes in order to bring their argument into view, starting with the 'recent publication' they mention – 'Government Lawyers, the Civil Service Code, and the Rule of Law' – a paper the three of them authored, and for which Wolfson again provided a Foreword.[66]

This publication was triggered by a report in the *Times* newspaper that, at the time that the government was considering how to respond to the Supreme Court's Rwanda judgment, civil servants were considering resisting any response that did not comply with international law on the basis of their code of conduct as set out in the Civil Service Code. That, the authors said, suggested 'a very worrying level of ignorance amongst some civil servants about some constitutional fundamentals, including about what the Civil Service Code actually provides, the relationship between international law and the rule of law in our legal system, and the proper role of the government lawyer'.[67] They pointed out that all the Code says is that civil servants must 'comply with the law and uphold the administration of justice' and so does not mention explicitly international law. Hence, they claimed, the Code refers to

> the only law that has effect as such in the UK, UK domestic law, and to the administration of the justice which that law delivers. It would be manifestly absurd to suggest – although it appears that perhaps it has been – that 'complying with the law and upholding the administration of justice' extends to refusing to collaborate with government proposals to change what has to be complied with and upheld. Nor do the codes allow the invention of principles which either limit, directly or indirectly, the capacity of an elected Parliament to change UK law if it so wishes, or prejudice the legitimacy of any request by government to Parliament for such a change.[68]

This background is the first bit necessary to begin to understand the last sentences of the third and final extract from the section of 'Safety of Rwanda (Asylum and Migration)' on the rule of law and international law.

> **Extract 3**
> The core of the rule of law in our constitution is that 'Ministers can neither claim any immunity, by virtue simply of their office, from the

66 Ekins, Laws, and Casey, 'Government Lawyers, the Civil Service Code, and the Rule of Law'.

67 Ibid at 8

68 Ibid at 10.

> rules of common law, nor by any decree or order impose a legal duty (or relieve anyone of a legal duty), except to the extent that an Act of Parliament authorizes them to do so'.[69] The integrity of our constitution is put in jeopardy when civil servants and Ministers assume that legislation that is, or risks being found to be, incompatible with the UK's international obligations cannot legitimately be put before Parliament or enacted.[70]

The quotation within the quotation is from a short publication on the Policy Exchange site by John Finnis, the intellectual force behind the UK branch of common good ideology.[71] It was occasioned by the issue I discussed in Chapter 1 in introducing the war against law in the UK.

Recall that in 2015 David Cameron's Conservative government quietly dropped from the Ministerial Code the phrase 'to comply with the law including international law and treaty obligations', leaving only 'an overarching duty on ministers to protect the integrity of public life'.[72] Cameron's amendment was greeted with consternation by senior lawyers. In contrast, Finnis welcomed the move, claiming that the former statement of duty was an assertion 'at odds with the fundamentals of British constitutional law'. The replacement, a duty 'to comply with the law', is 'constitutionally sound, and removes the threat that the earlier assertion posed to the Rule of Law'.[73] He saw the 'threat' thereto as follows:

> To say that Ministers can change the legal rights or obligations of anyone in the realm simply by entering into or ratifying an international treaty is to challenge that most fundamental principle of our constitutional law, and thus challenges also the Rule of Law. To say that Ministers can by treaty change the legal rights or duties of present or future Ministers is equally, and for precisely the same reason, quite contrary to our law. But this is what the 2010 Code formula seemed to imply by asserting that the law with which Ministers have an overarching duty to comply includes international law and treaty obligations.
>
> Our law does *not* 'include' treaty obligations not given legal force by Parliament. So the 1997/2010 assertion was (no doubt by good faith confusion) unconstitutional and a threat to the Rule of Law. . . .

[69] John Finnis, 'Ministers, International Law, and the Rule of Law' (Nov 2 2015) online: *Judicial Power Project* <https://judicialpowerproject.org.uk/ministers-international-law-and-the-rule-of-law/>.

[70] Ekins, Laws, and Casey, 'Safety of Rwanda (Asylum and Migration) Bill' at 13.

[71] Finnis, 'Ministers, International Law, and the Rule of Law'.

[72] Diane Taylor, 'Lawyers Express Concern over Ministerial Code Rewrite' (Oct 22 2015) online: *The Guardian* <www.theguardian.com/law/2015/oct/22/lawyers-express-concern-over-ministerial-code-rewrite>.

[73] Finnis, 'Ministers, International Law, and the Rule of Law'.

> The first responsibility of anyone who appeals to the Rule of Law is to distinguish between what is law and what is not law (but rather convention, or guidelines, or advice, or political agreement . . .). When Lord Bingham in his book *The Rule of Law* (2010) said that the Code's assertion, as it then stood, was 'binding' on Ministers, he spoke in a way that no judge or lawyer should speak.[74]

The best explanation, in Finnis's view, of the old and 'constitutionally mistaken' statement of obligation is that it was 'a confusingly compressed reminder to Ministers of the standing, morally grounded UK *policy* of complying with its treaty obligations, of encouraging other states to do likewise, and of supporting the due extension of customary international law and appropriate international institutions'.[75] So here Finnis was claiming that compliance with international law is not something legal, but a mere policy choice, which prepares the way for the supposed knockout punch, the true message of 'Safety of Rwanda (Asylum and Migration) Bill', Finnis's claim that international law is not really law:

> International law remains, like it or not, a *defective example of law*. The criteria for its formation and identification remain opaque, controverted, and manipulable without redress. It is subject to serious problems of free riding and other forms of bad faith. If we can speak of the Rule of Law in the international domain, we must accept, as Lord Bingham as good as admitted in his book, that it is only a Rule by imperfect analogy with the law of the land – if only for lack of courts with sufficient jurisdiction to identify and enforce it.[76]

If Finnis were right, there would be no need to make the argument that the Rwanda Bill complied with international law, or to make the pious proclamations about compliance with international law in the Rwanda Treaty. For if international law is not really law, it becomes entirely irrelevant to a discussion of the legal obligations of the UK and its officials, whether they be ministers or civil servants. That those arguments and the proclamations are made even as the common good lawyers wish to deny international law's relevance and even nature as law is just a vivid example of the double-speak in which some lawyers and the Conservative governments in this century have engaged.

Moreover, Finnis misrepresented what Bingham said in his book. Rather than 'as good as' admitting that international law is 'defective

[74] Ibid. His emphasis.
[75] Ibid. His emphasis.
[76] Ibid. My emphasis.

law', Bingham said that the 'analogy' between the situation of domestic law and of international law 'even if not exact, makes plain . . . why we should favour strict compliance with the law'.[77] The 'even if' does not suggest that there is a problem with international law because the analogy between domestic and international law is flawed. Indeed, that the analogy is flawed is undeniable because there is no international legislature, no centralized enforcement mechanism, and the International Court of Justice does not have compulsory jurisdiction to decide disputes between states.

However, Bingham's argument was that we should *not* focus on these disanalogies in working out why international law is law – why it binds states. Rather, we should suppose that the international legal order is a legal order and that its law is genuine law that binds states because it is what makes peaceful coexistence on decent terms possible. This is its core similarity with the domestic law that binds individuals in their interactions with each other and the state in its interactions with the individuals subject to its control. Both the domestic and international legal order offer an alternative to what Bingham said, more than a little elliptically, is 'the rule of the jungle' – that is, an arbitrary and unpredictable rule, no more tolerable in the small, domestic setting than it is in the larger, international one. As Bingham summed up this train of thought: 'The rule of the jungle is no more tolerable in a big jungle.'[78]

The issue is not, however, that it would be nice if only we thought that. In that case, the obligations of international law would be no more than a kind of moral code, and thus not legally enforceable, which is precisely what Finnis urges in this short publication:

> if Ministers so conduct themselves that the UK violates a treaty, they obviously must account to their colleagues and to Parliament both for making the UK internationally liable, and for putting in question the UK's settled policy of upholding what corresponds to the Rule of Law in the international domain. That 'must' is not legal, but an important principle of responsible government of our constitutional form.[79]

But that is not the case and, by stating that it is, Finnis also misrepresented the situation of UK domestic law. He didn't misrepresent it altogether, as he couldn't help but acknowledge that international law,

[77] Tom Bingham, *The Rule of Law* (London: Allen Lane, 2010) at 112.
[78] Ibid.
[79] Finnis, 'Ministers, International Law, and the Rule of Law'.

despite its alleged 'defective' nature, does exist and does have a presence in UK law, though his acknowledgement is very reluctant, as can be seen in his overuse of emphasis in this passage:

> Still, some rules of 'customary' international law correspond to parts of our common law, some other rules have been adopted by Act of Parliament, and there is a legal *presumption* that Parliament intends not to defy or ignore international law or the UK's treaty obligations. But *none of this* imposes on Ministers (or civil servants) anything comparable to their personal obligation as citizens and Ministers to *comply with the law*, that is, with the law of the land.[80]

Finnis's implicit claim that customary international law is binding only when it corresponds to parts of the common law is false. This is a mealy-mouthed description of the place of international law in the constitutional tradition to which Finnis and the other common good lawyers constantly proclaim their fidelity. They distort that tradition so that they can make preposterous claims such as Finnis's that Bingham 'spoke in a way that no judge or lawyer should speak'. In addition, the slippage from the comparison of the obligations of ministers to the 'personal obligation' of citizens is at the same time mysterious and misleading. Ministers are officers of the state and as such have responsibilities and duties that are different and more onerous than the responsibilities and duties they have as ordinary citizens. Let me quote back at Finnis with a shift in emphasis his acknowledgement that there is 'a *legal* presumption that Parliament intends not to defy or ignore international law or the UK's treaty obligations'.

Finnis emphasizes 'presumption' because the point of the term 'legal presumption' is to indicate that the presumption can be rebutted by explicit and unambiguous expressions of Parliament's intention to defy international law. I emphasize 'legal' instead because it tells us that in the absence of such an explicit and unambiguous expression of intent by Parliament, the UK's public officials are under a legal duty to comply with international law. This requires judges to interpret 'the law of the land' as including relevant international law. By necessary implication, ministers and other public officials have a legal duty to implement statutory directives in accordance with relevant international law.

We have seen that the provisions in the Rwanda Bill discussed in this chapter, all of which made their way into the Act, did explicitly and

[80] Ibid. His emphasis.

unambiguously defy international law, thus rebutting the presumption. Moreover, for the most part, the Bill prohibited judges from scrutinizing whether officials were acting within the scope of their authority. We have also seen that the common good lawyers want to affirm both that the Bill did not defy international law and that Parliament is entitled to defy international law. As I have set out in this chapter, they go so far as to argue that the Bill could and should have gone further in its defiance and yet would have remained in compliance with both the rule of law and international law.

Most importantly, however, they reveal their belief that there is ultimately nothing to defy since international law is 'defective law' – that is, not really law. However, they cannot put their belief on that basis because to do so would amount to a blatant defiance of both the law of the land and their constitutional tradition. So for the most part they stick with double-speak in the hope of avoiding a confrontation with the incoherence the Rwanda Act introduced into the UK constitutional order. The incoherence arises because the Rwanda Act creates a space within the UK constitutional order where the law of the land does not reach. This is an important point. Quite apart from the question of whether the Act violates the rule of law, it is clear that the space in which the executive would act in implementing it is a lawless space. Not only is relevant law disapplied, but also there is almost no independent review possible of whether the officials implementing the Act are acting illegally. In fact, the Act grants them license to act illegally and all but strips the judges of authority to say so.

'All but' because, as we have seen, section 4 declarations of incompatibility were still possible as well as applications to the European Court of Human Rights for a Rule 39 interim measure. In addition, the courts could review whether 'the Republic of Rwanda is not a safe country for the person in question'. These were the cracks through which the light of the rule of law would have got in; cracks which the common good lawyers wanted closed for precisely this reason, but which a sufficient number of Conservative members of Parliament insisted on keeping open in order to preserve the façade of the rule of law. Indeed, Ekins and his co-authors almost admit the implications of their argument when they say in support of their bid to get the Bill amended to preclude section 4 challenges that leaving section 4 in place installs 'an important internal contradiction [in the Bill], which significantly weakens its force'. What they do not see, or if they see it will not admit, is that eradicating that contradiction would have made the legislation into an even more draconian assault on the rule of law.[81]

An accurate response to the Rwanda Bill would have required the common good lawyers to admit that the Bill usurped the judicial function and in so doing imperilled the rule of law. They could then have debated on frank terms those lawyers who argued that the Bill was unconstitutional to the point where for the first time in UK history judges should regard themselves as authorized to strike down the statute as invalid. That they so diligently tried to put rule of law lipstick on this porcine law has a significance that goes far beyond the scope of the Rwanda Act.

The Act targeted perhaps the most vulnerable group in any society, non-citizens with a precarious claim to have any more rights than the mere right to make an asylum claim. It might thus appear that even if the Act had been implemented, while the rule of law would have been subverted, democracy was not at stake, since the individuals harmed were as far removed from the status of citizen as it is possible to be. Indeed, the common good lawyers and their allies regard dealing with 'illegal migrants', their favourite term for asylum seekers, in this lawless way as part of their project for restoring the 'democratic' control of the British people over their borders.

But one need only look, first, across the Atlantic to the US to see how removing the rights of the less vulnerable group is always a process which begins with targeting the most vulnerable but continues until one gets to the point of declaring the citizens one doesn't like the internal 'enemy' who don't deserve the law's protection. And then one can look, second, at the rhetoric of Conservative Party and the Reform Party to see what the Rwanda Act presaged for the UK if the far right comes to power.

But far from admitting that the Bill usurped the judicial function and in so doing imperilled the rule of law, Ekins and his co-authors have this to say:

> It is wildly irresponsible for lawyers to invite the Supreme Court to overthrow the fundamental rule of our constitution – or to suggest that such an unconstitutional act, which would be tantamount to a constitutional revolution, would be a justified response to Parliament enacting legislation that makes it lawful to remove persons to Rwanda. We doubt very much that the Supreme Court would entertain this course of action, which would invite and warrant intense political criticism of the Court,

[81] Ekins, Laws, and Casey, 'Safety of Rwanda (Asylum and Migration) Bill' at 14.

> and would and should lead to far-reaching parliamentary action to reverse the Court's attack on the fundamentals of the constitution.[82]

But I will show that it is they who are wildly irresponsible in their 'attack on the fundamentals of the constitution', as is the Bill they supported except for the fact that they thought that the attack was not sufficiently savage. However, I already indicated that my conclusion will not be that the statute was so fundamentally flawed that judges would have been entitled to invalidate it. I am prepared with Hermer to recognize that the Rwanda Act was a valid statute of a sovereign parliament. It is easy to agree with him that the clause in the Act which states that '[i]t is recognised that . . . the Parliament of the United Kingdom is sovereign' is 'otiose' because no one contests that fact. The issue is only what follows from that fact. It is, that is, more difficult to show that the assertion of sovereignty was not only otiose but also 'crass', because that requires showing in what way it perpetrated 'constitutional heresies'. And I now turn to that task.

[82] Ibid at 24.

4

Heresy vs Heresy: Debating the Rule of Law

4.1 Through Thick and Thin

My task in this chapter is to begin to set out the argument that the Rwanda Act, as Attorney General Richard Hermer charged, contained 'constitutional heresies' by focusing on the issue of the thin versus thick definition of the rule of law. The discussion will take us some distance into legal and political theory, but only so far as to engage with these issues, as members of the House of Lords engaged on 26 November 2024 in a debate on 'The Rule of Law', in which the main topic was Hermer's Bingham Lecture.[1]

Here's how things stand so far. I have been working provisionally with the thin definition of the rule of law, which requires no more than that officials obey the rules laid down by the superior authority of Parliament. As long as those rules are clear, so that citizens can know in advance what

[1] House of Lords, 'Rule of Law: Hansard, Volume 841' (Nov 26 2024) online: *UK Parliament* <https://hansard.parliament.uk/lords/2024-11-26/debates/D5A3DAF2-1DF8-46CC-BA01-A23FD6A59095/RuleOfLaw>. Note that in the wake of this debate, The House of Lords Constitution Committee published on 11 March 2025 a call for written evidence for an inquiry into the rule of law, inviting interested individuals and organizations to submit their views on this issue. See 'Rule of Law Inquiry Launched by Lords Constitution Committee' (Mar 11 2025) online: *UK Parliament* <https://committees.parliament.uk/committee/172/constitution-committee/news/205702/rule-of-law-inquiry-launched-by-lords-constitution-committee/>.

My own submission was based on early drafts of this chapter and the next. See David Dyzenhaus, 'Written Evidence (ROL0045)' (Apr 20 2025) online: *UK Parliament* <https://committees.parliament.uk/writtenevidence/140668/pdf/>.

Several common good lawyers, including John Finnis and Richard Ekins, and their allies, gave evidence. The refrain of their evidence is that one should adopt the thin conception of the rule of law because it represents the apolitical consensus.

For the report, see House of Lords Constitution Committee, 'Rule of Law: Holding the Line between Anarchy and Tyranny' (Nov 20 2025) online: *UK Parliament* <https://committees.parliament.uk/committee/172/constitution-committee/news/210496/constitution-rule-of-law-report-publication/>. I think it fair to say that the Report politely rejects the efforts made by the common good lawyers to instil their ideology in it.

the law is and can guide their actions by the law, the rule of law is in place, whatever the content of the rules. On this definition, there may seem to be nothing wrong with the Rwanda Act from the perspective of the rule of law, as the deportation rule consigns asylum seekers to a certain fate. As a matter of law, they know that they will be rendered to Rwanda, where they will get permanent residence regardless of the merits of their claim to refugee status. As a matter of fact, if they know anything about Rwanda, they will also know that to be rendered there is to be consigned to a country with a bad record of disrespect for human rights, so that they will be deterred from seeking asylum in the UK.

That might be morally crazy and against the spirit and the letter of human rights law, the law to which the UK is committed both internationally and domestically. But in the common good lawyers' view, it is not legally speaking crazy. Rather, they claim, it is consistent with the rule of law from an internal perspective, from the perspective of the UK's constitutional tradition. They also claim that it is consistent with the rule of law from the perspective of international law because the UK is a dualist state in which international law has direct effect – becomes a matter of the internal obligation of officials and the legal rights of people within the UK – only as long and so long as Parliament decrees that is the case.

However, we have seen that those claims are wrong. The Rwanda Act introduced a gross incoherence into the constitutional order. It did so by usurping the judicial function of testing the proposition that a country is a 'safe' place to which to render asylum seekers, by disapplying large parts of UK law, and by ousting almost altogether the jurisdiction of the courts to review its implementation. The last chapter already provides ample evidence in this regard, as the arguments made by the common good lawyers are so weak that they help to display the incoherence. Indeed, we saw that their real claim is that international law is not really law, since it is 'defective law'.

As will become clear in this chapter and the next, the claim that international law is not really law is based on the common good lawyers' most foundational claim of all – that parliamentary sovereignty by definition requires the view that international law is not really law. I noted in the Introduction that Hans Kelsen, the great Austrian philosopher of law, advised at the end of his 1920 book on sovereignty in both international law and domestic law that the 'concept [of sovereignty] should be radically repressed', both because there is no theoretical need to rely on it in understanding the ideas necessary for a complete theory of a constitutional order and because it is politically pernicious, tied as it is to nasty assertions of nationalism.[2] I also pointed out that in an influential paper in 2003, 'Sovereignty's Blight', the UK human rights lawyer Murray Hunt, on whom I relied often in the preceding chapter, argued that 'English lawyers' weakness for the alluring idea of "sovereignty" as a foundational concept' continued to 'blight contemporary public law and to prevent its evolution into a mature system regulating the exercise of power in a modern polity'.[3]

In the Introduction, I suggested that in an important sense, both Kelsen and Hunt are right. A pernicious and nationalistic conception of sovereignty has played an enormous role in the debates around Brexit and Rwanda, as it continues to do in politics in the UK and elsewhere in the world. However, one cannot get rid of the word, not least because it is such an essential tool in the kit of the political right, but also because it figures in any account of the UK constitution in which the principle of parliamentary supremacy or sovereignty is about Parliament's place as the ultimate source of law in the constitutional order.

I will from now on for the most part slightly switch my terminology, from talk of a contest of 'definitions' when it comes to the contest between a thin and a thick definition of the rule of law to talk of a contest of 'conceptions'. The first way of talking seeks a definitive formulation with clear boundaries limiting the scope of the concept (and therefore poses a false binary of what's in and what's out). In contrast, the second way conceives of the issues as interpretive understandings of what the core of the idea means, informed by the actual practice of participants – lawyers, judges and officials – rather than abstract theorizing. On this view, while the concept of the rule of law transcends to some extent time and place, particular conceptions are also tied to some extent to time and place. For example, the right to a fair trial has changed in meaning quite radically in the twentieth century and its meaning varies from jurisdiction to jurisdiction.[4]

In Chapter 2, I remarked on the distinction between a 'heretic' and an 'apostate'. An 'apostate' abandons their faith altogether. A heretic by

[2] Hans Kelsen, *Das Problem der Souveränität und die Theorie des Völkerrechts: Beitrag zu Einer Reinen Rechtslehre* (Aalen: Scientia Verlag, 1981) at 320 (My translation).

[3] Murray Hunt, 'Sovereignty's Blight: Why Contemporary Public Law Needs the Concept of "Due Deference"' in Nicholas Bamforth and Peter Leyland, eds, *Public Law in a Multi-Layered Constitution* (Oxford: Hart Publishing, 2003) 337 at 339.

[4] Ian Langford, 'Fair Trial: The History of an Idea' (2009) 8 *Journal of Human Rights* 37.

contrast adheres to a doctrine contradictory to at least one single and central principle of their faith. And if the common good lawyers are heretics because of their advocacy of the Rwanda Plan as consistent with the rule of law when in reality it is not, that is because they do so often express their allegiance to the concept of rule of law and to its place in the UK constitutional tradition. That allegiance is what they share with Hermer and other human rights lawyers who figure in my book, whatever their otherwise stark differences.

But while they may share allegiance to a bunch of 'concepts' – the rule of law, sovereignty, and so on – they differ in their particular *conceptions* thereof – that is, in the content they give to the particular concept. Here my argument encounters the problem that the thin definition states that one has the rule of law as long as the rules are properly enacted, whatever the content of the rules. So it may seem that the common good lawyers can deny that they ascribe any content at all to the rule of law.

Their denial is on its face odd. As I remarked at the end of Chapter 1, the reason I call them 'common good lawyers' rather than the 'Judicial Power Project lawyers' is so that we keep in mind that the Judicial Power Project is merely a vehicle for the Common Good Project. And the political agenda of the Common Good Project is to put in place a state that will enforce 'the natural law', understood as the moral virtues of an illiberal religious tradition, often presented as a very conservative and very controversial understanding of Catholicism. We were in Chapter 3 deep within the realm of legal arguments, a realm in which the thin definition is useful to the common good lawyers both because it clears the way for transforming the UK constitutional order into an order of executive rule and because it gives them some common ground with the many lawyers who take for granted that the thin definition is correct. In this chapter and the next we begin our journey back to the interaction between law and politics, so that in Chapter 6 we can return fully to discussion of the role of the politics of the 'common good' in the rule-of-law debate occasioned by the Rwanda Act.

In denying that they ascribe any content at all to the rule of law, the common good lawyers rely, as I have suggested, and will come back to later in this chapter, on the philosophical tradition of thinking about the law known as 'legal positivism'. A central tenet of this tradition is that all there is to law is what has been properly enacted or 'posited', so that the law can have any content. If that's right, it will seem illicit to claim that the concept of the rule of law includes respect for human rights and international law. But, as we will see, no one, neither positivist philosophers of law nor even the common good lawyers, can stick to the claim that the rules can have any content.[5]

In fact, as I will argue, everyone has a more or less thick conception of the rule of law and disagreements about how thick the conception should be are at the same time philosophical and fundamentally political in nature. The disagreements reflect different interpretations of how best to go on in our legal practices in light of our experience of those practices, for all there is to philosophy of law is a more abstract account of our already existing practices. Such an account will not be 'value-neutral'. It will take a stand on the issue of the best interpretation of our practices, one that is not merely faithful to the past, to tradition, but also informs, as I just suggested, how we should best go on. The main advantage, then, in moving away from talk of contest of definitions is that a definition in the kind of contested context in which debates about the rule of law take place is always a 'persuasive definition'.[6] It builds its victory in an argument into its verbal formulation. In contrast, a contest of conceptions accepts that each conception is advanced as an exercise of political advocacy about why it is the most productive way in which to go forward while remaining faithful to the past. It does this by offering contestable reasons about why the conception will in fact advance the 'common good' of all, instead of seeking to avoid the contest by defining the terrain of argument by stipulating a definition that excludes one's opponents from the contest.

We will soon see that these otherwise abstruse sounding observations on the methodology of philosophy of law became live issues in the debate that followed Hermer's Bingham Lecture. But I want to set the stage for that debate, first, by reintroducing the thin versus thick definition of the rule-of-law dispute, this time conceived as a contest of conceptions, with each allied to clearly political conceptions of democracy. Second, as I will show, this exercise will take us back to A. V. Dicey's discussion of constitutional fundamentals.

And as we go through this contest of conceptions, it is most important to recall that the Judicial Power Project operates in tandem with the Common Good Project. As I have again suggested, the former makes the 'legal' arguments that if successful clear the way for a change in the constitutional order such that the 'ruler', that is the executive, can

[5] I will slightly qualify this claim later, as some lawyers on the left also purport to advocate the thin definition.

[6] See Charles Leslie Stevenson, 'Persuasive Definitions' (1938) 47 *Mind* 331.

'promulgate the common good', an ideology of anti-liberal and generally reactionary principles claimed to embody 'the natural law' of the 'classical tradition'. In other words, the thin conception of the rule of law which the common good lawyers and their political allies in the House of Lords espouse is the Trojan horse that conceals the common good agenda, one committed to a much more substantive or thicker conception of the rule of law than Bingham's since it is about enforcing what it conceives as 'the natural law'. Indeed, it is so thick that, as the two concluding chapters will show, it ceases to be a conception of the rule of law at all, and becomes the legitimizing ideology that prepares the way for authoritarian rule. It is also important to bear in mind that, in making this argument, I acknowledge that the Judicial Power Project's political allies in the House of Lords, notably Lord Wolfson, likely reject this objective.

4.2 Democracy and the Rule of Law

Ronald Dworkin, one of the leading philosophers of law and politics of the post-war period, was also the leading practitioner of the 'interpretive' methodology just sketched, one that is highly controversial in philosophy of law, indeed in philosophy more generally. So much so that John Gardner, Dworkin's successor in the chair in philosophy of law in Oxford, liked to claim that Dworkin was not a real philosopher.[7] I will come back to this point later because, as we will see, Gardner's position on the rule of law, or more accurately a misrepresentation of his position, was relied on in the House of Lords debate in the main attack on Hermer.

In this section, I want to draw attention to Dworkin's distinction between the majoritarian conception of democracy, according to which the legitimate decision is the one the majority happens to vote for, whatever its content, and a liberal conception, according to which decisions by the majority are legitimate only if they respect certain fundamental rights. Both conceptions have an obvious foothold in the practices of the world's democracies. But they offer different prescriptions as to the design of our political and legal institutions and thus as to how we should best go on in our political and legal practices.[8]

[7] For example, Gardner once said that Dworkin is not a philosopher, but a 'theoretically ambitious lawyer': John Gardner, 'The Legality of Law' (2004) 17 *Ratio Juris* 168 at 173.

[8] Ronald Dworkin, 'Introduction: The Moral Reading and the Majoritarian Premise' in *Freedom's Law: The Moral Reading of the American Constitution* (Cambridge, MA: Harvard University Press, 1996) 1.

Notably, for our purposes, majoritarians favour parliamentary sovereignty so as to ensure that the majority can exercise its will unhindered by other institutions, especially judges. In contrast, Dworkin and others favour a written constitution that both entrenches essential rights and gives authority to judges to strike down as invalid statutes that violate rights. This liberal conception is more complex than its majoritarian rival. It says that a necessary condition of democratic legitimacy is that the decision is made by a majority. But that is not sufficient, they suggest, since a further condition is that the decision respects all those rights which citizens must have for them to be able to participate fully in the democratic process. The list of rights includes the right to vote, the right to free speech and, more controversially, the right to equal concern and respect, because if that right is undermined so is one's ability to participate fully in the life of the political community. They favour, then, a constitution which entrenches rights because they suppose that is the best kind of constitutional arrangement available for the protection of the rights citizens must have in a democracy.

Given Dworkin's distinctively liberal conception of democracy, it is no surprise that his conception of the rule of law is thick. Indeed, he argued for a 'rights' conception of the rule of law that

> assumes that citizens have moral rights and duties with respect to one another, and political rights against the state as a whole. It insists that these moral and political rights be recognized in positive law, so that they may be enforced *upon the demand of individual citizens* through courts or other judicial institutions of the familiar type, so far as this is practicable. The rule of law on this conception is the ideal of rule by an accurate public conception of individual rights.[9]

And he opposed his conception to the thin conception advocated by legal positivists, which he called 'the rulebook conception', because it distinguishes 'between the rule of law and substantive justice'. His conception, in contrast, 'requires, as part of the ideal of law, that the rules in the rule book capture and enforce moral rights'.[10]

I will return to this distinction later in the chapter, highlighting for the moment that the majoritarian conception of democracy has something important in common with the thin conception of the rule of law. Just as the majoritarian conception has it that laws can have any content, so the

[9] Ronald Dworkin, 'Political Judges and the Rule of Law' in *A Matter of Principle* (Cambridge, MA: Harvard University Press, 1985) 9 at 11–12. His emphasis.

[10] Ibid.

thin conception has it that laws with any content are consistent with the rule of law as long as they are made in accordance with the formal criteria for what counts as a valid law. It follows, as both the majoritarians and the common good lawyers urge, that the laws made by a democratic parliament are both legitimate and consistent with the rule of law, whatever their content.

Suppose, however, that the UK Parliament enacts a statute that declares the Prime Minister dictator for life and says that from now on he will announce his laws orally at a weekly press conference. That statute would be obviously inconsistent with any conception of democracy and the rule of law because it does away with both. And so it poses a clear problem for majoritarian democrats as well as for the thin conception of the rule of law. Now the Rwanda Act may not seem at first sight as dramatic as this imaginary statute. But I will be arguing that it poses the same kind of problem, and that it is illicit to try to hide that fact by relying on the technique of persuasive definition, by offering a definition that builds its victory in an argument into its verbal formulation. The shift from a contest of definitions to a contest of conceptions, to what is moreover a contest of *political* conceptions, is important if we are to prevent the common good lawyers from declaring victory through such definitions.

While I now begin to move away from the thin conception, it will continue to play a role in my argument. This is because Hermer and the other human rights lawyers agree with the common good lawyers that the elements of the rule of law that figure in the thin conception are part of the concept of the rule of law. Where they most obviously disagree is on whether international law and human rights are also part of the correct conception of the rule of law – that is, on whether the thin conception should be made thicker or more substantive, as Bingham, and Hermer following him, urge. This allows the common good lawyers and their allies to suggest that the area of agreement represents the apolitical consensus on the rule of law and that any attempt to move beyond it is both an attempt to smuggle one's political views into the concept and against the UK constitutional tradition.

However, as I will show, the insistence on the thin conception and nothing more is also political. But it does not follow that we are left with a contest of conceptions in which victory can be declared by the side that can point to the area of consensus. This is the move that those who substitute persuasive definition for good argument attempt to make. Rather, once we shift to a contest of political conceptions of the concept of the rule of law, progress can be made by argument that builds on while reflecting our practices and experience.

4.3 Back to Dicey's Constitutional Fundamentals

In Chapter 3, I briefly discussed Richard Ekins's Atkin Lecture with the title, 'Human Rights and the Rule of Law', subsequently published on Policy Exchange.[11] The lecture was just one in a series of attacks by Ekins and others on the European Court of Human Rights, and its practice of issuing 'interim measures' under Rule 39, the kind of judicial injunction which puts a temporary stop to the implementation of a policy until its legality can properly be adjudicated. In the lecture, Ekins purports to pay homage to Lord Atkin, who is regarded as one of the great common law judges, most famous for his dissent in *Liversidge v Anderson*,[12] a case on detention during the Second World War, which Ekins describes as follows:

> In *Liversidge*, as many of you will know, a majority of the House of Lords held that indefinite detention was lawful if the Home Secretary merely thought that he had good cause to detain a person. Lord Atkin dissented on the grounds that the legislation clearly made it a condition of the authority to detain that the Home Secretary in fact had good cause to detain a person, not just that he thought that he had good cause.[13]

Ekins raises this dissent because, as he points out, it is sometimes seen as the precursor to the House of Lords' 2004 decision in *Belmarsh*, which concerned the detention of foreigners considered to be threats to national security, and which is considered the most significant decision of the UK's highest Court on the basis of the Human Rights Act 1998.[14] As Ekins says, the 'point of comparing the two cases is to suggest that the House of Lords in *Belmarsh* followed the example set by Lord Atkin's courageous dissent in 1941, protecting liberty in dangerous times'. But, he claims,

> This is not a plausible comparison. The legislation under consideration in the *Belmarsh* case applied to foreign terror suspects rather than British

[11] Richard Ekins, 'Human Rights and the Rule of Law' (Apr 17 2024) online: *Policy Exchange* <https://policyexchange.org.uk/wp-content/uploads/Human-Rights-and-the-Rule-of-Law.pdf>.

[12] *Liversidge v Anderson* [1942] AC 206.

[13] Ekins, 'Human Rights and the Rule of Law' at 13.

[14] *A and others v Home Secretary* [2004] UKHL 56.

> terror suspects because it involved detention pending deportation, albeit in circumstances where there was an obstacle to deportation at the present time. The majority of the House of Lords ignored the deportation context, partly because of the way in which the case was presented by the Attorney General.[15]

He continues:

> The case is thus not an improvement on *Liversidge v Anderson* so much as a distorted echo of it. In *Liversidge*, the majority of the Court misread the legislation because of its view about wartime conditions; in *Belmarsh*, the Court misread the legislation, perhaps because of the Attorney General's litigation tactics and the temptation to stand in judgement over the government's policy. The leading case under the Human Rights Act is thus a failure of disciplined adjudication.[16]

Ekins's characterization of these decisions is inaccurate. Lord Atkin's judgment in *Liversidge* depends on exactly the kind of reasoning that the common good lawyers usually deplore. He held that the fact that the detentions could only be made if there was 'reasonable cause' to suspect the detainees of being a threat to national security meant that judges were entitled to review the detentions to check that there was in fact such cause. The majority held that in the context of wartime emergency, judges had no business second-guessing the government. It was this conception of the judicial role that led to Atkin's famous charge against his fellow judges that they were 'more executive minded than the executive'.[17]

The common good lawyers usually deplore such reasoning because they regard it as typical of the kind of judicial 'overreach' that infringes upon Parliament's sovereign law-making power. For the same reason, they deplore even more strongly section 3 of the Human Rights Act 1998.[18] As we have seen, that section imposes a statutory duty on judges

[15] Ekins, 'Human Rights and the Rule of Law' at 15.

[16] Ibid at 16.

[17] *Liversidge v Anderson*, at 244.

[18] For example, many of the cases analysed in Richard Ekins, Stephen Laws, and Conor Casey, 'The Impact of the Human Rights Act 1998 in Twenty Five Cases' (Nov 11 2024) online: *Policy Exchange* <https://policyexchange.org.uk/wp-content/uploads/The-Impact-of-the-Human-Rights-Act-1998.pdf>. This document comes adorned with their usual endorsements, for example: 'The debate on the Human Rights Act is often long on invective but short on analysis. This paper provides a wealth of focussed research and cogent argument, and is a valuable contribution to the on-going debate'. Signed by Lord Wolfson of Tredegar KC, former Minister of Justice.

to do what had previously been their duty at common law – to interpret legislation so as to make it consistent with protected rights. So Ekins should have been as scathing about Atkin's lack of 'discipline' as he usually is of judges when they decide on the basis of section 3. But far from doing that in his Atkin Lecture, he chides the judges in *Belmarsh* for *not* basing their reasoning on section 3:

> Strikingly, the Court did not consider the relevance of section 3 of the Human Rights Act, which would have forced the Court to confront the fact that the legislation could have been interpreted compatibly with the Convention right to liberty insofar as it only authorised detention with a view to deportation. The legislation required the Government to show to the court's satisfaction, every three months, that it was attempting to overcome obstacles to deportation. This was a condition on the authority to detain. The Court overlooked the condition in its haste to denounce the merits of the legislation. In so doing it failed to give the applicants their legal rights, a state of affairs in which the applicants were complicit insofar as the main aim of the litigation was precisely to secure the Court's political support in denouncing the legislation.[19]

This is also not accurate. The issue in *Belmarsh* arose because the UK had imprisoned without trial non-citizens who were considered to be threats to national security, but who could not be deported because of the risks they faced in their home countries. Officially, they were not 'imprisoned', but only 'detained' until such time as they could safely be deported, under the Anti-terrorism, Crime and Security Act 2001, one of the many statutes that countries enacted in the panic about terrorism after 9/11. But the detention in the high-security Belmarsh prison which gave the case its name was in effect indefinite, as the government had recognized in issuing an 'order' 'derogating' from the Article of the European Convention on Human Rights which prohibited such detentions.[20] Such derogation orders, orders suspending the operation of certain rights, were permitted in times of emergency under Article 15 of the Convention.[21] The government had thus recognized that such

19 Richard Ekins, 'Human Rights and the Rule of Law' at 15–16.

20 Article 5: 'Everyone has the right to liberty and security of person. No one shall be deprived of his liberty save in the following cases and in accordance with a procedure prescribed by law: … (f) the lawful arrest or detention of … a person against whom action is being taken with a view to deportation.'

21 Article 15(1): 'In time of war or other public emergency threatening the life of the nation any High Contracting Party may take measures derogating from its obligations under this Convention to the extent strictly required by the exigencies of the situation, provided that such measures are not inconsistent with its other obligations under international law.'

detentions could not be interpreted as consistent with protected rights, as confirmed by precedent binding on the Court,[22] thus making section 3 of the Human Rights Act 1998 wholly irrelevant.

The judges did not, then, 'overlook' anything. Indeed, for them to have reasoned on the basis that the detention was not in substance indefinite would have been a judicial fiat, equivalent to the legislative fiat in the Rwanda Act that declared Rwanda to be safe. The majority of the Court accepted that it was for the government to decide whether there was a situation of emergency and whether that situation required a derogation. But that left open the question of whether the response to the emergency was appropriate, in particular the extent of the derogation. The main issue for them was thus whether the extent of the derogation could be justified as proportionate to the threat that the detainees posed to national security. Here the Court found that, because the state was dealing with similar threats posed by UK nationals without detaining them, the detentions were disproportionate, and hence incompatible with protected rights.

Since *Belmarsh* is the judicial punching bag of choice for the common good lawyers, so should Atkin's dissent in *Liversidge* be their target, just as Bingham's *The Rule of Law* is their favourite punching bag when it comes to criticism of advocacy of a thick conception of the rule of law. So one should be most surprised to find Ekins in another part of his Atkin Lecture paying homage to Bingham as 'the greatest judge of his generation'.[23] This sudden praise for Bingham is astonishing not only because of the common good lawyers' general disdain for Bingham's

[22] *A and others v Home Secretary*, at paras 8 and 9.

[23] Ekins, 'Human Rights and the Rule of Law' at 12. In his Foreword, Wolfson was more circumspect, indicating the real view of the Judicial Power Project that both Atkin and Bingham were bad judges:

> If Lord Atkin was one of the greatest judges of his generation, the same must be true of the late Lord Bingham. In addition to his many judgments of the highest importance, his book, *The Rule of Law*, published shortly before his death in 2010, has been immensely influential – and not only because of its well-chosen title. However, there is no authority in legal philosophy, and Professor Ekins is quite right to put to the test Lord Bingham's claim that one of the eight principles of the rule of law is that the law must 'afford adequate protection of fundamental human rights'. The problem with Lord Bingham's account, Professor Ekins shows, is that it runs together two separate ideals, the rule of law and human rights, and, more controversially, takes human rights to be almost indistinguishable from European human rights law.

book, but also because *Belmarsh* is, as Ekins says, the 'leading case' under the Human Rights Act 1998, widely regarded as the most important human rights decision of the House of Lords during the time Bingham was senior Law Lord, and head of the Court.[24]

Since Bingham gave the leading opinion, he must be exemplary of Ekins's 'undisciplined judge' – a judge who makes decisions on political not legal grounds, thus setting himself up as an 'enemy of the people'. As we have seen, this was the charge levelled at judges in the infamous *Daily Mail* headline, 'Enemies of the People', a charge which Ekins was accused of associating himself with because of the 'inflammatory' nature of his critiques of the judiciary. Recall that he denied his association with this charge by saying he didn't 'mean that the judges aren't engaged with legal reasons or doing their best to adjudicate the case before them'.[25] However, his use of the language of 'discipline' in his Atkin Lecture is ominous. A few years before he had made the astonishing claim that the judges of the UK Supreme Court who interpreted an ouster clause – a statutory provision that limits or even precludes the court's authority to review the implementation of a statute – as not ousting all judicial review should be removed from office, a step which he asserted would not compromise judicial independence.[26] He thus advocated for a tactic Hungary and Poland (during the rule of the Law and Justice Party) successfully deployed of using mechanisms of judicial discipline to ensure a compliant judiciary at the same time as maintaining a façade of the rule of law.

Why then did Ekins choose to deem Bingham in the Atkin lecture the 'greatest judge of his generation'? It is because, as Ekins says, '[i]n his highly influential book, *The Rule of Law*, [Bingham] . . . makes clear that there are no plausible legal grounds for British judges to abandon

Wolfson, Foreword to Richard Ekins, 'Human Rights and the Rule of Law' at 5. As I argue in the text, the problem with Wolfson's account is that he ignores the fact that it is the UK Parliament that has run 'together two separate ideals, the rule of law and human rights' with the result that human rights are 'almost indistinguishable from European human rights law'.

24 Ibid at 14.

25 Ken Macdonald and Tim Owen, 'Double Jeopardy: The Law and Politics Podcast – Episode 29: Richard Ekins – Judges and Political Power' (May 2 2023) online: *Apple Podcasts* <https://podcasts.apple.com/de/podcast/episode-29-richard-ekins-judges-and-political-power/id1633485236?i=1000611450876&l=en-GB>.

26 Richard Ekins, 'Do Our Supreme Court Judges Have Too Much Power?' (May 14 2019) online: *The Spectator* <www.spectator.co.uk/article/do-our-supreme-court-judges-have-too-much-power-> at 9.

parliamentary sovereignty and that the rule of law cannot reasonably be deployed as a justification for judges to act in this unconstitutional, unlawful, indeed lawless way'.[27]

Bingham thus gets this rare, perhaps unique accolade from a common good lawyer because Ekins supposes, as he put it in another paper, that in *The Rule of Law* Bingham 'denounced his colleagues' constitutional heresy' in *Jackson*, a House of Lords decision, in which two of the judges raised as a theoretical possibility that Parliament could enact a statute that undermined the rule of law to the extent that they would have to consider invalidating it.[28] The result is that we have in place competing claims of heresy, with both Hermer and Ekins accusing the other side of heresy, with Bingham allegedly on Ekins's side.

To adjudicate between these claims, we need first to go to the pages of *The Rule of Law* on which Ekins relies. There Bingham quoted this passage from Lord Steyn's judgment in *Jackson*:

> The classic account given by Dicey of the doctrine of the supremacy of Parliament, pure and absolute as it was, can now be seen to be out of place in the modern United Kingdom. Nevertheless, the supremacy of Parliament is still the general principle of our constitution. It is a construct of the common law. The judges created this principle. If that is so, it is not unthinkable that circumstances could arise where the courts may have to qualify a principle established on a different hypothesis of constitutionalism. In exceptional circumstances involving an attempt to abolish judicial review or the ordinary role of the courts, the Appellate Committee of the House of Lords or a new Supreme Court may have to consider whether this is [a] constitutional fundamental which even a sovereign Parliament acting at the behest of a complaisant House of Commons cannot abolish.[29]

Bingham also quoted Lady Hale's statement in *Jackson* that 'The courts will treat with particular suspicion (and might even reject) any attempt to subvert the rule of law by removing governmental action affecting the rights of the individual from all judicial scrutiny'.[30]

[27] Ekins, 'Human Rights and the Rule of Law' at 12.

[28] *Jackson v Attorney General* [2005] UKHL 56. Richard Ekins, Stephen Laws, and Conor Casey, 'Safety of Rwanda (Asylum and Migration) Bill' (Dec 11 2023) online: *Policy Exchange* <https://policyexchange.org.uk/publication/safety-of-rwanda-asylum-and-migration-bill/> at 24.

[29] Tom Bingham, *The Rule of Law* (London: Allen Lane, 2010) at 166.

[30] Ibid at 167.

But Bingham did not do anything as strong as 'denouncing' Steyn and Hale. He merely said that he could not accept these observations as 'correct'. He did say that these and other observations 'have also been described by one acerbic commentator as "unargued and unsound", "historically false" and "jurisprudentially absurd"'.[31] But here he was merely describing, with a hint of disapproval in his use of 'acerbic', the reaction of the academic he was quoting, who did in fact denounce Steyn and Hale. Bingham's point seems clearly to be that one reason to avoid such observations is that it will provoke some acerbic sorts into making denunciations. The 'acerbic' academic was none other than Richard Ekins,[32] which meant that he bestowed on his own position the aura of the 'greatest judge of his generation'.

In addition, it is clear from the whole argument of Bingham's book that his disagreement with his colleagues was limited to just two matters. First, he disagreed with Steyn's claim that parliamentary supremacy or sovereignty is a principle invented by judges with the result that judges can unmake it. Second, he rejected the tentative thought expressed by both Steyn and Hale that, in the dramatic circumstance of Parliament enacting a statute like the Rwanda Act, one that explicitly and gravely affects individual rights and removes entirely judicial scrutiny of the statute's implementation, judges might consider rejecting it. But he was far from disagreeing with Hale's claim that the courts should treat such a statute with 'particular suspicion'.

Moreover, on closer inspection, the points on which Bingham in fact disagreed with Hale and Steyn reveal a very different position from that presupposed by talk of denunciation, one that entails a much stronger claim than the one implied by the passage he quoted from Steyn. He said that it is 'of course true that the principle of parliamentary sovereignty cannot without circularity be ascribed to statute, and the historical record reveals no such statute'. He continued:

> But it does not follow that the principle must be a creature of the judge-made common law which the judges can alter: if it were, the rule could be altered by statute, since the primary characteristic of any common law rule is that it yields to a contrary provision of a statute. To my mind, it has been convincingly shown that the principle of parliamentary sovereignty has been recognized in this country not because the judges have invented

[31] Ibid.

[32] Ibid, quoting from Richard Ekins, 'Acts of Parliament and the Parliament Acts' (2007) 123 *Law Quarterly Review* 91 at 103.

> it but because it has been accepted as such by judges and others officially concerned in the operation of our constitutional system.[33]

The stronger claim is that parliamentary sovereignty is a constitutional fundamental beyond the reach of both judges *and* Parliament. It is so 'because it has been accepted as such by judges and others officially concerned in the operation of our constitutional system'. If Bingham is correct in this claim, it should follow that the rule of law, the other constitutional fundamental we saw Dicey identify in Chapter 2, is also beyond the reach of both Parliament and judges because its status is also due to the fact that 'it has been accepted as such by judges and others officially concerned in the operation of our constitutional system'.

That claim needs to be elaborated because it raises certain problems that require resolution. For Bingham's alternative seems just as vulnerable to the charge of circularity he made against Steyn's position since he is saying that the principle is accepted because it is accepted. In addition, it is not at all clear what my 'beyond the reach' means. While still vague at this point in this chapter, the idea is linked to the claim in the preceding chapter that a statute such as the Rwanda Act that undermines constitutional fundamentals introduces an incoherence into the constitutional order. Dicey himself played with such an idea when he made claims such as that 'martial law' – the idea that the military may by law do anything it supposes necessary in an emergency – is 'unknown to the law of England'.[34] As I have argued elsewhere, his point seems to be that a space in which the executive or the military or any arm of government can do as it pleases is not legally 'cognizable' – cannot be grasped within the language of legality and constitutionalism.[35]

The rest of this chapter and the next will make these claims more precise and, in so doing, prepare the way for an argument that the kind of circularity in Bingham's 'because it has been accepted as such by judges and others officially concerned in the operation of our constitutional system' is not flawed. Rather, it presupposes a methodology of philosophical argument of the sort Dworkin proposed, and which Dicey also employed, as do lawyers generally who work within the common law

[33] Bingham, *The Rule of Law*, at 167.

[34] AV Dicey, *Introduction to the Study of the Law of the Constitution* (Indianapolis: Liberty Fund, 1982) at 182.

[35] David Dyzenhaus, 'The Puzzle of Martial Law' (2009) 59 *University of Toronto Law Journal* 1.

tradition, that is, the very tradition to which the common good lawyers so repeatedly express their allegiance.

4.4 Philosophy of Law in the House of Lords

When I introduced Bingham in Chapter 2, I observed that he rejected the thin conception of the rule of law, which he rightly took to be implicit in this passage from one of the most influential essays on this topic of the last century, Oxford legal philosopher Joseph Raz's 'The Rule of Law and Its Virtue':

> A non-democratic legal system, based on the denial of human rights, on extensive poverty, on racial segregation, sexual inequalities, and religious persecution may, in principle, conform to the requirements of the rule of law better than any of the legal systems of the more enlightened Western democracies. . . . It will be an immeasurably worse legal system, but it will excel in one respect: in its conformity to the rule of law . . . The law may . . . institute slavery without violating the rule of law.[36]

Bingham's discussion occurs within chapter 7, 'Human Rights', in the section in which he set out the fifth of the eight principles he identified as giving us the content of the rule of law – 'The law must afford adequate protection of fundamental human rights'. In response to Raz, he said that, 'while one can recognize the logical force of Professor Raz's contention, I would roundly reject it in favour of a "thick" definition, embracing the protection of human rights within its scope'.[37] But Bingham gave no reasons for his rejection. Instead, he offered this example:

> A state which savagely represses or persecutes sections of its people cannot in my view be regarded as observing the rule of law, even if the transport of the persecuted people to the concentration camp or the compulsory exposure of female children on the mountainside is the subject of detailed laws duly enacted and scrupulously observed. So to hold would be to strip 'the existing constitutional principle of the rule of law' affirmed by section 1 of the Constitutional Reform Act 2005 and widely recognized in the laws of other countries around the world, of much of its virtue.[38]

[36] Joseph Raz, 'The Rule of Law and Its Virtue' in *The Authority of Law*: *Essays on Law and Morality* (Oxford: Clarendon Press, 1983) 210 at 211. See Bingham, *The Rule of Law*, at 66–67.
[37] Bingham, *The Rule of Law*, at 67.
[38] Ibid at 67.

In recognizing 'the logical force of Professor Raz's contention', offering an example that in effect duplicated those Raz had provided, and in pitting one 'definition' against another, Bingham fell into the trap that awaits all who play the definitional game. For Raz had argued that the virtue of the rule of law is an instrumental virtue.[39] He offered the analogy of a knife. The virtue of a knife is sharpness, but one can do morally abominable things with a sharp knife. The rule of law's virtue is not then a moral virtue. It is, we could say, formal in that it offers clear guidance to those subject to the law. But that too is purely instrumental. Raz's examples seem to illustrate his point that what may be a moral vice from the human rights perspective may be a virtue from the perspective of the rule of law. Or, to put the point in the way I have so far, a statute can be morally but not legally crazy. And if that argument is 'logically sound', one cannot oppose it by offering a competing definition.

Moreover, in his Bingham Lecture, Hermer did little better in these reflections on the dispute, even though he avoided talk of 'definition' and used 'conception':

> Parliamentary sovereignty is one of the fundamental features of our constitution and the ultimate legal authority of Parliament to make or unmake any law is crystal clear. However, viewing the rule of law through this distorting lens of ultimate decision-making authority alone risks mistaking it for a purely formal, and thin, conception of 'rule by law'.
>
> As lawyers know, Parliament's authority in our constitution is legal authority, an authority that requires that Parliament maintains in its legislation the ideals of the rule of law, of government under law, one of the contributions to the modern world of which we in the UK are justly proud. And as I (following Lord Bingham) have explained, those ideals are much thicker and more substantive than the thin gruel of a formal conception of 'rule by law'.[40]

In putting things in this way, Hermer followed Bingham in walking into the trap of the definitional game. This was amply pointed out by members of the House of Lords hostile to the thick conception, specifically by Lord David Wolfson and Lord Guglielmo Verdirame who both attempted to debunk Bingham's thick or substantive conception of the rule of law.

[39] Raz, 'The Rule of Law and Its Virtue' at 226.

[40] Richard Hermer, 'The Rule of Law in an Age of Populism' (Oct 14 2024) online: *Bingham Centre for the Rule of Law* <www.biicl.org/documents/12532_bingham_lecture_2024.pdf> at 6–7.

We encountered Wolfson in the last chapter through his Foreword to Richard Ekins's Atkin Lecture earlier that year, 'Human Rights and the Rule of Law'. By the time of the debate in the House of Lords, Labour was in power, and Wolfson had been appointed as Shadow Attorney General – that is, Hermer's counterpart in the Conservative official opposition. Verdirame is a high-profile practising international lawyer. His chamber's website says that 'he is working on two books: one on the relationship between international law and national law; and the other (entitled "*Can Liberty Last?*") on the future of political liberty'. It also states that he is 'a (non-party affiliated) member of the House of Lords, where he focuses on debates and legislation within his wider field of expertise (international law, foreign affairs and defence, arbitration, constitutional law and the protection of fundamental liberties)'.[41]

One does not often encounter philosophical argument in parliamentary debates and, for the most part, it was a debate conducted in the politest of terms. For example, the debate was begun by Baroness Angela Smith of Cluny, her first speech to that august body as the newly appointed Advocate General for Scotland. She opened the debate by 'moving' that 'This House takes note of the importance of the rule of law'. She then offered a passionate defence of Bingham's conception of the rule of law.[42]

She was immediately followed by Wolfson, who sought to offer a demolition of just that conception. Nevertheless, he began by saying that 'it is a privilege and a pleasure to begin by welcoming the noble and learned Baroness, Lady Smith of Cluny, the Advocate-General, to her place, and to congratulate her on a very fine maiden speech. Given her illustrious background, both personal and professional, we expected a great deal from her – but she met and indeed exceeded those expectations'.[43] After the initial display of politeness, however, the gloves come off.

For example, both Wolfson and Verdirame used the occasion to take some political potshots at Hermer. Wolfson brought the conflict between Israel and Palestine twice into his speech in a way that could be taken to imply that Hermer, who like Wolfson is Jewish, is on the 'wrong' side of that conflict.[44] And Verdirame suggested, just as obliquely, that Hermer

[41] 'Lord Verdirame' online: *Twenty Sussex* <www.twentyessex.com/people/guglielmo-verdirame/>.

[42] House of Lords, 'Rule of Law' at column 620.

[43] Ibid at column 628.

[44] Ibid. Wolfson first expressed his displeasure at Hermer for refusing to say whether the UK would grant Prime Minister Netanyahu immunity from the arrest warrant against him issued by the International Criminal Court. Hermer had said that the decision would

was courting 'demagoguery' because he had said to a journalist 'we need to be militant about our belief in the rule of law ... We should be shouting it from the rooftops'.[45] But the prize in this regard goes to Baron Keith Stewart of Dirleton, a former Advocate General of Scotland, who, unlike his successor who opened the debate, sided with Wolfson in rejecting Bingham. He saw fit to warn as follows: 'Let us be careful lest the public come to echo the call of the rioters in "Henry VI", "first ... let's kill all the lawyers"'.[46] In other words, Hermer should drop his allegiance to the rule of law lest he be lynched. And he is, as I write, being subject to a virtual lynching, as the common good lawyers in concert with the right-wing media are launching daily attacks on him, urging the Prime Minister to fire him. One can't help but be reminded yet once more of the infamous *Daily Mail* headline declaring judges to be 'Enemies of the People'.

I will not, however, dwell further on these moments because my concern is more with the philosophical argument. For Wolfson and Verdirame, in venturing quite deep into philosophy of law against the backdrop of the Rwanda Act, provide a unique opportunity for rejecting the position they share with the common good lawyers, especially Ekins. We have already seen this closeness between Ekins and Wolfson, and

be for the courts, not for him. Wolfson went on to say, speaking about pro-Palestinian political activity:

> I have spoken before about my astonishment that a sign calling for jihad on the streets of London was regarded by the police as not requiring any further investigation. Last week's *Jewish Chronicle* reported that a sermon that called for the destruction of Jewish homes and was delivered two weeks after the 7 October massacre was originally not deemed by the Metropolitan Police to meet the criminal threshold, once the context – I emphasise 'the context' – was taken into account. After something of an uproar, the police have said that they are now reviewing their earlier decision.
>
> I am well aware of the difficult job that the police have. We on this side of the House – and, I am sure, all of us on all sides – support the police in the work they do. But to maintain public confidence, we need to make sure that justice is done and seen to be done. That applies from the moment when there is a knock on the door by a police officer, right up to the handing down of a sentence by a judge.

House of Lords, 'Rule of Law' at column 620. Nothing here was of direct relevance to the debate and it is hard to explain other than as making a personal point about Hermer.

45 Ibid at column 643.

46 Ibid at column 654.

Verdirame has co-authored Judicial Power Project papers with Ekins, as he announced in his intervention in the debate, including one in support of the removal of international law from the Ministerial Code.[47]

Wolfson started the main part of his intervention by setting out his version of the thin conception:

> At its heart, the rule of law means that the state is governed by laws and that everyone in the state, and the state itself, is subject to those laws. The core features of the rule of law are not now in doubt. They include that everybody is subject to the same laws; wealth, power, status or privilege provide no special protection. Governments and public officials are subject to the law. They must exercise their powers lawfully. The law must be accessible and clear. Disputes should be determined by independent courts and tribunals. A vibrant and independent legal profession is necessary to promote liberty under the rule of law. Without the rule of law, underpinned by an independent judiciary and the courts, much else would fail to prosper. It is one of the foundations that supports economic activity, wider prosperity and a settled society. In short, the rule of law, independent courts and an independent judiciary are not optional extras or simply a service, but one of the foundations on which everything else is built.[48]

He then proceeded to his attack:

> We have heard Lord Bingham's name mentioned already, and I suspect that we will hear it many more times. Of course, he wrote a book on the subject, *The Rule of Law*, published in 2010. If you entitle your book, 'The Rule of Law', people will think that is what it is: the rule of law is what he says it is. I read with interest the recent lecture given by the noble and learned Lord, the Attorney-General, at the Bingham Centre, which is named after him. However, Lord Bingham's view of the rule of law is a very expansive or 'thick' view. It is not shared by many others. . . .
>
> The problem with Lord Bingham's expansive view of the rule of law, as Professor Gardner wrote in a trenchant review in the *London Review of Books*, is that it includes within the rule of law 'the full range of human rights: not just those ensuring due process of law for all, but also those concerned with . . . life, privacy, association, property and assembly'.
>
> On that approach, it is very hard to leave logical space for regimes that respect the rule of law but are otherwise notably illiberal; for example,

[47] Richard Ekins and Guglielmo Verdirame, 'The Ministerial Code and the Rule of Law' (Nov 6 2015) online: *UK Constitutional Law Blog* <https://ukconstitutionallaw.org/2015/11/06/richard-ekins-and-guglielmo-verdirame-the-ministerial-code-and-the-rule-of-law/>.

[48] House of Lords, 'Rule of Law' at column 625.

> they forbid gay relationships or organised religion. I would not want to live in a country like that, but is it right that such a state would not have the rule of law? Where you end up, as Professor Gardner put it, is the conceit that 'no country has the rule of law unless it would be morally suitable to join the Council of Europe'.
>
> We do the rule of law a disservice if we try to cram within it any and every social good. Not every social good is a human right, and not all human rights are part of the rule of law. The rule of law with its traditional limits is important enough in itself. It does not need to encompass or express every conceivable legal or social good.[49]

Wolfson did not refer here to Raz. But in quoting from John Gardner's review of Bingham's book, he relied as much on Raz, for Gardner, at that time Professor of Jurisprudence in Oxford, channelled Raz's position in his review, without naming him.

In choosing these excerpts, Wolfson picked the more condescending moments in Gardner's review and made no mention of the fact that these are but moments in an otherwise highly laudatory account. For Gardner largely expressed great admiration for Bingham's work as judge, the book, and Bingham's understanding of the content of the rule of law. He did say of Bingham's discussion of Raz that as 'philosophy this would be high comedy'. Wolfson did not, however, quote this most condescending remark, perhaps because Gardner immediately qualified it by saying of Bingham's conception of the rule of law that as 'the work of a judge it is . . . quite impeccable'.[50] And Gardner elaborated this combination of condescension and praise in the conclusion to his review:

> The Rule of Law is not only a moral ideal for government and law, but also a core doctrine of the United Kingdom constitution, recently reasserted by Act of Parliament. *The Rule of Law* does double service as a lively tour of some of the contemporary and historical debates about the moral ideal and as an introduction to some problems about the constitution that have been pressingly and sometimes disturbingly live in

[49] Ibid. On 25 March 2025, at an event hosted by Policy Exchange, Lord Wolfson delivered a lecture, 'The Rule of Law: At Home, Abroad – and in Westminster' (Mar 25 2025) online: *Policy Exchange* <https://policyexchange.org.uk/events/the-rule-of-law-at-home-abroad-and-in-westminster/>. It is clearly intended as a riposte to Lord Hermer's lecture, 'The Rule of Law in an Age of Populism'. Wolfson's lecture does not do much more than gather together points made in print by Finnis, Ekins, and Casey and so does not add to the discussion in the text.

[50] John Gardner, 'How to Be a Good Judge' (Jul 8 2010) online: *London Review of Books* <www.lrb.co.uk/the-paper/v32/n13/john-gardner/how-to-be-a-good-judge>.

> important recent cases in the higher courts in England. In its first role, as we saw, Bingham's book goes slightly out of its depths. In its second role, however, the book is completely in its element. One could not wish for a better guide to the place of the Rule of Law in the English courts and in the United Kingdom constitution than Tom Bingham, who has done so much, in his long and distinguished period of high judicial office, to protect it. And the book shows us how: by good judgment, a peerless grasp of doctrine, and a strong moral compass, not by the highfalutin pretensions of the philosopher judge, to which Bingham (unlike some of his colleagues in the higher judiciary) has never been much attracted.[51]

Verdirame's intervention in the House of Lords debate has the same structure and substance as Wolfson's, though it is free of Wolfson's condescension:

> I will focus my remarks on the meaning of the expression 'the rule of law' and on international law. In his essay, 'The Rule of Law and Its Virtue', Joseph Raz began with a warning: 'Not uncommonly when a political ideal captures the imagination of large numbers of people its name becomes a slogan used by supporters of ideals which bear little or no relation to the one it originally designated'.
>
> Raz went on to argue for what is sometimes described as the thin conception of the rule of law. It was thin, not because he did not believe in other values such as democracy, human rights and international law, but because he wanted to set forth a viable and coherent conception of the rule of law that did not conflate the rule of law and the rule of *good* law. The latter, as he put it, would require 'a complete social philosophy'.[52]

Verdirame then explained:

> Inflating the concept of the rule of law to accommodate other ideals, wishes and causes, however worthy, is a bad idea for at least two reasons. First, we will not be able to agree on it, as today's debate shows. The thicker the conception of the rule of law, the more politicised the rule of law will become. The scope and interpretation of some fundamental rights, and the ways in which conflicts between rights should be resolved, are an example. Those issues will remain contested. ...
>
> Secondly, the key features of the rule of law are legal certainty, clarity and predictability – that is the very first principle of the rule of law, according to Lord Bingham. By expanding the rule of law to include democracy – a list of fundamental rights that is itself unsettled and ever expanding – as well as every rule of international law, we end up with an all-encompassing,

[51] Ibid at 10–11.

[52] House of Lords, 'Rule of Law' at column 643. His emphasis.

> panoptic concept of the rule of law that itself becomes a source of unclarity, uncertainty and unpredictability; in other words, we end up with a conception of the rule of law that does not advance the rule of law. As anticipated by Raz, when the concept of the rule of law is bloated in this way, there is also a risk that it becomes a perfunctory slogan.[53]

This is an adept summary of Raz's complex argument and its implications. However, in a later essay, 'The Law's Own Virtue', Raz listed Bingham's eight principles and said: 'There is a considerable overlap between these and my list, but two glaring omissions in mine are the inclusion of adequate protection of fundamental human rights and requiring compliance by the state with its obligations in international law.'[54] Raz of course was suggesting that he was correct to omit human rights and international law. But he had to include the others because in the earlier 'The Rule of Law and Its Virtue', the essay on which Verdirame relied, he had set out an extensive list of principles of the rule of law that included equivalents (and more) to the six principles on Bingham's list that Raz here explicitly endorsed.[55] It follows that Raz's conception of the rule of law, while it excludes protection of human rights and respect for international law, includes much that is very different from the thin definition of the rule of law on which the common good lawyers purport to rely. It is, to labour the point, itself thick, although in some respects thinner than Bingham's.

When it comes to these respects, the common good lawyers and their allies in Wolfson and Lord Verdirame would of course be happy to have Raz confirm their view that adequate protection of fundamental human rights and compliance by the state with its obligations in international law are not intrinsic to the rule of law. But even if that is right, it leaves untouched the fact that the common good lawyers with whom they are so closely allied defended as consistent with the rule of law the deportation rule in the Rwanda Act that, as I will now show, violated six of the principles on Bingham's list, including four out of the six that Raz supposes *must* figure on his *own* list.

Here's Bingham's complete list.

(1) 'The law must be accessible and so far as possible intelligible, clear and predictable'.[56]

[53] Ibid.
[54] Joseph Raz, 'The Law's Own Virtue' (2019) 39 *Oxford Journal of Legal Studies* 1 at 9.
[55] Raz, 'The Rule of Law and Its Virtue' at 214–19.
[56] Bingham, *The Rule of Law*, at 37.

(2) 'Questions of legal right and liability should ordinarily be resolved by application of the law and not the exercise of discretion'.[57]
(3) 'The laws of the land should apply equally to all, save to the extent that objective differences justify differentiation'.[58]
(4) 'Ministers and public officers at all levels must exercise the powers conferred on them in good faith, fairly, for the purpose for which the powers were conferred, without exceeding the limits of such powers and not unreasonably'.[59]
(5) 'The law must afford adequate protection of fundamental human rights'.[60]
(6) 'Means must be provided for resolving, without prohibitive cost or inordinate delay, bona fide civil disputes which the parties themselves are unable to resolve'.[61]
(7) 'The adjudicative procedures provided by the state should be fair'.[62]
(8) 'The rule of law requires compliance by the state with its obligations in international law as in national law'.[63]

It should be clear that the Rwanda Act was precisely such a statute. It violated principles 2 and 3 because, in disapplying protected rights, it did not do away with the laws that protect rights, but made the law ordinarily applicable to asylum seekers completely inaccessible to them. In addition, principle 2 was violated because, as we saw, ministers were given an unlimited discretion to decide whether to obey injunctions issued by the European Court of Human Rights, a feature of the Act which also made it in violation of principle 4. Principle 7 is violated because the Act exempted its implementation from adjudicative procedures with the very limited exceptions that we saw the common good lawyers wanted excised from the Bill.

To say that the Act violated principle 5 – human rights – and principle 8 – international law – is an understatement, which is why the common good lawyers engaged in the exercise I analysed in the last chapter. As we saw, they claimed that there was no violation because violating human rights and international law is consistent with respecting both. At the same time, they suggested that in the case of international law there is

57 Ibid at 48.
58 Ibid at 55.
59 Ibid at 60.
60 Ibid at 66.
61 Ibid at 85.
62 Ibid at 90.
63 Ibid at 277.

nothing there to violate because it is 'defective law'. That these two principles are the only ones they deny form part of the rule of law is most important. The denial, they think, is required by the thin conception, whereby officials must obey the rules laid down by the superior authority of the supreme Parliament, whatever the content of the rules. And if, as Bingham's thick conception asserts, the rule of law requires adequate protection of fundamental human rights and compliance by the state with its obligations in international law, rules that have a content that violates these requirements will also violate the rule of law.

But, as I already suggested, the thin conception is *not* thin in the sense that the common good lawyers and their allies deploy it. Since the Rwanda Act violated so many principles that are in common between the two conceptions, one does not, as these lawyers suppose, have the rule of law as long as the rules are clear and enacted in a valid statute such as the Rwanda Act. For the thin conception is itself thick, merely less thick than Bingham's because it expunges principles 5 and 8. Why are these two to be expunged?

In 'The Law's Own Virtue', Raz said that that there are 'various reasons to dissent from Lord Bingham's list. For current purposes, the important one is that it is not a principle or a doctrine, but an assembly of diverse principles, with diverse rationales behind them'.[64] He was thus willing to endorse six of Bingham's principles because he considered them derivable from a 'principle or doctrine', which he stated as uniting the 'conditions whose satisfaction is required to make it possible for those subject to the law to find out what it is, and thereby make it possible for the government (which aims to guide people's behaviour) to know how to govern, and for those subject to it to know how they are governed'.[65]

That does not yet give us any reason to adopt that doctrine or conception of the rule of law, something we need to know given that it is controversial and rejected by prominent lawyers such as Hermer and Bingham as insufficient because it is thought to exclude international law and human rights from its list of rule-of-law principles. Indeed, as we will see in Chapter 5, Raz does have a reason, based on his theory of law, which is as controversial as any claim in the debate about the meaning of the rule of law. So it is question-begging to discount Bingham's conception of the rule of law because one happens to adopt a premise that by

[64] Raz, 'The Law's Own Virtue' at 9.
[65] Ibid.

definition excludes it, especially when, as I will show, that premise is itself part of a controversial political position.

Consider that when Bingham and Hermer suppose that the excluded principles must be on the list, they do so in part because as a matter of fact that is what the existing law of the UK requires, notably, the Human Rights Act 1998. The result is that the practices over time of lawyers and judges have both reflected these principles and more deeply embedded them in the substratum of the legal order, in, one might say, the 'unwritten constitution'. Recall from Chapter 2 that the UK constitution is often said to be 'unwritten' in that it is not contained in any one written document as is the case with the Constitution of the US. Rather, it consists of principles found in a muddle of judgments and statutes rendered and enacted over the course of centuries. Because much of its content is gleaned from judgments in a 'common law system', one in which judgments on a matter today stand as precedents or authoritative pronouncements binding on courts in the future – it is also often said to be a 'common law constitution'. It is for these reasons that the *Encyclopaedia Britannica* could plausibly claim that Dicey's book 'is considered part of the British constitution'.[66]

In making the supposition that the excluded principles must be on the list, Bingham and Hermer are therefore at one with Dicey, and his statement of the third feature of the rule of law in the UK context, which it is fitting to quote yet again:

> There remains yet a third and a different sense in which the 'rule of law' or the predominance of the legal spirit may be described as a special attribute of English institutions. We may say that the constitution is pervaded by the rule of law on the ground that the general principles of the constitution (as for example the right to personal liberty, or the right of public meeting) are with us the result of judicial decisions determining the rights of private persons in particular cases brought before the Courts; whereas under many foreign constitutions the security (such as it is) given to the rights of individuals results, or appears to result, from the general principles of the constitution.[67]

But Raz would reject Dicey's third feature for the same reason he criticizes Bingham: that Dicey had not derived his third feature 'from a principle or a doctrine' since it is a mere 'assembly of diverse principles,

[66] 'Albert Venn Dicey' (Jul 20 1998) online: *Encyclopedia Britannica* <www.britannica.com/biography/Albert-Venn-Dicey>.

[67] Dicey, *Introduction to the Study of the Law of the Constitution*, at 119.

with diverse rationales behind them'. In Chapter 5, I show both that there are good reasons to reject Raz's rejection of this feature and of two of Bingham's principles of the rule of law. I also show that their presence is the dimension of the UK constitutional tradition that explains why the Rwanda Act perpetrated, as Hermer claimed, constitutional heresies, though, as we have seen, it was not heretical enough for the common good lawyers as they wanted it to exclude judicial review even further.

5

Sovereignty, International Law, the Rule of Law

5.1 The Politics of the Thin Conception

We saw in the last chapter that even the thin conception of the rule of law is thick in that it includes six out of Lord Bingham's eight principles. The common good lawyers may still insist that it is these six that attract consensus so that to include human rights and international law is to abandon apolitical agreement and smuggle in one's preferred morality. However, as I will now show, the thin conception is as political as any other. To insist on it while not acknowledging that fact is not only, as we saw in the last chapter, out of step with A. V. Dicey's 'the legal spirit' of the UK constitution, but also an attempt to win the thin versus thick contest by persuasive definition, by offering a definition that builds its victory in an argument into its verbal formulation.

This book is not the place to go too far into the depths of philosophy of law, in particular the legal theory of the leading figure to present a defence of the thin conception of the rule of law. For Joseph Raz, while one of the most brilliant philosophers of law of the post-war period, is also one of the most difficult. It suffices to know that what lies behind the 'doctrine' that drives Raz's influential work on the rule of law is his view that the concept of authority requires that the content of an authoritative directive, for example a parent giving an order to a child, must be determinable without the child having to work out for itself what the order requires.[1]

Contrast, for example, 'Be good today at school!' with 'Go to sleep right now!' The first order does not do the job because the child must work out using their own judgment what to do, while the second does because what the parent intended is determinable as a matter of fact. Note how this claim connects to the thin conception of the rule of law,

[1] Joseph Raz, 'Authority, Law, and Morality' in *Ethics in the Public Domain: Essays in the Morality of Law and Politics* (Oxford: Oxford University Press, 1994) 194.

stated as that rules contained in a valid statute are by definition consistent with the rule of law, whatever their content. For in order for the condition of 'whatever their content' to be met, the rules must have a content that one can determine by factual tests – that is, without having to rely on one's own judgment about what is required.

On this view of authority, a legal rule determines a matter authoritatively only if its content can be worked out as a matter of fact. Here we can contrast a law that says to people 'Drive carefully!' or 'Take all reasonable care!' with one that says 'Drive on the left-hand side of the road!' or 'Do not exceed 40 miles per hour on this stretch!' Raz well knew, as we all know, that many of the laws that play an important part in our lives are in fact more like the first two of these pairs, even though, as we also know, it is as important in many areas of our social lives that many laws that govern our interaction with each other look more like the second two. So something goes wrong if we have a concept of legal authority which insists that law is only law properly so called if it is like the second pair because, unlike the first, the content of the injunctions is factually determinable. It would thus be wrong to deem the first pair 'defective law', as we saw John Finnis says of international law.[2] And where it goes wrong is that it is driven by Raz's 'doctrine' about authority, not by an attempt to make sense of existing practices, one that deploys the interpretive methodology I sketched in the last chapter which works off our existing practices.

At this point, we need a quick excursion into the history of legal and political ideas in the UK in order to understand why legal positivism goes hand in hand with a thin but still political conception of the rule of law. The term 'law properly so called' is John Austin's.[3] He was the dominant figure in philosophy of law in England in the nineteenth century and one of the founders of the tradition of legal positivism. And it is to that tradition that Raz and John Gardner belonged – the two philosophers on whom members the House of Lords relied in the debate on the rule of law in order to attack Bingham's thick conception, and thus also Attorney General Richard Hermer for his endorsement of Bingham.[4]

[2] John Finnis, 'Ministers, International Law, and the Rule of Law' (Nov 2 2015) online: *Judicial Power Project* <https://judicialpowerproject.org.uk/ministers-international-law-and-the-rule-of-law/>.

[3] John Austin, *Lectures on Jurisprudence or The Philosophy of Positive Law*, 5th edition (London: John Murray, 1885) volume 1.

[4] Raz and Gardner followed Hart in that all three purported to reject large parts of that tradition, in particular its 'command theory' of law. I have argued that they did not

Austin had that view because he advanced a 'command theory' of law in which law is the commands of a legally unlimited sovereign to whom those subject to the law have 'a habit of obedience'.[5] The sovereign is the one habitually obeyed by most of his subjects, and his commands motivate this 'habit of obedience' by threatening punishments for non-compliance. In addition, Austin stipulated that commands must have a factually determinable content. In putting forward this theory, Austin was following in the footsteps of the eighteenth-century philosopher Jeremy Bentham, the other founder of legal positivism as well as of utilitarianism, the political philosophy that holds that society should be organized so as to maximize the greatest amount of happiness of the greatest number.[6]

Bentham didn't just happen to found two unconnected traditions. In his general theory, legal institutions established on the model of the command theory of law make it possible to organize society in such a way that the promise of the greatest happiness of the greatest number can be realized. The way to gauge what policies will serve this purpose is to consult the people whose happiness is to be served. This, in turn, requires putting in place a well-functioning democracy in which the elected representatives of the people will make policies that accord with the actual preferences of those who elected them to office. They make such laws by majority voting, just as they were elected by majority voting, so that the policies of the law reflect at least the preferences of the majority of the population. Once embedded in law, the policies are faithfully implemented by officials. To enable both faithful implementation and rule-following by citizens, the laws must have a clear, factually determinable content. In addition, Bentham feared, with reason, that judicial elites would obstruct the process of social reform needed to ensure the greatest happiness of the great number by using principles allegedly derived from the common law to impose their views on the law. He thus advocated marginalizing the role of judges in the legal order to the greatest extent possible.

All this is important to know if one wishes to understand the true origins of the thin *definition* of the rule of law. To repeat: it requires no

succeed in freeing themselves from those parts of the tradition – David Dyzenhaus, *The Long Arc of Legality: Hobbes, Kelsen, Hart* (Cambridge: Cambridge University Press, 2022).

[5] Austin, *Lectures on Jurisprudence*, at 220–21.

[6] Jeremy Bentham, *A Fragment on Government* [1776] (Cambridge: Cambridge University Press, 1988) at 10.

more than that officials obey the rules laid down by the superior authority of Parliament. As long as those rules are clear, so that citizens can know in advance what the law is and can guide their actions by the law, the rule of law is in place whatever the content of the rules. But, as we can now see, it is not a mere definition. It is the *conception* of the rule of law that serves the majoritarian conception of democracy introduced in the last chapter, itself a political conception of how to design our institutions in the service of an ideal – the utilitarian ideal of the greatest happiness of the greatest number.

It is this set of ideas that are at the heart of legal positivism, the philosophical tradition that still dominates Oxford and beyond, since law is simply what is in fact 'posited' or put in place by those with authority to make law, the instrument of those best placed to gauge what will serve the common good understood as the happiness of the individuals in a society. These ideas, as Austin recognized, give rise to the claim that both international law and constitutional law are not really law because if either of them were law, the sovereign would no longer be legally unlimited, no longer able to implement the unadulterated preferences of the majority.[7]

However, in the post-war period, the politics of this conception were obscured when H. L. A. Hart, as Professor of Jurisprudence in Oxford, adopted from his positivist predecessors the view that the law can have any content, all the while rejecting the command theory on two grounds. First, he advanced a conceptual argument to show that law cannot be reduced to the simple model of commands plus coercion for disobedience since law also requires that officials accept its rules as right in some sense. In other words, law operates as a system of authority as well as one of force. Hart summed up this idea in perhaps the most famous sentence of post-war philosophy of law: 'Law surely is not the gunman situation writ large.'[8]

Second, to support the conceptual argument, Hart pointed to facts about actual legal practice, such as the existence of many laws that do not look like commands backed by threats of punishment. Instead, they make it possible for people to make binding rules for themselves to structure the nature of their interactions – for example, through contracts. And just as such laws empower people to make law for themselves, so there are fundamental rules in any legal order that empower bodies like

[7] Austin, *Lectures on Jurisprudence*, at 177, 204.

[8] HLA Hart, 'Positivism and the Separation of Law and Morals' in *Essays in Jurisprudence and Philosophy* (Oxford: Clarendon Press, 1983) 49 at 59.

parliaments to make law for everybody. It follows from this kind of law that even a sovereign parliament is not legally unlimited, since, in order to make law, it must comply with certain fundamental criteria that at least legal officials accept as the marks of a valid law.[9] And here we should note that when, as we saw in the last chapter, Lord Bingham criticized Lord Steyn for suggesting that judges had created the principle of parliamentary sovereignty, he relied on Hart's analysis for his own claim that 'the principle of parliamentary sovereignty has been recognized in this country not because the judges have invented it but because it has been accepted as such by judges and others officially concerned in the operation of our constitutional system'.[10]

Hart emphasized that these departures from his positivist predecessors did not affect their thesis that the law can have any content, and hence that rules with any content can be perfectly consistent with the rule of law. But because he advanced primarily a conceptual argument for this thesis, the politics of the thin conception became invisible. It was that invisibility that allowed the thin conception to appear as a neutral definition, hovering above politics. In turn, that gave the common good lawyers and their allies a resource to claim that any attempt to argue for a thicker definition is political and therefore somehow tainted. In addition, as we saw in the last chapter with both Lord Wolfson and Lord Verdirame, their allies also help themselves to the claim that to allow any moral content into the rule of law is to embark on a slippery slope which bottoms out in the whole of one's moral position getting poured into the rule of law, exactly the point of Gardner's condescending remarks about Bingham's *The Rule of Law*, on which Wolfson relied.[11]

Now, slippery-slope arguments by themselves do nothing. What matters is not the existence of a slope, because they exist everywhere. It is whatever force propels things down the slope that matters. So we need to ask, what is the force in the legal positivist contention, as repeated by Wolfson and Verdirame in the House of Lords' debate, that allowing a bit of morality in allows all of morality in. That force cannot be the thin definition of the rule of law that follows from positivistic

[9] Ibid at 59–61. Hart elaborated these criticisms and his own theory of legal order in 1961 in 'The Foundations of a Legal System' in *The Concept of Law*, 2nd edition (Oxford: Clarendon Press, 1994) 100.

[10] Tom Bingham, *The Rule of Law* (London: Allen Lane, 2010) at 167.

[11] House of Lords, 'Rule of Law: Hansard, Volume 841' (Nov 26 2024) online: *UK Parliament* <https://hansard.parliament.uk/lords/2024-11-26/debates/D5A3DAF2-1DF8-46CC-BA01-A23FD6A59095/RuleOfLaw> at column 625.

ideas, because to accord it force in and of itself would be to play the definitional game in which the odds are unfairly stacked against all rivals. If there is any force to this definition, it comes from the claims on which Raz relied, including that the 'law may … institute slavery without violating the rule of law'.[12]

I call this a 'claim' rather than an 'example' because Raz merely asserted this proposition, as he relied on assertions when he said that a 'non-democratic legal system, based on the denial of human rights, on extensive poverty, on racial segregation, sexual inequalities, and religious persecution may, in principle, conform to the requirements of the rule of law better than any of the legal systems of the more enlightened Western democracies'.[13] It is hardly unusual for philosophers of law not to ask whether the examples they choose to illustrate their arguments do in fact serve their purpose. When one does ask, as I will now show, interesting features of the examples come to light which vastly complicate claims such as the 'law may … institute slavery without violating the rule of law'. Moreover, we will see that this specific example provides an instructive analogy with what the Rwanda Act sought to achieve.

5.2 Apartheid South Africa and Enslavement

Recall that in the House of Lords debate Lord Wolfson said that on Bingham's 'approach, it is very hard to leave logical space for regimes that respect the rule of law but are otherwise notably illiberal'.[14] I agree. But the issue is not 'logical space'. Rather, it is actual legal space, the space of a functioning legal order, a topic to which I can without exaggeration say I have devoted a long academic career, going back at least to the time when I was a graduate student at Oxford in the 1980s, writing a doctoral thesis about philosophy of law and adjudication in my native country, apartheid South Africa; as it happens, a thesis supervised by three of the figures we have encountered in this book – Ronald Dworkin, John Finnis and Joseph Raz.[15]

[12] Joseph Raz, 'The Rule of Law and Its Virtue' in *The Authority of Law: Essays on Law and Morality* (Oxford: Clarendon Press, 1983) 210 at 211.

[13] Ibid.

[14] House of Lords, 'Rule of Law' at column 625.

[15] Dworkin was my main supervisor, but he had a half-time appointment at New York University Law School. When he was away, I worked with either Raz or Finnis. For the record, they were all in different ways excellent supervisors, as I amply acknowledged in my thesis and the book that came from it: David Dyzenhaus, *Hard Cases in Wicked Legal*

Note that these very issues arose in Hermer's response at the end of the House of Lords debate in his bid to show why a 'thick conception of the rule of law is the one that is true to rule-of-law values'. He drew on what he said was an 'analogy' of apartheid in South Africa:

> Under apartheid, the laws were very clear. There was certainty as to the contents of those laws. Those laws were passed by a Parliament; those laws were adjudicated upon by an independent judiciary, including some brilliant lawyers who afterwards sat in your Lordships' House – one still does. That, I suggest, was not a country that operated according to the rule of law. That was rule by law. As the right reverend Prelate the Bishop of Norwich set out in his brilliant and insightful speech, fundamental human rights have to be an integral part of what we understand to be the rule of law as distinct from ruled by laws.[16]

In making this point, Hermer was responding to Lord Stewart, whom we encountered earlier in his warning that Hermer was in danger of being lynched for his defence of the rule of law. Stewart had this to say about apartheid South Africa:

> The House will be aware that, over the years and centuries, eminent lawyers in different times, working within noble legal traditions, have bent their talents and learning to erecting a framework for what to us, but not to them, seemed to be morally indefensible concepts. The obvious examples that I can give would be the use of Roman law in erecting a framework around the concept of slavery, or the role of lawyers in South Africa who did not honourably distance themselves from the exercise, working within the noble Roman Dutch tradition, in building a structure for apartheid.[17]

However, Hermer was wrong to suppose that the rule of law was absent in apartheid South Africa, and Stewart's description of the role of lawyers in this era is not accurate. In fact, throughout the apartheid era, the most 'eminent lawyers' were doing the opposite of what Stewart claimed; they were, that is, doing human rights work against the regime. His and Hermer's mistakes will help to develop the philosophical argument for the thick conception of the rule of law. I start with apartheid South Africa and move from there to legalized enslavement.[18]

Systems: South African Law in the Perspective of Legal Philosophy (Oxford: Clarendon Press, 1991); 2nd edition as *Hard Cases in Wicked Legal Systems: Pathologies of Legality* (Oxford: Oxford University Press, 2010).

16 House of Lords, 'Rule of Law' at column 676.

17 Ibid at column 653.

18 I rely in this section on the analysis in 'The Politics of Legal Space', chapter 5 of Dyzenhaus, *The Long Arc of Legality*, 297.

The apartheid regime maintained throughout its existence a formal commitment to the rule of law. It thus answered to what I have called the 'compulsion of legality' – a requirement that state action be capable of showing that it is legally authorized.[19] It is just one way of describing an important implication of a commitment to the rule of law – that the state undertakes that its officials must be able to show that their decisions are authorized by law. In addition, all inhabitants of apartheid South Africa were subject to the same general law. The racial laws of apartheid carved out vast exceptions to the rule of general law by creating the legal regimes that dominated the lives of black South Africans, subjecting them to severe discrimination. These regimes relegated black South Africans – the majority of the population – to an inferior status in almost all aspects of life. Nevertheless, the ideal that all South Africans were equal before the law – the specifically legal ideal of human dignity[20] – was maintained as an abstract ideal of the legal order throughout the apartheid era, even as particular laws made it ever clearer that the animating political ideology of the ruling party was one of white supremacy.[21]

To be both within the legal community in some respects and without for others is to occupy a highly problematic legal status, that of the second-class citizen. The status of second-class citizenship is much more *legally* – as opposed to morally – problematic than the status of enslavement, provided the enslaved persons are relentlessly consigned to the status of objects or things. This is because second-class status introduces an innate tension or instability into a legal order. For if one is legally recognized as having equal status before the law in some respects but not others, the parts of the law that seem to relegate one to inferior status are thrown into question by those that do not whenever a challenge is brought to the former.

An example is the Group Areas Act 1950, a statute that gave to officials the authority to set aside an area of South Africa for residence by one racial group and made it a criminal offence for members of other groups to reside there. The validity of the statute could not be challenged on the basis of its violation of the right of all South Africans to equality because

[19] David Dyzenhaus, 'Preventive Justice and the Rule-of-Law Project' in Andrew Ashworth, Lucia Zedner, and Patrick Tomlin, eds, *Prevention and the Limits of the Criminal Law* (Oxford: Oxford University Press, 2013) 9.

[20] See Jeremy Waldron, 'How Law Protects Dignity' (2012) 71 *Cambridge Law Journal* 200.

[21] Dyzenhaus, *Hard Cases in Wicked Legal Systems*; David Dyzenhaus, *Judging the Judges, Judging Ourselves: Truth, Reconciliation and the Apartheid Legal Order* (Oxford: Hart Publishing, 1998).

the South African constitutional order followed the principle of parliamentary sovereignty, modelled on the UK. However, when officials designated the biggest and best areas for white South Africans, their decisions could be and were challenged on the basis that the statute did not give officials the authority to act unreasonably in implementing the statute by creating a situation of gross inequality for racial groups.

The idea of second-class citizenship does not pertain to your political standing in the sense of X is a citizen of the UK. Rather, it pertains to your legal standing, your standing before the law to require that an official who makes a decision that affects your interests be able to show that the decision was legally authorized. As long as an individual has such standing, even if it is marked by inequality, human rights lawyers can exploit the tensions intrinsic to the presence of second-class status within a legal order to try to improve the legal situation of those who are subject to legalized oppression and injustice. It was in fact a key strategy of the 'eminent lawyers' of apartheid South Africa, pre-eminently Arthur Chaskalson, who through his human rights work did much to maintain respect for the ideal of the rule of law even during the worst periods of state oppression – work which earned him the position of first Chief Justice of the post-apartheid constitutional order.[22]

Those who control ultimate law-making authority have available to them two strategies to try to pre-empt such human rights lawyering. They can either increase the substantive injustice by altogether depriving the disfavoured group of legal status, that is, in enslaving them by declaring them to be 'things' owned in the same way as the owner owns any property, or by attacking procedural justice, that is, by ousting those procedures that permit judges to supervise the implementation of the law. And of course they can use both methods simultaneously. I will start with substantive injustice.

In the House of Lords debate, Baron Richard Keen of Elie KC, a Conservative peer, also embraced the thin conception of the rule of law as part of the general onslaught on Hermer, and offered more detail than Raz about the alleged consistency of slavery with the rule of law:

> The Roman republic developed a sophisticated legal system and courts which made citizens of Rome subject to the law and not the rule of tyrants. At the same time, it embraced slavery and had a well-developed

[22] Stephen Ellman, *Arthur Chaskalson: A Life Dedicated to Justice for All* (Montgomery, AL: New South Books, 2019).

> jurisprudence dealing with all aspects of slavery. Slavery was subject to the rule of law in the Roman republic and not the whim of individuals. Both master and slave were the subject of law. I give that example in order to emphasise that while the rule of law as properly understood and expressed by Aristotle is clear, it is not to be confused with our perception of or belief in human rights. We consider the concept of slavery to be abhorrent. It does not follow that a society which embraced slavery had abandoned the rule of law.[23]

Keen's description is accurate, but only to a point. All systems of legal enslavement, systems in which the status of being an enslaved person is created by law, encounter tensions because it is very difficult to use law to permanently consign a human being to the status of a thing. The development of the Roman law of slavery is in fact a prime example in this regard, as when enslaved persons assumed tasks on behalf of their masters, such as entering into contracts, it became difficult to maintain them in the class of things without any rights. In addition, the possibility of manumission – the emergence of an enslaved person by dint of an act of the owner from non-status to full status – made it more difficult to maintain the legal category of non-status.[24]

An example closer in time is even more instructive. In the antebellum US, 'Fugitive Slaves' who fled from enslavement in southern states to freedom in abolitionist northern states were required to be returned to their owners by two legal provisions. First, by the constitutional compact which established the Union through a set of compromises which permitted and secured enslavement without mentioning it by name, referring instead to 'property'. Second, by the federal Fugitive Slave Acts which sought to overcome the resistance by abolitionists in northern states to the return of fugitive slaves, a resistance that was often fought out by legal means in the courts.

The abolitionists and those judges who listened sympathetically to their arguments were often inspired by the ruling of the Court of King's Bench in the 1772 case of *Somerset v Stewart*, which held that an enslaved person brought to England could not be compelled to leave and was entitled to a writ of *habeas corpus*. Lord Mansfield stated in his judgment a wide-reaching jurisprudential basis for his decision: 'The state of slavery is of such a nature that it is incapable of being introduced

[23] House of Lords, 'Rule of Law' at column 673.
[24] See Alan Watson, *Roman Slave Law* (Baltimore: Johns Hopkins University Press, 1987).

on any reasons, moral or political, but only positive law . . . It's so odious, that nothing can be suffered to support it, but positive law.'[25]

A writ is the command of a court to the state, and *habeas corpus* – Latin for 'have a body' – requires, as Dicey explained, that any imprisoned person 'be actually brought before the Court' so that the court can have 'knowledge of the reason why he is imprisoned; and then having him before the Court, either then and there set him free or else see that he is dealt with in whatever way the law requires, as, for example, brought speedily to trial'.[26] Dicey thus argued that the writ is a crucial part of the rule of law since it helps to ensure that the law is enforced.[27]

In the US, the ability to litigate on the basis of Lord Mansfield's dictum operated in the shadow cast by the Constitution's Articles which permitted enslavement. Yet it also operated in the light cast by the Preamble of the Constitution, which promised justice and freedom for all. The Constitution's internal inconsistency on the question of enslavement created a tension within the legal order it created. This tension was exacerbated by the fact that local statutes also regulated the situation of enslaved persons brought into the North, for example by mandating that enslaved persons who stayed with their owners beyond a prescribed period of time in the North be freed.

Especially pertinent for my argument in this book are the problems attending the capture of fugitive slaves in the North who contested their rendition in court. When lawyers sought their release through applications for *habeas corpus* or other legal devices, were the fugitive slaves litigating as free legal subjects in a space in which slavery had been abolished, or were they pieces of property which, once certified as such, required rendering back to the South? This tension pitted the claims of the Constitution about justice and freedom against the claim of the South that its private property law regime should govern. But the legal situation was made even more complex by other considerations.

First, international law was itself in play. The anti-enslavement principle in *Somerset's Case* was seen by abolitionists and argued in court by their lawyers to be one common to international law and to US law

[25] Andrew Lyall, *Granville Sharp's Cases on Slavery* (Oxford: Hart Publishing, 2017) 233. For extensive discussion of the influence of Lord Mansfield's dictum, see James Oakes, *Freedom National: The Destruction of Slavery in the United States, 1861–1865* (New York: WW Norton, 2014).

[26] AV Dicey, *Introduction to the Study of the Law of the Constitution* (Indianapolis: Liberty Fund, 1982) at 129.

[27] Ibid at 130–39.

since the Constitution was argued to include such principles despite the tension within it created by the combination of the enslavement-permitting property Articles with the promise of freedom.[28] Finally, within the North, 'personal liberty' laws were enacted which sought to ensure that fugitive slaves were given all the procedural rights of a free person when they litigated, which significantly improved their chances of a favourable verdict.

Southern politicians seeking to address these tensions enacted a new federal Fugitive Slave Law in 1850 which, as Andrew Delbanco says, 'denied the most basic right enshrined in the Anglo-American tradition: habeas corpus – the right to challenge, in open court, the legality of their detention'.[29] Delbanco describes it as an 'act without mercy'. It forbade defendants to testify in their own defence, ruled out trial by jury, and disallowed all forms of exonerating evidence including rape, beatings and other kinds of abuse, put the power of extradition in the hands of federal officers, criminalized the act of sheltering a fugitive, and required local authorities to assist the claimant in recovering his property. Once ownership was proven according to the property laws of the South, the enslaved person was rendered back to captivity. Only proof that the person was not owned in the eyes of that law, such as emancipation papers signed by the owner, would save the enslaved persons from this fate.[30]

The 1850 law had two important and interrelated dimensions. First, it sought to turn public law cases about liberty into pure private law matters about who owned property with a foreordained result. Second, it sought to ensure that result by reducing the public law dimension of the litigation by stripping litigants' procedural rights to the bone. The 1850 law sought, that is, to deal with the problem of the status of fugitive slaves claiming legal standing before Northern courts by stripping litigants of the procedural rights that made it possible to present their case. It thus sought to deal with the internal legal tensions of the US constitutional order by making it almost impossible to raise these in a judicial forum. But that attempt served only to intensify political tensions in the North, often leading to violent resistance to the enforcement of the law, given

[28] It was also argued to be part of 'natural law', that is the moral/legal principles that bind all nations, and something like the equivalent in international law today, briefly discussed in Chapter 2, of *jus cogens*.

[29] Andrew Delbanco, *The War Before the War: Fugitive Slaves and the Struggle for America's Soul from the Revolution to the Civil War* (New York: Penguin Books, 2018) at 5.

[30] I follow Delbanco, ibid at 5.

that the legal avenues of resistance had been nearly extinguished.[31] In addition, new liberty laws were enacted in the North which sought to ensure jury trials for fugitive slaves in the face of the 1850 law, which, as one Southern senator complained, amounted to a 'practical denial of the whole right of the slaveholder over his slave, if he gets beyond the Jurisdiction of his own State'.[32] The ensuing political tensions were a significant cause of the civil war.

5.3 Enslavement and the Rwanda Act

The fugitive slave example is highly instructive for an appreciation of just how legally crazy the Rwanda Act was because it highlights a feature of the way in which rulers use law as an instrument of injustice that is usually neglected. Recall at this point that, in his chapter on parliamentary sovereignty, Dicey quoted with approval his philosopher cousin Leslie Stephen's claim that '[i]f a legislature decided that all blue-eyed babies should be murdered, the preservation of blue-eyed babies would be illegal'. Dicey added Stephen's qualification: 'but legislators must go mad before they could pass such a law, and subjects be idiotic before they could submit to it'.[33] So he seemed clearly to indicate that the law can be morally arbitrary – that is, cruel or even evil – and override protections in other laws against such cruelties, and yet be perfectly valid. As a result, whatever judges think of the mental states of the legislators who enacted the law or of the subjects who submit to it, their constitutional duty is to apply it and not to listen to any lawyer who would argue otherwise.

However, Dicey did not remark on the fact that any such statute would find itself in conflict with other parts of the law; for example, statutes and common law principles about the best interests of the child and the state's role as the ultimate guardian of their interests. The only way for the legislature to prevent judges finding themselves in the difficult situation of dealing with such tensions is to take them out of the picture altogether by an ouster clause, one that explicitly deprives them of the authority to scrutinize officials' implementation of the statute to check

31 RJM Blackett, *The Captive's Quest for Freedom: Fugitive Slaves, the 1850 Fugitive Slave Law, and the Politics of Slavery* (New York: Cambridge University Press, 2018). See also James Oakes's very perceptive review, 'The Power of Running Away' (Dec 6 2018) online: *New York Review of Books* <www.nybooks.com/articles/2018/12/06/fugitive-slaves-power-of-running-away/>. My account is deeply indebted to Oakes.

32 Ibid.

33 Dicey, *Law of the Constitution*, at 33.

that the officials are acting within the scope of their legal authority. To put the point more abstractly, what we can think of as the procedural dimension of the rule of law is as, if not more important than its substantive dimension. Moreover, those who espouse the thin conception are committed to conceding all of these points, although they wish to avoid confronting the consequences of that concession.

Consider from the last chapter that when in the House of Lords debate on the rule of law, Wolfson selected parts of John Gardner's review of Bingham's *The Rule of Law*, he omitted that Gardner not only fully endorsed Bingham's view of the content of the rule of law, but also went even further than Bingham. Indeed, Gardner endorsed the very claims made by Lord Steyn and Lady Hale that judges might have to consider invalidating a statute that flagrantly violated the rule of law, claims which in that chapter we saw Richard Ekins and his coauthors denounce as 'constitutional heresy'.[34] Gardner said that, in the passages from Steyn's and Hale's judgments that so upset Ekins, the judges were

> not thinking of an act of Parliament that merely violates human rights. No doubt they agree that Parliament is constitutionally at liberty to do that much. As they make clear, they are thinking of an act of Parliament that purports to oust the jurisdiction of the courts to rule on questions of law arising under that same act. Consider, for example, an act of Parliament that says that it is deliberately obscure and must not be clarified by the courts. I hope Bingham would agree that in spite of this provision the courts would have to go on applying – and thereby necessarily clarifying – the act, for that is the very least that the doctrine of parliamentary sovereignty requires. It requires the courts to apply parliamentary legislation, whatever its merits. If Bingham would accept this then he is on the side of Steyn and Hale after all. He is committed to upholding an act of Parliament as law even when it demands not to be upheld.[35]

Gardner continued:

> It is only Bingham's 'thick' account, then, that makes it seem as if the Steyn and Hale view is at odds with the constitutional doctrine of parliamentary sovereignty. If we jettison the extra baggage with which Bingham weighs down the ideal, we see that the rule of law and the

[34] Richard Ekins, Stephen Laws, and Conor Casey, 'Safety of Rwanda (Asylum and Migration) Bill' (Dec 11 2023) online: *Policy Exchange* <https://policyexchange.org.uk/publication/safety-of-rwanda-asylum-and-migration-bill/> at 24.

[35] John Gardner, 'How to Be a Good Judge' (2010) 32 *London Review of Books*, online: <https://johngardnerathome.info/pdfs/binghamreview.pdf> at 8–9.

> doctrine of parliamentary sovereignty are as one in requiring judges to disregard, and thereby invalidate, certain imaginable provisions of an act of Parliament. For those provisions prevent acts from entering the law, and the doctrine of parliamentary sovereignty says that all acts of Parliament, however immoral, have to enter the law. The doctrine of parliamentary sovereignty cuts against invalidating acts of Parliament on human rights grounds, but not against invalidating them on rule of law grounds.[36]

However, whether Gardner is right that 'human rights grounds' do not count depends in the UK context on the content of the unwritten constitution, on what Dicey called 'the predominance of the legal spirit . . . a special attribute of English institutions'. Recall that Dicey continued that 'the Constitution is pervaded by the rule of law on the ground that the general principles of the Constitution (as for example the right to personal liberty, or the right of public meeting) are with us the result of judicial decisions determining the rights of private persons in particular cases brought before the Courts'.[37] The content of the unwritten UK constitution comes, that is, from the decisions of judges interpreting the legal material, both statutes and past judicial decisions, relevant to the particular matter they must decide.

The important point here for a correct understanding of the rule of law is that when rulers use law as an instrument of substantive injustice, especially when that injustice is one that undermines the status of a group of individuals as equal before the law, that will invariably bring that part of the law into conflict with other parts. Such conflicts create a problem for those charged with interpreting the law, especially judges. They must try to reconcile those parts of the law that enshrine protection of rights with those that either strip away that protection or undermine it. Therefore, to ensure that the executive can implement the substantive injustice free of the legal constraints that are applicable, rulers should also deprive judges of their authority to review implementation.

To be effective, an attack on certain kinds of substantive justice must therefore be accompanied by an attack on procedural justice. The Rwanda Act did both, and more. It both deprived judges of their review authority with narrow exceptions and disapplied the law the judges would have relied on in exercising their authority. It was thus even more draconian from the procedural perspective of the rule of law than the

36 Ibid at 9.

37 Dicey, *Law of the Constitution*, at 119.

Fugitive Slave Acts. And from the substantive perspective of the rule of law, there is also a similarity between the two statutes: both demanded the rendition of human beings from a space where their rights were protected to one where they weren't. The Fugitive Slave Acts required rendering human beings from a legally constructed space in which they had a right to liberty equal to that of all other human beings to a space where they were considered a thing, to be used at the pleasure of the person deemed to be their owner. The Rwanda Act required rendering human beings from a legally constructed space in which they had the right to demand that their claim to be asylum seekers be properly processed to a space in which they were subject to the power of a state with an atrocious human rights record. They were rendered, that is, to a space where they were at the mercy of a state not known for its mercy.

It is the procedural dimension of the rule of law – the right to have the legality of state action against you fully determined in a judicial procedure – that opens up the cracks where the light gets in, as we saw in Chapter 3 in the common good lawyers' panic about the slivers of judicial review that remained in the Rwanda Act. I have sketched in my previous work how the compulsion of legality can set in motion two very different 'cycles of legality'.[38] In one 'virtuous cycle', the institutions of legal order cooperate in devising controls on public actors that ensure that their decisions comply with the principle of legality, understood as a substantive conception of the rule of law. In the other 'empty' cycle, the content of legality is understood in an ever more formal or vacuous manner, resulting in the mere appearance or even the pretence of legality. With this second cycle, the compulsion of legality results in the subversion of the kinds of values associated with a substantive conception of the rule of law, notably the individual interest in equality and liberty. When judges play a role in sustaining an empty cycle, they might make things worse from the perspective of the rule of law by placing what a UK judge, Sullivan J, memorably described as a 'thin veneer of legality' over the 'reality' of 'executive decision-making, untrammelled by any prospect of effective judicial supervision'.[39]

One has to be alert in analysing these cycles to the presence of not only legal 'black holes' – Lord Steyn's famous description of Guantanamo Bay as a space devoid of legal controls[40] – but also legal 'grey holes'. In the

[38] Dyzenhaus, 'Preventive Justice and the Rule-of-Law Project' at 98.

[39] *Re MB* [2006] EWHC 1000 (Admin) [2006] HRLR 29 (2006) 150 at para 103.

[40] Johan Steyn, 'Guantanamo Bay: The Legal Black Hole' (2004) 53 *International and Comparative Law Quarterly* 1.

latter, there are legal controls, but these are not substantive enough to give the affected individuals any real protection. There is just enough legality to provide the government with a basis to claim that it is still governing in accordance with the rule of law, and thus to garner some legitimacy.[41] Since these holes are in substance black, their existence can be even more dangerous for the rule of law than full-blown black holes. A little bit of legality might, that is, be more lethal to the rule of law than none since it allows the government to pretend that it is abiding by the rule of law. But that bit of legality also affords human rights lawyers and judges the opportunity to try to turn the grey hole into something better by building more substance into the legal controls. They accept, that is, that the government and the legislature have committed themselves to ruling through the rule of law and use that commitment as a legitimating basis for finding that the legislature must have intended real not sham controls. Ironically, as we saw in the last chapter, all this was completely appreciated by the common good lawyers, who sought as a result to persuade the Conservative government of the day to close nearly all the cracks, thus producing the near total darkness of a black hole. As I remarked in the last chapter, they thus showed that their project is not so much about curbing 'judicial power', a 'Judicial Power Project', as it as about giving unlimited power to the executive.

5.4 Through Thick and Thin Again

Some very important things follow. First, even those who purport to espouse a thin conception of the rule of law cannot avoid commitment to both the substantive and the procedural dimensions of the rule of law. For they cannot stick with the part of the thin conception that posits that as long as those rules are clear, the rule of law is in place *whatever the content of the rules.*

Recall that when it comes to substance, Verdirame said in the House of Lord debate:

> The thicker the conception of the rule of law, the more politicised the rule of law will become. The scope and interpretation of some fundamental rights, and the ways in which conflicts between rights should be resolved, are an example. Those issues will remain contested. I agree with the noble

[41] See David Dyzenhaus, *The Constitution of Law: Legality in a Time of Emergency* (Cambridge: Cambridge University Press, 2006).

> and learned Lord, Lord Etherton, that a fair trial is the obvious exception because it is intertwined with the rule of law.[42]

But if the right to a fair trial is intertwined with the rule of law, it is inconsistent with the rule of law to deny that right. That raises the question 'why?' and the answer will have something to do with a value like the inherent dignity of all before the law.[43] And we are then firmly on the slippery slope that the thin conception is supposed to prevent us from sliding down.

It follows, second, that if the rule Parliament enacts undermines the procedural dimension of the rule of law, one also cannot stick with the 'whatever the content' part of the thin conception, as Wolfson himself explained:

> Governments and public officials are subject to the law. They must exercise their powers lawfully. The law must be accessible and clear. Disputes should be determined by independent courts and tribunals. A vibrant and independent legal profession is necessary to promote liberty under the rule of law. Without the rule of law, underpinned by an independent judiciary and the courts, much else would fail to prosper.[44]

For once that concession is made, we are again on the slippery slope, though not one that allows every conceivable human right to flood in. Rather, only those rights come in that have been recognized by UK legal institutions as relevant to the determination of the scope of official authority, notably Parliament in its statutes and the judiciary in their judgments.

Notice that the rights come into play because of a right that the legal order recognizes, not because a judge or Parliament has chosen to recognize that right but because such a right is presupposed by commitments intrinsic to legal order, a right without which one could not claim that there was either legal order or the rule of law. This is the right of an individual subject to the power of the state to demand that an official who purports to be exercising authority over that individual is in fact acting on the basis of an authority grounded in law. Access to judicial review or its equivalent – for example, an expert administrative tribunal – is essential to

42 House of Lords, 'Rule of Law' at column 643.

43 Waldron, 'How Law Protects Dignity'. Some will claim that trials are merely instrumental, to ensure that the rules are accurately applied to the accused. But that claim squeezes the trial into the command theory of law.

44 House of Lords, 'Rule of Law' at column 625.

the rule of law, as every proponent of the thin conception will admit. And they should then also concede that such access is required in large part because otherwise those subject to state power would not be able to vindicate their legally-protected rights, a concession that makes their conception of the rule of law substantive.

Now it is obviously the case that the content of these rights is different today from what it was centuries ago, or even before instruments such as the European Convention on Human Rights entered into force, or before the Human Rights Act 1998. In addition, the institutional machinery has changed. As we saw in Chapter 2, there is the European Court of Human Rights; the Judicial Committee of the House of Lords became the Supreme Court; the Joint Committee on Human Rights was established in Parliament to monitor the state's compliance with rights, as was the House of Lords Constitution Committee to 'keep under review the operation of the constitution'; and there is much more besides. Finally, we have seen that the Human Rights Act 1998 made a difference to the remedies available to judges when faced with an Act of Parliament that violated human rights, in that under section 3 judges are under a formal duty to interpret statutes in a way that makes them consistent with a legislative intention to respect rights, while section 4 places them under a formal duty to make a declaration of incompatibility if they are unable to do so.[45]

I use 'formal' here to signal that the change made by sections 3 and 4 is not that major – not a change in the constitution to the place of Parliament as the supreme or ultimate legal authority. In the past, judges thought of themselves as under a duty at common law to interpret statutes so as to render them consistent with legally protected rights. And if a statute could not be so interpreted, it was often the case that they felt obliged in their judgments to highlight this fact, as a signal to both Parliament and the public that something had gone wrong, not only morally but also legally. They would issue, that is, what we can think of as an informal declaration of incompatibility.

Recall from the preceding chapter the Second World War detention case *Liversidge v Anderson*. Lord Atkin's complaint in his dissent that his fellow judges had proved themselves to be 'more executive minded than the executive' was directed at the fact that they had done the legislature's

[45] It may be the case that the judges of the Supreme Court, under the direction of Lord Reed, are now 'editing the Human Rights Act out of existence', because 'they regard it as an unwelcome remnant of a past era'. See Conor Gearty, 'Unwelcome Remnant' (2025) 47 *London Review of Books* 11 at 14.

work for it in reading into the statute a provision that said that judges could not review the executive's decisions to detain individuals suspected of being a threat to national security.[46] Lord Atkin's dissent echoes an earlier one by Lord Shaw in *Halliday*, a decision on wartime detention of such suspects during the First World War.[47] Shaw started with the assumption that Parliament must be taken to intend that its delegates act in accordance with the rule of law, which meant that it had to explicitly authorize any departures from the rule of law. The judicial stance, in his view, should be that 'if Parliament had intended to make this colossal delegation of power it would have done so plainly and courageously and not under cover of words about regulations for safety and defence'. For judges to allow the right to be violated is, he said, to '"revolutionize" the constitution'. It amounts to what he called a 'constructive repeal of *habeas corpus*', a repeal by the executive which is then ratified by judges. He would, he said, have come to his conclusion even if the language of the statute 'had been much more plain and definite than it is'.[48]

Notice that when judges issue either informal or formal declarations of incompatibility they are not denying parliamentary sovereignty, understood as Parliament's power to override a constitutional principle. Rather, they are pointing out that, in overriding the principle, Parliament has introduced an incoherence into the legal order which needs attention. In other words, they are saying that can does not imply ought. I'm referring here to the maxim 'ought implies can', usually attributed to the philosopher Immanuel Kant. It tells us that if a certain action is impossible for someone to perform, that person does not have a moral obligation to do it. Whatever the merits of the maxim, and whether Kant actually espoused it, it is clear that its opposite is not true. Can does not imply ought. I can in fact murder you, but I ought, morally speaking, not to. But what about Parliament? Parliament can legislate in contravention of international law and the rule of law. But it ought not to. Is this a moral or a legal ought, or both?

The common good lawyers do not confront these questions squarely. As we have seen, at times they argue that Parliament can but perhaps ought not to. At other times, they argue that what Parliament can do is legitimate for Parliament to do. They therefore assert that can implies

[46] *Liversidge v Anderson* [1942] AC 206 at 244.
[47] *R v Halliday, ex parte Zadig* [1917] AC 260.
[48] Ibid at 292–94.

ought.[49] At yet other times, they argue that there is neither a legal nor moral ought at stake as human rights and international law are the moral code of the liberal left cosmopolitan elite which this elite falsely claims to be law so that it can impose the rule of lawyers on the rule of politics – on those who represent the sovereign British people.

In fact, this last answer was a theme of the onslaught on Hermer in the House of Lords debate and has been echoed in a recent essay by Conor Casey and Yuan Yi Zhu on Policy Exchange,[50] which was subsequently picked up in the media in a sustained attack on Hermer.[51] Casey and Zhu's polemic provides rich evidence of the common good lawyers' ability to proclaim allegiance to the rule of law while turning it into whatever the government of the day says it is. In a nutshell, Suella Braverman, the far-right Conservative politician, had as Attorney General watered down the risk advice that government lawyers should give to ministers about the legality of proposed policies. Hermer restored the advice and articulated a more robust understanding of what it entails.[52] As Dominic Grieve KC, Attorney General in the Conservative government of David Cameron from 2010 to 2014, pointed out in a letter to the *Times* on 20 February 2025, Hermer was being castigated for doing his job:

[49] While Ekins acknowledges that legislatures may make mistakes when it comes to the determination of people's rights, he also argues that because Parliament has the 'capacity' to deliberate about rights and come to the right answer, we should accept that its statutes are in fact the product of such deliberation, and therefore legitimate, because by definition rights-respecting. Richard Ekins, 'Legislation as Reasoned Action' in Grégoire Webber, Paul Yowell, Richard Ekins, Maris Köpcke, Bradley W Miller, and Francisco J Urbina, eds, *Legislated Rights: Securing Human Rights Through Legislation* (Cambridge: Cambridge University Press, 2018) 86. This 'argument' was relied on in a curious dissent in the Canadian Supreme Court: *Frank v Canada* 2019 SCC 1 at para 134, which sought to upturn decades of constitutional law by putting the Canadian constitution in the service of the common good, as conceived by Ekins and the other common good lawyers the judges cited, among them some of the editors of the book.

[50] Conor Casey and Yuan Yi Zhu, 'From the Rule of Law to the Rule of Lawyers? The Problem with the Attorney General's New Legal Risk Guidelines' (Nov 26 2024) online: *Policy Exchange* <https://policyexchange.org.uk/wp-content/uploads/From-the-Rule-of-Law-to-the-Rule-of-Lawyers.pdf>.

[51] Eleni Courea, 'Deeply Unfair: How Attorney General Became a Lightning Rod for Criticism of Starmer' (Feb 13 2025) online: *The Guardian* <www.theguardian.com/politics/2025/feb/13/attorney-general-richard-hermer-lightning-rod-for-criticism-of-starmer>.

[52] See 'Attorney General's Legal Risk Guidance' (Nov 6 2024) online: *Gov.UK* <https://assets.publishing.service.gov.uk/media/672b7189abb279b2de1e8c59/AG_s_Legal_Risk_Guidance_2024.pdf>.

> Sir, It is the duty of attorneys general, in accordance with their oath, to apply their legal knowledge to the furtherance of the policy aims of government. But it is also the duty of attorneys to speak truth to power. As the government is subject to the rule of law and committed to upholding international law to which our country has adhered, that inevitably includes pointing out when a policy is likely to be found to be unlawful. To attack Lord Hermer for his advice, as Lord Glasman and others have done ('MPs press for ethics investigation into Hermer', Feb 17), is to 'kill the messenger'. It won't itself change the law or the risk of government falling foul of it if it disregards the advice.[53]

The most absurd example reads like something from QAnon or Infowars, or the latest salvo from the political thugs who hold high office or seek so to hold in the once stable democracies of the West. But it appeared on *GB News*, the UK equivalent of *Fox News*, owned, as we saw in Chapter 1, by the same man who is one of the funders of Policy Exchange. It was penned by a Conservative MP, Alex Story.[54] Taking Casey and Zhu's piece as his inspiration, he claimed:

> international law, without the protection of domestic law, is profoundly undemocratic and a recipe for perpetual external interference in one's internal affairs, the corollary of which is eventual conflict. In the minds of Hermer and of internationalists on whose behalf he seems to be speaking, no borders and no sovereignty exist. ... It is a Marxist worldview, accepted by very few outside Richard Hermer's narrow circle of friends, ... In my opinion, Hermer should be impeached before our country sinks further into the orbit of sundry international (and deeply suspect) organisations, such as the United Nations, only to disappear Pluto-like out of the galaxy of nations.

But even once-respectable newspapers, newspapers that have long ceased to be 'conservative' such as the *Times* and the *Telegraph*, joined the chorus of abuse against Hermer, with the latter claiming that Hermer had 'capitulated' to international law.[55] And it is to that charge that I now turn.

[53] Dominic Grieve, 'Rewriting of History by Putin and Trump' (Feb 20 2025) online: *The Times* <www.thetimes.com/comment/letters-to-editor/article/the-times-letters-rewriting-of-history-by-trump-and-putin-3msvhktgm>.

[54] Alex Story, 'Starmer's Attorney General Stripped the UK of Her Sovereign Rights – and You Didn't Even Notice' (Jan 2 2025) online: *GB News* <www.gbnews.com/opinion/keir-starmer-attorney-general-richard-hermer>.

[55] Nick Gutteridge, 'Attorney General's Speeches Provide Clues as to Why Starmer Has Capitulated to International Law' (Jan 18 2025) online: *The Telegraph* <www.telegraph.co.uk/politics/2025/01/18/attorney-general-speeches-keir-starmer-international-law/>.

5.5 International Law and the Rule of Law

As I pointed out in Chapter 3, it is quite difficult to work out the common good lawyers' stance on international law because they move between three different positions. First, they claim that it is fine for the UK to break its international law commitments because that is consistent with the constitutional status of international law in the UK, a dualist jurisdiction. It is also therefore consistent with the rule of law. Second, they claim that because the UK is a dualist jurisdiction, international law recognizes that its obligations bind within the jurisdiction only if Parliament has made that the case by enacting an incorporating statute. As a result, there is no departure from international law in breaking international law. Finally, they claim that there is nothing there to break because international law is not really law.

All three claims are incorrect in regard to the UK's constitutional tradition. I rely here on the argument of a paper 'Is International Law a Part of the Law of England?' – an address to the Grotius Society in 1939 by Hersch Lauterpacht, at that time Whewell Professor of International Law in Cambridge, and with a good claim to being the most influential scholar in his field in the twentieth century. There, Lauterpacht took as his epigraph the following lines from Blackstone's *Commentaries*:

> [T]he law of nations (whenever any question arises which is properly the object of its jurisdiction) is here adopted in its full extent by the common law, and is held to be a part of the law of the land. And those acts of parliament, which have from time to time been made to enforce this universal law, or to facilitate the execution of its decisions, are not to be considered as introductive of any new rule, but merely declaratory of the old fundamental constitutions of the kingdom; without which it must cease to be a part of the civilized world.[56]

There is a double irony here. First, the Grotius Society is named after Hugo Grotius, the Dutch humanist we already encountered in Chapter 1, and it was founded in 1915, amongst other things, 'to advance the study of international law'. Grotius is principally known as the father of modern international law, yet, as we saw in that chapter, Policy

[56] Sir William Blackstone, *Commentaries on the Laws of England*, fifth chapter of the Fourth Book, quoted in Lauterpacht, 'Is International Law a Part of the Law of England?' in Elihu Lauterpacht, ed, *Hersch Lauterpacht International Law: Collected Papers: The Law of Peace, Part 1, International Law in General* (Cambridge: Cambridge University Press, 2009) volume 2, 537.

Exchange has appropriated his name to bestow an annual prize on politicians for their achievements in subverting international law and the rule of law.

Second, Sir William Blackstone (1723–1780) was, as I have previously remarked, one of the great figures in the common law tradition, whose *Commentaries on the Laws of England* was 'the dominant law book in England and America in the century after its publication and played a unique role in the development of the fledgling American legal system'.[57] It is for this reason that Ekins was happy to cite Blackstone in his 'Protecting the Constitution' for the proposition that the 'constitution's guardians are not the courts'.

> Its guardians, as Blackstone said several centuries ago, are parliamentarians, who should act now to guard the constitution *from* judicial overreach, and from the instabilities and threats to good governance that result from that overreach. Parliament's duty is to depoliticise the courts, to prevent litigation from becoming politics by other means, and to protect the courts from political controversy.[58]

But Blackstone never said anything like that. He did say that 'as the English constitution lasts, we may venture to affirm, that the power of parliament is absolute and without control'.[59] But he also had the following to say about the judiciary, which Ekins somehow omits:

> In this distinct and separate existence of the judicial power, consists one main preservative of the public liberty; which cannot subsist long in any state, unless the administration of common justice be in some degree separated both from the legislative and also from the executive power. Were it joined with the legislative, the life, liberty, and property, of the subject would be in the hands of arbitrary judges, whose decisions would be then regulated only by their own opinions, and not by any fundamental principles of law; which, though legislators may depart from, yet judges are bound to observe.[60]

Blackstone here recognized the very same tension I highlighted in previous chapters between the constitutional fundamental of parliamentary

[57] Sir William Blackstone, *Commentaries on the Laws of England: A Facsimile of the First Edition of 1765–1769* (Chicago: University of Chicago Press, 1979) volume 1 at iii.

[58] Richard Ekins, 'Protecting the Constitution: How and Why Parliament Should Limit Judicial Power' (Dec 28 2019) online: *Policy Exchange* <https://policyexchange.org.uk/wp-content/uploads/2020/01/Protecting-the-Constitution.pdf> at 8–9. His emphasis.

[59] Blackstone, *Commentaries on the Laws of England*, at 156–57.

[60] Ibid at 259.

sovereignty and that of the rule of law under the guardianship of judges. For he tells us that for the legislature to usurp the judicial function, or to transfer it to the executive, is to endanger 'the life, liberty, and property, of the subject'. Where Blackstone differed from Dicey is in his estimation of international law. For Blackstone included in the passage cited by Lauterpacht, as Bingham was later to do, international law obligations as part of the 'law of the land', thus suggesting that reviewing the state's adherence thereto is part of the judiciary's role.

On this basis, Lauterpacht argued that this view of international law, and of the judicial role in upholding it, was consistent with the doctrine of parliamentary sovereignty. He pointed out that there is a commonly accepted rule that judges are to interpret statutes 'so as not to be in conflict with international law'.[61] Any affirmation of the absolute sovereignty of parliament is, given this rule of statutory construction, a 'theoretical affirmation', one which has 'the probably not unintended effect of stressing the duty of judges to do their utmost to interpret statutes so as not to impute to the Legislature the intention of disregarding international law'.[62] In other words, Lauterpacht suggested that there is an innate connection between the idea of parliamentary sovereignty and the judiciary's role in ensuring that Parliament respects international law in its law-making. Judges should not impute an intention to Parliament to override the principles of the unwritten constitution, which includes principles of both domestic law and international law, because to do that would be to undermine the structure – the constitutional order – in which Parliament has its place as the ultimate legal authority.

Lauterpacht argued further that the English insistence on an incorporating statute to give effect to international law is not the result of the claim that international law is not part of domestic law. Rather, it was a reaction to the uncertainty of international law in particular areas. That is, where the requirements of international law are uncertain, and given that international law is part of the law of the land, the way to resolve uncertainty is for Parliament to clear up the uncertainty.[63] In Lauterpacht's view, the doctrine of incorporation is not, as dualist theories have it, about the incorporation of particular norms of international law by statute, but about the incorporation of the whole of international law by a legal order. He stressed that there is an act of will

[61] Lauterpacht, 'Is International Law a Part of the Law of England?' at 542.
[62] Ibid at 543.
[63] Ibid at 546.

of the individual state on which such incorporation depends. But that act, he argued, is a general submission to international law. While it is a voluntary one, as long as it lasts it 'has the effect of elevating to the authority of a legal rule the unity of international and municipal law'.[64] From the 'point of view of municipal law' – that is, what I call 'domestic law' – that submission may, Lauterpacht said, be 'validly refused or withdrawn, but the sanction of such action must be, in Blackstone's words, that the State would "cease to be part of the civilized world"'.[65]

So much, Lauterpacht suggested, is required as soon as one begins to move beyond the common good lawyers' Austinian image of sovereignty as the absolute unlimited authority of an 'uncommanded commander', the figure of thought in the command theory of law that says that the sovereign is legally unlimited. As Lauterpacht argued, the root of dualism is to be found in the rise of such positivistic doctrines of absolute state sovereignty.[66] But just as it is not asserted in the UK tradition that the common law fails to be part of the law of the land because statutes may override it, so, Lauterpacht insisted, one should reject the claim that international law is not part of the law of the land because statutes may override it. He claimed that at that moment of overriding, the 'fundamental jurisprudential identity' of law with its aspirations is in peril,[67] including at least in part the law's aspiration to protect human rights, an aspiration that we have seen was firmly embedded in UK constitutional law in the post-war period.

Voluntary submission is needed to maintain what Lauterpacht called 'a fundamental jurisprudential identity' between domestic law and international law.[68] That identity is manifested in various ways, including the dualist recognition of the importance of international law in the interpretation of statutes, of the force of customary international law in the absence of an explicit statutory override, and of the category of *jus cogens* or mandatory norms.

As I have explained elsewhere, the upshot is that the academic debate between dualism and monism as theories of the place of international law in domestic law is beside the point. Dualism and monism are not competing theories. Rather, they are different practical ways in which a

[64] Ibid at 549.
[65] Ibid.
[66] Ibid at 555.
[67] Ibid at 558–59.
[68] Ibid.

constitutional order can choose to manage its recognition of the binding force of the obligations of international law. Notably, the same goes for a domestic legal order's recognition of constitutional law: either, as in the UK, one has parliamentary sovereignty, in which case constitutional principles exert their force mainly in disciplining what officials may lawfully do in implementing a statute, or one has an arrangement, as in the US, where the judges have the authority to invalidate statutes that they find to be in conflict with constitutional principle. In both cases, with both international law and with constitutional law, the UK arrangements recognize that these kinds of law are law properly so called.[69]

The common good lawyers and the right-wing media have a different view. They share Austin's position that international law is not really law. But they extend the position in claiming that both human rights law and international law are just foreign moral codes that cosmopolitan elites of 'lefty lawyers' want to impose on the British people. We know that Dicey accepted that constitutional law is not defective law, but rejected international law. In accepting constitutional law, he departed from Austin, who rejected both international law and constitutional law as no more than moral codes pretending to be law, not law 'properly so called', in his terms, or 'defective law' in Finnis's. But Dicey was compelled to move away from Austin in regard to constitutional law because his view of the rule of law as a constitutional fundamental compelled that move. For the same reason he should have accepted the claim about international law. That he did not had the result that Austin's theory of law as the commands of a legally unlimited commander remained a disturbing presence in his theory, as it does in legal positivism to this day, as we will see in the next section, in which I return to the topic of parliamentary sovereignty.

5.6 The Paradox of Sovereignty Dissolved

In Chapter 2, in introducing the constitutional fundamental of parliamentary sovereignty in the UK constitutional order, I mentioned that the paradox of sovereignty arises if one holds, as Dicey did, that Parliament has the 'right to make or unmake any law whatever; and further, that no person or body is recognised by the law of England as having a right to override or set aside the legislation of Parliament'.[70] For that might be

[69] Dyzenhaus, *The Long Arc of Legality*, chapter 4.

[70] Dicey, *Law of the Constitution*, at 3–4. It also arises with Blackstone's famous claim that 'as the English constitution lasts, we may venture to affirm, that the power of parliament

taken to entail that Parliament can enact a law that binds its law-making authority into the future. We saw that the philosopher John Mackie pointed out that this problem is the equivalent of the philosophical problem of God's omnipotence. For example, can God create a stone so heavy that he could not lift it?[71]

Mackie's own solution to the puzzle turned on two sets of distinctions. First, a distinction between 'first order laws' and 'second order laws'. First order laws are the laws Parliament makes to govern individuals and subordinate bodies, such as the officials who deal with asylum seekers. Second order laws are 'laws about laws', 'laws governing the actions of the legislature itself'. The other distinction, built on the first, is between what he called 'first order sovereignty' – 'sovereignty (1)' – which is 'unlimited authority to make first order laws' and 'second order sovereignty' – 'sovereignty (2)' – which is 'unlimited authority to make second order laws'. He then argued that we cannot 'without contradiction mean both that the present parliament has sovereignty (2) and that every parliament at every time has sovereignty (1), for if the present parliament has sovereignty (2) it may use it to take away the sovereignty (1) of later parliaments. What the paradox shows is that we cannot ascribe to any continuing institution legal sovereignty in an inclusive sense'.[72]

By 'inclusive sense', Mackie meant that Parliament's authority includes the authority to give up part or all of its authority. In order to be a 'continuing' legal institution, a parliament must abide by the second order laws that give it its character as such. But, as I suggested in calling this section 'The Paradox of Sovereignty Dissolved', it follows that he is not so much providing a solution as denying what the paradox affirms, and what makes it in the first place a paradox – that there could be a parliament subject to no legal limit. But notice that he is not denying that there could be such a thing as a sovereign parliament – a body with ultimate legislative authority. Mackie's solution was influential, notably on H. L. A. Hart.[73] But unlike Mackie, Hart suggested that it was possible to have a Parliament with sovereignty (2). In that, he disagreed with Mackie and opened the conceptual space for the common good lawyers to argue that the UK Parliament has

is absolute and without control'. Blackstone, *Commentaries on the Laws of England*, at 156–57.

[71] JL Mackie, 'Evil and Omnipotence' (1955) 64 *Mind* 200 at 211–12.

[72] Ibid at 211–12.

[73] HLA Hart, *The Concept of Law*, 2nd edition (Oxford: Clarendon Press, 1994) at 148–54.

sovereignty (2), exactly the argument made by Ekins in his essays on this set of issues.[74]

Dicey, as I have suggested, offered no explicit solution to the puzzle raised by the paradox. Indeed, as we have seen, his example of the statute that requires the execution of blue-eyed babies indicates that he thought there was none, which also seems to help the common good lawyers to suppose that what parliament can do, parliament legitimately does. However, in what could be a direct answer to the very existence of the common good lawyers' Judicial Power Project, Dicey observed as follows:

> The fact that the most arbitrary powers of the English executive must always be exercised under Act of Parliament places the government, even when armed with the widest authority, under the supervision, so to speak, of the Courts. Powers, however extraordinary, which are conferred or sanctioned by statute, are never really unlimited, for they are confined by the words of the Act itself, and, what is more, by the interpretation put upon the statute by the judges. Parliament is supreme legislator, but from the moment Parliament has uttered its will as lawgiver, that will becomes subject to the interpretation put upon it by the judges of the land, and the judges, who are influenced by the feelings of magistrates no less than by the general spirit of the common law, are disposed to construe statutory exceptions to common law principles in a mode which would not commend itself either to a body of officials, or to the Houses of Parliament, if the Houses were called upon to interpret their own enactments. … In England judicial notions have modified the action and influenced the ideas of the executive government. By every path we come round to the same conclusion, that Parliamentary sovereignty has favoured the rule of law, and that the supremacy of the law of the land both calls forth the exertion of Parliamentary sovereignty, and leads to its being exercised in a spirit of legality.[75]

To explain this important passage, I draw on a recent book by Yuval Levin, a prominent figure in American conservatism, *American Covenant: How the Constitution Unified Our Nation – And Could Again.*[76] Early in the book, Levin points out that a common approach

[74] Richard Ekins, 'Constitutional Principle in the Laws of the Commonwealth' in John Keown and Robert P George, eds, *Reason, Morality, and Law: The Philosophy of John Finnis* (Oxford: Oxford University Press, 2013). See also Richard Ekins, 'Legislative Freedom and Its Consequences' in Richard Johnson and Yuan Yi Zhu, eds, *Sceptical Perspectives on the Changing Constitution of the United Kingdom* (Oxford: Hart Publishing, 2023) 55.

[75] Dicey, *Law of the Constitution*, at 273.

[76] Yuval Levin, *American Covenant: How the Constitution Unified Our Nation – And Could Again* (New York: Basic Books, 2024).

to the separation of powers between the legislative branch, the judicial branch and the executive branch makes the mistake of imagining that 'there is a fungible commodity called "power" that the different branches of our government exercise, so that the question is who has less or more of it'. That's a mistake, he argues, since each branch is 'expected to exercise its authorities differently, and for a different purpose'.[77] The legislature makes laws that authorize and channel public power, the executive implements that power, while the judiciary performs a legality check; it checks that the executive has not acted outside the limits of its legal authority in particular cases.

The common good lawyers make exactly that mistake since they regard the judiciary as having grabbed legislative power from the legislature when what the judges are doing is exercising a qualitatively different power – checking on whether the executive is staying within the limits of their delegated authority. So much is evident in the manifesto for the Judicial Power Project which I quoted in Chapter 1. Recall that they say that 'the judicial power has a central, strategic place in any well-ordered constitutional arrangement: no state is well-governed without an independent judiciary, exercising legal and constitutional authority to adjudicate disputes, including disputes between citizens and officials, fairly and in accordance with settled positive law'.[78] But the place is not accurately described as 'strategic'. It is one thing to note that judges, like any person who holds public office, are capable of overstepping their legitimate authority. It is quite another to misdescribe their authority in a bid to delegitimize what they not only legitimately do, but also are under a duty to do.

As Dicey thought, and as Levin explains, judges have a constitutional role which has to do with guardianship of legality. Moreover, such guardianship is not confined to policing the boundaries of 'settled positive law', since it includes guardianship both of positive law and of the principles embedded in it. It is only if one is prone to making this mistake, or wishes to pretend that it is not a mistake because the pretence serves a political purpose, that one will also suppose that as long as Parliament enacts a clear rule like the deportation rule, one which exempts the executive from scrutiny, that is consistent with the rule of law and therefore legitimate.

[77] Ibid at 25.

[78] 'About the Judicial Power Project' online: *Judicial Power Project* <https://judicialpowerproject.org.uk/about/>.

The same mistake is made by many on the left, such as Martin Loughlin whose views I sketched at the end of Chapter 2.[79] And both the left and the right are helped in this view by legal positivists whose understanding of the rule of law cannot escape the legacy of Bentham and Austin, who saw law as a mere instrument of power. Dicey, in contrast, worked up his conception of the rule of law from the actual practices of legality prevailing in the UK at the time he produced the first edition of his *Introduction to the Study of the Law of the Constitution*, just as Bingham did for his time in *The Rule of Law*, though he was of course working on practices that had evolved in the post-war human rights era.

This is more than a perfectly respectable legal methodology. It is the methodology at work in a common law legal order which makes its arguments inductively rather than deductively. It is also a perfectly respectable philosophical methodology despite the efforts of some to discredit it.[80] And, as I have suggested from Chapter 2 on, not only is Dicey a reliable guide if one is interested, as the common good lawyers so frequently claim to be, in the constitutional 'tradition' of the UK, but also to the UK's present. His understanding of sovereign authority is not derived, as in Raz, from a concept of authority that stands outside our practices, but is worked up from the conceptions of legal authority within our practices. The legal orders of the societies that we tend to group together under labels such as 'the liberal democracies of the West' cannot do without the concept of sovereign authority because these legal orders presume as a constitutional fundamental that there is a source of ultimate legal authority, a parliament. But each parliament in such a liberal democracy must exercise its ultimate authority in ways that maintain its authority.

Thomas Hobbes, the greatest political philosopher to write in English, put forward much the same view in *Leviathan* in 1651.[81] He identified several 'rights' of sovereignty which if the sovereign gives up have the

[79] Martin Loughlin, *Against Constitutionalism* (Cambridge, MA: Harvard University Press, 2022).

[80] For example, John Gardner, *Law as a Leap of Faith* (Oxford: Oxford University Press, 2012) at 24, who accused Ronald Dworkin and Gerald Postema, both of whom work with such a methodology, of creating a 'fundamentally anti-philosophical climate'. See Postema's fine treatment in *Law's Rule: The Nature, Value, and Viability of the Rule of Law* (New York: Oxford University Press, 2022) and the pioneering work of Martin Krygier, for example, 'Well-Tempered Power: "A Cultural Achievement of Universal Significance"' (2024) 16 *Hague Journal on the Rule of Law* 479.

[81] Thomas Hobbes, *Leviathan* (Cambridge: Cambridge University Press, 2014).

effect of making the sovereign no longer sovereign. For that reason he advocated that one should treat any sovereign act that seems to give up sovereignty as void.[82] That is more or less what UK judges do when they encounter an ouster clause. Because such a clause, in purporting to remove the authority of judges to check that the officials are acting legally, removes any check on the officials' authority, judges must do something in order to *preserve* Parliament's authority. They do not declare the provision that contains the ouster clause invalid, but rather find ways to explain why the clause is 'inoperable or void in the sense of being empty any practical legal effect'.[83]

The last quotation comes from the leading work on Dicey's constitutional thought by the Canadian public law scholar Mark Walters, who is suggesting here the solution Dicey should have offered, based on his constitutional theory, to the paradox of sovereignty. But, as I just indicated, it is not so much a solution to the paradox as a dissolution of it. Helpful is another observation from Walters's book, that Dicey's blue-eyed baby passage has been misconstrued since his point was that 'Parliament *could not make* such a law'.[84] He explains:

> It could not make such a law because of certain limits inherent within the very nature of parliamentary sovereignty and sovereign authority generally. As Stephen stated earlier in the passage quoted by Dicey, it could not make such a law 'because the legislature is the product of a certain social condition'. This was Stephen's main point and the reason why Dicey quoted the passage.[85]

Thus, when Dicey followed Stephen he was gesturing at the basis of the constitutional fundamentals, nothing more, but also nothing less than, as we saw Bingham say, that the fundamentals have been 'accepted as such by judges and others officially concerned in the operation of our constitutional system'.[86]

I recognize that the idea that 'the legislature is the product of a certain social condition' is rather vague. But in the context of this chapter and of my discussions more generally of parliamentary sovereignty and the rule of law, I can give it content by drawing on Ernst Fraenkel's astute analysis

[82] Ibid, chapter 18 at 127.

[83] Mark Walters, *A V Dicey and the Common Law Constitutional Tradition: 'A Legal Turn of Mind'* (Cambridge: Cambridge University Press, 2020) at 294.

[84] Ibid at 203. His emphasis.

[85] Ibid. Footnotes omitted. His emphasis.

[86] Bingham, *The Rule of Law*, at 167.

of the Nazi state. In *The Dual State*, Fraenkel argued that the Nazi state was a 'Dual State' which consisted of two states that existed side by side. On the one side was the 'normative state', which contained whatever remained of the law and institutions of the Weimar legal order together with the statutory regimes enacted after 1933 and implemented through those institutions. On the other side was the 'prerogative state', which consisted of the apparatus of the Nazi Party wherein the leader's will (his actual will or his will as interpreted by subordinate officials) was the ultimate source of authority.[87] Fraenkel observed that the law of the normative state governed its subjects only as long as officials in the prerogative state did not find such government inconvenient. Put positively, a Nazi official could override the law or the institutions of the normative state whenever this was thought to be in the interests of the Nazi Party.

Fraenkel contrasted the Dual State with what we can think of as the 'Rule-of-Law State', which he took to be a state in which all official action is subject to law, the officials are answerable for their actions before the ordinary courts, and the law to which they are answerable includes both the positive law that authorizes their actions and legal principles embedded in the law protective of individual rights.[88] He concluded that the rule of law did not obtain in Nazi Germany because the protections of the normative state were subject to the discretion of Nazi officials in the prerogative state.[89]

The Rule-of-Law State is at one end of the continuum of legality. As long as a state is on that continuum, those who are subject to its law will be part of a 'jural community' – the community of legal subjects bound together by law. These bonds are in the first place constituted by the enacted or positive law made by the state. However, they are also constituted by fundamental legal principles, both the principles of the rule of law that will be found in any state committed to governing in accordance with law and the particular principles that the state has committed to over time. To the extent that the state chooses to violate these principles, it will both undermine the bonds and move the state closer to the other end of the continuum, until the point where it falls right off, as Fraenkel argued the Dual State did.

[87] Ernest Fraenkel, *The Dual State: A Contribution to the Theory of Dictatorship* [1941], 2nd edition (Oxford: Oxford University Press, 2017).

[88] Ibid at 156.

[89] Ibid at 70–71.

It is important to know that Fraenkel's book is based on a particularly rich experience, his legal practice in Berlin from 1933 to 1938, which he was permitted to do despite being Jewish (and socialist) because of his frontline service in the First World War.[90] In his Preface to the 1974 German edition of *The Dual State*, Fraenkel said that in the final phase of his legal practice in Berlin he frequently described his work to friends as that of a 'switchman'.

> That is, I regarded it an essential part of my efforts to ensure that a given case was dealt with under the auspices of the 'normative state', and not end up in the 'prerogative state'. Colleagues with whom I was on friendly terms confirmed that they, too, had repeatedly worked towards making sure that their clients were punished in a court of law.[91]

The metaphor is stark of the railway switchman desperately trying to keep his client on the train on the legal track where the possible destinations are known and either welcome or tolerable because the prerogative track leads to somewhere unknowable except for the fact that the journey will be cruel and the destination more than likely fatal. Moreover, from what is known about the detail of Fraenkel's legal victories, Douglas Morris has suggested that they did not depend on the residual legal rights available within the normative state. Rather, they depended entirely on the effective use of legal procedures to Fraenkel's clients' advantage in cases in which judges were not subject to direct pressure from officials in the prerogative state or were prepared to try to resist such pressure and do their jobs.[92] This was all that was possible because the 'always cramped space' of the normative state contracted as the Nazi grip on power increased until the point when 'the normative state meant not the rule of law but the technical administration of the law'.[93] So even the legal track offered a rather shaky ride.

In the context of a Dual State, then, it is not possible to be a human rights lawyer – to belong to the group of lawyers committed above all to trying to vindicate the rights of their clients using whatever resources their legal order offers, even in the face of those parts of the enacted law that either altogether explicitly deny them rights or that make it

[90] See Douglas G Morris, *Legal Sabotage: Ernst Fraenkel in Hitler's Germany* (Cambridge: Cambridge University Press, 2020).

[91] Fraenkel, *The Dual State*, at xix.

[92] Douglas G Morris, 'The Dual State Reframed: Ernst Fraenkel's Political Clients and His Theory of the Nazi Legal System' (2013) 58 *Leo Baeck Institute Year Book* 5.

[93] Ibid at 5 and 19.

procedurally difficult, even apparently impossible to vindicate the rights which the law does offer them. In short, the Dual State does not offer an arena of legality in which such lawyers can make arguments on behalf of their clients.

It is easy to see how in the dramatic circumstances of a Dual State, the change from legal order to prerogative order is also a change in the social condition. Indeed, in a state where people are subject to rule by executive order and deprived of the resources that in a Rule-of-Law State allow one to hold officials to account, not only the social condition has radically changed, but there is no longer rule by a legislature that is the 'product' of the old social condition. Now I am not claiming that the Rwanda Act would by itself have turned the UK into a Dual State. But it did create a pocket of virtual lawlessness within the legal order – a space in which those subject to the state's power would be deprived of the right to contest exercises of that power. The common good lawyers' arguments analysed in Chapter 3 to the effect that this pocket should have been made almost completely lawless are part of their project of changing the order and the social condition of the UK to the point where the executive can promulgate their conception of the common good. The successful introduction of such a pocket into the legal order does not, then, create a prerogative state. But it allows for a mode of exercising prerogative power that puts a Rule-of-Law State onto the Dual State path.[94]

Once we can see why a Rule-of-Law State and a certain range of social conditions are dependent on each other, we can also appreciate why it was unproblematic for Bingham, as I pointed out in the preceding chapter, to forward a circular argument, saying in effect that the principle of parliamentary sovereignty is accepted because it is accepted. For circularity can be a virtue, as we can see by resorting yet again to Walters, this time in an essay on the idea of the 'unwritten constitution'. There, Walters makes a useful distinction between 'linear' and 'circular' theories of law.[95] Linear theories assume 'that the authority of legal norms can be traced back along a line of increasingly higher norms until

[94] It is telling that Fraenkel's analysis of the Dual State is now considered relevant to developments in Trump's US. See Amanda Taub, 'The Frightening Precedents for Trump's "Legal Abyss": The "Dual-State Theory" Explains How Authoritarians Bend the Law to Their Will' (May 3 2024) online: *New York Times* <www.nytimes.com/2025/05/03/world/trump-dual-state.html?searchResultPosition=1>.

[95] Mark Walters, 'The Unwritten Constitution as a Legal Concept' in David Dyzenhaus and Malcolm Thorburn, eds, *Philosophical Foundations of Constitutional Law* (Oxford: Oxford University Press, 2016) 33.

an originating source is located. Law from this perspective is held up by a string, and someone or something must hold the end of that string'.[96] Circular theories, in contrast, 'do not need to address the problem of infinite regress': 'Law from this perspective is embedded within a network of interlocking strands of normative value that bend back upon themselves never reaching an end. The relevant image on this account is not a string but a web of strings shaped into a globe or sphere.'[97]

Stephen in fact put forward just such a theory in the pages that precede the blue-eyed baby passage. Like Hart many years later, he emphasized that law cannot be understood solely in terms of coercion since 'coercion itself is only possible by virtue of the co-operation which implies the existence of every other social motive'.[98] He continued: 'We may say of any stone in an arch that it is the keystone, if by abstracting it the arch would fall into ruin, and coercion is in that sense a keystone in the social structure; but so are all the other forces which are essential to the structure as soon as it attains any permanence or magnitude'.[99] That insight led him to observe of constitutions that '[i]n reality, . . . the power of making a constitution presupposes a readiness to act together and accept certain rules as binding, and thus again implies a whole set of established customs, such as are necessary to the constitution and authority of a representative body'.[100] And that observation in turn prepared the way for the real point of the blue-eyed baby passage, which in Stephen's book follows directly after these lines:

> Lawyers are apt to speak as though the legislature were omnipotent, as they do not require to go beyond its decisions. It is, of course, omnipotent in the sense that it can make whatever laws it pleases, inasmuch as a law means any rule made by the legislature. But from the scientific point of view, the power of the legislature is of course strictly limited. It is limited so to speak, both from within and without; from within, because the legislature is the product of a certain social condition, and determined by whatever determines the society; and from without, because the power of imposing laws is dependent upon the instinct of subordination, which is itself limited.[101]

[96] Ibid.

[97] Ibid at 2.

[98] Leslie Stephen, *The Science of Ethics* (London: Smith, Elder, & Co, 1882) at 142.

[99] Ibid.

[100] Ibid at 143.

[101] Ibid.

The command theory of law is obviously a linear theory since it presupposes the legally unlimited sovereign at the apex of the legal hierarchy. That puts the sovereign not only outside of the law, but also outside of the 'social condition' of the time. In fact, Bentham – a radical reformer – was clear that this was his aim. In his hands, the command theory of law was intended as an instrument that would take a wrecking ball to the traditions that sustained the elites of his day who were holding back social reform.

More to the point of the main theme of my book is that the command theory of law is the legal theory of the common good lawyers, though they add a significant twist to it. Recall that Bentham and Austin designed the command theory of law as the legal theory of parliamentary sovereignty. By contrast, the common good lawyers' theory is only a pretend theory of parliamentary sovereignty. Indeed, it is only a pretend *legal* theory. As we have seen, Lord Atkin's accusation in his dissent in *Liversidge* that his fellow judges were 'more executive minded than the executive' and Lord Shaw's in *Halliday* that to allow the detention regulation to stand was to revolutionize the constitution are just as accurately levelled at the common good lawyers and their allies in the House of Lords and in the right-wing media. Their command theory is a theory that makes the executive the uncommanded commander of the society, so that the person at its head can 'promulgate the common good',[102] a good which requires taking a wrecking ball to the 'social condition' of the UK – to the very tradition of constitutional government to which they so constantly proclaim their fidelity.

I remarked at the end of Chapter 3 that because the Rwanda Act targeted perhaps the most vulnerable group in any society, non-citizens with a precarious claim to have any more rights than the mere right to make an asylum claim, it might seem that even if the Act had been implemented, while the rule of law would have been subverted, democracy was not at stake. That is, the individuals harmed were as far removed from the status of citizen as it is possible to be. But, as I also remarked, one need only look, first, across the Atlantic to the US to see how removing the rights of less vulnerable groups is always a process which begins with targeting the most vulnerable but continues until one gets to the point of declaring the citizens one doesn't like the internal 'enemy' who don't deserve the law's protection. And then one can look, second, at

[102] 'The Common Good Project' online: *The University of Oxford* <www.law.ox.ac.uk/the-common-good-project/common-good-project>.

the rhetoric of Conservative Party, the Reform Party and some of the leaders of Blue Labour to see what the Rwanda Act presaged for the UK if the far right come to power. This is not a novel danger.

In the nineteenth century, Governor Edward Eyre, the British governor of Jamaica, declared martial law in one area to deal with a rebellion, and among other brutal acts kidnapped a politician and rendered him to that area so that he could be executed after a show trial. In reaction, John Stuart Mill and others formed the Jamaica Committee, an effort to bring Eyre and two of his officials to justice in the UK. Mill, at that time a member of Parliament, and his allies failed for complex reasons. The point I want to take from this episode is that Mill and his allies, while concerned about what Eyre had done in Jamaica, also saw clearly that if the rule of law were not asserted for colonial rule, Eyre's tactics could come to be seen as legitimate for the state in dealing with political opposition within the UK.[103]

More recently, in the wake of the terrorist attacks on the US of 11 September 2001, many countries adopted legislation with special legal regimes for suspected terrorists that created severe problems for the rule of law on any conception.[104] Quite apart from these problems, there was a justified fear that these regimes might affect the way the state decided to deal with very different problems. As one of my colleagues perceptively put it at that time, we need 'to attend to the law's role in producing the alien within'.[105] For if we do not so attend, if our state uses law to render the most vulnerable – the 'aliens' or asylum seekers – rightless so that they can be dealt with as the executive pleases, the rule of law is undermined in a way that will inevitably lead to undermining the constitutional order of democracy.

The sovereignty of Parliament which the UK-based common good lawyers have made their mantra is not the Parliament as it has been conceived by the great authorities in the constitutional tradition these lawyers purport to uphold. Important as Lord Bingham was, he is in a

[103] For a wonderful account, see RW Kostal, *A Jurisprudence of Power: Victorian Empire and the Rule of Law* (Oxford: Oxford University Press, 2005). See also my response to Kostal: David Dyzenhaus, 'The Puzzle of Martial Law' (2009) 59 *University of Toronto Law Journal* 1.

[104] David Dyzenhaus, *The Constitution of Law: Legality in a Time of Emergency* (Cambridge: Cambridge University Press, 2006).

[105] Audrey Macklin, 'Borderline Security' in Kent Roach, Ron Daniels, and Patrick Macklem, eds, *The Security of Freedom: Essays on Canada's Anti-Terrorism Bill* (Toronto: University of Toronto Press, 2001) 383 at 398.

long line of succession from Sir Edward Coke (1552–1634), Sir William Blackstone (1723–1780) through to Dicey. There are of course differences between the figures within the tradition, but its guiding theme is summed up in the title of a book by its foremost post-war exponent, Trevor Allan, *The Sovereignty of Law: Freedom, Constitution, and Common Law*.[106]

When I introduced Dicey in Chapter 2, I pointed to his description of the '[t]wo features' which have 'at all times since the Norman Conquest characterised the political institutions of England'. The first is the 'omnipotence or undisputed supremacy throughout the whole country of the central government', while the second, 'closely connected with the first, is the rule or supremacy of law'.[107] I emphasized the double occurrence of 'supremacy' – the fact that Dicey first talks about the 'undisputed supremacy ... of the central government', not of Parliament. It suggests that parliamentary sovereignty is equated with the supremacy of law over all state action and there is a vision driving his picture of the UK constitutional order as one of government according to law. As the ultimate source of law, Parliament has the most important role in this constitutional structure. But the thing to emphasize is that it is a role *within* a structure, the *legal* structure of the UK constitutional order. And so, as I said, difficult questions arise if Parliament does something that appears to damage the structure by enacting a law that undermines the constitution.

It has taken from Chapter 2 to this chapter to vindicate my claim that the Rwanda Act is just such a law, as vivid an example as Stephen's blue-eyed baby statute. I have thus completed the task of showing that, while the common good lawyers make their arguments in the language of the law, they have a troubled relationship with the law and the legal authorities they claim as the basis for these arguments. And so now I have the support I needed for my conclusion, first, that their arguments are a kind of camouflage for their political agenda and, second, that their political agenda has itself a troubled relationship with the rule of law. Indeed, the 'ancient constitution' they often claim to be in the business of restoring is

[106] Trevor Allan, *The Sovereignty of Law: Freedom, Constitution, and Common Law* (Oxford: Oxford University Press, 2013). For an astonishing attempt by a common good lawyer to assimilate Allan's liberal theory of the rule of law into the agenda of the Common Good Project, see Michael Foran, 'Common Law and the Common Good' in Geneviève Cartier and Mark D Walters, eds, *The Promise of Legality: Critical Reflections on the Work of TRS Allan* (Oxford: Hart Publishing, 2025) 197.

[107] Ibid at 107.

in reality a new kind of order, one with only a tenuous claim to be a constitutional order. The Judicial Power Project turns out to be just a vehicle for the Common Good Project. I now turn to showing how the political agenda is to put in place a state that will enforce 'the natural law', understood as the moral virtues as portrayed in their illiberal distortion of what they misleadingly refer to as the 'classical tradition'.

6

The Political Theology of the Parallel Universe

> A tyranny devoted to pernicious ends has no self-sufficient *reason* to submit itself to the discipline of operating consistently through the demanding processes of law, granted that the rational point of such self-discipline is the very value of reciprocity, fairness, and respect for persons which the tyrant, *ex hypothesi*, holds in contempt.[1]

My epigraph contains the best short account I know of why a tyrant will avoid submitting itself to the rule of law. The reason is simply that the ideologies of tyrannical regimes – their conceptions of the 'common good' – are incompatible with 'the demanding processes of law'. Its author is John Finnis and I will now proceed to show why his conception of the common good, and more generally the conception in 'common good constitutionalism', amount to just such an ideology.

In Chapters 3 and 4, I spent some time on Richard Ekins's Atkin Lecture, 'Human Rights and the Rule of Law', a talk he gave during the time the Rwanda Bill was before Parliament.[2] I suggested that rather than regard the lecture as a 'tour de force' – Lord Wolfson's description in his fulsome Foreword to it – we should regard it as a tour of someone who dwells in a parallel universe, a world akin to the one we live in, yet also distinct because it operates according to some different fundamental laws. In this, my final chapter, I will set out, to the extent possible, the constitution of that universe.

Those who dwell in it sometimes like to describe it as 'the political constitution'. Recall that Ekins defended himself against the charge of accusing judges of being 'enemies of the people' in their decisions during the Brexit saga by saying that he didn't

1 John Finnis, *Natural Law and Natural Rights* (Oxford: Clarendon Press, 1980) at 273. His emphasis.

2 Richard Ekins, 'Human Rights and the Rule of Law' (Apr 17 2024) online: *Policy Exchange* <https://policyexchange.org.uk/wp-content/uploads/Human-Rights-and-the-Rule-of-Law.pdf>.

> mean that the judges aren't engaged with legal reasons or doing their best to adjudicate the case before them. Of course not. But I think that the choices, the decisions that have been made in both those cases, especially in the second, ... do involve legal reasoning and an approach to high profile, clearly as they were, constitutional controversies that is incompatible with long settled constitutional law and does encourage politicization of litigation and an undermining of the techniques of the political constitution, which the law has otherwise been pretty careful to protect.[3]

However, the common good lawyers' ideology is not really constitutional in any legal sense. Rather, it is a 'political theology', a set of religious doctrines weaponized for political ends in a still largely secular era in which one must make pacts with allies not from one's faith community.

I can only set out the content to some extent for a reason I mentioned in the Introduction and elaborated in Chapter 1. Answers about the content of the ideology of common good advocates, including the common good lawyers of the Judicial Power Project, are hard to come by. They are mostly vague about it and define it negatively, against what one can broadly describe as liberalism. I thus suggested the label for them of 'negatively prescriptive theorists' to convey that their ideology is for the most part an 'anything-but' one, in their case anything-but-liberalism. This is a label I settled on in past work on German legal and political thought of the 1920s and 1930s to describe Carl Schmitt, the German authoritarian political and legal theorist who is hugely influential today.[4]

The task of elaborating the content is made even more difficult by several other factors. For one thing, unlike Harvard Law professor Adrian Vermeule, their main US collaborator in the Common Good Project they share, the UK common good lawyers are not as forthcoming as Vermeule about the content of their ideology. Indeed, Vermeule is a bit of an outlier even among the right-wing academic ideologues in the US in the extent to which he is prepared to reveal both his debt to Schmitt and his 'integralist' vision of the duty of the state coercively to impose a reactionary ideology, allegedly derived from the Catholic natural law tradition, on

[3] Ken Macdonald and Tim Owen, 'Double Jeopardy: The Law and Politics Podcast – Episode 29: Richard Ekins – Judges and Political Power' (May 2 2023) online: *Apple Podcasts* <https://podcasts.apple.com/de/podcast/episode-29-richard-ekins-judges-and-political-power/id1633485236?i=1000611450876&l=en-GB>.

[4] David Dyzenhaus, 'The Politics of the Question of Constituent Power' in Martin Loughlin and Neil Walker, eds, *The Paradox of Constitutionalism: Constituent Power and Constitutional Form* (Oxford: Oxford University Press, 2007) 129 at 130–34.

society.[5] Moreover, there is no evidence that John Finnis, the main common good lawyer in the UK, has ever read Schmitt. Finally, Richard Ekins has featured so prominently in these pages because of his leading role in the Judicial Power Project since it was founded in 2015. But unlike Finnis he does not express political positions on the culture war issues such as abortion, immigration and the way in which Muslim immigrants are producing children at a rate that will swamp the local population, same-sex marriage, sexual relations between consenting male adults, and so on. Rather, he and his co-authors for the Judicial Power Project provide the arguments that will clear the way for an executive to promulgate and enforce policies on such issues, unhindered by judges, lawyers and human rights commitments in both domestic and international law.

Recall that the Judicial Power Project is the legal face of the political Common Good Project. As Chapters 2–5 show, its lawyers make their arguments in the language of the law not in the language of politics. Indeed, they like to accuse their opponents of making political arguments because of these lawyers' commitments to human rights and international law – to, as we have seen, a thick or substantive conception of the rule of law. They also claim that they themselves adopt the thin conception of the rule of law, one based on a politically neutral consensus about the rule of law which is true to the ancient constitution. But, as we have seen, the thin conception of the rule of law is neither thin nor apolitical nor true to the UK constitutional tradition. Rather, it is a stripped-down version of the thin conception. It requires only that law be used as a blunt instrument of rule to pass in clear terms legally unlimited power to the executive so that the executive can 'promulgate the common good'. And as we will see in this chapter, this is the common good according to 'the natural law', in some sense the thickest conception of the rule of law on offer, but in fact a political theology antithetical not only to liberalism, but also to democracy and the rule of law.[6]

[5] See Matt Sleat, *Post-Liberalism* (Cambridge: Polity, 2026) and Laura K Field, *Furious Minds: The Making of the MAGA New Right* (Princeton, NJ: Princeton University Press, 2025). For a critique from within Catholicism, see Jason Blakely, 'The Integralism of Adrian Vermeule: Not Catholic Enough' (Oct 5 2020) online: *Commonweal* <www.commonwealmagazine.org/not-catholic-enough>. Blakely ends his essay with: 'Until Vermeule reckons with Catholic teachings he finds inconvenient, his "Catholic integralism" will lack theoretical integrity and should not be described as Catholic. I'll leave it to others to decide what description might be more fitting'.

[6] See Richard Ekins, 'Political Polarization and the Rule of Law' (2025) 19 *Law & Ethics of Human Rights* 201 in which he sanctimoniously characterizes his and the Judicial Power

For this reason, a return to my observations about Schmitt in the Introduction and Chapter 1 is easy to justify. Schmitt is relevant not only because he is a direct influence on Vermeule, but also because he, better than anyone else in the twentieth century, set out the logic of the 'legal' (in substance anti-legal) argument often deployed by the common good lawyers, arguments that depend on inaccurate and misleading claims about the law. Moreover, Schmitt was hardly the first to come up with such an argument. Well before Schmitt in the twentieth and Vermeule in the twenty-first century argued that the head of the executive is the true guardian of the constitution when it comes to decisions on existentially important matters, the English barrister W. F. Finlason put forward the same argument in several publications during the Jamaica controversy about the rule of law in the control of the British Empire briefly sketched at the end of the last chapter.[7] It is, that is, the logic of the argument one will adopt if one wants to destroy the rule of law from within. It is also the kind of argument that one will come up with if one wishes to put in place a secular basis for an anything-but-liberalism ideology.

Besides these considerations, there is the genealogical link between Schmitt and Finnis through Eric Voegelin, the other German authoritarian thinker I mentioned in the Introduction and Chapter 1. As I pointed out, Voegelin adopted Schmitt's legal theory wholesale in 1936 in a book in support of the fascist Austrian state established by Engelbert Dolfuss in 1934 in his bid to crush both the Nazi Party and the socialists of 'Red Vienna'.[8] That link is most important because it is not merely genealogical, as I will show through my focus on Finnis.

I remarked in the Introduction that Finnis remains the most politically influential legal scholar of the post-war period. He may well be eclipsed in this century by Vermeule, if Vermeule assumes the role of 'crown jurist' to Trump or later to J. D. Vance, the equivalent to the role that

Project's attempts to politicize and undermine the rule of law as an attempt to save it and to prevent polarization. Astonishingly, he clearly believes his own rhetoric, hence the tone.

7 For example, WF Finlason, *A Treatise on Martial Law: As Allowed in Time of Rebellion; with Practical Illustrations Drawn from the Official Documents in the Jamaica Case and the Evidence Taken by the Royal Commission of Enquiry with Comments, Constitutional and Legal* (London: Stevens & Sons, 1866). For discussion, David Dyzenhaus, 'The Puzzle of Martial Law' (2009) 59 *University of Toronto Law Journal* 1.

8 Eric Voegelin, *The Authoritarian State: An Essay on the Problem of the Austrian State* [1936] (Columbia: University of Missouri Press, 1989) volume 4 of *Collected Works*. See also David Dyzenhaus, '"Immanentizing the Eschaton" Eric Voegelin, Hans Kelsen, and the Debate over Secular Religion' in Sander Verhaegh, ed, *American Philosophy and the Intellectual Migration* (Berlin: De Gruyter, 2025) 279.

Schmitt sought and got after 1933. But as Matt Sleat effectively shows in *Post-Liberalism*, in general the common good advocates in the US seem to be happy to inveigh against liberalism as if the ideas of a few figures are somehow responsible for all the ills of the world neoliberalism created, without much evidence that they themselves have engaged with the leading texts of liberal political philosophy.[9]

Finnis, in contrast, as I remarked in the Introduction, is a brilliant scholar, of great depth and range, one of the founders of 'new natural law theory'. As a result, close attention to his work best displays the tensions in the Common Good Project. There is, however, one important distinction to keep in mind between Schmitt and Voegelin in their view of the justification for the state's right to enforce some illiberal ideology on those subject to its power. While Schmitt thought that it was enough for justification that the ideology is sufficiently illiberal, Voegelin suggested that the ideology correspond with 'transcendent' truth, with 'transcendence' apparently coming from some unspecified Christian theology. But I will show that in debate about this distinction, Schmitt has the better argument because in the modern world, the debate must take place on what I call the 'secular plateau'.

This is the terrain where you cannot count on all your allies accepting that your truth as to religious beliefs is true also for them. Indeed, you cannot count on them having any view as to religious truth, perhaps even, as is quite commonly the case in the modern age, rejecting any idea that there could be such a truth, at least one that can be asserted as the basis for a state-imposed religion. Since I can meet Finnis and other common good advocates on the secular plateau – the terrain on which they are compelled to argue by the world in which we all live – I will make no attempt to engage in arguments internal to Christian theology.

Indeed, if it were necessary to so engage, I would have to recuse myself since I have no competence in this area. I will, however, call attention briefly to the fact that Finnis's interpretation of the Catholic natural law tradition is far from uncontroversial within his faith community, and even within the much smaller community of those arguing for revising our practices in light of teachings based on the integralist view of the Catholic natural law tradition.[10]

[9] Sleat, *Post-Liberalism*.

[10] See Brian McCall, '"What Good Is John Finnis?" Assessing the Personal and Common Good in *Natural Law and Natural Rights*' (2020) 83 *Persona y Derecho* 637. See also Brian McCall, *The Architecture of Law: Rebuilding Law in the Critical Tradition* (Notre Dame,

It is worth noting that Finnis has been working in this tradition for many years, and is regarded as a or the lead thinker in it. But Finnis has never as far as I know referred to Vermeule, and the latter refers to Finnis only once in his *Common Good Constitutionalism*, and not only is his reference entirely perfunctory, but also he did not see fit to place Finnis on his list of 'essential treatments of natural law'.[11] For Vermeule and his fellow 'integralists', Finnis is far too liberal since he will not endorse the state's use of law to enforce his religious beliefs on others. But, as we will see later, this feature marks little or no difference between Finnis and the integralists because the religious beliefs that at least some integralists would want the state to use coercion to impose on all can always be imposed in Finnis's position under the guise of being required to maintain peace, order and 'public morals'.[12]

When push comes to shove, it seems clear that when it comes to the division within the Catholic faith, it is not so much between Finnis and Vermeule but between, on the one side, Catholics who have made their peace with or fully accept liberalism and democracy and, on the other, the anti-liberals like Vermeule and Finnis. Just one telling example is the contrast between Finnis's hostility to immigrants, about which we will see

IN: University of Notre Dame Press, 2018). In an earlier work, McCall advocated among other measures prohibiting women from wearing trousers as only skirts are sufficiently modest. Brian McCall, *Building the City of God: Living as Catholics in a Secular Age* (New York: Angelico Press, 2014) at 70–71. However, he also says, at 71, that 'the softness of the femininity is underscored by the flowing nature of a skirt with its fluid movement', which conjures up a rather different image of men drawn to the movement of what lies beneath. In the last chapter, 'Politics: Life of the Perfect Society', he argues for reconstituting the family, politics and the economy under the 'source of all law and justice. Christ the King'. See ibid at 276.

The leading philosophical voice in integralism is Thomas Pink, who advances the peculiar position that the state should be involved in enforcing Catholic doctrine, but only on the baptized. See Thomas Pink, 'The Right to Religious Liberty and the Coercion of Belief: A Note on *Dignitatis Humanae*' in John Keown and Robert P George, eds, *Reason, Morality, and Law: The Philosophy of John Finnis* (Oxford: Oxford University Press, 2013) 427. Pink's view of Finnis's work on Catholic doctrine is perhaps indicated by the astonishing feat in this chapter, in a volume of essays in honour of Finnis, of not deigning to mention Finnis.

11 Adrian Vermeule, *Common Good Constitutionalism* (Cambridge: Polity, 2022) at 188 note 10. The perfunctory reference is at 200, note 115. Note that McCall's *The Architecture of Law* is on Vermeule's list and it contains the same intemperate attack on Finnis as his 'What Good Is John Finnis?'

12 For an excellent account of these debates, see Kevin Vallier, *All the Kingdoms of the World – On Radical Religious Alternatives to Liberalism* (New York: Oxford University Press, 2023).

much in this chapter, and the words of the late Pope this year in his 'Letter of the Holy Father Francis to the Bishops of the United States of America'.[13]

Francis was speaking to the mass deportation programme that the Trump administration is currently undertaking not only illegally but also in defiance of the lower courts, and his words were understood to be a direct rebuke to J. D. Vance's fatuous attempt to justify Trump's inhumanity on the basis of Catholic doctrine.[14] But the late Pope's words are just as apt for the Rwanda Act, which in one respect was even worse than Trump's programme since it gave the veneer of legality to mass deportation in a way that violated both of the UK's constitutional fundamentals of parliamentary sovereignty and the rule of law. He said in part:

> I have followed closely the major crisis that is taking place in the United States with the initiation of a program of mass deportations. The rightly formed conscience cannot fail to make a critical judgment and express its disagreement with any measure that tacitly or explicitly identifies the illegal status of some migrants with criminality. At the same time, one must recognize the right of a nation to defend itself and keep communities safe from those who have committed violent or serious crimes while in the country or prior to arrival. That said, the act of deporting people who in many cases have left their own land for reasons of extreme poverty, insecurity, exploitation, persecution or serious deterioration of the environment, damages the dignity of many men and women, and of entire families, and places them in a state of particular vulnerability and defenselessness.
>
> This is not a minor issue: an authentic rule of law is verified precisely in the dignified treatment that all people deserve, especially the poorest and most marginalized. The true common good is promoted when society and government, with creativity and strict respect for the rights of all – as I have affirmed on numerous occasions – welcomes, protects, promotes and integrates the most fragile, unprotected and vulnerable. This does not impede the development of a policy that regulates orderly and legal migration. However, this development cannot come about through the privilege of some and the sacrifice of others. What is built on the basis of

13 Pope Francis, 'Letter of the Holy Father Francis to the Bishops of the United States of America' (Feb 10 2025) online: *Vatican* <www.vatican.va/content/francesco/en/letters/2025/documents/20250210-lettera-vescovi-usa.html>.

14 Jan-Werner Müller, 'What Did Pope Francis Think of JD Vance? His View Was more than Clear' (Apr 23 2025) online: *The Guardian* <www.theguardian.com/commentisfree/2025/apr/23/pope-francis-jd-vance-meeting>.

> force, and not on the truth about the equal dignity of every human being, begins badly and will end badly.
>
> Christians know very well that it is only by affirming the infinite dignity of all that our own identity as persons and as communities reaches its maturity. Christian love is not a concentric expansion of interests that little by little extend to other persons and groups. In other words: the human person is not a mere individual, relatively expansive, with some philanthropic feelings! The human person is a subject with dignity who, through the constitutive relationship with all, especially with the poorest, can gradually mature in his identity and vocation. The true *ordo amoris*[15] that must be promoted is that which we discover by meditating constantly on the parable of the 'Good Samaritan' (cf. *Lk* 10:25–37), that is, by meditating on the love that builds a fraternity open to all, without exception.

6.1 The Politics of the Judicial Power Project

My claim about the genealogical link between Finnis and Voegelin is not based on extensive discussions of Voegelin in Finnis's work. There are only six references to Voegelin in *Natural Law and Natural Rights*,[16] Finnis's major contribution to philosophy of law, and thirteen in the five volumes of Finnis's collected essays. None of these is substantial other than in an essay of 1971, 'Revolutions and Continuity of Law',[17] and in one of 2009, 'Hart as a Political Philosopher'. The second is his attack on H. L. A. Hart, Finnis's former supervisor in Oxford, and the leading English philosopher of law of his time.[18]

Similarly, in the volume of twenty-seven essays published in honour of Finnis in 2013, a volume in which some of the leading scholars of our

[15] At this point, Francis was responding directly to JD Vance, who had sought to justify the programme in an interview with Sean Hannity, Trump's main alt-right media booster, that it is a 'Christian concept', by saying that it is located in the idea of *ordo amoris*, or right ordering of love, that 'love and compassion start with family, then extend to neighbours, then nation, and, last and least, reach fellow human beings as such'. See Müller, 'What Did Pope Francis Think of JD Vance?' For an argument to similar effect in Finnis, see his 'Migration Rights' in John Finnis, *Human Rights and the Common Good: Collected Essays Volume III* (Oxford: Oxford University Press, 2011)116 at 118–19.

[16] Finnis, *Natural Law and Natural Rights.*

[17] John Finnis, 'Revolutions and Continuity of Law' reprinted in *Philosophy of Law: Collected Essays Volume IV* (Oxford: Oxford University Press, 2011) 407.

[18] John Finnis, 'Hart as a Political Philosopher' in *Philosophy of Law: Collected Essays Volume IV* 257 at 278.

time paid tribute to his contribution,[19] 'Voegelin' does not appear in the index, an omission not only of a name, but also a sign of the authors' lack of interest in, indeed even acknowledgement of, Finnis's philosophy of history – his understanding both of the relationship between politics, religion and community in the modern era and of the role of history in political and moral argument. The only attention to something like Finnis's thought in this regard is Richard Ekins's contribution, 'Constitutional Principle in the Laws of the Commonwealth'.[20] But Ekins did little more than summarize the more legal aspects of Finnis's engagement with history over the years.

The one exception is in Finnis's careful response to the essays in the book, especially to Ekins. There one finds one significant reference to Voegelin's most influential work, *The New Science of Politics*, first published in 1952.[21] There is also for the first time as far as I'm aware in Finnis's vast body of work a short but highly significant discussion of Schmitt, though 'Schmitt' and 'Voegelin' do not appear in the index.[22] Such lack of attention by the scholars who contributed to this volume is remarkable given Finnis's own ample acknowledgement of his debt to Voegelin, though in his attack on Hart he did bury it in a footnote. There he acknowledges in particular the impact on him of *The New Science of Politics*:

> Not long after Hart had asked me to contribute a book to his series, and to call it *Natural Law and Natural Rights*, I read this book and the contemporaneous article on Oxford political philosophers. My book articulates a philosophical theory offering to supply the element missing, as Voegelin's article observes, in virtually all the Oxford political philosophers, the element he named ('The Oxford Political Philosophers' at 103, 109), I think obscurely, 'a science of principles' and 'philosophical anthropology'.[23]

Both this footnote and Finnis's discussion of Schmitt support the argument of a paper that sharply contrasts with the treatment of the twenty-seven other contributors, which I regard as the most insightful analysis

[19] Notably, Joseph Raz, 'Value: A Menu of Questions' and Jeremy Waldron, 'What Is Natural Law Like?' in John Keown and Robert P George, eds, *Reason, Morality, and Law: The Philosophy of John Finnis* (Oxford: Oxford University Press, 2013) 13 and 73.

[20] Ekins, 'Constitutional Principle in the Laws of the Commonwealth' in ibid 396.

[21] Eric Voegelin, *The New Science of Politics* (Chicago: University of Chicago Press, 1952); Finnis, 'Reflections and Responses' in Keown and George, eds, *Reason, Morality, and Law* 459 at 530 and 582–83.

[22] Finnis, 'Reflections and Responses' at 576, 582–83.

[23] Finnis, 'Hart as a Political Philosopher' at 278, note 52. The reference is to Eric Voegelin, 'The Oxford Political Philosophers' (1953) 3 *Philosophical Quarterly* 97.

yet published of Finnis's scholarly trajectory: Coel Kirkby's, 'Abysmal Jurisprudence'.[24] For Voegelin is central to Kirkby's analysis of what we can think of as Finnis's turn to history as a normative resource, as a repository of moral, political and legal value.

The 'abyss' in Kirkby's title refers to the 'abysmal' theory of history that Finnis took from Voegelin, with the abyss, Kirkby says, 'a metaphor for the meaninglessness of our temporal world and its history'.[25] However, as Kirkby points out, Voegelin also argued 'that wise men could access the timeless moral truth that transcended' this messy meaningless world and he shows how Finnis, during a long career, self-consciously took on the role of providing advice to politicians, even acting at times as council to the government, in order to guide them in their service to his understanding of such transcendent truth.[26]

Kirkby thus begins his account with Finnis's lecture – 'Judicial Power: Past, Present and Future' – at the launch of the Judicial Power Project in 2015.[27] The Project, recall, was launched at the initiative of Dean Godson, the director of Policy Exchange, a right-wing think tank. It opened in 2015 with an introductory speech by Michael Gove, then Minister of Justice, who said that he considered the project 'one of the most important pieces of work by any think tank and academic institution in Britain today'. In Chapter 1, I claimed that in retrospect one can see that Gove expressed this view because his government, in addition to Godson, Ekins and Finnis, understood the project as providing the legal inspiration and the arguments for the war against law to come, helped by the lustre imparted by Oxford professors driving the project. While Chapters 3 to 5 of my book now fully support this claim, Kirkby's description of the lecture explains why it was appropriate for the launch of this project, an explanation that is required because without it, the lecture is utterly puzzling.

Take, for example, the podcast with which I began Chapter 3, in which Tim Owen and Ken Macdonald, the two senior human rights lawyers

24 Coel Kirkby, 'Abysmal Jurisprudence: On the Genesis of John Finnis's Practical Guide to Statesmen' (2024) 74 *University of Toronto Law Journal* 119. For the record, I am the editor of this journal. It was subject to our usual rigorous process of anonymized peer review by two well-established scholars.

25 Ibid at 123.

26 Ibid.

27 John Finnis, 'Judicial Power: Past, Present and Future' (Oct 21 2015) online: *Policy Exchange* <https://policyexchange.org.uk/blogs/john-finnis-judicial-power-past-present-and-future/>.

who interviewed Ekins, suggested that Ekins's claim about judges was so out of touch with reality that he must be living in a parallel universe.[28] They began the podcast, as they often do, by asking their interviewee about what brought him to his legal career and in particular about Finnis's influence on him. Ekins responded that Finnis was a 'major intellectual influence on me' and that he had 'benefited from his wisdom and advice on all manner of things across my doctorate and thereafter. And I did speak to him after I decided with Policy Exchange to set up the project. And he gave a barnstorming lecture in October 2015, which we may touch on'.[29]

But Owen and Macdonald clearly could not make head or tail of the lecture despite having read it, as well as other work by Ekins, in preparation for their podcast. They noted that Finnis started with a lot of references to Sir Francis Bacon (1561–1626), a philosopher and lawyer who held high political office during a turbulent political career, including serving as Attorney General.[30] Ekins explained that the references were there because the launch was held in Gray's Inn, one of the four London 'Inns of Court' – professional associations of barristers and judges – of which Bacon was one of the most illustrious members. But Owen and Macdonald were more interested in trying to work out the link between the ten opaque 'theses' Finnis expounded and Ekins's own philosophy, which they characterized as 'quite a sort of ideological set of beliefs', applied by Ekins 'across the board to all the recent developments in what you regard as the development of an impermissible degree of judicial power, which is contrary to your vision of the rule of law and particularly parliamentary sovereignty'. And they wondered both why Finnis appeared so 'disdainful' of judges since he both gave them an essential role in upholding constitutional order and was utterly unclear about the limits of that role, other than suggesting, as they surmised, that the role is 'incredibly narrow and technical'.[31]

Finally, they were curious about the fact that Finnis's lecture could hardly have appeared to what must have been a rather bewildered audience as 'barnstorming', as the kind of low-altitude daring tricks performed by stunt pilots from which the metaphor comes. For Finnis discussed his theses at a very high altitude in relation to a bunch of cases

[28] Macdonald and Owen, 'Double Jeopardy – Richard Ekins'.
[29] Ibid.
[30] Daniel R Coquillette, *Francis Bacon* (Edinburgh: Edinburgh University Press, 1992).
[31] Macdonald and Owen, 'Double Jeopardy – Richard Ekins'.

in a way that made his message more than obscure to his audience, though as Owen noted, he finished as 'a sort of Ignatius Loyola or Karl Marx or Mao Tse Tung of the Judicial Power Project'.[32]

Owen was referring to a call to arms at the end of Finnis's lecture:

> Why, then, is the drift everywhere towards the subjection of legislative power, directly or indirectly, to judicial power? Why do many judges in many jurisdictions ever more confidently give judgments assuming the roles of constitution makers and legislators? Answers must remain speculative; the causes are various. One cause is hidden in that word 'jurisdiction' I used just then when I meant countries, political and civic communities of households, families, people. Discourse in law schools and courts increasingly locates its participants in a universe of standards of correct thought and decision, and of the incorrect and unacceptable, *which are generated and shared among persons who speak as if they were nowhere in particular.* And they can carry on this discourse, and make, commend or recommend the corresponding judicial decisions for whole countries and sets of countries with amazingly little pushback by those whom our constitutions still firmly designate as the makers of the law that shapes its people's future. Why is some pushback in order? Why was and is that historic constitutional distribution of responsibilities sound?[33]

I have emphasized 'which are generated and shared among persons who speak as if they were nowhere in particular' because these words are key to understanding the whole passage – indeed, the whole lecture, but also both the agenda of the Judicial Power Project and how it is driven by the Common Good Project. For the target of all three is the group that Finnis, in a flight of rhetoric with troubling historical resonances, clearly understood as rootless cosmopolitan lawyers – scholars, judges and practising human rights lawyers, who are sapping the strength of the British people.

Because of such flights of rhetoric, Macdonald put it to Ekins that the Judicial Power Project is 'actually a political project as much as a legal philosophical project. In other words, you're all coming from a political ideology, which is familiar also in the United States, in some sections of the Republican Party. And although it is dressed up in legal language, what's really going on here is a political project to rebalance power in the modern democratic state'. Ekins dismissed this criticism as 'unfair'. The lecture, he claimed was

[32] Ibid.

[33] Finnis, 'Judicial Power: Past, Present and Future' at 27–28.

> a very thoughtful reflection on the history and of the common law tradition and the foundations of a proper judicial role in our Constitution. And to that extent, I think it's not ideological. It's a thoughtful exposition of a principled position which has long roots in and cross-party roots, I should add. I thought that it's somehow – and I have heard this line of criticism before, of course – the thought that somehow it's carrying water for the Conservative Party is deeply unfair and just ignorant, I think – not that I'm implying either of you are ignorant – but about the history of our Constitution, in which this is scarcely a recent phenomenon or exclusive to one side of the divide. Clement Attlee would approve, I hope.[34]

In referring to Clement Atlee, who as the UK post-war Labour prime minister was responsible for the legislative reforms that put in place the welfare state, Ekins was attempting to show the commonality between the Judicial Power Project's hostility to judges and the UK, with, as we saw it described in Chapter 3, 'a tradition of dissent' consisting of 'left-leaning scholars ... deeply resentful of what they saw as conservative judges twisting the pliable rules of statutory interpretation to favour the existing order, privileging the rich and the powerful, and defeating the purposes of statutes intended to further the interests of the workers, the homeless, and the least well-off in society'.[35]

However, as I pointed out at the end of the preceding chapter, in contrast to the left tradition's command theory of law, which makes Parliament the uncommanded commander of the society, the common good lawyers opt for the executive, so that the person at its head can 'promulgate the common good'.[36] Consider that Conor Casey and Adrian Vermeule have co-authored a defence of common good constitutionalism, in which one of the charges they claim to rebut is that their ideology promotes 'executive authoritarianism'.[37] 'There is', they say, 'simply no substance to these kinds of arguments'.[38] But they then go on to directly contradict their own assertion:

34 Macdonald and Owen, 'Double Jeopardy – Richard Ekins'.

35 Michael Taggart, 'Prolegomenon to an Intellectual History of Administrative Law: The Case of John Willis and Canadian Administrative Law' (2005) 43 *Osgoode Hall Law Journal* 257.

36 'The Common Good Project' online: *The University of Oxford* <www.law.ox.ac.uk/the-common-good-project/common-good-project>.

37 Conor Casey and Adrian Vermeule, 'Myths of Common Good Constitutionalism' (2022) 45 *Harvard Journal of Law & Public Policy* 104 at 132.

38 Ibid.

> we agree with the premise that – unlike diffuse and procedurally cumbersome legislative assemblies, or low-capacity judicial bodies – hierarchical bureaucracies with very wide regulatory reach, when *commanded by an energetic and motivated political executive*, are better suited to promoting the integration of substantive and valuable moral precepts into legal ordinances. From the perspective of common good constitutionalism, then, a core advantage of *an executive-led separation of powers* above other ways of allocating authority is that it can allow *the executive to better infuse the technocratic work of the administrative state with an explicit political vision oriented to the common good*, aligning its extensive regulatory outputs to goals conducive to this end.[39]

Given that, I do agree with Ekins that to accuse the Judicial Power Project of 'carrying water for the Conservative Party' is 'ignorant'. But it is so only in that the accusation ignores that the project is not performing menial tasks for its masters in the Conservative Party. Rather, it is driving its own agenda through the medium of the Conservative Party – that is, the agenda of the Common Good Project in which 'the ruler' 'promulgates the common good' for a society, with the common good understood by a small group of scholars in elite universities as a kind of weaponized version of Catholicism, a political theology. And if the Reform Party comes to power at the next general election, as the current polls suggest, the fit between its policies and both the ideology of the Common Good Project and the legal 'reforms' the Judicial Power Project proposes will be close to seamless. It is to understand that project and how it operates in combination with the Judicial Power Project that we need to turn to Schmitt and Voegelin.

6.2 Liberalism as 'Gnosticism'

In this regard, Kirkby's account of Finnis's lecture at the launch of the Judicial Power Project goes a long way to solving the puzzle that confronted Macdonald and Owen in their attempt to understand the lecture. Kirkby says:

[39] Ibid at 135. My emphasis. For an effective critique, see Jan-Werner Müller, '"Common Good Constitutionalism": Rule of Law, Rule by Law, or Something Else Entirely?' (2025) 87 *Law and Contemporary Problems* 47. Müller's argument shows that what the common good lawyers are aiming at is 'something else entirely', that is, executive rule. See especially, 63–64.

> In a sweeping history starting with Francis Bacon and Edward Coke, . . . [Finnis] set out his ideal of judicial power within the British constitutional order. Yet Finnis chose to end his story with the *Wheat Case* (1915), a relatively minor decision of the High Court of Australia. In his reading, the majority's decision exemplified the corrupting modern idea of judicial authority as an exclusive and expansive institutional power. He vilified the High Court's decision as 'a judicial mini-*coup d'état*', one of a series of similar judicial cases across the British Empire and its successor states that 'were the rotten foundations of the judicial doctrine of separation of powers'. Finnis claimed that this doctrine was championed by a contemporary cosmopolitan elite – 'persons who speak as if they were nowhere in particular' – to impose their 'universe of standards of correct thought and decision' against the wishes of 'political and civic communities of households, families, people'. These enemies of the people corrupted and expanded judicial power beyond its legitimate function under the rule of law to resolve specific disputes. In so doing, Finnis concluded, the UK Supreme Court was acting on this misconceived notion of judicial power to thwart the will of a national community that was pursuing its common good through Brexit.[40]

Kirkby's focus thereafter is on the way in which Finnis, first, turned to Thomism – to Thomas Aquinas and the Catholic natural law tradition – for inspiration to contest the relentlessly secular legal positivism dominant in Oxford partly due to the towering figure of Hart, his doctoral supervisor. However, such a turn does not suffice in a secular world in which one wishes to intervene in practical politics, and that necessitated Finnis's turn to Voegelin and his philosophy of history. As Kirkby explains, Finnis turned to history 'as the ultimate foundation for his Thomist theory of natural law and as the practical guide for collective political action by conservative Catholics and their allies against their Cold War enemies',[41] which I should clarify means not only the Soviet bloc, but also liberalism, the demon within.

For in *The New Science of Politics* Voegelin argued that the history of ideas in the West should be read as a clash between various 'Gnostic' ideologies, which he defines so as to include liberalism, which is a secularized religion. He took Gnosticism to be the creed that the earthly world is created by an evil lesser god and that only a select few have access to the divine, which they can facilitate bringing to earth through some apocalypse that will allow for creation of a perfect society. On this

40 Ibid at 120.
41 Ibid at 138.

view, Stalinism, Nazism and liberalism are equally Gnostic. All of these, in his most famous claim, seek to 'immanentize the eschaton', to bring about the end times on earth.[42]

Kirkby of course knows of the references to Voegelin that span Finnis's career. But he did not rely on any of these references to make his argument, since he can show that Voegelin's philosophy of history is the inspiration for Finnis's most foundational accounts of the nature of constitutional order. His argument is effective because there is no other way to explain Finnis's body of work other than by invoking the philosophy of history of the figure who was such a constant influence on him. However, my concerns in this book are rather different from Kirkby's. I need to explain the way in which the Common Good Project combines with and underpins the Judicial Power Project – to explain how the anti-legal logic of argument of the first is underpinned by the political theology of the second. I'll start with some context for one of the two substantial quotations from Voegelin in Finnis, in his essay 'Revolutions and Continuity in Law'.

6.3 Finnis: Commander of the British Empire

In Chapter 1, I noted that Finnis was so important in one significant political battle, the executive's battle with Parliament to take the UK out of the European Community, that Conservative Prime Minister Boris Johnson rewarded him in 2019 in the Queen's Birthday Honours, making him a 'Commander of the British Empire'. While a CBE has for the most part lost its connotation of an honour bestowed on someone who did his bit in the age of imperialism, that connotation is, as I suggested, particularly appropriate for Finnis.

His essay 'Revolutions and Continuity in Law' was one of the major interventions in the debates in constitutional theory and philosophy of law sparked in UK law journals by the Rhodesian High Court's decision in *Madzimbamuto v Lardner-Burke*.[43] The question for the Court arose because Ian Smith's white minority government had illegally broken away from Britain in 1965 by issuing a Unilateral Declaration of Independence (UDI), thus asserting Rhodesia's sovereignty. The main purpose of UDI was to maintain a system of racist domination roughly similar to the one across the border in apartheid South Africa.

[42] Voegelin, *The New Science of Politics*, at 119, 166.
[43] *Madzimbamuto v Lardner-Burke* (1968) 2 SA 284 (RAD).

In 1965, Smith's government replaced the old 1961 Constitution. The new Constitution made two major changes. First, it purported to constitute the sitting Rhodesian High Court as the High Court of Rhodesia. Second, it abolished the minimal political safeguards for the black majority in the 1961 Constitution.[44]

In *Madzimbamuto*, the Rhodesian High Court was faced with a challenge to Daniel Madzimbamuto's detention under emergency power regulations. Although he had been initially detained before 1965, his continued detention was under emergency regulations issued under the 1965 Constitution. Madzimbamuto's wife claimed that both the declaration of the state of emergency and the detention order were invalid because the government was illegal. With one dissent, the majority rejected the challenge. Two of the judges in the majority, including Chief Justice Beadle in the main judgment, relied on Hans Kelsen's legal theory.

We have encountered Kelsen a couple of times through his claim that the concept of sovereignty 'should be radically repressed', both because he thought that there is no theoretical need to rely on it and that it is politically pernicious, tied as it is to nasty assertions of nationalism.[45] In Chapter 5, I argued that legal theory can't do without the idea of sovereignty because the constitutional order of a modern legal state requires an institution that has ultimate legal authority. But I also argued that sovereignty is not pernicious as long as it is understood as ultimate *legal* authority, not unlimited power, since it is power that must be exercised legally.

Kelsen in fact expressed a quite similar view in that he argued that at the basis of every legal order is a *Grundnorm* – a basic norm – which constitutes the authority of the ultimate legislative institution.[46] And the Court's decision became known as the 'Grundnorm case' because two of the judges in the majority reasoned that they could rely on Kelsen to avoid confronting the dilemma which Madzimbamuto's lawyer presented to them: they had to decide between accepting the 1961 Constitution or the 1965 one, with the latter choice entailing that

[44] Claire Palley, *The Constitutional History and Law of Southern Rhodesia, 1888–1965* (Oxford: Clarendon Press, 1966) at 751; though, as she points out at 628, the protection of rights and liberties under the 1961 Constitution was precarious at best.

[45] Hans Kelsen, *Das Problem der Souveränität und die Theorie des Völkerrecht: Beitrag zu Einer Reinen Rechtslehre* (Aalen: Scientia Verlag, 1981) at 320. My translation.

[46] Hans Kelsen, *Introduction to the Problems of Legal Theory* (Oxford: Clarendon Press, 1992).

the judges had joined the revolutionary overthrow of the old order by legitimizing the new one.

Beadle took Kelsen's argument to be that a successful legal revolution takes place when the usurping government is effective. At that point, he reasoned, the basic norm which authorizes the Constitution is simply presupposed and the judges were doing nothing more than recognizing this fact, not playing a role in bringing it into existence.[47] In particular, Beadle suggested that this 'Kelsenian' reasoning made possible a 'positivist' and politically neutral approach – one which looked to the way law is rather than how it ought to be. The approach did not, he suggested, lead to the conclusion that the revolution had been successful. However, it was successful enough for him to consider the government to have *de facto* if not *de jure* authority, authority in fact, if not legitimate authority.[48] The issue, he claimed, was not whether the change had come about by illegal revolution, but only the efficacy of the new government.[49]

In his essay, Finnis endorsed the conclusion reached by the majority, but not their positivistic reasoning. He argued that both Kelsen's *Grundnorm* and the equivalent in Hart's philosophy of law cannot explain the way in which a legal order continues through time since they both assume that there is no more to legal order than a set of valid rules. I won't assess the merits of his argument here since my focus is on his alternative.[50] He found it in Voegelin and he referred to Voegelin's essay, 'The Nature of the Law', at that time not published, saying: 'As Eric Voegelin has pointed out, the existence in continuity of a legal system can no more be explained by reference simply to sequences of sets of valid rules than can motion, as Zeno discovered, be explained by reference to sequences of points'.[51]

Finnis's point here is that a legal system's identity over time cannot be explained by reference simply to a set of rules, as it will depend on something more substantive. As he said:

[47] For example, *Madzimbamuto* at 315–17.

[48] Ibid at 322–26.

[49] Ibid at 328.

[50] Finnis was, I think, right about Hart but mistaken in his understanding of Kelsen, since he assumed that Kelsen's model of law is static, a system of valid rules at a particular point in time, whereas Kelsen emphasized the dynamic aspect of legal order. See my *The Long Arc of Legality: Hobbes, Kelsen, Hart* (Cambridge: Cambridge University Press, 2022) for argument on this score.

[51] Finnis, 'Revolutions and Continuity in Law' at 428, note 57. Voegelin's 'The Nature of the Law' was subsequently published in Voegelin, *The Nature of Law and Related Legal Writings* in *The Collected Works of Eric Voegelin* (Baton Rouge: Louisiana State University Press, 1991).

> Legal, like pre-legal, social rules have no common identity or basis of existence in time save that of the group of human beings which accepts them. In times of crisis, the lawyer is obliged to admit that his judgments rest on a critical assessment of the identity of an object which normally he regards as 'artificial and anomalous' and legally barely intelligible – viz. the great 'unincorporated society' in which he lives.

He followed that by claiming:

> As soon as the Rhodesian judges had decided that Rhodesia was, as a matter of 'fact', a distinct society with its own accepted power structure and intelligible commonweal, not merely a fragment of imperial power and commonweal, their decision (if not their reasoning) became almost inevitable. The reason for this inevitability was expressed, as we saw, by lawyers of Edward IV: 'it is necessary that the realm should have a king under whose authority laws should be held and upheld'. It is indeed possible to speak of a legal system growing, flourishing, and withering away – but only if one considers it as something importantly more than a set of rules, however profoundly analysed.[52]

As I have pointed out elsewhere, this claim in context is far more radical than anything to be found in the majority judgments.[53] The 'distinct society' was that of the white minority who 'accepted' the oppressive 'power structure' because it was 'intelligible' to them as serving their economic and caste interests. The 'king' whose 'authority' was 'necessary' in order that 'laws should be held and upheld' was the government headed by Smith which had ruptured the old constitutional order because it somewhat restrained their supremacist view of the order of things, the rule of the white minority over the black majority, an aspect of the context Finnis did not mention in his essay.

A bit later in his essay, Finnis asked the question in the abstract to which he thought the High Court had given an answer – 'What is the relevant unit which has an identity and thus a history?' In his view, '[w]e can say very little', though he found that Voegelin says a lot, for it is here that we get the first substantial quotation in Finnis's work from Voegelin:

> the society in the whole extension of its historical course, with its cycle of constitutional sub-forms, was well established [for Plato and Aristotle] as a unit of inquiry. Moreover, since it was recognized that the cycle of forms applied not only to one particular polis, e.g. Athens, but was typical within

52 Finnis, 'Revolutions and Continuity of Law' at 429. Footnote and paragraph break omitted.

53 Dyzenhaus, *The Long Arc of Legality*, at 439–40.

> a range of variations for all Hellenic poleis, even the single polis was already superseded as the ontological unit and had given way to the Hellenic society, organized as a manifold of poleis, as the unit of empirical inquiry . . . the process was well under way in which the object of inquiry expands from the order of the concrete societies to civilizations which belong to the same type of order, and ultimately to the order of history of a mankind which is no finite unit of observation at all as it extends indefinitely into the future.[54]

I have little idea of what this means, which I confess is generally my reaction to Voegelin's esoteric musings. But I think that the important point has to do with the idea of 'the order of the concrete societies', an idea that Voegelin took up at the end of his essay 'The Nature of the Law', to which Finnis told us in his footnote reference he was 'much indebted'.

In a section with the title 'The Legal Order and the Historically Concrete Society', Voegelin emphasized that 'law has its function in the concrete ordering of society'.[55] But the idea of the concrete is nowhere explained in Voegelin's 'The Nature of the Law'. Indeed, the whole essay is devoid of explanation as it consists of one bald assertion after another. It does, however, resonate with the idea of 'concrete order thought', adopted by Schmitt in 1934. Concrete order thought, at least in Schmitt's version, is a way of thinking about the law antithetical to both liberal democratic constitutionalism and legal positivism. As Schmitt put it, the state 'is only one organ of the *Führer* of the movement', who will put in place a concrete order 'that will measure up to the numerous tasks of the governmental, *völkisch*, economic, and ideological conditions and to the new form of community'.[56]

It is most significant that Finnis himself acknowledged many years later this kind of resonance in his response to Ekins's rather anodyne treatment of the historical dimension of his thought in the volume of essays in his honour. There he set out the 'ground' of political community – the basis for continued identity over time – in a 'consensus':

> a shared willingness to assent to a normative proposition: that our realm and its people, as a historic and continuing community, should (as it can) defend and promote the rights and well-being of its members by common acknowledgement of the fundamental principles and rules (not least

[54] Finnis, 'Revolutions and Continuity in Law' at 431, quoting from Eric Voegelin, *Order and History*, volume 3, *Plato and Aristotle* (Chapel Hill, NC: Louisiana State University Press, 1957) at 334.

[55] Voegelin, 'The Nature of the Law' at 67–68.

[56] Carl Schmitt, *On the Three Types of Juristic Thought* (Westport, CT: Praeger, 2004) at 98.

> parliamentary supremacy) by which it has lived since the time – now very many centuries ago – when it first began to understand itself as this realm and people and to govern itself accordingly.[57]

This set of observations brought Finnis directly to Schmitt in a long paragraph. I will break it into two parts to display the tension that is otherwise obscured by Finnis's presentation of the second as part of a seamless whole with the first and indicate the significant footnotes, which I will discuss in the text, with * and **. Here is the first part:

> The injustice, unconcealed furor, and consequent wickedness and horrors of the *Gleichschaltung* ('bringing into line', a euphemism) instigated by the National Socialist regime, and ideologized by its prime scholarly juristic theorist Carl Schmitt, as a forcible means to the *Gleichartigkeit* or *Artgleichheit* of national homogeneity as ground for the unrestricted domination of the people by the Executive,* have understandably** deterred or dampened inquiry and reflection about the preconditions for the emergence and sustainability of the shared understandings and trust that make possible and stable the widely shared disposition whose articulable content is a constitution. But that justified caution is no sufficient justification for carelessness about those preconditions.[58]

And here's the second:

> The 'constitutional patriotism' that some recent, mostly German theorists (not least in reaction to the Nazi exploitation and deformation of patriotism) have proposed as a reputable replacement for patriotism, should rather be regarded as one element in the central case(s) of reasonable and affective patriotism, itself a necessary condition for constitutional government and political liberty. That is to say, a reasonable patriotism includes an understanding that a broadly worthy constitution, in its place in the sequence of constitutional forms of our constitution, is one of the fine things – our patrimony and social capital – to which it is good to be attached, in large measure because one is *grateful* that these things were *made to be*, and are *there for us all* in our infancy, maturity and, we hope, in any later dependency.[59]

This part is a reference to an idea popularized by Jürgen Habermas, the most important German post-war philosopher, explained by one scholar as involving 'citizens developing (critical and reflexive) loyalty and attachment to their country's constitution. Citizens interpret the

[57] Finnis, 'Reflections and Responses' at 581.

[58] Ibid at 562. The German words in italics both convey 'utter similarity' or 'radical sameness'.

[59] Ibid. His emphasis.

principles found in their constitution – which represent universal moral norms, and might be found in any liberal-democratic constitution – in the light of their community's unique historical experience'.[60] Since among other foils, Habermas was intent on combating Schmitt's pernicious ideas, designed to bring about authoritarian rule,[61] one might infer that in moving from Schmitt to Habermas, Finnis was relying on Habermas to reject Schmitt. But that is not the case.

In the footnote in the first part, which I indicated with **, Finnis elaborates on 'understandably' as follows:

> But, I believe, needlessly and even damagingly. Excessive recoil of this kind took some time to become prevalent: in September 1957, for example, the Australian Catholic Bishops all spoke with undisguised appreciation of national homogeneity (as something to be valued and retained, not, of course, to be imposed), and of the need for 'cultural pluralism' to give way, after a generation or so, to 'complete cultural integration'. Though perhaps speaking more or less *ultra vires*,[62] as Catholic bishops fairly often do, their grasp of the problem of conditions for common and public good was firmer than many of their successors, who seem relatively inattentive to what John Paul II in 2005 called a tenet of Catholic social doctrine: that 'the family and the nation are both natural societies' which cannot in human history be replaced by anything else; he went on to suggest that the proper remedy for 'unhealthy nationalism' includes essentially a reasonable patriotism.[63]

So Finnis was here saying that we should adopt as the foundation of our constitutional order a Schmittian idea of the 'national homogeneity' of the people in a political project that will replace cultural pluralism with 'complete cultural integration'. One must thus ask how such a project could be accomplished 'reasonably', or subject to his qualification – 'as something to be valued and retained, not, of course, to be imposed' – given that it is no different in substance from these sentences from Schmitt that Finnis quoted in the footnote placed at * in the first part:

> German law and the German state no longer ... rest on the empty and formal 'equality of all before the law' or the deceptive phrase 'equality of

[60] Daffyd Huw Rees, 'Constitutional Patriotism' in Amy Allen and Eduardo Mendiata, eds, *The Cambridge Habermas Lexicon* (Cambridge: Cambridge University Press, 2019) 66 at 67.

[61] See Jan-Werner Müller, *Constitutional Patriotism* (Princeton, NJ: Princeton University Press, 2007).

[62] Finnis means here 'not in their official capacity'.

[63] Finnis, 'Reflections and Responses' at 562, note 344.

> all that has a human face', but on the real homogeneity and substantial nature of the entire German people, unified in itself and homogeneous. *Gleichartigkeit* [homogeneity of type/race] is something more, and something more profound than *Gleichschaltung*, which is but a means and an instrument for *Gleichartigkeit* ... The decisions concerning magistrates, doctors and lawyers purify public life from non-Aryan elements foreign to the race.[64]

As we will see, a mark of Finnis's reflections on the need to achieve complete cultural integration on the basis of national homogeneity, something like Schmitt's 'substantive homogeneity of the people', is a squeamishness about means and a vagueness about ends. But my point here is not that he is trying to conceal anything. Rather, it is that he is unwilling to face up to the radical implications of his positions, for example his position on immigration – in large part a process in which people from countries that once formed part of the vast British Empire have sought to take up residence in the metropole. He may also be unwilling to confront too directly the doctrine of free exercise of religion that became the official policy of his faith when the document *Dignitatis Humanae* was adopted by the Second Ecumenical Council of the Vatican in the mid-1960s. However, he was willing to say that the adoption of this doctrine may have the result of favouring or permitting 'the causing of much odious treason and misery'.[65]

6.4 Means and Ends

In his vehement criticism of the liberal views of his former supervisor Hart, Finnis claimed that

> Hart's normative political philosophy has little indeed to say about the inter-relations of common good, justice and liberty in a nation whose liberty-minded citizens have largely given up procreating – or rather,

[64] Finnis's reference, ibid at 562, note 343, is: 'Faye, *Heidegger*, 153, quotes a writing of Schmitt in May 1933'. This book was omitted from the bibliography. The French original is Emmanuel Faye, *Heidegger: L'Introduction du Nazisme dans la Philosophie: Autour des séminaires inédits de 1933–1935* (Paris: Albin Michel, 2005) at 252. '*Gleichschaltung*' was the term used in the late 1930s for the process whereby all the organs of state were coordinated so as to achieve the goal of homogeneity, a similar idea to what we saw Casey and Vermeule refer to as an 'executive-led separation of powers' – Casey and Vermeule, 'Myths of Common Good Constitutionalism' at 135.

[65] See John Finnis, 'Towards Vatican II's Centenary: Your Next Fifty Years' (2016) 14 *Ave Maria Law Review* 1 at 6.

> bearing children at a rate consistent with their community's medium-term survival, and whose law, considered in its much-obscured implications, marks out for them a path towards, first the loss of national self-determination; and then their own *replacement*, as a people, by other peoples, more or less regardless of the incomers' compatibility of psychology, culture, religion or political ideas and ambitions, or the worth or viciousness of those ideas and ambitions; and finally to the ruinous loss of most or much that Hart worked for, or took for granted, as precious.[66]

This is, as is typically the case with Finnis, a long and complex sentence. I have emphasized 'replacement' in it because his dire empirical diagnosis of the existential danger facing the UK has much in common with the 'Great Replacement Theory', a term coined two years later by the French novelist turned white supremacist Renaud Camus, which has since become a trope of the far right,[67] especially in countries where there is a falling birth rate in the native population.

The *Encyclopaedia Britannica* explains the theory as 'a far-right conspiracy theory alleging, in one of its versions, that left-leaning domestic or international elites, on their own initiative, or under the direction of Jewish co-conspirators, are attempting to replace white citizens with nonwhite (i.e., Black, Hispanic, Asian, or Arab) immigrants'.[68] It is hardly surprising, then, that advocates of the Great Replacement Theory include racists of all kinds, some openly expressing antisemitic and neo-Nazi views, views that Finnis himself would of course reject. Moreover, in the context of an essay in which he is criticizing what he clearly regards as the naïve liberalism of Hart, one could surmise that he sees the empirical phenomenon as resulting from a series of disjointed and ill-reasoned policies and tragic social developments, in particular, family planning, birth control, the entry of women into the workplace, the rise of 'equality' of the sexes, the demise of the traditional family, combined with a lax and ill-reasoned immigration and refugee regime that permits the movement of non-Christian, non-white peoples into Europe. He might be taken, that is, to be arguing that Hart is an example of someone who may have had good intentions, but who failed to see the bad implications of his liberalism.

[66] Finnis, 'Hart as a Political Philosopher' at 278. My emphasis.

[67] Brian Duignan, 'Replacement Theory' (Aug 23 2025) online: *Encyclopaedia Britannica* <www.britannica.com/topic/replacement-theory>.

[68] Ibid.

However, while this may be true of Finnis's sentiments in regard to Hart, it must also be taken into account that the paragraph with which he began this part of his essay reads as follows:

> European states in the early twenty-first century move ever more clearly out of the social and political conditions of the 1960s into a trajectory of demographic and cultural decay; *circumscription* of political, religious, and educational speech and associated freedoms; *pervasive untruthfulness* about equality and diversity; *population transfer and replacement by a kind of reverse colonization*; and resultant internal fissiparation foreshadowing, it seems, ethnic and religious inter-communal miseries of hatred, bloodshed, and political paralysis reminiscent of late twentieth century Yugoslavia's or the Levant's. So the time seems ripe for a wider reflection on late twentieth-century political philosophies *so characteristic, so suasive, so victorious, as Hart's.*[69]

The words I have emphasized taken together suggest a deliberate policy hidden from the public by the elite behind the policy and which Hart's liberalism has at least served to facilitate.

In regard to means, consider what Finnis had to say in 2009, the same year in which, as we saw in the Introduction, he explicitly advocated a version of the Great Replacement Theory:

> Confronted by the grave warnings thus issuing from courts of great pan-European authority, citizens of countries whose Muslim population is increasing very rapidly by immigration and a relatively high birth rate may ask themselves whether it is prudent, or just to the children and grandchildren of everyone in their country, to permit any further migratory increase in that population, or even to accept the presence of immigrant, non-citizen Muslims without deliberating seriously about a possible reversal – humane and financially compensated for and incentivized – of the inflow. Such thoughts, and the corresponding proposals that might be put forward for reflective deliberation, could not rightly be described as extreme.[70]

So here we have Finnis praising the European Court of Human Rights, no longer as the common good lawyers usually like to portray it – a 'foreign' court imposing an un-British conception of human rights on the British people; rather, it is a court of 'great pan-European authority', delivering a 'stern warning'.[71]

69 Finnis, 'Hart as a Political Philosopher' at 274. My emphasis.

70 Finnis, 'Endorsing Discrimination between Faiths' at 439–40.

71 Thomas Adams, 'The Politics of Judicial Power' (Nov 11 2015) online: *UK Constitutional Law Blog* <https://ukconstitutionallaw.org/2015/11/11/thomas-adams-the-politics-of-judicial-power/>.

The cases to which Finnis was referring concerned a Turkish ban on Refah, an Islamist political party.[72] But the case that Finnis mainly discusses in this essay – *Begum* – is one decided by the House of Lords which concerned a challenge to a dress code imposed by a school board in a majority-Muslim school in England.[73] While the House of Lords upheld the ban, Finnis argued that the judges only alluded to the real political threat posed by Muslims, a threat which had explicitly been identified by the European Court of Human Rights:

> To read *Refah* reflectively, aware of Europe's demographic trends and immigration policies, is to wonder whether the future of democracy and the rule of law, and of much else besides, is not imperilled here and now by the relentless defaming of all who try to initiate public deliberation about political and legislative action to counter, effectively, the bad and ever-increasingly unavoidable effects of those trends and policies.[74]

Finnis thus leaves us in the dark as to what means are to be adopted to deal with this peril. But, given his influence on the Judicial Power Project, spearheaded by Ekins, and given, as we saw in Chapters 3–5, the way in which that Project proves itself to be an Executive Power Project, we can know that whatever means he contemplated are to be unconstrained by the rights commitments of UK law. Judges will be told to get out of the way by statutory command so that they are either forced into the severely constrained role that Finnis and Ekins consider appropriate or even ousted from having any role at all, which is what Ekins advocated for the Rwanda Act.

So much for means, but what about ends? And with this question, we come back to the problem of negatively prescriptive theory, or anything-but-liberalism. As I noted in the Introduction and Chapter 1, the issue is not so much that any particular common good advocate fails to offer any content. Each has something to say, though they are often rather, sometimes very, vague when it comes to content; and there are minor disagreements about many issues, mainly about how far the state should be able to go in using coercion on citizens to force them to be virtuous, for

[72] *Refah Partisi (No 1) v Turkey* (2002) 35 EHRR 3 and *Refah Partisi (No 2) v Turkey* (2003) 37 EHRR 1.

[73] *R (on the application of Begum) v Denbigh High School Governors* [2007] 1 AC 100. For a response to Finnis, and a very different analysis of the decision, see David Dyzenhaus, 'Proportionality and Deference in a Culture of Justification' in Grant Huscroft, Bradley Miller, and Grégoire Webber, eds, *Proportionality and the Rule of Law: Rights, Justification, Reasoning* (Cambridge: Cambridge University Press, 2014) 234.

[74] Finnis, 'Endorsing Discrimination between Faiths' at 441.

example by requiring people to adhere to a very conservative version of Catholicism.

Finnis is in the category of vague, at least in his writings for a more general audience.[75] Consider, for example, his analysis of Islam, which he thinks justifies a ban on wearing its religious symbols, since 'the use of a religious symbol to manifest one's personal belief can threaten the rights of others only if it is associated with a definite and particular kind of religious culture':

> a religious culture must have one or more of a cluster of features: a disrespect for equality (here the equality of females, especially girls and young women); a denial of immunity from coercion in religious matters (including matters of apostasy from that religion or rejection of all religion), the immunity now central to Christian political teaching; a mandating, encouragement, or permission of intimidation of apostates, backsliders and others; and a treatment of all arenas, educational or political, as in principle subject to threatening pressure, indeed compulsion, in the name of religious truths and precepts and of promoting adherence to them.[76]

In these lines, Finnis declared his allegiance to religious toleration, in keeping with the *Dignitatis Humanae*, the document I mentioned above, the Second Ecumenical Council of the Vatican's declaration on Religious Freedom. He also seemed to suggest a firm commitment to both equality of women and freedom from coercion in religious matters. But in the same essay, he justified using state force against Muslims, who are all tarred with the same brush of wishing to coerce others into adhering to a very conservative and coercive version of their religion. Ironically, this is exactly the charge that used to be levelled at Catholics.[77] Unfortunately, the charge can be levelled again today if one takes, as one definitely should not, the 'hard integralism' advocated by the likes of Vermeule and J. D. Vance to portray accurately the teachings of the Church. That is, one should not take as accurate a distorted version of the faith, one which advocates a crude kind of nationalism in the guise of religion, and which we saw the late Pope utterly reject in a direct rebuke to Vance.

75 When Finnis writes for an audience that he takes to be broadly sympathetic to his more right-wing views, there is a marked difference in tone and substance. See, for example, Finnis, 'Towards Vatican II's Centenary: Your Next Fifty Years'.

76 Finnis, 'Endorsing Discrimination between Faiths' at 434–35.

77 John T McGreevy and R Scott Appleby, 'Catholics, Muslims, and the Mosque Controversy' (Aug 27 2010) online: *New York Review of Books* <www.nybooks.com/online/2010/08/27/catholics-muslims-mosque-controversy/>.

Here I adopt a useful distinction between 'soft' and 'hard' 'integralism', elaborated by Xavier Foccroulle Ménard and Anna Su.[78] Relying on Thomas Crean and Alan Finister's *Integralism: A Manual of Political Philosophy*,[79] they note that the 'temporal power' – that is, the state – of the hard integralists may intervene if 'for example, the parents cause grave psychological neglect or harm in "instructing [their children] in theft or idolatry, or sexual perversion"'. Foccroulle Ménard and Su comment that '[o]n their face, idolatry and sexual pervasion would include many lifestyles, values and behaviors which, in modern liberal societies, are being taught to children by parents informed by their religion, other than Catholicism, or even by their atheism'.[80] More dramatically, hard integralists hold that

> Within Christendom, not only must the ruler keep his realm free from doctrines which reason itself knows to be gravely contrary to the truth, but also 'from all heresies and other opinions solemnly condemned by the Church'. Among other policies, idolaters, atheists, all the unbaptized as well as adherents of heretical and schismatic bodies must generally be excluded from legislative positions, and higher executive and judicial offices. Only the baptized will be recognized with official citizenship, in contrast to the unbaptized who will receive certain civil rights and when applicable, particular law.[81]

In contrast, according to Foccroulle Ménard and Su, '[u]nder soft integralism, the Catholic natural law tradition informs state policies and actions without actively enforcing positive laws that restrict individuals in their liberal freedom, for prudential and subsidiarity reasons',[82] where 'prudence' will require the ruler to take into account practical considerations and 'subsidiarity' that some measure of freedom must be allowed at each level of implementation. For example, within families, parents should have the freedom to decide how to integrate their children into the life of virtue. As a result, '[g]iven these guiding principles and the

[78] Xavier Foccroulle Ménard and Anna Su, 'Liberalism, Catholic Integralism, and the Question of Religious Freedom' (2022) 47 *Brigham Young Law Review* 1171. For an excellent critique of integralism, see Micah Schwartzman and Jocelyn Wilson, 'The Unreasonableness of Catholic Integralism' (2019) 56 *San Diego Law Review* 1039.

[79] Thomas Crean and Alan Finister, *Integralism: A Manual of Political Philosophy* (London: Eurospan, 2020).

[80] Foccroulle Ménard and Su, 'Integralism' at 1206.

[81] Ibid at 1207, quoting from Crean and Finister, *Integralism: A Manual of Political Philosophy*, at 116.

[82] Foccroulle Ménard and Su, 'Integralism' at 1216.

Church's policy change with regard to secular states in *Dignitatis Humanae*, we can see that an approximation of religious freedom similar to what we see under some liberal regimes is possible or at least plausible under a soft integralist regime'.[83] However, Foccroulle Ménard and Su also point out that whether we get the 'tyrannical Christian state' of the hard integralists or the milder state of the soft integralists can't be told in advance. All will depend on the doctrines of the men in charge of the Church at the time.[84]

All this is small comfort for anyone of a liberal disposition, as I will explain by returning to Finnis. Finnis does not style himself an integralist and he indicated strongly at several points in *Natural Law and Natural Rights* his support for the good of 'autonomy' – of leaving it to individuals to decide for themselves how to lead their lives.[85] He also has advocated the state tolerating a limited plurality of lifestyles, with the limitation exercised by their compatibility with what he calls 'basic goods'.[86] Moreover, in his book on his main source of ethical inspiration in Aquinas, Finnis suggested that Aquinas's position is 'not that readily distinguishable from the "grand simple principle" (itself open to interpretation and diverse applications) of John Stuart Mill's *On Liberty*'.[87] So at these points in his work, Finnis seemed to endorse, in a somewhat qualified way, Mill's 'Harm Principle'.

Such endorsement would be surprising because, as I explained in Chapter 1, the 'Harm Principle' holds that the state may use coercion against individuals only to prevent them from harming each other. The principle thus requires that the state should be entirely 'neutral' – take no stand – on the question of what is best for the individual. It is for the individual alone to decide what (if any) religion to practise, whether or not to bear children, what kind of intimate relations they want, including sexual relations, and so on. And it is this vision of the liberal state as neutral between conceptions of the good life that common good advocates regard as 'the demon within', as the most totalitarian of ideologies because, for example, it requires Catholics and others to privatize their religion, to regard its practice as a matter for their personal choice.

[83] Ibid.
[84] Ibid at 1217–18.
[85] Finnis, *Natural Law and Natural Rights*, at 168–69.
[86] Ibid at 118–25.
[87] John Finnis, *Aquinas: Moral, Political, and Legal Theory* (Oxford: Oxford University Press, 1998) at 228.

Common good advocates oppose liberalism because it requires them, first, to regard some of their most fundamental beliefs as holding for their community of faith alone with no thought that these should be imposed by the state on others. It requires them, second, to accept both that the adherents of other faiths and atheists have equal standing in the life of the secular state and that those with ways of life antithetical to their religion are equally entitled to live those lives as they see fit. Moreover, as the common good advocates see it, liberalism is totalitarian not only in that it requires Catholics amongst others to accept that truth for them in some fundamental matters is not truth for others. Even more troubling to the common good advocates is that liberalism also demands toleration of a plurality of other belief systems, some of which contradict their own, a phenomenon that will inevitably have the effect of undermining their own belief systems. In particular, Mill celebrated the 'experiments in living' made available in a liberal society because these enable individuals to make informed choices as to how to live.[88] But, for common good advocates, the availability of a menu of options about how to live endangers certain communities of faith since their members will inevitably be attracted to experiments in ways that require leaving the fold.

However, Finnis did not really endorse anything like the harm principle. Everything turns on his qualification – that individuals should be able to 'constitute themselves' 'by their own private efforts and initiatives' even if they would do better through participating in the 'public enterprise', as long as they can do so without 'injuring (either by act or omission) the common good'.[89]As Finnis made clear in the same work, 'public order' is 'an aspect of the common good' and to be equated with 'public morality'.[90] And this conception of public order makes him at best a soft or squeamish integralist.

For example, in his essay 'Religion and State', speaking again of the House of Lords decision in *Begum*, Finnis said:

> If a religion treats coercion of its own adherents, of potential adherents, or of anyone else as permissible, let alone mandatory, it is a standing incitement to violate the rights of others and public order, and those who adhere to it faithfully are rightly liable, in principle, to be kept, where

[88] John Stuart Mill, *On Liberty* in Mill, *Collected Works*, JM Robson, ed (Toronto: University of Toronto Press, 1977) volume 18, chapter 2.

[89] Finnis, *Natural Law and Natural Rights*, at 169.

[90] Ibid at 216–17.

> morally possible, as far as is necessary from political communities that acknowledge the right to religious freedom.[91]

As in Finnis's advocacy of remigration, albeit 'humane and financially compensated for and incentivized', we get a vague description of what such measures would be like in practice. The limit suggested by 'Where morally possible, as far as is necessary' allows for too much flexibility in the future. It may turn out to be no limit at all if some Trump- or Farage-like leader gets to decide on what constitutes a threat to public order. Recall that Finnis thought that the important truth in Schmitt's idea of substantive homogeneity was also stated in the Australian bishops' 'undisguised appreciation of national homogeneity (as something to be valued and retained, not, of course, to be imposed), and of the need for "cultural pluralism" to give way, after a generation or so, to "complete cultural integration"'.[92] And if 'complete cultural integration' is one's moral goal, that goal will largely determine what means are necessary to reach it.

Important in this regard is how capacious the category of 'public order' is in Finnis's hands. Public order does not extend to banning gay sexual activity in private, but it seems to extend to some indeterminate category of prohibitions using unspecified means on *any* public manifestations of gay identity. In 'Law, Morality, and "Sexual Orientation"' Finnis wrote:

> A political community which judges that the stability and protective and educative generosity of family life are of fundamental importance to the whole community's present and future can rightly judge that it has compelling reasons for judging that homosexual conduct – a 'gay life-style' – is never a valid, humanly acceptable choice and form of life, in denying that same-sex partners are capable of marrying, and in doing whatever it *properly* can, as a community with uniquely wide but still subsidiary functions . . . to discourage such conduct.[93]

91 John Finnis, 'Religion and State' in *Religion and Public Reasons, Collected Essays: Volume V* (Oxford: Oxford University Press, 2011) 80 at 99.

92 Finnis, 'Reflections and Responses' at 562, note 344.

93 John Finnis, 'Law, Morality, and "Sexual Orientation"' in *Human Rights and Common Goods: Collected Essays: Volume III* (Oxford: Oxford University Press, 2011) 334 at 344. His emphasis. See also Finnis's excellent obituary of Joseph Raz for the British Academy 'Joseph Raz 21 March 1939–2 May 2022' (Apr 10 2025) online: *The British Academy* <www.thebritishacademy.ac.uk/documents/5716/Memoirs-22-12-Raz.pdf> 308 at 339, in which, clearly stung by the fact that Raz must have considered him to be a 'bigot', he seeks to defend the views which Raz condemned on the basis that they are 'intended purely to protect public morals and formation of the young against a deformation (of reason) damaging to individual well-being and this people's continuance'.

So yet again one gets the vague constraint in the emphasis on '*properly*'. The state should take measures to force gay men back into the closet, but do so 'properly'.

I will now show that this vagueness about both means and ends confronts Finnis with the same problem that faced Lord Devlin in one of the major public debates in the UK about the state's role in using law to enforce morality in the 1960s, a debate which culminated amongst other things in the decriminalization of sex between consenting male adults. As we will see, the problem has to do with making arguments based on revealed or religious truth on what I will call the 'secular plateau', a metaphor for a pluralistic society in which, in order to make any headway, your arguments must appeal to potential allies who do not share what you take as your revealed truth.[94]

6.5 Schmitt and Voegelin on the Secular Plateau

Patrick Devlin (1905–1992) was one of the leading judges in the UK of the post-war period. He entered the public eye when he gave a lecture arguing against the recommendation of a Conservative government-appointed commission of inquiry – the Wolfenden Report – that sexual relations between men should be decriminalized.[95] He argued that any society has a distinct identity based on its sense of core moral values, its

[94] I have adapted the term 'secular plateau' from the political theory of Ronald Dworkin. See Dworkin, 'Comment on Narveson: In Defense of Equality' (1983) 1 *Social Philosophy and Policy* 24 at 25.

[95] Patrick Devlin, 'Morals and the Criminal Law' in *The Enforcement of Morals* (London: Oxford University Press, 1965) 1. For an excellent discussion of the ensuing debate, see Nicola Lacey, 'Patrick Devlin, "The Enforcement of Morals (1965)"' in Chloë Kennedy and Lindsay Farmer, eds, *Leading Works in Criminal Law* (London: Routledge, 2024) 82. At 84, Lacey explains that there is a 'certain elusiveness, an ambiguity or opaqueness in many of the positions … [Devlin] adopted on matters ranging from the substantive conclusions of the Wolfenden Report, through the constitutional scope for judges to develop the common law, to the very conception of morality which he argued the law should enforce. His relationship to Catholicism is also of interest, given the explicit invocations of Christian morality throughout the text. A Catholic by upbringing, Devlin abandoned his training for the priesthood and renounced his faith; his wife, conversely, converted to Catholicism, and their children were raised as Catholics. Towards the end of his life, he rediscovered his faith, in the words of his wife, "and really the violence of it, as if it had been pent up all these years", asked to see a priest and took the rites of the church, but declined to take communion – a sacrament available in Catholic doctrine only to those who do not believe themselves guilty of grave sin – "because I am not worthy"'. As Richard Wollheim memorably put it, see Lacey at 92, Devlin veers between 'anthropological' and 'absolutist' views of morality and Lacey says

sense of appropriate public morality, and that, just as it is entitled to protect itself against treason in the form of political subversion, so it is entitled to protect itself against moral subversion, including using the coercive instrument of criminal law. His test for what should be considered on the list of core moral values was what the 'man in the street' considered crucial to the maintenance of his society as a distinct society.[96]

As he put it:

> In England, we believe in the Christian idea of marriage and therefore adopt monogamy as a moral principle. Consequently, the Christian institution of marriage has become the basis of family life and so is part of the structure of our society. It is there not because it is Christian. It has got there because it is Christian, but it remains there because it is built into the house in which we live and could not be removed without bringing it down. ... [A] non-Christian is bound by it not because it is part of Christianity but because, rightly or wrongly, it has been adopted by the society in which he lives. It would be useless for him to stage a debate designed to prove that polygamy was theologically more correct and socially preferable; if he wants to live in the house, he must accept it as built in the way in which it is.[97]

Devlin's lecture, later published in a short book, was met by a stern response from Hart. Hart pointed out that Devlin identified a society with a list of the values which happened to have popular support at that time. That, Hart pointed out, led to the absurd claim that any change in the values on that list meant a change in the nature of that society. Hart was also concerned about the authoritarian dimension of Devlin's views on the legal enforcement of morality, and so advocated a return to Mill's 'Harm Principle', which he somewhat reformulated.[98]

Devlin, we should note, did at the end of his lecture try to temper his moral authoritarianism by coming up with a list of what he called 'elastic principles', for example that enforcement should be by the least intrusive means and leave individuals with as much liberty as possible.[99] But given that the very elasticity of the principles meant that whether and how they

that this 'strange combination of absolutism and populism is a distinctive and perplexing aspect of Devlin's text'.

96 Devlin, 'Morals and the Criminal Law' at 14–15; HLA Hart, *Law, Liberty and Morality* (London: Oxford University Press, 1963).

97 Devlin, 'Morals and the Criminal Law' at 9.

98 Ibid at 51–52, 77–81.

99 Ibid at 16–20.

would be applied would depend on how the powerful gauged the moral outrage of some portion of the population, these principles were utterly platitudinous.

Finnis's attack on Hart is framed by Hart's debate with Devlin. He ended the attack with a page and a half full of quotations from and references to Voegelin, taken straight from *The New Science of Politics*. In particular, he invoked Voegelin as the source for three possible explanations for the alleged 'deficiencies of political philosophies such as Hart's'.[100]

The first explanation, in which the quotations within the quotation are from Voegelin's *The New Science of Politics*, is that these deficiencies were encouraged by:

> the inclination to take one's society's existence, especially when it has had 'a long and glorious history', for granted 'as part of the order of things', 'an inclination to disregard the structure of reality, of relaxing into the sweetness of existence, of a decline of civic morality, of a blindness to obvious dangers, and a reluctance to meet them with all seriousness', the mood of late, disintegrating societies no longer willing to fight for their existence (an existence which is also a precondition for their serving the common good of peoples and territories beyond their own).[101]

The second explanation is that these 'political-philosophical deficiencies' were encouraged by the

> *contrasting* predispositions mentioned by Voegelin . . . predispositions to an *activism* shaped by a kind of faith, such as liberal or Marxist or National Socialist beliefs in essentially inevitable cultural progress. After all, Mill's activist 'doctrine of liberty', as Hart called it, confessedly rested on just such a faith, in 'the salutary *permanent* effects of freedom'[102] – that is, we should now say, on sub-rational, spiritually disordered faith in a course of history that had brought societies such as ours up to a plateau of progress from which there *would not be* a falling off.[103]

The third is that Hart's position amounted to 'no more than Oxford philosophers' standard bad practice of discussing, say, Plato's or Mill's "theories" and "doctrines" with a kind of detachment from their deepest truth-conditions'.[104]

[100] Finnis, 'Hart as a Political Philosopher' at 278–79, quoting from Voegelin, *The New Science of Politics*, at 168.

[101] Ibid at 278–79, quoting from Voegelin, *The New Science of Politics*, at 168.

[102] The quotation is from Mill, *On Liberty*. Finnis's emphasis.

[103] Finnis, 'Hart as a Political Philosopher' at 279. His emphasis.

[104] Ibid.

Finally, Finnis suggested that perhaps all three explanations are operating: 'All are encouraged by aversion to acknowledging reality's full range and partly transcendent structure, the deep aversion which I mentioned in the first sentences of sec. I's last paragraph',[105] that is, that Hart 'lacked the ... belief ... that moral judgments can be really true'.[106] Finnis did not cite Voegelin in support of the third explanation. But the obscure reference to 'transcendent structure' is pure Voegelin, and speaks to the one difference between Schmitt and Voegelin, which is nicely illustrated by a return to the debate that framed Finnis's attack.

Finnis, although he shared Devlin's view of society's right to use law to enforce morality, criticized both Hart and Devlin for making what he regarded as the same fatal mistake, evidenced by what he called 'Hart's resolute nonengagement with any part of the real case for those condemnations and their direct or indirect enforcement'.[107] As we have just seen, Devlin thought that it was appropriate in the UK that the public morality that would be enforced would be a basically Christian set of values, because of the place of Christianity in UK history. But he did not insist on the truth of Christian doctrines. They just happened to be doctrines central to his own society's history, just as he may have thought that in the UK it was appropriate as a matter of history for Parliament to make such decisions, but would not have stipulated that all societies should adopt parliamentary democracy as their mode of government.[108]

Finnis rejected this aspect of Devlin's position because it substitutes 'moral beliefs' for 'the concern for truth'.[109] He returned to this theme in his attack on Hart in which he chastised his former supervisor for his 'evasion or oversight of all questions of activities affecting public morality, as distinct from the truly private acts of consenting adults'.[110] Such evasion, Finnis claimed, 'results in thoroughgoing neglect of the question what conditions of procreation and education and self-understanding are needed to sustain political culture, and philosophy, and indeed the political community itself in face of threats external or internal'. It also

105 Ibid.

106 Ibid referring to his essay at 259.

107 Finnis, 'Hart as a Political Philosopher' at 274.

108 Ibid at 25.

109 John Finnis, 'Human Rights and their Enforcement' in John Finnis, *Human Rights and Common Goods: Collected Essays: Volume III* (Oxford: Oxford University Press, 2011) 19 at 27.

110 Finnis, 'Hart as a Political Philosopher' at 277.

results in a 'liberalism that consciously evades "material" moral issues, as controversial or non-neutral, is prone indeed to evade essential facts, causalities, inter-dependencies, and the like, even when these tend to determine outcomes fundamentally'.[111]

However, Finnis was unable to distance himself even in this one respect from Devlin because, while his argument was based on what he regards as the revealed truth of Catholicism, he was forced by the secular world he rails against to make his argument on what I called the secular plateau. Consider one of his favourite themes – control of sexuality, in particular homosexuality. In a typical intervention, 'Marriage: A Basic and Exigent Good', he began by explicitly stipulating that sexual relations are immoral if not between a husband and wife for the purpose of procreation. One is allowed to enjoy sex, but only within that context.

In support of this claim, Finnis of course did not appeal only to Catholic theologians. For example, for his premise that homosexual conduct is 'intrinsically shameful, immoral and indeed depraved or depraving', he claimed that '[a]ll three of the greatest Greek philosophers, Socrates, Plato, and Aristotle, ... rejected the linchpin of modern "gay" ideology and lifestyle'.[112] But that premise is as weak as one for the justice of enslaving people that begins with 'all three of the greatest Greek philosophers, Socrates, Plato, and Aristotle, accepted that it was perfectly just to enslave'. What's interesting about it is only that Finnis on occasion feels the need to reach outside of his faith community for support because he knows that the appeal to revealed truth will fall on stony ground when it is made to people outside.[113]

More important is that Finnis also made an appeal to empirical evidence. He accused Hart of neglecting the 'malign results' of the

[111] Ibid at 277.

[112] Finnis, 'Law, Morality, and "Sexual Orientation"' at 336.

[113] Finnis does not help his audience when it comes to clarifying the link he supposes exists between natural law and Catholicism. For example, he writes: 'the divine revelation constitutive of Christianity – the central form of which ... must be Catholicism – is the central event of human history and became the bearer of what is sound in the philosophical tradition of moral and political (and therefore legal) philosophy inaugurated, masterfully, by Plato and Aristotle'. See John Finnis, 'Grounding Human Rights in Natural Law' (2015) 60 *American Journal of Jurisprudence* 199 at 200, 201. Yet he thought natural law could be explained without a religious basis since he also writes, ibid: natural law theory 'differs from, even when it coincides in moral judgment with, bodies of moral teaching self-identified as part of a divine revelation addressed to everyone'. See John Finnis, 'Reason, Revelation, Universality and Particularity in Ethics' (2008) 53 *American Journal of Jurisprudence* 23.

decriminalization of homosexuality, which he claimed 'include the misery induced by the side effects of efforts, even successful efforts, to suppress and contemn one's own or others' reactions to want of *fides* [fidelity]'. He added that 'the miseries to be counted extend also to the wider effects of sexual "liberation" on children in their years of radical dependency, vulnerability, and need; and on those killed or damaged by damaged children; and quite generally on the vulnerable'.[114] However, he presented no evidence for these sweeping claims, which seem akin to the Emperor Justinian's claim, reported by Hart in his response to Devlin, that homosexuality causes earthquakes.[115]

It is for more help on the secular plateau that Finnis turned first to Voegelin and later to Schmitt, despite the fact that, as Finnis himself notes, Voegelin was 'no follower of ... [Aquinas's] faith or philosophy'.[116] This claim is even more true of Schmitt since he is like Devlin in that any illiberal basis will do for achieving the common good. In fact, a remarkable feature of the influence of both Voegelin and Schmitt on the ideologies of those on the far right who base their beliefs ultimately in a religious worldview is that neither Voegelin nor Schmitt professed commitment to any faith. Schmitt was born into a Catholic family but was excommunicated when he married a second time after failing to get a nullification of his first marriage from the Vatican. Thereafter, he had a troubled relationship with Catholicism.[117] And Voegelin in his memoir denied a commitment to any faith. He said that he has in his files documents labelling him 'a Communist, Fascist, a National Socialist, an old liberal, a new liberal, a Jew, a Catholic, a Protestant, a Platonist, a neo-Augustinian, a Thomist, and of course a Hegelian – not to forget that I was supposedly strongly influenced by Huey Long'. (Long was the American politician who was either revered as a populist hero who took up left-wing causes or despised as a ruthless demagogue.) But Voegelin regarded these labels as just proof of the fact that he was toiling away as a 'scientist' 'who 'honestly wants to explore the structure of social reality'.[118]

[114] Finnis, 'Hart as a Political Philosopher' at 270–74.

[115] Hart, *Law, Liberty, and Morality*, at 50.

[116] John Finnis, 'Introduction' in *Intention and Identity: Collected Essays: Volume II* (Oxford: Oxford University Press, 2011) 1 at 14, note 20.

[117] Reinhard Mehring, 'A "Catholic Layman of German Nationality and Citizenship"? Carl Schmitt and the Religiosity of Life' in Jens Meirhenrich and Oliver Simons, eds, *The Oxford Handbook of Carl Schmitt* (Oxford: Oxford University Press, 2014) 73.

[118] Eric Voegelin, *Autobiographical Reflections* (Columbia: University of Missouri Press, 2011) at 73–74. Revised Edition with Glossary. Volume 34 of *Collected Works*.

Finnis of course differs and, as Kirkby notes, his project is not a Schmittian one of 'moral indifference and sovereign supremacy' since, in his view, 'a sovereign had a moral obligation ... to promote the common good necessary for the full flourishing of its community'.[119] And that common good, Finnis emphasized, is merely instrumental in that it serves ultimately what he takes to be the transcendent truth of the Catholic Church.[120] But while Finnis's position might not be Schmittian in that he is confident in his grip on the truth of his doctrines, his resort to Schmittian ideas of homogeneity that I highlighted earlier is necessitated by the secular plateau. Here a recent book about philosophy of law by a young political theorist and common good advocate is instructive.

In *The Nature of Law: Authority, Obligation, and the Common Good*, Daniel Mark defends a Finnisian account of the moral obligation to obey the law.[121] Mark, who says he is 'a disciple' of Robert George,[122] Finnis's influential former student at Princeton, goes carefully through the complex arguments for and against there being such an obligation: with the Oxford legal positivists Hart and Raz arguing against, and the Oxford natural lawyer Finnis arguing for, such an obligation.

Mark acknowledges that in a secular democratic society, one cannot base one's account of the moral obligation to obey the law wholly on a divine source. So he opts for Schmitt, citing Schmitt's claim in *Political Theology* that '[a]ll significant concepts of the modern state are secularized theological concepts not only because of their historical development – in which they were transferred from theology to the theory of the state, whereby, for example, God became the omnipotent lawgiver – but also because of their systematic structure, the recognition of which is necessary for a sociological reconsideration of these concepts'.[123] From this observation, Mark concludes that for Schmitt 'divine authority is *the* starting point for thinking about the authority of the state'[124] and he follows Schmitt in supposing that with this starting point we must conceive law on the model of command. The last chapter of his book has the title 'We the Sovereign' and Mark here embraces Schmitt because

119 Kirkby, 'Abysmal Jurisprudence' at 154.
120 Finnis, 'Reflections and Responses' at 510–18.
121 Daniel Mark, *The Nature of Law: Authority, Obligation, and the Common Good* (Notre Dame, IN: University of Notre Dame Press, 2024).
122 Ibid at ix.
123 Ibid at 225, quoting from Carl Schmitt, *Political Theology: Four Chapters on the Concept of Sovereignty* (Chicago: University of Chicago Press, 2005) at 36.
124 Mark, *The Nature of Law*, at 225. His emphasis.

he is a 'strident critic of neutrality', 'insists on law's normativity (its directness towards substantive ends)', and frames law's normativity 'in a way that resonates with our idea of law's necessary relationship with the common good'.[125] He also suggests that Schmitt, while not arguing for democracy, 'helps us to see how a nondemocratic theory of authority and obligation aimed at the good properly accommodates democratic structures and ends'.[126]

Mark insists that he, like Schmitt, is not a legal positivist even though he recognizes that his command theory of law is like the one the legal positivist John Austin put forward in the nineteenth century. Recall from the preceding chapter that on this theory, law is the commands of a legally unlimited sovereign to whom those subject to the law have 'a habit of obedience'.[127] The sovereign is the one habitually obeyed by most of his subjects, and his commands motivate this 'habit of obedience' by threatening punishments for non-compliance. In addition, Austin stipulated that commands must have a factually determinable content.

But recall also that legal positivists suppose that both law and the rule of law can have any content. Since the content may be morally atrocious, they argue that there can be no moral obligation to obey the law just because it is the law. And if that's what the command model entails, – law understood as the instrument of any ideology – how can one fold it into a non-positivist philosophy of law? Stated even more broadly, the puzzle is how common good lawyers and common good advocates more generally can combine Schmitt, a command model of law, illiberalism, non-positivism and democracy in one position.

There is a three-part solution to this puzzle. The first has to do with the legal logic of the position, more accurately with its anti-legal Schmittian logic. Schmitt often seemed to be involved in a careful elaboration of the history and theory of the legal constraints on delegated authority to respond to an emergency – that is, of a 'commissarial dictator', one who has constitutionally limited emergency powers on commission from the people, by contrast with a 'sovereign dictator', one who is free from any legal limit.[128] But he also argued that sovereign

[125] Ibid at 298–99.

[126] Ibid at 35.

[127] Ibid at 220–21.

[128] Carl Schmitt, *Dictatorship: From the Origin of the Modern Concept of Sovereignty to Proletarian Class Struggle* [1922] (Cambridge: Polity, 2014).

dictatorship can always assert itself against the law, including the law of the emergency regime, because legally unlimited and illimitable 'constituent power' is always present in a constitution.[129]

Recall from Chapter 1 that the manifesto for the Judicial Power Project identifies the judiciary as both the main threat to and guardian of the rule of law in the UK, in that it claims that '[j]udicial overreach increasingly threatens the rule of law and effective, democratic government', and that 'the judicial power has a central, strategic place in any well-ordered constitutional arrangement: no state is well-governed without an independent judiciary, exercising legal and constitutional authority to adjudicate disputes, including disputes between citizens and officials, fairly and in accordance with settled positive law'. It also suggests that the 'British constitutional tradition has [. . .] long centred on a disciplined account of the proper scope of judicial authority, which has been held rightly subject to the legislature's final authority to choose the content of the law and not to undermine the executive's constitutional responsibility to choose how best to act within the scope of its lawful powers'.[130]

This conception of the judicial role in constitutional order was the main theme of Finnis's inaugural lecture for the Judicial Power Project which began with the references to Francis Bacon which we saw puzzled Macdonald and Owen. Finnis dwelt in this part of his lecture on Bacon's rivalry with Sir Edward Coke (1552–1634), one of the great figures among the common law jurists, a rivalry that was both personal and political.[131] Finnis portrayed the rivalry as a great jurisprudential or legal-philosophical one about the role of judges in claiming as follows:

> Bacon's essay 'Of Judicature' or the office and responsibility of a judge, published in 1612, written like most of his essays after he became Solicitor General in 1607, and intended like the others to be the fruit of experience not book-learning, begins and almost ends by calling upon judges to abstain from law making or from disturbing the established boundaries of rights and properties, the landmarks; and to be content with their high responsibility, right or prerogative of interpreting and applying the laws, not novelties. But far from being against novelties, he himself urged, over two decades, that extensive law reform and ambitious rationalization of

129 See ibid at 110–11, and the dark formulation of the idea of sovereign dictatorship, at 119.

130 'About the Judicial Power Project' online: *Judicial Power Project* <https://judicialpowerproject.org.uk/about/>.

131 For a vivid account, see the novel by Jesse Norman, *The Winding Stair* (London: Biteback Publishing, 2023).

> England's chaotic common and statutory law be undertaken – only not in the exercise of judicial power.[132]

But here Finnis rather exaggerated Bacon's opposition to judges, as we can see by quoting the first and last parts of Bacon's essay:

> Judges ought to remember that their office is *jus dicere* and not *jus dare* – to interpret law and not to make or give law; . . . Let them be lions, but yet lions under the throne, being careful not to check or oppose any points of sovereignty. Let not judges also be so ignorant of their own right as to think there is not left to them, as a principal part of their office, a wise use and application of laws; for they may remember what the apostle says of a greater law than theirs: *Nos scimus quia lex bona est, modo quis ea utatur legitime.* 'We know that the law is good if a man uses it lawfully'.[133]

Contra Finnis, nothing in these lines distinguished Bacon sharply from Coke on judges, as we can see by referring to a book which Finnis said in a footnote to his invocation of Bacon we should look to 'above all' if we want to understand 'Bacon as jurist'.[134] For Daniel Coquillette's book is in severe tension with the claims made by Finnis in his lecture since he argues at length that Bacon and Coke were not far apart on what he calls the 'slow evolution of judge-made law'.[135] Moreover, even if, as the famous line from Bacon's essay states, the judges are 'under the throne', they are yet 'lions'. They are, that is, not 'mice', to evoke a letter a judge wrote to Lord Atkin after he had delivered his dissent in *Liversidge*,[136] the case discussed in the preceding chapter on wartime detention. Mr Justice Stable said of the majority that they had 'reduced the stature of the Judiciary with consequences that the nation will one day bitterly regret'. 'Bacon', the judge continued, 'said the Judges were the Lions under the throne, but the House of Lords has reduced us to mice squeaking under a chair in the Home Office'.[137] And, as we can see from Chapters 3–5, that is precisely the aim of the common good lawyers of the Judicial Power Project, though in the case of the Rwanda Act, their aim was more to silence the judges almost altogether

132 Finnis, 'Judicial Power: Past, Present and Future' at 5.

133 Sir Francis Bacon, 'Of Judicature' (1983) 9:3 *Judging* 64.

134 Finnis, 'Judicial Power: Past, Present and Future' at 5, note 5.

135 Coquillette, *Francis Bacon*, at 284–92.

136 *Liversidge v Anderson* [1942] AC 206.

137 Stable J quoted in Geoffrey Lewis, *Lord Atkin* (London: Butterworths, 1983) at 152.

so that the Home Office could render asylum seekers to Rwanda without the annoyance of judicial squeaks.[138]

That Bacon hardly differed from Coke on judges does not mean that they agreed on other matters. As Coquillette makes clear, Bacon was, as Finnis claimed, much more of an ardent law reformer than Coke. But, according to Coquillette, Bacon's 'legal ideology' was very different from what I have shown to be the ideology of the common good lawyers, since he did not harken back to some mythical past, a 'tradition' which somehow turns out to be that of 'the natural law'. Instead, he laid the basis for Jeremy Bentham and John Austin some centuries later in propounding an ideology that was 'secular, utilitarian, and "progressive"'.[139] Coquillette does acknowledge that Bacon's law reform projects had an 'authoritarian' side, but emphasizes that he was no 'lawless totalitarian', indeed was not 'opposed to "the rule of law", even in the broad sense of a liberal, common law judicial system'.[140]

In contrast, Schmitt scorned the rule of law, and, as we have seen, the common good lawyers, while they seek to borrow from Bentham's heirs on the left in claiming that they are all about restoring Parliament's authority, put forward arguments that will result in Parliament handing unlimited power to the executive. Mark at times seems completely aware that the aim of such projects is to hand unlimited power to the executive. However, in a telling passage, he acknowledges that in accepting Schmitt's legal theory, he has also accepted that the sovereign's authority is 'without legal restraints', but adds as a comfort that there are still 'moral constraints' – the 'moral substance at stake that justifies the use of emergency powers'.[141]

This 'comfort' brings me to the second part of the solution to the puzzle of how Mark can endorse Schmitt, a command model of law, illiberalism, non-positivism and democracy. He supposes that a

[138] Ironically, Finnis himself is highly critical of the judges in the majority in *Liversidge* for being more executive-minded than the executive itself, in the course of arguing that the judges in *Miller 2*, the decision on prorogation discussed in Chapter 4, were 'more parliament-minded than parliament itself'. John Finnis, '*Brexit* and the Balance of our Constitution' in *Judicial Power and the Balance of Our Constitution: Two Lectures by John Finnis* (London: Policy Exchange, 2018) online: <https://judicialpowerproject.org.uk/wp-content/uploads/2018/01/Judicial-Power-and-the-Balance-of-Our-Constitution.pdf> 134 at 157–58.

[139] Coquillette, *Francis Bacon*, at 291.

[140] Ibid at 284–86.

[141] Mark, *The Nature of Law*, at 319.

command model of law is non-positivist if one stipulates that the only proper use to which that instrument of law may be put is to impose the true morality on those subject to the law. For Mark, as for other common good advocates, that requires, as we saw Finnis tell us, that 'cultural pluralism' would give way, after a generation or so, to 'complete cultural integration'.[142]

In this regard, Mark's avoidance of even a mention in his book of Schmitt's authoritarian inclinations let alone his opportunistic career as a Nazi is remarkable. He does, however, wish to ward off the critique of Finnis as authoritarian by claiming that Finnis 'considers the obligation to obey the law to be of a piece with limited authority'.[143] He quotes in support a typically complex sentence from one of Finnis's essays: 'The reason . . . for taking the law seriously to the full extent of its tenor and intended reach – and never regarding it as giving *no* reason for doing what it commands – is a reason connected with that irreducible multiformity of human goods (and that plurality of human persons) which imposes intrinsic limitations on human practical reasoning and makes nonsense (and injustice) of totalitarian projects'.[144]

Mark fails to notice here that Finnis talks of 'totalitarian' not 'authoritarian' projects and there is of course a real distinction between a regime that imposes total ideological control on the population and one that allows for a limited amount of pluralism. But I will now elaborate my claim from Chapter 1 that those who advocate authoritarianism cannot make this distinction in a principled way, a failing that can have dramatic implications for politics. This elaboration provides the third and final part of the solution to the puzzle about how Mark, and common good lawyers more generally, can combine Schmitt, a command model of law, illiberalism, non-positivism and democracy in one position.

6.6 A Christian Vision for Kingdom Politics

Finnis, as we have now seen on several occasions, wished to temper his moral authoritarianism with 'not, of course, to be imposed'. But as we have also seen, these qualifications are empty because his idea of public order or public morality is so capacious that coercion will play a role.

142 Finnis, 'Reflections and Responses' at 562, note 344.

143 Mark, *The Nature of Law*, at 294.

144 John Finnis, 'Law as Coordination' in *Philosophy of Law: Collected Essays Volume IV* (Oxford: Oxford University Press, 2011) 66 at 72–73.

He would no doubt respond, first, that his understanding of 'complete cultural integration' is not incompatible with a limited form of pluralism, with the limit set by the compatibility of the tolerated groups with the ideology enforced by the state. As one of his sympathizers once put it to me after we both attended a seminar on his work, 'Finnis would not prohibit Anglicans from going to Mass'. In other words, in so far as other faith communities in the Christian tradition, indeed, even the Judeo-Christian tradition, are not incompatible with Finnis's own take on religion, they will be tolerated. That's what makes Finnis's project authoritarian not totalitarian.

The same may be true of Vermeule's 'integralism', though it's not clear to what extent Jews will be tolerated. For example, in *The Josias*, an online journal 'founded by a small community seeking to articulate an authentically Catholic political stance from which to approach the present order of society',[145] Vermeule reported the following:

> The most interesting conversation I've had lately in an academic setting was with a colleague – a man of the left who thinks of himself as 'secular', but who is in fact animated by a vibrant faith in the progress of history – who asked me to lunch and pressed the question 'in a fully Catholic polity, the sort you would like to bring about, what would happen to me, a Jew?' (Nothing bad, I assured him).[146]

But what does 'nothing bad' entail? Consider that in Crean and Finister's *Integralism: A Manual of Political Philosophy* they assert that '[in] a formally Catholic society, not only idolaters and atheists must be generally excluded from the legislature, and from the higher executive and judicial offices, but also all the unbaptised, as well as all adherents of heretical and schismatic bodies'[147] and that '[s]ince a citizen, simply speaking, is a subject endowed with certain rights and duties within a society because of his presumed willing of that society's common good, only someone who professes the gospel, as taught by the Church, can be a citizen simply speaking within Christendom'.[148] As one commentator put it: 'So, Jews out of Congress, the executive, and the courts.'[149]

[145] 'What Is the Josias?' online: *The Josias* <https://thejosias.com/about/>.

[146] Adrian Vermeule, 'According to Truth' (Jul 19 2018) online: *The Josias* <https://thejosias.com/2018/07/19/according-to-truth/>.

[147] Crean and Finister, *Integralism: A Manual of Political Philosophy*, at 117.

[148] Ibid at 118.

[149] Cole S Aronson, 'The Integralists and Us' (Fall 2023) online: *The Jewish Review of Books* <https://jewishreviewofbooks.com/philosophy/14786/the-integralists-and-us/#>. It is in this context that one can appreciate the point of American public intellectual Leon

However much Finnis may differ from Vermeule on such issues, they have the same response to challenges about the authoritarian implications of their positions on the common good: natural law theory sets a limit on the ideology the state may enforce. But here we should remember from my Introduction the point made about Schmitt's 'negatively prescriptive theory', aka anything-but-liberalism. As I explained, Schmitt's example shows that to adopt such a theory may force one to accept as legitimate whatever political force happens to fill the empty space of the common good. All such theorists have of course their own visions of how to fill that space, for example the vision of a somewhat tolerant state-imposed version of Catholicism that some among the common good lawyers espouse. But because they have to forge alliances with others who belong to different faiths, as well with yet others who have a secular basis for their right-wing ideology, what unites them is anything-but-liberalism, so whatever will happen to fill the space does the trick. Put differently, it is difficult, even impossible, to make principled distinctions between the ideologies of these 'furious minds', as Laura K. Field has aptly called them, and as she has effectively shown, the more moderate among them are inevitably dragged towards the more extreme.[150]

Mark's attempt to shore up Finnis's philosophy of law with Schmitt so that it does not appeal to more than a group of nationalistic or far-right Catholics is necessary only because common good lawyers and advocates must make their arguments on the secular plateau. I have adapted the term 'secular plateau' from the political theory of Ronald Dworkin, the liberal political and legal philosopher we encountered in Chapter 4. In an influential article, Dworkin argued that different liberal theories are best understood as competing conceptions of the abstract egalitarian principle that every citizen has a right to be treated with equal concern and respect by their own government. Hence, he suggested that the abstract egalitarian principle can be thought to provide 'a kind of plateau in political argument'.[151] I can help myself to this label because for Dworkin the

Wieseltier's comment on Vermeule's '(Nothing bad, I assured him)': 'His parenthetical assurance is not good enough. He might just as well have winked. The roots of his quasi-theocratic ideal are rotten with Jew-hatred, and so are some of his intellectual and political allies, as he might trouble himself to notice on his next visit to Budapest or Warsaw'. Leon Wieseltier, 'Christianism' (2022) 2 *Liberties* 326 at 356.

150 Field, *Furious Minds.*

151 Ronald Dworkin, 'Comment on Narveson: In Defense of Equality' (1983) 1 *Social Philosophy and Policy* 24 at 25.

plateau is secular as well as egalitarian on the supposition that whatever the differences between rival political ideologies, they all will start from a commitment to some conception of equality. Common good advocates, however, will refuse to compete on the plateau conceived as egalitarian because they will not regard it as a level terrain where every argument starts off on the same terms.

On their view, that competition is rigged against them because it excludes them from privileging their illiberal conception of the common good, one that will seek to restore relationships of inequality that they regard as part of the natural order of things. But they cannot refuse to compete on the secular plateau conceived more abstractly, as detached from a commitment to equality, for reasons of what we can think of as 'realpolitik'. By realpolitik, I mean the set of practical considerations that any ideological position faces in any still-functioning democratic system in which as a matter of fact there is a plurality of groups with different ideologies, and one must form an alliance with at least some of these if one is to have any hope of the state using law to impose anything like one's own ideology. And that forces common good advocates into alliances with other illiberals who may not share anything like their purported squeamishness about means or their vagueness about ends. I say 'purported' because my case study of the Rwanda saga shows such squeamishness and vagueness seem to vanish when it comes to putting in place the mechanisms of state power for achieving such ends.

What has brought about this state of affairs? It is worth noting that when Voegelin in 1952 published *The New Science of Politics* he did not convey the same degree of moral panic that in the twenty-first century seems to infect Finnis and others on the right. For he ended his book by asserting that 'the American and English democracies which most solidly in their institutions represent the truth of the soul, are at the same time existentially the strongest powers', though he did warn that it 'will require all our efforts to kindle this glimmer into a flame by repressing Gnostic corruption and restoring the forces of civilization'.[152]

These concluding observations of *The New Science of Politics* were made at a time when one could view these two democracies as not only having triumphed over the Nazis, but also as superior in force to the Communist bloc. More significantly, within the couple of pages that precede the observations, Voegelin suggested that what makes English

[152] Voegelin, *The New Science of Politics*, at 189.

democracy distinctive is that it 'preserved the institutional culture of aristocratic parliamentism as well as the mores of a Christian commonwealth, now sanctioned as national institutions'. Similarly, while the American Revolution was 'strongly affected by the psychology of the enlightenment', it also 'had the good fortune of coming to its close within the institutional and Christian climate of the *ancien régime*'.[153] These two democracies had not, as the French and German revolutions had done, brought about 'modernity without restraint' – that is, liberalism run amok.[154]

What Voegelin clearly had in mind was that the substantive homogeneity of a majority Christian and white political community was in place, ruled over by an aristocratic elite which would remain in power because of the longstanding institutional arrangements in which people trusted. The pages are then a somewhat disguised wink to those in the know. The majority of the population thought that they had – and they trusted in – rule by the stable democratic institutions that made up the body politic of 'we, the people'. In reality, they were living in the Christian climate of the *ancien régime* – the common good promulgated by their rulers under the guise of democracy. However, even this 'glimmer' was under threat. The Protestant Reformation and its liberal successors had radically undermined transcendentalist traditions and the glimmer had to be nurtured into a shining light that could guide radical political change if it were not to be extinguished altogether.

The sense that the glimmer could be extinguished of course went far beyond Voegelin. It animated the career of William F. Buckley, who was directly inspired by Voegelin and whose thought continues to be a huge influence on the ideology of the intellectuals in the MAGA movement.[155] And it explains why by the late 1950s, and definitely into the 1960s, a sense of moral panic set in among conservatives, the climate in which the Hart–Devlin debate took place and in which Finnis started writing. Since then, climate change has been even more severe. It has become 'modernity without restraint': in the US, the era ushered in by the Civil Rights Movement, the Warren Court and feminism; in our century, the election of a black President, the Me Too and Defund the Police movements, trans rights, and so on – whatever features of contemporary societies get

[153] Ibid at 188.

[154] Ibid at 189.

[155] See Sam Tannenhaus, *Buckley: The Life and the Revolution that Changed America* (New York: Random House, 2025). This is in terms of size and detail a monumental book, but it fails at any point to get to grips with Buckley's ideas.

grouped under the adjective 'woke' and which, as a result, become the targets in a culture war.

For a while such changes seemed unstoppable. Consider one of the most influential works of the late twentieth century, Catholic moral philosopher Alasdair MacIntyre's *After Virtue: A Study in Moral Theory*.[156] First published in 1981, MacIntyre criticized the liberal world in which he lived along lines that have become familiar – that is, for the loss of meaning in a world in which individuals are abandoned to find their own meaning in a neoliberal market economy. He also thought that it was possible to construct a different kind of economic, political and moral order, informed by a deeply conservative ethics of virtue best articulated for him in the doctrines of the Catholic Church in which each individual has a given role and status within a well-defined and highly determinate system.

This kind of society, MacIntyre argued, was not to be created by a political movement which would overthrow the existing order, whether peacefully through the mechanisms of democracy or by violent revolution. Nor would it be the case that the goal of such a community would be enforced by the state. Rather, taking as his example the existence of monasteries in the dark ages, in our own dark age, with the 'barbarians', as he famously said on the last page of his book, already within our frontiers and 'governing us for quite some time', the only viable political option seemed to be to build small communities of virtue whose practices would inspire both growth and emulation.[157]

Fast forward to 2012 and we find much the same sentiment, though with a glimmer of hope for climate change in the right direction, in the political imagination of the right. It is in 'A Christian Vision for Kingdom Politics', a blog post by Joshua Hawley just before Obama was elected to his second term in office.[158] At that time, Hawley, a graduate of Stanford and Yale, was an associate professor of law. Since 2018 he has been a Republican senator, a pillar of the MAGA movement. He became infamous in 2020 for saluting the 6 January insurrectionists on his way into the Capitol to lead the Republican effort to prevent

[156] Alasdair MacIntyre, *After Virtue: A Study in Moral Theory*, 3rd edition (Notre Dame, IN: University of Notre Dame Press, 2007).

[157] Ibid at 262–63.

[158] Joshua Hawley, 'A Christian Vision for Kingdom Politics: Immanentize the Eschaton!' (Oct 26 2023) online: *Patheos* <www.patheos.com/blogs/philosophicalfragments/2012/10/26/christian-vision-for-kingdom-politics/>.

Biden's certification as President only to be caught on video scuttling fearfully away after the mob he had cheered on broke into building.

I will reproduce almost all of Hawley's post because it so beautifully traces the trajectory of the political theology of the far right – from despair at liberalism's victory to hope that the state can be drafted into a project where its vision of the common good can be enforced. He began with this sketch of Voegelin's centrality to the political theology of the right:

> Eric Voegelin was a German-American émigré who wrote several volumes of high-toned philosophy in the 1950s which were read by approximately zero members of the American public – save a certain William F. Buckley, Jr. When the irrepressible founder and editor of *National Review* happened upon Voegelin's first monograph, *The New Science of Politics*, he discovered a condemnation of utopian ambition in politics that delighted him. Politics turns totalitarian, Voegelin explained, 'when a Christian transcendental fulfillment becomes immanentized. Such an immanentist hypostasis of the eschaton, however, is a theoretical fallacy'. Right. In short order, Buckley had converted that jumble of theory-speak into a whimsical political slogan: 'Don't let them immanentize the eschaton!' Or, broadly: Beware of all political programs that aim to create utopias. . . .
>
> Eventually Buckley had the phrase printed on t-shirts and buttons and it became a favorite of conservative political writers. But I wonder, ten days before a presidential election in which evangelicals will again be called upon to fulfill their duties as citizens: Isn't immanentizing the eschaton *precisely* what Christian citizens should be doing?[159]

Hawley continued with this diagnosis of the times:

> Through the 1980s and '90s evangelicals sought to turn back the forces of secularization. Groups like the Moral Majority and the Christian Coalition pressed for laws recognizing Christianity's unique place in American life, including laws that would allow prayer in public schools and Christian displays in public places.
>
> They advocated a constitutional amendment to overturn *Roe v. Wade*. In the main, the idea was to resurrect America's Christian identity, to win from the public and from the government recognition of 'Christian values', and reaffirmation of Christianity's special place in American history and culture. The aim was, in a sense, to 'convert' both society and government.

[159] Ibid.

> That approach is due for a rethink. For one thing, it depends on a Christian social hegemony that is likely lost for good. Believing Christians no longer constitute an overwhelming majority of the American public, nor do they occupy the commanding heights of culture, entertainment, and academia. As a sheer projection of demographic destiny, they are unlikely to do so anytime soon.[160]

So here one finds the same sentiment that we just got from MacIntyre – that one reason not to try to impose a Christian vision for 'Kingdom Politics' is that it's not politically feasible. But Hawley then added a qualification:

> It's far from clear that restoring Christian social authority is an appropriate aim of *politics* in the first place. The conversionist approach tends to confuse the distinct missions of church and state – is it really the role of government, for instance, to promote 'Christian values' or refurbish America's Christian heritage? – even as it fails to provide much guidance as to what, exactly, government is supposed to be doing.[161]

Moreover, 'advancing God's kingdom does not mean abandoning constitutional government in favor of theocracy or using the state to convert non-believers. On the contrary, a kingdom-inspired approach to politics would give up trying to Christianize the state altogether'.

> Rather than seek to Christianize the state and use it to restore a Christian social consensus, believing citizens should call the state to its true purpose – to serve justice, and by extension, the kingdom of God. This is Christians' role in politics, and their service, both to the Lord and to their fellow man. For the principles of the kingdom and the social life it envisions are not for Christians only, but for all people. The kingdom life *is* the common good. And Christians should offer it winsomely, creatively, heartily once again.[162]

If we fast forward from 2012 to 2020 and the insurrection, or to now and Hawley's role in a Senate in which he has voted to confirm all of Trump's far-right picks for cabinet positions, none of whom seem squeamish about either means or ends, we can see that once a 'Christian social hegemony' seems feasible, with insurrectionists now occupying 'the commanding heights of culture … and entertainment' and able to bully various institutions into submission, the qualifications

[160] Ibid.
[161] Ibid. His emphasis.
[162] Ibid.

and squeamishness can be abandoned.[163] And, as I have claimed throughout the book, if you enter the alliance of negatively prescriptive theorists, you will find that you have abandoned whatever principles might have prompted any past squeamishness about means and vagueness about ends.[164] But, and this is the third and final part of the solution to the puzzle, common good advocates don't have to abandon democracy, at least in name, which is why they can put forward a position that combines democracy with Schmitt, a command model of law, illiberalism and non-positivism.

In Voegelin's memoir, he remarked scornfully that '[t]he Austrian veering toward Mussolini as a protection against the worst evil of Hitler apparently was beyond the comprehension of ardent Marxists, who could do nothing but yell "Fascism"'.[165] He also said that his 1934 Schmittian book in praise of Austrian fascism was his 'first major attempt to understand that an authoritarian state that would keep radical ideologists in check was the best possible defence of democracy'.[166]

Voegelin's followers today do not, however, have to 'veer towards Mussolini', since they have learned a lesson about democracy that was unavailable to the likes of Voegelin and Schmitt in the 1930s. Their main teacher is Victor Orbán and he has taught that the political space of authoritarianism need not exclude democracy as long as the version of democracy is 'illiberal democracy'. This is a democracy whose institutions have been hollowed out or captured so that, first, the return of the ruler in periodic elections is guaranteed to the extent possible and, second, institutions such as parliaments and the judiciaries are disabled from mediating the promulgation of the common good.

163 Ibid.

164 One finds exactly the same movement in the work of common good advocate Patrick Deneen. In the Conclusion to his *Why Liberalism Failed* (New Haven, CT: Yale University Press, 2018) he argued that while the liberal project needed reform, its 'foundation should not be abandoned' (at 182). Much like MacIntyre, he argued not for regime change but for fostering practices in 'local settings' and for cultivating 'virtuosity in households' (at 198). (Curiously, MacIntyre's *After Virtue* seems to have escaped his attention.) But, as we saw in Chapter 1, if we fast forward to Patrick Deneen, *Regime Change: Towards a Postliberal Future* (New York: Sentinel, 2023), it appears that in the MAGA era, virtuosity can be cultivated and enforced nationally. See also Adrian Vermeule, 'A Christian Strategy' (Nov 1 2017) online: *First Things* <https://firstthings.com/a-christian-strategy/>.

165 Voegelin, *Autobiographical Reflections*, at 68.

166 Ibid at 9.

There is, then, no need to introduce anything more authoritarian because illiberal democracy suffices. One simply puts in place the system described by two American political scientists as competitive authoritarianism, a 'hybrid regime' that differs from the fascist regimes of the mid twentieth century mainly in that it combines features of democratic and authoritarian rule. As I mentioned in Chapter 1, the leading example is Orbán's Hungary in which, in their summary, his government 'packed the Constitutional Court, limited opposition media access both by politicizing state-run media and by coopting much of the private media, and gerrymandered electoral districts to lock in the ruling party's control of parliament'.[167] And, at the risk of stating the obvious, a parliament subject to this degree of control does little more than provide a façade of democracy over the blunt instrument of unconstrained executive power.

In Chapter 4, I drew attention to Dworkin's distinction between the majoritarian conception of democracy, according to which the legitimate decision is the one the majority happens to vote for, whatever its content, and a liberal conception, according to which decisions by the majority are legitimate only if they respect certain fundamental rights. As I remarked, both conceptions have an obvious foothold in the practices of the world's democracies. But they offer different prescriptions as to the design of our political and legal institutions and thus as to how we should best go on in our practices.[168] In particular, the majoritarian conception favours parliamentary sovereignty and a thin conception of the rule of law.

In the UK, the common good lawyers adopt the majoritarian conception because it can be transformed into one of unlimited executive power, exactly the transformation the Judicial Power Project seems designed to achieve. My analysis of the debate over the Rwanda Act, the rule of law, and more generally constitutionalism in a democracy is the evidence for my claim in Chapter 1 that the Judicial Power Project's manifesto is the sheep's clothing for the wolf of the Common Good Project, whose illiberal agenda is revealed through this chapter's account of the thought of John Finnis, its major intellectual figure in the UK. But, we need to

[167] Steven Levitsky and Lucan Way, 'The New Competitive Authoritarianism' (2020) 31 *Journal of Democracy* 51 at 54. For the book, see Levitsky and Way, *Competitive Authoritarianism: Hybrid Regimes after the Cold War* (Cambridge: Cambridge University Press, 2012).

[168] Ronald Dworkin, 'Introduction: The Moral Reading and the Majoritarian Premise' in *Freedom's Law: The Moral Reading of the American Constitution* (Cambridge, MA: Harvard University Press, 1996) 1.

note, exactly the same result can be and has been largely achieved in a constitutional order like that of the US, one with an entrenched constitution which protects a list of liberal rights and freedoms. All one needs is a supine Supreme Court with a large majority of judges appointed because they share the ideology of the ruler.[169]

It is that feature of the US legal order that explains the biggest difference between the common good lawyers on that side of the Atlantic and their counterparts in the UK, the willingness of Vermeule to accord to judges a role that the UK common good lawyers oppose, and which brings them in this one respect closer to Schmitt than Vermeule. In his *Common Good Constitutionalism*, Vermeule purports to adopt a Dworkinian interpretive methodology to show that the principles that lie under the surface of US positive constitutional law are the political ideology of his integralism.[170] His exploitation of Dworkin is glib, but more importantly absurd since his ideology is incompatible with any plausible version of constitutionalism. It results, as I have shown in this book, in the elevation of the legally unlimited executive to the status of ultimate source of legal authority. That Vermeule is prepared to give to judges this pseudo-Dworkinian role, in contrast to the common good lawyers in the UK, has, as I just suggested, everything to do with the fact that the far right in the US can count on the majority of their Supreme Court both to give the executive a free hand and to decide against the liberal precedents put in place by the Warren Court.

The result in both legal orders is that one gets neither the rule of law nor democratic constitutional order. Rather one gets 'organ sovereignty', the supremacy of the executive. This term was coined by Hermann Heller, one of the leading public law and legal theorists of Weimar-era Germany, to describe Schmitt. In his 1927 book on sovereignty in public and international law, Heller pointed out that Schmittian logic is born of a wish to replace legal theory with a 'political theology' in which the executive is endowed with magical powers.[171] It is an anti-legal theory

[169] See Leah Litman, *Lawless: How the Supreme Court Runs on Conservative Grievance, Fringe Theories, and Bad Vibes* (New York: Atria, 2025). On the role of the Federalist Society in bringing about this state of affairs, a clear model for the Judicial Power Project, see Amanda Hollis-Brusky, *Ideas With Consequences: The Federalist Society and the Conservative Counterrevolution* (New York: Oxford University Press, 2015).

[170] See for example, Vermeule, *Common Good Constitutionalism* at 95–97.

[171] Hermann Heller, *Sovereignty: A Contribution to the Theory of Public and International Law*, David Dyzenhaus, ed, Belinda Cooper, trans (Oxford: Oxford University Press, 2019) at 101–4.

according to which the will of the executive is made the source of law on the most important constitutional issues.

6.7 Conclusion

Schmitt began *Political Theology* with the famous sentence 'Sovereign is he who decides on the exception', by which he wished to convey that the political sovereign is the one capable of making a decision both about when there is an emergency, in the sense of a disruption to the social, political or moral order, and about how effectively to respond to it.[172] That effectively makes the 'sovereign' an uncommanded commander who stands outside the legal order with the legitimacy to act at will against the law. The success of his actions is gauged only by the criterion of whether he succeeds in making the distinction which Schmitt claimed as the essential distinction of 'the political', the distinction between 'friend and enemy', the distinction which establishes who is in the 'substantively homogeneous' 'people' and who is out.

This argument came to the fore in Schmitt's explicit claim in 1932 that the President – the head of the executive, is the 'guardian' of the constitution,[173] so that when it came to the limits on executive power to act under the emergency powers provision of the Weimar Constitution, Article 48, these were to be determined in a process of unilateral executive interpretation. This is exactly as J. D. Vance and Adrian Vermeule are suggesting in their response to the attempts by judges in the hierarchy below the Supreme Court to uphold both the rule of law and the authority of the legislative branch against Trump's sweeping assertions of executive power, attempts which will prove futile if Republican legislators continue in their cultish devotion to Trump and the Supreme Court continues to thwart these attempts, often on its 'shadow docket', its decisions announced without offering any reasons.[174]

[172] Schmitt, *Political Theology* at 5.

[173] Carl Schmitt, 'The Guardian of the Constitution: Schmitt on Pluralism and the President as the Guardian of the Constitution' in Lars Vinx, *The Guardian of the Constitution: Hans Kelsen and Carl Schmitt on the Limits of Constitutional Law* (Cambridge: Cambridge University Press, 2015) 125.

[174] Charlie Savage and Minho Kim, 'Vance says "Judges Aren't Allowed to Control" Trump's "Legitimate Power"' (Feb 9 2025) online: *New York Times* <www.nytimes.com/2025/02/09/us/politics/vance-trump-federal-courts-executive-order.html>. For the 'shadow docket', see Alicia Bannon, 'Supreme Court Must Explain Why It Keeps

In this regard, Schmitt's theory of the judicial role supposes that judges adjudicate properly only when they subsume the facts of a case to the determinate content of a statute. The independence of judges depends on such a role being available to them and so they are incapable of resolving the political disputes that face the person who occupies the role of the guardian of the constitution.[175] Such disputes, Schmitt asserted, have to be resolved not by a higher authority but by what he called a 'neutral third'[176] – in his view, the President of the Reich because he alone could take political decisions in the name of the 'whole of the political unity' of the German people. On this point, Schmitt rested his final claim that the President has a democratic legitimacy that judges lack.[177]

This final claim should of course provoke astonishment in anyone who values democracy. If democracy is reduced to a bond established by a supreme leader between himself and a portion of the population that answers to his vision of the substantive homogeneity of the *Volk*, then any successful authoritarian is by definition a democrat and the countries we took to be good examples of well-functioning democracies were fake. Such astonishment is important to keep in mind when we notice that in common good writings, whether by lawyers like Finnis, Ekins and Vermeule, or political theorists such as Patrick Deneen, talk of 'democracy' is rare, mentioned usually as an afterthought. Democracy becomes little more than an attempt to dignify an anti-democratic theory or regime, as in 'German Democratic Republic', the official title of the East German post-war regime. But in the midst of astonishment it is important to keep in mind that a Schmittian understanding of 'democracy' or its equivalents, for example, 'the sovereignty of the people' or 'the people's will', is the understanding that goes with Schmitt's conception of the judicial role and the role of the executive in political order.

Exactly that conception of the judicial role is, as we can now see, the role the Judicial Power Project seems to accord to judges. We can also see that the point of giving the executive this 'constitutional' role is to destroy the liberal democratic constitutional order, as Hans Kelsen, at that time Schmitt's colleague on the Cologne Law Faculty, pointed out in the

Ruling in Trump's Favor' (Aug 14, 2025) online: <www.brennancenter.org/our-work/analysis-opinion/supreme-court-must-explain-why-it-keeps-ruling-trumps-favor>.

175 Schmitt, 'The Guardian of the Constitution' at 117–20.

176 Ibid at 151–60.

177 Ibid at 168–73.

1930s.[178] Up until 1933, Schmitt was legal adviser to General Kurt von Schleicher, who had a central part in the demise of the Weimar Republic as President Paul von Hindenburg's 'closest confidant'. As historian Christopher Browning has recently pointed out, Schleicher had two goals: 'ousting Germany's unpopular, presidentially appointed chancellor, Heinrich Brüning, and harnessing Hitler's popularity to carry out an authoritarian revision of the democratic Weimar Constitution that Germany's upper class conservative nationalists did not have sufficient popular support to achieve on their own'.[179]

Browning titles his essay – clearly intended as a meditation on Trump's US today – 'Hitler's Enablers' because these figures prepared the way for the Nazi seizure of power by destroying the institutions that stood in Hitler's way, even as they tried to outmanoeuvre him. One of the most consequential steps in this destruction was the federal government's coup against the state of Prussia in 1932. Prussia was not only by far the most powerful and largest state in the federal system, but also the main bastion of social democratic resistance to the extreme right. The coup was masterminded by Schleicher and Schmitt and saw the federal government taking control of Prussia's machinery of government by invoking the emergency powers provision of the Weimar Constitution. They alleged that the Prussian government was unable to contain unrest on the streets, unrest which the federal government had itself connived to provoke.

Schmitt appeared on behalf of Schleicher in the court challenge that the social democrats and others brought to the validity of the declaration of emergency. He argued that the Court that heard the matter had no jurisdiction to decide such a highly charged political question. The Court rejected this argument, but nonetheless gave the federal government most of what it wanted: control over the internal machinery of Prussian government. Schmitt was nevertheless highly distressed by what he regarded as the Court's failure to understand that the emergency powers provision ousted judicial control altogether, thus precluding the

[178] Hans Kelsen, 'Who Ought to Be the Guardian of the Constitution' [1931] in Lars Vinx, ed and trans, *The Guardian of the Constitution: Hans Kelsen and Carl Schmitt on the Limits of Constitutional Law* (Cambridge: Cambridge University Press, 2015) 174. Kelsen was responding to Carl Schmitt, 'The Guardian of the Constitution' [1931] in ibid at 79.

[179] Christopher Browning, 'Hitler's Enablers' (Nov 7 2024) online: *New York Review of Books* <www.nybooks.com/articles/2024/11/07/hitlers-enablers-the-death-of-democracy-benjamin-carter-hett/>.

Court from deciding at all, and by the fact that the Court decided that Prussia could retain its representation in the upper house of the German Parliament.[180]

Hitler had Schleicher murdered in the 'Night of the Long Knives' in late June of 1934, which marked him as special enemy of the Nazis because nearly all of the many others who died that night were Nazi Party members who were perceived as dangerous rivals within the Party. Given Schleicher's distinction in this respect and Schmitt's closeness to him, one might have expected that Schmitt would have suffered a similar fate. But he wormed his way into the regime's good books, largely by taking to writing virulently pro-Nazi and antisemitic tracts. This included one in 1934 titled 'The Führer – Guardian of Law' which praised the statute Hitler had caused to be enacted to legalize the June assassinations retrospectively, including the murder of Schmitt's friend Schleicher.[181] He thus managed to establish himself as the 'Kronjurist' – crown jurist – to the Nazis until he fell out of favour later in the decade.

This tale speaks to Schmitt's despicable character. But that he was able to make this transition to Nazi legal propagandist highlights the point of my distinction between authoritarian political and legal theory and more extreme, even totalitarian theories, notoriously the Nazi variety. People on the less extreme side of the political spectrum that goes from right-wing authoritarian to fascist to totalitarian find it difficult, maybe impossible, to draw principled differences between their position and the positions of others. For Schmitt, like his aristocratic friends, despised the uncouth Austrian corporal with his biological views about Jewish inferiority in contrast to their more educated 'cultural' racism. But because he and his political friends yearned for a post-liberal future, what Leo Strauss in a 1932 review of one of Schmitt's books called the 'horizon beyond liberalism', once that future had arrived they had no reason in principle to reject its totalitarian content.[182] The messiah is whoever happens to win power – 'Sovereign is he who decides on the exception'. And as we saw in Chapter 3, there is a strong echo of Schmitt's distress at the Court's decision about the coup against Prussia

[180] David Dyzenhaus, 'Legal Theory in the Collapse of Weimar: Contemporary Lessons?' (1997) 91 *American Political Science Review* 121.

[181] Carl Schmitt, 'Der Führer Schutzt das Recht' in *Positionen und Begriffe in Kampf mit Weimar, Genf, Versailles* (Berlin: Duncker & Humblot, 1988) 199.

[182] Leo Strauss, 'Comments on Carl Schmitt's *Der Begriff des Politischen*' reproduced in Carl Schmitt, *The Concept of the Political* (New Brunswick, NJ: Rutgers University Press, 1976) 81 at 104–5.

in the common good lawyers' reaction to the Rwanda Act, which in their view did not go far enough since it did not totally oust judicial review of the statute's implementation in that it left open a few extremely limited avenues for challenge.

In the leading work on Carl Schmitt's influence in Europe after the war, Jan-Werner Müller titles one chapter 'Integral Europe and the Rise of the European New Right(s)'.[183] He begins with the observation that '"Integrity" was one of Carl Schmitt's keywords. For him, integrity was inextricably linked to the concept of order'. This combination of integrity and order 'came to be at the heart of the New Right movements which arose in Europe during the 1970s and especially the 1980s' and they replaced the 'fascist primacy of the political with a primacy of the cultural. Where fascist parties in the first part of the twentieth century had sought to capture the state, these movements placed an emphasis on first shaping a society's self-image'.[184] As he sets out, Schmitt was by no means the only or even the main inspiration for what Müller calls the 'integralist insurgency'. Nor, as he makes clear was its source of inspiration mainly religious. And he comments at the end of the chapter that for both the old and the new right, 'the sources of both integration and integrity often remained obscure or downright mystical'.[185] The difference that comes from fast forwarding from 2003 – the year of publication of his book – to the present is that the right has in the US captured the state so that those who have been waging the battle on the cultural front can now jostle with others in the competition to use the instruments of the state, including the blunt instrument of its coercive powers, to impose their values on society.

In the volume of essays in honour of Finnis, one of the more critical contributions is Leslie Green's essay on the issues that occupied Hart and Devlin in their debate about state-enforced morality. There, Green speaks to the fear that Finnis's view of the state and law as the instrument of his grip on moral truth provides a thought experiment in which a new party – the 'Natural Law Party' – 'now has five reliable votes in the Supreme Court or has just swept Parliament'.[186] The fear, Green

[183] Jan-Werner Müller, *A Dangerous Mind: Carl Schmitt in Post-War European Thought* (New Haven, CT: Yale University Press, 2003) at 207.

[184] Ibid.

[185] Ibid at 218.

[186] Leslie Green, 'The Nature of Limited Government' in Keown and George, eds, *Reason, Morality, and Law* 186 at 200.

suggests, is not that you are going to get what he describes as a 'tsunami of civic republicanism', by which he means the kind of theory which seeks to establish increased democratic control over all our institutions, private as well as public, in order to achieve the equality of all citizens. Rather, as he explains,

> The fear is more likely to be that we are in for a loss of liberty in personal life, especially in sexual conduct, that discrimination on grounds of sex and sexual orientation will get a lot worse, and that our criminal justice system will take on a hard, retributive character. That is, the distrust of natural law morality has less to do with a fear of public morality than with a fear of the morality it will make public. To speak bluntly, the worry is that the values it wants to see in the public sphere are anti-liberal and anti-humanist (not just ante-liberal and ante humanist).[187]

Interestingly, Finnis in his response did not deny this claim. Rather, he simply asserted that politics is about setting your vision of moral truth against another, in his case against what he sums up in a list of the pet hates of the far right as 'millennial judgments' about '(xeno-, Islamo-, homo-, trans- . . .) "phobic" violations of "identity" rights and egalitarian "diversity" values'.[188]

We can now see that Finnis's culture war requires the war against law I have set out in these pages. There may be no better way to understand the political stakes in this war than by seeing how it is fought out on concrete issues in which the very meaning of the rule of law is in play. But it would be wrong for me to leave on a note which suggests that all we need is the rule of law properly understood and sincere commitment to the cause of human rights to fight these battles. As the odd alliance between the far right and elements of the left sketched in Chapter 1 should tell us, we are in this war because of the inability of liberal democrats thus far to respond to challenges that face the majority of people, both in the societies of the West and elsewhere.

The moral panic about immigration that so occupies Finnis and the far right, but also it sometimes seems a large proportion of the population in these societies, is in part the product of falling birth rates.[189] Falling birth rates may also account for yet another moral panic about control over

[187] Ibid.

[188] Finnis, 'Reflections and Responses' at 530.

[189] See Ivan Krastev and Stephen Holmes, *The Light that Failed: Why the West is Losing the Fight for Democracy* (New York: Pegasus Books, 2019) and Richard Seymour, *Disaster Nationalism: The Downfall of Liberal Civilization* (London: Verso, 2025).

sexuality, which results in the right's obsession with abortion, homosexuality, trans rights and putting women back into the traditional role of housewife and mother. But there is also a concern about rising inequality that gets displaced onto both immigration and control over sexuality. Finnis, Vermeule and other common good advocates purport to offer meaning to people who live their lives in the wreckage created by the neoliberal forces that swept our world after the collapse of the Soviet Union. To fight back, to fight against having their particular substantive conception of the good forced upon us, we will need more than a commitment to the rule of law, human rights and democracy. Such commitments will have to be anchored in a moral vision that provides a genuine alternative. The vision will go beyond Mill's 'Harm Principle' to show how an attempt to establish a more just and more equal society out of the wreckage requires the framework of the rule of law and human rights that the Judicial Power and Common Good Projects are working so hard to destroy. At the same time, it must show how that framework of the rule of law and human rights cannot be maintained without a profound commitment to the greater social, economic and political equality of all.

That's the challenge.

BIBLIOGRAPHY

Books and Articles

Allan, Trevor, *The Sovereignty of Law: Freedom, Constitution, and Common Law* (Oxford: Oxford University Press, 2013).

Austin, John, *Lectures on Jurisprudence or The Philosophy of Positive Law*, 5th edition (London: John Murray, 1885), volume 1.

Bacon, Sir Francis, 'Of Judicature' (1983) 9:3 *Judging* 64.

Beller, Steven, *A Concise History of Austria* (Cambridge: Cambridge University Press, 2006).

Bentham, Jeremy, *A Fragment on Government* [1776] (Cambridge: Cambridge University Press, 1988).

Bingham, Tom, *The Rule of Law* (London: Allen Lane, 2010).

Blackett, RJM, *The Captive's Quest for Freedom: Fugitive Slaves, the 1850 Fugitive Slave Law, and the Politics of Slavery* (New York: Cambridge University Press, 2018).

Blackstone, Sir William, *Commentaries on the Laws of England: A Facsimile of the First Edition of 1765–1769* (Chicago: University of Chicago Press, 1979) volume 1.

Casey, Conor, and Adrian Vermeule, 'Myths of Common Good Constitutionalism' (2022) 45 *Harvard Journal of Law & Public Policy* 104.

Chia, Joyce, and Savitri Taylor, 'A Masterclass in Evading the Rule of Law: The Saga of Scott Morrison and Temporary Protection Visas' (2021) 44 *University of New South Wales Law Journal* 4.

Collini, Stefan, *Public Moralists: Political Thought and Intellectual Life in Britain 1850–1930* (Oxford: Clarendon Press, 2006).

Coquillette, Daniel R, *Francis Bacon* (Edinburgh: Edinburgh University Press, 1992).

Crean, Thomas, and Alan Finister, *Integralism: A Manual of Political Philosophy* (London: Eurospan, 2020).

Delbanco, Andrew, *The War before the War: Fugitive Slaves and the Struggle for America's Soul from the Revolution to the Civil War* (New York: Penguin Press, 2018).

Deneen, Patrick, *Why Liberalism Failed* (New Haven, CT: Yale University Press, 2018).

Regime Change: Towards a Postliberal Future (New York: Sentinel, 2023).

Devlin, Patrick, 'Morals and the Criminal Law' in *The Enforcement of Morals* (London: Oxford University Press, 1965) 1.

Dicey, AV, *Introduction to the Study of the Law of the Constitution* [1915] (Indianapolis *Women's Health Organization*, 597 *US* 215 (2022).: Liberty Fund, 1982).

Drakeley, Rhys, 'Loophole or Law-Breaking? Rwanda Plan's Inconsistency with International Refugee Law' (2023) 4 *York Law Review* 141.

Dworkin, Ronald, 'Comment on Narveson: In Defense of Equality' (1983) 1 *Social Philosophy and Policy* 24.

'Political Judges and the Rule of Law' in *A Matter of Principle* (Cambridge, MA: Harvard University Press, 1985) 9.

'Introduction: The Moral Reading and the Majoritarian Premise' in *Freedom's Law: The Moral Reading of the American Constitution* (Cambridge, MA: Harvard University Press, 1996) 1.

Dyzenhaus, David, *Hard Cases in Wicked Legal Systems: South African Law in the Perspective of Legal Philosophy* (Oxford: Clarendon Press, 1991); 2nd edition as *Hard Cases in Wicked Legal Systems: Pathologies of Legality* (Oxford: Oxford University Press, 2010).

'Legal Theory in the Collapse of Weimar: Contemporary Lessons?' (1997) 91 *American Political Science Review* 121.

Legality and Legitimacy: Carl Schmitt, Hans Kelsen, and Hermann Heller in Weimar (Oxford: Clarendon Press, 1997).

Judging the Judges, Judging Ourselves: Truth, Reconciliation and the Apartheid Legal Order (Oxford: Hart Publishing, 1998).

The Constitution of Law: Legality in a Time of Emergency (Cambridge: Cambridge University Press, 2006).

'The Politics of the Question of Constituent Power' in Martin Loughlin and Neil Walker, eds, *The Paradox of Constitutionalism: Constituent Power and Constitutional Form* (Oxford: Oxford University Press, 2007) 129.

'The Puzzle of Martial Law' (2009) 59 *University of Toronto Law Journal* 1.

'Preventive Justice and the Rule-of-Law Project' in Andrew Ashworth, Lucia Zedner, and Patrick Tomlin, eds, *Prevention and the Limits of the Criminal Law* (Oxford: Oxford University Press, 2013) 9.

'Proportionality and Deference in a Culture of Justification' in Grant Huscroft, Bradley Miller, and Grégoire Webber, eds, *Proportionality and the Rule of Law: Rights, Justification, Reasoning* (Cambridge: Cambridge University Press, 2014) 234.

The Long Arc of Legality: Hobbes, Kelsen, Hart (Cambridge: Cambridge University Press, 2022).

'"Immanentizing the Eschaton": Eric Voegelin, Hans Kelsen, and the Debate over Secular Religion' in Sander Verhaegh, ed, *American Philosophy and the Intellectual Migration* (Berlin: De Gruyter, 2025) 279.

Ekins, Richard, 'Acts of Parliament and the Parliament Acts' (2007) 123 *Law Quarterly Review* 91.

'Constitutional Principle in the Laws of the Commonwealth' in John Keown and Robert P George, eds, *Reason, Morality, and Law: The Philosophy of John Finnis* (Oxford: Oxford University Press, 2013) 396.

'Legislation as Reasoned Action' in Grégoire Webber, Paul Yowell, Richard Ekins, Maris Köpcke, Bradley W Miller, and Francisco J Urbina, eds, *Legislated Rights: Securing Human Rights through Legislation* (Cambridge: Cambridge University Press, 2018) 86.

'Legislative Freedom and Its Consequences' in Richard Johnson and Yuan Yi Zhu, eds, *Sceptical Perspectives on the Changing Constitution of the United Kingdom* (Oxford: Hart Publishing, 2023) 55.

'Political Polarization and the Rule of Law' (2025) 19 *Law & Ethics of Human Rights* 201.

Ellman, Stephen, *Arthur Chaskalson: A Life Dedicated to Justice for All* (Montgomery, AL: New South Books, 2019).

Faye, Emmanuel, *Heidegger: L'Introduction du Nazisme dans la Philosophie: Autour des séminaires inédits de 1933–1935* (Paris: Albin Michel, 2005).

Feldman, David, 'Democracy, Law, and Human Rights: Politics as Challenge and Opportunity' in Murray Hunt, Hayler Hooper, and Paul Yowell, eds, *Parliaments and Human Rights: Redressing the Democratic Deficit* (Oxford: Hart Publishing, 2015) 95.

Field, Laura, *Furious Minds: The Making of the Maga New Right* (Princeton, NJ: Princeton University Press, 2025).

Finlason, WF, *A Treatise on Martial Law: As Allowed in Time of Rebellion; with Practical Illustrations Drawn from the Official Documents in the Jamaica Case and the Evidence Taken by the Royal Commission of Enquiry with Comments, Constitutional and Legal* (London: Stevens & Sons, 1866).

Finnis, John, *Natural Law and Natural Rights* (Oxford: Clarendon Press, 1980).

'"Shameless Acts" in Colorado: Abuse of Scholarship in Constitutional Cases' (1994) 7 *Academic Questions* 10.

Aquinas: Moral, Political, and Legal Theory (Oxford: Oxford University Press, 1998).

'Reason, Revelation, Universality and Particularity in Ethics' (2008) 53 *American Journal of Jurisprudence* 23.

'Endorsing Discrimination between Faiths: A Case of Extreme Speech' in Ivan Hare and James Weinstein, eds, *Extreme Speech and Democracy* (Oxford: Oxford University Press, 2009) 430.

Human Rights and the Common Good: Collected Essays Volume III (Oxford: Oxford University Press, 2011).

'Human Rights and Their Enforcement' 19.

'Law, Morality, and "Sexual Orientation"' 334.

'Introduction' in *Intention and Identity: Collected Essays: Volume II* (Oxford: Oxford University Press, 2011) 1.

Philosophy of Law: Collected Essays Volume IV (Oxford: Oxford University Press, 2011).

'Hart as a Political Philosopher' 257.

'Law as Coordination' 66.

'Revolutions and Continuity of Law' 407.

'Religion and State' in *Religion and Public Reasons, Collected Essays: Volume V* (Oxford: Oxford University Press, 2011) 80.

'Reflections and Responses' in John Keown and Robert P George, eds, *Reason, Morality, and Law: The Philosophy of John Finnis* (Oxford: Oxford University Press, 2013) 459.

'Grounding Human Rights in Natural Law' (2015) 60 *American Journal of Jurisprudence* 199.

'Towards Vatican II's Centenary: Your Next Fifty Years' (2016) 14 *Ave Maria Law Review* 1.

Foccroulle Ménard, Xavier, and Anna Su, 'Liberalism, Catholic Integralism, and the Question of Religious Freedom' (2022) 47 *Brigham Young Law Review* 1171.

Foran, Michael, 'Rights, Common Good, and the Separation of Powers' (2023) 86 *Modern Law Review* 599.

'Common Law and the Common Good' in Geneviève Cartier and Mark D Walters, eds, *The Promise of Legality: Critical Reflections on the Work of TRS Allan* (Oxford: Hart Publishing, 2025) 197.

Fraenkel, Ernest, *The Dual State: A Contribution to the Theory of Dictatorship* [1941], 2nd edition (Oxford: Oxford University Press, 2017).

Ganz, John, *When the Clocks Broke: Con Men, Conspiracists, and How America Cracked Up in the Early 1980s* (New York: Farrar, Straus and Giroux, 2024).

Gardner, John, 'The Legality of Law' (2004) 17 *Ratio Juris* 168.

Law as a Leap of Faith (Oxford: Oxford University Press, 2012).

Gearty, Conor, 'Unwelcome Remnant' (2025) 47 *London Review of Books* 11.

Geoghegan, Peter, 'Making Media Great Again' (2025) 47 *London Review of Books* 25.

Glasman, Maurice, *Blue Labour* (Cambridge: Polity, 2022).

Green, Leslie, 'The Nature of Limited Government' in John Keown and Robert P George, eds, *Reason, Morality, and Law: The Philosophy of John Finnis* (Oxford: Oxford University Press, 2013) 186.

Guriev, Serge, and Daniel Treisman, *Spin Doctors: The Changing Face of Tyranny in the 21st Century* (Princeton, NJ: Princeton University Press, 2022).

Hart, HLA, *Law, Liberty and Morality* (London: Oxford University Press, 1963).

'Bentham and the Demystification of the Law' (1973) 36 *Modern Law Review* 2.

'Positivism and the Separation of Law and Morals' in *Essays in Jurisprudence and Philosophy* (Oxford: Clarendon Press, 1983) 49.

The Concept of Law, 2nd edition (Oxford: Clarendon Press, 1994).

Hayek, FA, *Law, Legislation and Liberty* (London: Routledge, 1990), volume I.

Haysom, Nicholas, and Clive Plaskett, 'The War Against Law: Judicial Activism and the Appellate Division' (1988) 4 *South African Journal on Human Rights* 303.

Hazony, Yarom, *The Virtue of Nationalism* (New York: Basic Books, 2018).

Heller, Hermann, *Sovereignty: A Contribution to the Theory of Public and International Law*, David Dyzenhaus, ed; Belinda Cooper, trans (Oxford: Oxford University Press, 2019).

Hobbes, Thomas, *Leviathan* (Cambridge: Cambridge University Press, 2014).

Hollis-Brusky, Amanda, *Ideas with Consequences: The Federalist Society and the Conservative Counterrevolution* (New York: Oxford University Press, 2015).

Hunt, Murray, *Using Human Rights Law in English Courts* (Oxford: Hart Publishing, 1997).

'Sovereignty's Blight: Why Contemporary Public Law Needs the Concept of "Due Deference"' in Nicholas Bamforth and Peter Leyland, eds, *Public Law in a Multi-Layered Constitution* (Oxford: Hart Publishing, 2003) 337.

Kelsen, Hans, *Das Problem der Souveränität und die Theorie des Völkerrechts: Beitrag zu Einer Reinen Rechtslehre* (Aalen: Scientia Verlag, 1981).

Introduction to the Problems of Legal Theory (Oxford: Clarendon Press, 1992).

'Who Ought to Be the Guardian of the Constitution' [1931] in Lars Vinx, ed and trans, *The Guardian of the Constitution: Hans Kelsen and Carl Schmitt on the Limits of Constitutional Law* (Cambridge: Cambridge University Press, 2015) 174.

Kirkby, Coel, 'Abysmal Jurisprudence: On the Genesis of John Finnis's Practical Guide to Statesmen' (2024) 74 *University of Toronto Law Journal* 119.

Kostal, RW, *A Jurisprudence of Power: Victorian Empire and the Rule of Law* (Oxford: Oxford University Press, 2005).

Krastev, Ivan, and Stephen Holmes, *The Light That Failed: Why the West Is Losing the Fight for Democracy* (New York: Pegasus Books, 2019).

Krygier, Martin, 'Well-Tempered Power: "A Cultural Achievement of Universal Significance"' (2024) 16 *Hague Journal on the Rule of Law* 479.

Lacey, Nicola, 'Patrick Devlin, "The Enforcement of Morals (1965)"' in Chloë Kennedy and Lindsay Farmer, eds, *Leading Works in Criminal Law* (London: Routledge, 2024) 82.

Lanchester, John, *Capital* (London: Faber and Faber, 2011).

Landau, David, 'Abusive Constitutionalism' (2013) 47 *UC Davis Law Review* 189.

Langford, Ian, 'Fair Trial: The History of an Idea' (2009) 8 *Journal of Human Rights* 37.

Lauterpacht, Hersch, 'Is International Law a Part of the Law of England?' in Elihu Lauterpacht, ed, *Hersch Lauterpacht International Law: Collected Papers: The Law of Peace, Part 1, International Law in General* (Cambridge: Cambridge University Press, 2009) volume 2, 537.

Legutko, Ryszard, *The Demon in Democracy: Totalitarian Temptations in Free Societies* (New York: Encounter Books: 2016).

Levin, Yuval, *American Covenant: How the Constitution Unified Our Nation – And Could Again* (New York: Basic Books, 2024).

Levitsky, Steven, and Lucan Way, *Competitive Authoritarianism: Hybrid Regimes after the Cold War* (Cambridge: Cambridge University Press, 2012).

'The New Competitive Authoritarianism' (2020) 31 *Journal of Democracy* 51.

Lewis, Geoffrey, *Lord Atkin* (London: Butterworths, 1983).

Litman, Leah, *Lawless: How the Supreme Court Runs on Conservative Grievance, Fringe Theories, and Bad Vibes* (New York: Atria, 2025).

Loughlin, Martin, *The British Constitution: A Very Short Introduction* (Oxford: Oxford University Press, 2013).

Against Constitutionalism (Cambridge, MA: Harvard University Press, 2022).

Lyall, Andrew, *Granville Sharp's Cases on Slavery* (Oxford: Hart Publishing, 2017).

Lynn, Ann, *Constitutional History of the UK* (Abingdon: Routledge, 2016) at 494.

MacIntyre, Alasdair, *After Virtue: A Study in Moral Theory*, 3rd edition (Notre Dame, IN: Notre Dame University Press, 2007).

Mackie, JL, 'Evil and Omnipotence' (1955) 64 *Mind* 200.

Macklin, Audrey, 'Borderline Security' in Kent Roach, Ron Daniels, and Patrick Macklem, eds, *The Security of Freedom: Essays on Canada's Anti-Terrorism Bill* (Toronto: University of Toronto Press, 2001) 383.

Mark, Daniel, *The Nature of Law: Authority, Obligation, and the Common Good* (Notre Dame, IN: Notre Dame University Press, 2024).

McCall, Brian, *Building the City of God: Living as Catholics in a Secular Age* (New York: Angelico Press, 2014).

The Architecture of Law: Rebuilding Law in the Critical Tradition (Notre Dame, IN: University of Notre Dame Press, 2018).

'What Good Is John Finnis? Assessing the Personal and Common Good in *Natural Law and Natural Rights*' (2020) 83 *Persona y Derecho* 637.

Mehring, Reinhard, 'A "Catholic Layman of German Nationality and Citizenship"? Carl Schmitt and the Religiosity of Life' in Jens Meirhenrich and Oliver Simons, eds, *The Oxford Handbook of Carl Schmitt* (Oxford: Oxford University Press, 2014) 73.

Mill, John Stuart, *On Liberty*, in Mill, *Collected Works*, JM Robson, ed (Toronto: University of Toronto Press, 1977), volume 18.

Morris, Douglas G, 'The Dual State Reframed: Ernst Fraenkel's Political Clients and His Theory of the Nazi Legal System' (2013) 58 *Leo Baeck Institute Year Book* 5.

Legal Sabotage: Ernst Fraenkel in Hitler's Germany (Cambridge: Cambridge University Press, 2020).

Müller, Jan-Werner, *A Dangerous Mind: Carl Schmitt in Post-War European Thought* (New Haven, CT: Yale University Press, 2003).

Constitutional Patriotism (Princeton, NJ: Princeton University Press, 2007).

'"Common Good Constitutionalism": Rule of Law, Rule by Law, or Something Else Entirely?' (2025) 87 *Law and Contemporary Problems* 47.

Norman, Jesse, *The Winding Stair* (London: Biteback Publishing, 2023).

Oakes, James, *Freedom National: The Destruction of Slavery in the United States, 1861–1865* (New York: WW Norton & Company, 2014).

Pabst, Adrian, *The Demons of Liberal Democracy* (Cambridge: Polity, 2019).

Postliberal Politics (Cambridge: Polity, 2021).

Palley, Claire, *The Constitutional History and Law of Southern Rhodesia, 1888–1965* (Oxford: Clarendon Press, 1966).

Pink, Thomas, 'The Right to Religious Liberty and the Coercion of Belief: A Note on *Dignitatis Humanae*' in John Keown and Robert P George, eds, *Reason, Morality, and Law: The Philosophy of John Finnis* (Oxford: Oxford University Press, 2013) 427.

Postema, Gerald, *Law's Rule: The Nature, Value, and Viability of the Rule of Law* (New York: Oxford University Press, 2022).

Raz, Joseph, 'The Rule of Law and Its Virtue' in *The Authority of Law: Essays on Law and Morality* (Oxford: Clarendon Press, 1983) 210.

'Authority, Law, and Morality' in *Ethics in the Public Domain: Essays in the Morality of Law and Politics* (Oxford: Oxford University Press, 1994) 194.

'Value: A Menu of Questions' in John Keown and Robert P George, eds, *Reason, Morality, and Law: The Philosophy of John Finnis* (Oxford: Oxford University Press, 2013) 13.

'The Law's Own Virtue' (2019) 39 *Oxford Journal of Legal Studies* 1.

Rees, Daffyd Huw, 'Constitutional Patriotism' in Amy Allen and Eduardo Mendiata, eds, *The Cambridge Habermas Lexicon* (Cambridge: Cambridge University Press, 2019) 66.

Sajó, András, 'Militant Rule of Law and Not-so-Bad Law' (2024) 16 *Hague Journal on the Rule of Law* 525.

Schepple, Kim Lane, 'Autocratic Legalism' (2018) 85 *University of Chicago Law Review* 545.

Schmitt, Carl, 'Der Führer Schutzt das Recht' in *Positionen und Begriffe in Kampf mit Weimar, Genf, Versailles* (Berlin: Duncker & Humblot, 1988) 199.

On the Three Types of Juristic Thought (Westport, CT: Praeger, 2004).

Political Theology: Four Chapters on the Concept of Sovereignty (Chicago: University of Chicago Press, 2005).

Constitutional Theory (Durham, NC: Duke University Press, 2008).

Dictatorship: From the Origin of the Modern Concept of Sovereignty to Proletarian Class Struggle (Cambridge: Polity, 2014).

'The Guardian of the Constitution' in Lars Vinx, ed and trans, *The Guardian of the Constitution: Hans Kelsen and Carl Schmitt on the Limits of Constitutional Law* (Cambridge: Cambridge University Press, 2015) 79.

'The Guardian of the Constitution: Schmitt on Pluralism and the President as the Guardian of the Constitution' in Lars Vinx, ed and trans, *The Guardian of the Constitution: Hans Kelsen and Carl Schmitt on the Limits of Constitutional Law* (Cambridge: Cambridge University Press, 2015) 125.

Schwartzman, Micah, and Jocelyn Wilson, 'The Unreasonableness of Catholic Integralism' (2019) 56 *San Diego Law Review* 1039.

Seymour, Richard, *Disaster Nationalism: The Downfall of Liberal Civilization* (London: Verso, 2025).

Simpson, AW Brian, *Human Rights and the End of Empire: Britain and the Genesis of the European Convention* (Oxford: Oxford University Press, 2010).

Sleat, Matt, *Post-Liberalism* (Cambridge: Polity, 2026).

Slobodian, Quinn, *Hayek's Bastards: Race, Gold, IQ, and the Capitalism of the Far Right* (New York: Zone Books, 2025).

Stephen, Leslie, *The Science of Ethics* (London: Smith, Elder, & Co, 1882) 142.

Stevenson, Charles Leslie, 'Persuasive Definitions' (1938) 47 *Mind* 331.

Steyn, Johan, 'Guantanamo Bay: The Legal Black Hole' (2004) 53 *International and Comparative Law Quarterly* 1.

Stolleis, Michael, *A History of Public Law in Germany: 1914–1945* (Oxford: Oxford University Press, 2004).

Strauss, Leo, 'Comments on Carl Schmitt's *Der Begriff des Politischen*' reproduced in Carl Schmitt, *The Concept of the Political* (New Brunswick, NJ: Rutgers University Press, 1976) 81.

Taggart, Michael, 'Prolegomenon to an Intellectual History of Administrative Law in the Twentieth Century: The Case of John Willis and Canadian Administrative Law' (2005) 43 *Osgoode Hall Law Journal* 257.

Tannenhaus, Sam, *Buckley: The Life and the Revolution That Changed America* (New York: Random House, 2025).

Templeman, Lord Sydney William, 'Treaty-Making and the British Parliament' (1991) 67 *Chicago-Kent Law Review* 459.

Tuck, Richard, *The Left Case for Brexit: Reflections on the Current Crisis* (Cambridge: Polity, 2020).

Vallier, Kevin, *All the Kingdoms of the World – On Radical Religious Alternatives to Liberalism* (New York: Oxford University Press, 2023).

Vermeule, Adrian, *Common Good Constitutionalism* (Cambridge: Polity, 2022).

Voegelin, Eric, *The New Science of Politics* (Chicago: University of Chicago Press, 1952).

'The Oxford Political Philosophers' (1953) 3 *Philosophical Quarterly* 97.

Order and History, volume 3, *Plato and Aristotle* (Baton Rouge: Louisiana State University Press, 1957).

The Authoritarian State: An Essay on the Problem of the Austrian State [1936] (Columbia: University of Missouri Press, 1989), volume 4 of *Collected Works*.

The Nature of Law and Related Legal Writings in *The Collected Works of Eric Voegelin* (Baton Rouge: Louisiana State University Press, 1991).

Autobiographical Reflections (Columbia: University of Missouri Press, 2011).

Waldron, Jeremy, 'How Law Protects Dignity' (2012) 71 *Cambridge Law Journal J* 200.

'What Is Natural Law Like?' in John Keown and Robert P George, eds, *Reason, Morality, and Law: The Philosophy of John Finnis* (Oxford: Oxford University Press, 2013) 73.

Wallington, Peter, 'Sovereignty Regained' (1974) 37 *Modern Law Review* 686.

Walters, Mark, 'The Unwritten Constitution as a Legal Concept' in David Dyzenhaus and Malcolm Thorburn, eds, *Philosophical Foundations of Constitutional Law* (Oxford: Oxford University Press, 2016) 33.

AV Dicey and the Common Law Constitutional Tradition: 'A Legal Turn of Mind' (Cambridge: Cambridge University Press, 2020).

Wasserman, Janek, *Black Vienna: The Radical Right in the Red City, 1918–1938* (New York: Cornell University Press, 2014).

Watson, Alan, *Roman Slave Law* (Baltimore: Johns Hopkins University Press, 1987).

Wieseltier, Leon, 'Christianism' (2022) 2 *Liberties* 326.

Web Sources

'A Conference in Washington, DC' online: *National Conservatism* <https://nationalconservatism.org/natcon-4-2024/>.

'About the Copernican Academy' online: *Copernican Academy* <https://akademiakopernikanska.gov.pl/o-akademii/>.

'About the Judicial Power Project' online: *Policy Exchange* <https://judicialpowerproject.org.uk/about/>.

'About Us' online: *Matrix Chambers* <www.matrixlaw.co.uk/about-us/>.

'About Us' online: *Voegelin View* <https://voegelinview.com/about-us/>.

'Act of Union 1707' online: *UK Parliament* <www.parliament.uk/about/living-heritage/evolutionofparliament/legislativescrutiny/act-of-union-1707/>.

Adams, Thomas, 'The Politics of Judicial Power' (Nov 11 2015) online: *UK Constitutional Law Blog* <https://ukconstitutionallaw.org/2015/11/11/thomas-adams-the-politics-of-judicial-power/>.

'Agreement between the Government of the United Kingdom and Great Britain and Northern Ireland and the Government of the Republic of Rwanda for the Provision of an Asylum Partnership to Strengthen Shared International Commitments on the Protection of Refugees and Immigrants' (Apr 30 2024) online: *Gov.UK* <www.gov.uk/government/publications/ukrwanda-agreement-for-the-provision-of-an-asylum-partnership-to-strengthen-shared-international-commitments-on-the-protection-of-refugees-and-migra>.

'Albert Venn Dicey' (Jul 20 1998) online: *Encyclopedia Britannica* <www.britannica.com/biography/Albert-Venn-Dicey>.

Andenas, Mads, and Eirik Bjorge, 'Carl Schmitt, International Law, and Constitutional Tradition in the United Kingdom' (Aug 6 2025) online: *Voelkerrechts* <https://voelkerrechtsblog.org/carl-schmitt-international-law-and-constitutional-tradition-in-the-united-kingdom/>.

Aronson, Cole S, 'The Integralists and Us' (Fall 2023) online: *Jewish Review of Books* <https://jewishreviewofbooks.com/philosophy/14786/the-integralists-and-us/#>.

'Attorney General' online: *Gov.UK* <www.gov.uk/government/ministers/attorney-general>.

'Attorney General's Legal Risk Guidance' (Nov 6 2024) online: *Gov.UK* <https://assets.publishing.service.gov.uk/media/672b7189abb279b2de1e8c59/AG_s_Legal_Risk_Guidance_2024.pdf>.

Badenoch, Kemi, 'Speech to the IDU in Washington' (Dec 9 2024) online: *Conservatives* <www.conservatives.com/news/kemis-idu-washington-speech>.

Bannon, Alicia, 'Supreme Court Must Explain Why It Keeps Ruling in Trump's Favor' (Aug 14 2025) online: *Brennan Center for Justice* <www.brennancenter.org/our-work/analysis-opinion/supreme-court-must-explain-why-it-keeps-ruling-trumps-favor>.

Blakely, Jason, 'The Integralism of Adrian Vermeule: Not Catholic Enough' (Oct 5 2020) online: *Commonweal* <www.commonwealmagazine.org/not-catholic-enough>.

Bradner, Eric, 'Conway: Trump White House Offered "Alternative Facts" on Crowd Size' (Jan 23 2017) online: *CNN* <https://edition.cnn.com/2017/01/22/politics/kellyanne-conway-alternative-facts>.

Browning, Christopher, 'Hitler's Enablers' (Nov 7 2024) online: *New York Review of Books* <www.nybooks.com/articles/2024/11/07/hitlers-enablers-the-death-of-democracy-benjamin-carter-hett/>.

Caird, J, R Hazell, and D Oliver, 'The Constitutional Standards of the House of Lords Select Committee on the Constitution' (London: The Constitution Unit, 2015) online: <www.ucl.ac.uk/constitution-unit/sites/constitution-unit/files/constitutional-standards-third-edition.pdf>.

Cameron, Chris, 'Trump Defends Tucker Carlson after Nick Fuentes Interview' (Nov 16, 2025) online: *New York Times* <www.nytimes.com/2025/11/16/us/politics/trump-tucker-carlson-nick-fuentes.html>.

Cameron-Chileshe, Jasmine, William Wallis, and Delphine Strauss, 'Sunak Attacks "Lefty Lawyers" amid Criticism of Small Boats Strategy' (Mar 8 2023) online: *Financial Times* <www.ft.com/content/246232b7-2f83-4698-a2bd-368e396913fe>.

'Canterbury Institute' online: *Canterbury Institute* <www.canterbury.institute/>.

Casey, Conor, and Yuan Yi Zhu, 'From the Rule of Law to the Rule of Lawyers? The Problem with the Attorney General's New Legal Risk Guidelines' (Nov 26 2024) online: *Policy Exchange* <https://policyexchange.org.uk/wp-content/uploads/From-the-Rule-of-Law-to-the-Rule-of-Lawyers.pdf>.

'Revisiting the British Origins of the European Convention on Human Rights' (May 20 2025) online: *Policy Exchange* <https://policyexchange.org.uk/publication/revisiting-the-british-origins-of-the-european-convention-on-human-rights/>.

'Constitution Committee' online: *UK Parliament* <https://committees.parliament.uk/committee/172/constitution-committee/>.

Courea, Eleni, 'Labour Peer Calls for "Arrogant" Attorney General to Be Sacked' (Feb 10 2025) online: *The Guardian* <www.theguardian.com/politics/2025/feb/10/labour-peer-maurice-glasman-attorney-general-richard-hermer-sacked-labour>.

'Deeply Unfair: How Attorney General Became a Lightning Rod for Criticism of Starmer' (Feb 13 2025) online: *The Guardian* <www.theguardian.com/politics/2025/feb/13/attorney-general-richard-hermer-lightning-rod-for-criticism-of-starmer>.

Donald, Alice, and Joelle Grogan, 'Explainer: The European Convention on Human Rights' (Jun 24 2022) online: *The UK in a Changing Europe* <https://ukandeu.ac.uk/explainers/the-european-convention-on-human-rights/>.

'Defeat in the Supreme Court' (Nov 17 2023) online: *Verfassungsblog* <https://verfassungsblog.de/defeat-in-the-supreme-court/>.

Downer, A, 'Foreword' in Richard Ekins, Stephen Laws, and Conor Casey, 'Safety of Rwanda (Asylum and Migration) Bill' (Dec 11 2023) online: *Policy Exchange* <https://policyexchange.org.uk/publication/safety-of-rwanda-asylum-and-migration-bill/>.

'Dr Conor Casey' online: *The University of Surrey* <www.surrey.ac.uk/people/conor-casey>.

Duignan, Brian, 'Replacement Theory' (Aug 23 2025) online: *Encyclopedia Britannica* <www.britannica.com/topic/replacement-theory>.

Dyzenhaus, David, 'Lawyer for the Strongman' (Jun 12 2020) online: *Aeon* <https://aeon.co/essays/carl-schmitts-legal-theory-legitimises-the-rule-of-the-strongman>.

'The Snake Charmers' (Mar 7 2022) online: *Verfassungsblog* <https://verfassungsblog.de/os5-snake-charmers/>.

'Schmitten in the USA' (Apr 20 2022) online: *Verfassungsblog* <https://verfassungsblog.de/schmitten-in-the-usa/>.

'Democracy or Apocalypse' (Sep 20 2022) online: *Aeon* <https://aeon.co/essays/eric-voegelin-hans-kelsen-and-the-debate-over-nazism>.

'Written Evidence (ROL0045)' (Apr 20 2025) online: *UK Parliament* <https://committees.parliament.uk/writtenevidence/140668/pdf/>.

Eddy, Melissa, '"Mother" of All Problems? Immigration Remark Reignites German Debate' (Sep 6 2018) online: *New York Times* <www.nytimes.com/2018/09/06/world/europe/immigration-germany-merkel.html>.

Ekins, Richard, 'Do Our Supreme Court judges Have too much Power?' (May 14 2019) online: *The Spectator* <www.spectator.co.uk/article/do-our-supreme-court-judges-have-too-much-power->.

'Protecting the Constitution: How and Why Parliament Should Limit Judicial Power' (Dec 28 2019) online: *Policy Exchange* <https://policyexchange.org.uk/wp-content/uploads/2020/01/Protecting-the-Constitution.pdf>.

'Rule 39 and the Rule of Law' (May 17 2023) online: *Policy Exchange* <https://policyexchange.org.uk/wp-content/uploads/Rule-39-and-the-Rule-of-Law.pdf>.

'Human Rights and the Rule of Law' (Apr 17 2024) online: *Policy Exchange* <https://policyexchange.org.uk/wp-content/uploads/Human-Rights-and-the-Rule-of-Law.pdf>.

'Lord Hermer Is Preposterously Wrong About International Law' (May 30 2025) online: *The Spectator* <www.spectator.co.uk/article/lord-hermer-is-preposterously-wrong-about-international-law/>.

Ekins, Richard, and Sir Stephen Laws, 'The Future of Human Rights Reform' (Oct 1 2025) online: *Policy Exchange* <https://policyexchange.org.uk/wp-content/uploads/The-Future-of-Human-Rights-Law-Reform_.pdf>.

Ekins, Richard, and Guglielmo Verdirame, 'The Ministerial Code and the Rule of Law' (Nov 6 2015) online: *UK Constitutional Law Blog* <https://ukconstitutionallaw.org/2015/11/06/richard-ekins-and-guglielmo-verdirame-the-ministerial-code-and-the-rule-of-law/>.

Ekins, Richard, Stephen Laws, and Conor Casey, 'Government Lawyers, the Civil Service Code, and the Rule of Law' (Dec 6 2023) online: *Policy Exchange* <https://policyexchange.org.uk/publication/government-lawyers-the-civil-service-code-and-the-rule-of-law/>.

Ekins, Richard, Stephen Laws, and Conor Casey, 'Safety of Rwanda (Asylum and Migration) Bill' (Dec 11 2023) online: *Policy Exchange* <https://policyexchange.org.uk/publication/safety-of-rwanda-asylum-and-migration-bill/>.

'The Impact of the Human Rights Act 1998 in Twenty Five Cases' (Nov 11 2024) online: *Policy Exchange* <https://policyexchange.org.uk/wp-content/uploads/The-Impact-of-the-Human-Rights-Act-1998.pdf>.

Elliott, Mark, 'Utterly Risible' (Sep 10 2020) online: *X* <https://twitter.com/profmarkelliott/status/1304076133827309569>.

'Could the Supreme Court Reject the Rwanda Bill as Unconstitutional?' (Dec 11 2023) online: *Public Law for Everyone* <https://publiclawforeveryone.com/2023/12/11/could-the-supreme-court-reject-the-rwanda-bill-as-unconstitutional>.

English, Rosalind, 'The UK Can, and Should, Leave the Human Rights Convention: Shadow AG's Advice Underlines Conservative Party's Policy' (Oct 7 2025) online: *UK Human Rights Blog* <https://ukhumanrightsblog.com/2025/10/07/the-uk-can-leave-the-human-rights-convention-shadow-ags-advice-underlines-conservative-partys-policy/>.

Fahrenthold, David A, 'Heritage Foundation Board Member Resigns Over Video Defending Carlson' (Nov 17 2025) online: *New York Times* <www.nytimes.com/2025/11/17/us/politics/heritage-foundation-tucker-carlson-nick-fuentes.html>.

Falconer, Charles, 'Lefty Lawyers, "Enemies of the People": How Upholding the Law Is a Crime in Some Eyes' (Aug 12 2023) online: *The Guardian* <www.theguardian.com/commentisfree/2023/aug/12/lefty-lawyers-enemies-of-people-upholding-law-a-crime>.

Fasel, Raffael, 'Ouster Clauses and the Silent Constitutional Crisis' (Feb 20 2024) online: *UK Constitutional Law Blog* <https://ukconstitutionallaw.org/2024/02/20/raffael-n-fasel-ouster-clauses-and-the-silent-constitutional-crisis/>.

Finnis, John, 'Judicial Power: Past, Present and Future' (Oct 21 2015) online: *Policy Exchange* <https://policyexchange.org.uk/blogs/john-finnis-judicial-power-past-present-and-future/>.

'Ministers, International Law, and the Rule of Law' (Nov 2 2015) online: *Judicial Power Project* <https://judicialpowerproject.org.uk/ministers-international-law-and-the-rule-of-law/>.

'*Brexit* and the Balance of Our Constitution' in *Judicial Power and the Balance of Our Constitution: Two Lectures by John Finnis* (London: Policy Exchange, 2018) online: <https://judicialpowerproject.org.uk/wp-content/uploads/2018/01/Judicial-Power-and-the-Balance-of-Our-Constitution.pdf>.

'Only One Option Remains with Brexit: Prorogue Parliament and Allow Us Out of the EU with No-Deal' (Apr 1 2019) online: *The Telegraph* <www.telegraph.co.uk/politics/2019/04/01/one-option-remains-brexit-prorogue-parliament-allow-us-eu/>.

'Joseph Raz 21 March 1939–2 May 2022' (Apr 10 2025) online: *The British Academy* <www.thebritishacademy.ac.uk/publishing/memoirs/22/raz-joseph-1939-2022/> 308.

Finnis, John, and Robert P George, 'An Enhanced Amicus Brief in Dobbs' (Nov 3 2021) online: *SSRN* <https://papers.ssrn.com/sol3/papers.cfm?abstract_id=3955231>.

Francis, Pope, 'Letter of the Holy Father Francis to the Bishops of the United States of America' (Feb 10 2025) online: *Vatican* <www.vatican.va/content/francesco/en/letters/2025/documents/20250210-lettera-vescovi-usa.html>.

Gardner, John, 'How to Be a Good judge' (Jul 8 2010) online: *London Review of Books* <www.lrb.co.uk/the-paper/v32/n13/john-gardner/how-to-be-a-good-judge>.

Gower, Melanie, Patrick Butchard, and CJ McKinney, 'Research Briefing: The UK–Rwanda Migration and Economic Development Partnership' (May 29 2024) online: *House of Commons Library* <https://commonslibrary.parliament.uk/research-briefings/cbp-9568/>.

Grieve, Dominic, 'Rewriting of History by Putin and Trump' (Feb 20 2025) online: *The Times* <www.thetimes.com/comment/letters-to-editor/article/the-times-letters-rewriting-of-history-by-trump-and-putin-3msvhktgm>.

Gutteridge, Nick, 'Attorney General's Speeches Provide Clues as to Why Starmer Has Capitulated to International Law' (Jan 18 2025) online: *The Telegraph* <www.telegraph.co.uk/politics/2025/01/18/attorney-general-speeches-keir-starmer-international-law/>.

Halliday, Josh, 'Ministerial Code: No 10 "Showing Contempt for International Law"' (Oct 25 2015) online: *The Guardian* <www.theguardian.com/law/2015/oct/26/ministerial-code-no-10-showing-contempt-for-international-law>.

Hawley, Joshua, 'A Christian Vision for Kingdom Politics: Immanentize the Eschaton!' (Oct 26 2023) online: *Patheos* <www.patheos.com/blogs/philosophicalfragments/2012/10/26/christian-vision-for-kingdom-politics/>.

Hermer, Richard, 'The Rule of Law in an Age of Populism' (Oct 14 2024) online: *Bingham Centre for the Rule of Law* <www.biicl.org/documents/12532_bingham_lecture_2024.pdf>.

'Attorney General's 2024 Bingham Lecture on the Rule of Law' (Oct 15 2024) online: *UK.Gov* <www.gov.uk/government/speeches/attorney-generals-2024-bingham-lecture-on-the-rule-of-law>.

'Attorney General's 2025 RUSI Annual Security Lecture' (May 29 2025) online: *UK.Gov* <www.gov.uk/government/speeches/attorney-generals-2025-rusi-annual-security-lecture>.

Hille, Peter, 'German "Remigration" Debate Fuels Push to Ban Far-Right AfD' (Jan 12 2024) online: *Deutsche Welle* <www.dw.com/en/german-remigration-debate-fuels-push-to-ban-far-right-afd/a-67965896>.

House of Lords, 'Rule of Law: Hansard, Volume 841' (Nov 26 2024) online: *UK Parliament* <https://hansard.parliament.uk/lords/2024-11-26/debates/D5A3DAF2-1DF8-46CC-BA01-A23FD6A59095/RuleOfLaw>.

House of Lords Constitution Committee, 'Rule of Law: Holding the Line Between Anarchy and Tyranny' (Nov 20 2025) online: *UK Parliament* <https://committees.parliament.uk/committee/172/constitution-committee/news/210496/rule-of-law-holding-the-line-between-anarchy-and-tyranny/>.

House of Lords Select Committee on the Constitution, 'Safety of Rwanda (Asylum and Immigration) Bill' (Feb 9 2024) online: *UK Parliament*

<https://committees.parliament.uk/publications/43291/documents/215532/default/>

'Human Rights (Joint Committee)' online: *UK Parliament* <https://committees.parliament.uk/committee/93/human-rights-joint-committee/>.

Hunt, Murray, 'Clause 54 of the Illegal Migration Bill: A Rule of Law Analysis for House of Lords Report Stage' (Jul 23 2023) online: *Bingham Centre* <https://binghamcentre.biicl.org/publications/clause-54-of-the-illegal-migration-bill-a-rule-of-law-analysis-for-house-of-lords-report-stage>

'Safety of Rwanda (Asylum and Immigration) Bill: A Preliminary Rule of Law Analysis for House of Commons Second Reading' (Dec 11 2023) online: *Bingham Centre for the Rule of Law* <https://binghamcentre.biicl.org/publications/safety-of-rwanda-asylum-and-immigration-bill-a-preliminary-rule-of-law-analysis-for-house-of-commons-second-reading>.

'Inaugural Grotius Prize Presented to Hon Scott Morrisson MP' (Nov 20 2023) online: *Policy Exchange* <https://policyexchange.org.uk/events/inaugural-grotius-prize-presented-to-hon-scott-morrison-mp/>.

'Iraq Inquiry Publishes Advice to Blair on War' (Jun 30 2010) online: *BBC* <www.bbc.com/news/10463844>.

Jenrick, Robert, 'Ending Judicial Activism' (Oct 7 2025) online: <www.conservatives.com/news/ending-judicial-activism>.

Joint Committee on Human Rights, 'Legislative Scrutiny: Illegal Migration Bill' (Jun 11 2023) online: *UK Parliament* <https://publications.parliament.uk/pa/jt5803/jtselect/jtrights/1241/report.html>.

'Judicial Power Project' online: *Judicial Power Project* <https://judicialpowerproject.org.uk/>.

'Kemi Badenoch Exposes the Laws and Treaties Holding Britain Back' (Jun 6 2025) online: *Conservatives* <www.conservatives.com/news/kemi-badenoch-exposes-the-laws-and-treaties-holding-britain-back?utm_source=substack&utm_medium=email>.

Kennedy, Maev, 'Tributes to Lord Bingham, "the Greatest Judge of Our Time"' (Sep 12 2010) online: *The Guardian* <www.theguardian.com/law/2010/sep/12/tributes-lord-bingham-judge-dies>.

Kettle, Martin, 'Does Starmer Believe in Anything, People Ask, and Now We Know: His Credo Is the Rule of Law' (Oct 17 2024) online: *The Guardian* <www.theguardian.com/commentisfree/2024/oct/17/keir-starmer-beliefs-attorney-general-rule-of-law>.

Kirkpatrick, David D, 'Robert P George, The Conservative Christian Big Thinker' (Dec 16 2009) online: *New York Times* <www.nytimes.com/2009/12/20/magazine/20george-t.html>.

Lilla, Mark, 'The Tower and the Sewer' (Jun 20 2024) online: *New York Review of Books* <www.nybooks.com/articles/2024/06/20/the-tower-and-the-sewer-why-liberalism-failed-deneen/>.

'Lord Verdirame' online: *Twenty Sussex* <www.twentyessex.com/people/guglielmo-verdirame/>.

Loughlin, Martin, 'Brexit and the English Constitution' (Nov 28 2023) online: *LSE Research Online* <http://eprints.lse.ac.uk/120882/1/Loughlin_Brexit_and_the_British_Constitution.pdf>.

Macdonald, Ken, and Tim Owen, 'Double Jeopardy: The Law and Politics Podcast – Episode 29: Richard Ekins – Judges and Political Power' (May 2 2023) online: *Apple Podcasts* <https://podcasts.apple.com/de/podcast/episode-29-richard-ekins-judges-and-political-power/id1633485236?i=1000611450876&l=en-GB>.

McGreevy, John T, and R Scott Appleby, 'Catholics, Muslims, and the Mosque Controversy' (Aug 27 2010) online: *New York Review of Books* <www.nybooks.com/online/2010/08/27/catholics-muslims-mosque-controversy/>.

Megerian, Chris, Lindsay Whitehurst, and Mark Sherman, 'Roberts Rejects Trump's Call for Impeaching Judge Who Ruled against His Deportation Plans' (Mar 19 2025) online: *AP News* <https://apnews.com/article/donald-trump-federal-judges-impeachment-29da1153a9f82106748098a6606fec39>.

Mitchell, Archie, and Kate Devlin, 'James Cleverly Refuses to Deny He Called Rishi Sunak's Rwanda Scheme "Batshit"' (Nov 16 2023) online: *The Independent* <www.independent.co.uk/news/uk/politics/james-cleverly-rwanda-scheme-batshit-sunak-b2448446.html>.

Müller, Jan-Werner, 'What Did Pope Francis Think of JD Vance? His View Was More Than Clear' (Apr 23 2025) online: *The Guardian* <www.theguardian.com/commentisfree/2025/apr/23/pope-francis-jd-vance-meeting>.

'Caeser Wept' (Dec 4 2025) online: *London Review of Books* <www.lrb.co.uk/the-paper/v47/n22/jan-werner-muller/caesar-wept?utm_campaign=4001961_20251206ICYMI%20-%20subs&utm_medium=email&utm_source=LRB%20email&dm_i=7NIQ,2DRXL,3EIBBA,4QOO2,1>.

Norton-Taylor, Richard, 'Chilcot Inquiry: Iraq Papers Show Lord Goldsmith's Warning to Tony Blair' (Jun 30 2010) online: *The Guardian* <www.theguardian.com/uk/2010/jun/30/chilcot-inquiry-lord-goldsmith-blair>.

Oakes, James, 'The Power of Running Away' (Dec 6 2018) online: *New York Review of Books* <www.nybooks.com/articles/2018/12/06/fugitive-slaves-power-of-running-away/>.

'Our Vision' online: *Bingham Centre for the Rule of Law* <https://binghamcentre.biicl.org/our-vision>.

Pearson, Elaine, 'Seven Years of Suffering for Australia's Asylum Seekers, Refugees' (Jul 16 2020) online: *Human Rights Watch* <www.hrw.org/news/2020/07/16/seven-years-suffering-australias-asylum-seekers-refugees>.

Pells, Rachael, 'Daily Mail's "Enemies of the People" Front Page Receives more than 1,000 Complaints to IPSO' (Nov 10 2016) online: *The Independent*

<www.independent.co.uk/news/media/daily-mail-nazi-propaganda-front-page-ipso-complaints-brexit-eu-enemies-of-the-people-a7409836.html>.

Phipps, Claire, 'British Newspapers React to Judges' Brexit Ruling: "Enemies of the People"' (Nov 4 2016) online: *The Guardian* <www.theguardian.com/politics/2016/nov/04/enemies-of-the-people-british-newspapers-react-judges-brexit-ruling>.

'Policy Exchange' online: *Policy Exchange* <https://policyexchange.org.uk/>.

Poole, Thomas, 'The Executive Power Project' (Apr 2 2019) online: *London Review of Books* <www.lrb.co.uk/blog/2019/april/the-executive-power-project>.

'Press Release: The European Court Grants Urgent Interim Measure in Case Concerning Asylum-Seeker's Imminent Removal from the UK to Rwanda' (Jun 14 2022) online: *European Court of Human Rights* <https://hudoc.echr.coe.int/app/conversion/pdf/?library=ECHR&id=003-7359967-10054452&filename=Interim+measure+granted+in+case+concerning+asylum-seeker%E2%80%99s+imminent+removal+from+the+UK+to+Rwanda.pdf>.

Ramzy, Austin, 'Kept from Australia, Refugee at Nauru Center Sets Himself on Fire' (Apr 27 2016) online: *New York Times* <www.nytimes.com/2016/04/28/world/australia/nauru-iranian-refugee-self-immolation.html>.

'Rule of Law Inquiry Launched by Lords Constitution Committee' (Mar 11 2025) online: *UK Parliament* <https://committees.parliament.uk/committee/172/constitution-committee/news/205702/rule-of-law-inquiry-launched-by-lords-constitution-committee/>.

Sales, Lord Philip, 'Purpose in Law and Interpretation' (Nov 19 2024) online: *UK Supreme Court* <https://supremecourt.uk/speeches/purpose-in-law-and-interpretation>.

Savage, Charlie, and Minho Kim, 'Vance Says "Judges Aren't Allowed to Control" Trump's "Legitimate Power"' (Feb 9 2025) online: *New York Times* <www.nytimes.com/2025/02/09/us/politics/vance-trump-federal-courts-executive-order.html>.

Savage, Michael, 'Goldsmith: Why I Changed My Mind on Iraq' (Jan 28 2010) online: *The Independent* <www.independent.co.uk/news/uk/politics/goldsmith-why-i-changed-my-mind-on-iraq-1881329.html>.

Steerpike, 'Blue Labour Founder Jets Off to Trump Inauguration' (Jan 16 2025) online: *The Spectator* <www.spectator.co.uk/article/blue-labour-founder-jets-off-to-trump-inauguration/>.

Steinbeis, Maximilian, 'Right Wing Crits' (Nov 15 2019) online: *Verfassungsblog* <https://verfassungsblog.de/right-wing-crits/>.

Story, Alex, 'Starmer's Attorney General Stripped the UK of Her Sovereign Rights – and You Didn't Even Notice' (Jan 2 2025) online: *GB News* <www.gbnews.com/opinion/keir-starmer-attorney-general-richard-hermer>.

Taub, Amanda, '"This Is Worse": Trump's Judicial Defiance Veers beyond the Autocrat Playbook' (Mar 20 2025) online: *New York Times* <www.nytimes

.com/2025/03/20/world/europe/trump-courts-defiance-autocrats-playbook.html?searchResultPosition=1>.

'The Frightening Precedents for Trump's "Legal Abyss": The "Dual-State Theory" Explains How Authoritarians Bend the Law to Their Will' (May 3 2024) online: *New York Times* <www.nytimes.com/2025/05/03/world/trump-dual-state.html?searchResultPosition=1>.

Taylor, Diane, 'Lawyers Express Concern Over Ministerial Code Rewrite' (Oct 22 2015) online: *The Guardian* <www.theguardian.com/law/2015/oct/22/lawyers-express-concern-over-ministerial-code-rewrite>.

'The Common Good Project' online: *University of Oxford* <www.law.ox.ac.uk/the-common-good-project/common-good-project>.

'The Grotius Prize – Presented to Giorgia Meloni' (Apr 28 2023) online: *YouTube* <www.youtube.com/watch?v=qdFDhcMtOtY>.

Tidman, Zoe, 'Home Secretary Suella Braverman Blames Protest Disruption on "Tofu-Eating Wokerati"' (Oct 19 2022) online: *Independent* <www.independent.co.uk/news/uk/politics/suella-braverman-just-stop-oil-tofu-b2205903.html>.

Trilling, Daniel, 'Starmer v Starmer: Why Is the Former Human Rights Lawyer so Cautious about Defending Human Rights?' (Jul 29 2025) online: *The Guardian* <www.theguardian.com/politics/2025/jul/29/keir-starmer-labour-party-human-rights-mixed-record-international-law>.

Tucker, Adam, 'The Rwanda Policy, Legal Fictions, and Parliament's Legislative Authority' (Nov 22 2023) online: *UK Constitutional Law Blog* <https://ukconstitutionallaw.org/2023/11/22/adam-tucker-the-rwanda-policy-legal-fictions-and-parliaments-legislative-authority/>.

'UK–Rwanda Treaty: Provision of an Asylum Partnership' (Dec 5 2023) online: *Gov.UK* <www.gov.uk/government/publications/uk-rwanda-treaty-provision-of-an-asylum-partnership/uk-rwanda-treaty-provision-of-an-asylum-partnership-accessible>.

'UK/Rwanda: Agreement for the Provision of an Asylum Partnership to Strengthen Shared International Commitments on the Protection of Refugees and Migrants' (Apr 30 2024) online: *Gov.UK* <https://assets.publishing.service.gov.uk/media/656f51d30f12ef07a53e0295/UK-Rwanda_MEDP_-_English_-_Formatted__5_Dec_23__-_UK_VERSION.pdf>.

Ungoed-Thomas, John and Antony Barnett, 'Revealed: UK Granted Asylum to Rwandan Refugees while Arguing Country Was Safe' (Jan 27 2024) online: *The Guardian* <www.theguardian.com/world/2024/jan/27/revealed-uk-granted-asylum-to-rwandan-refugees-while-arguing-country-was-safe>.

Vermeule, Adrian, 'A Christian Strategy' (Nov 1 2017) online: *First Things* <https://firstthings.com/a-christian-strategy/>.

'According to Truth' (Jul 19 2018) online: *The Josias* <https://thejosias.com/2018/07/19/according-to-truth/>.

'The Head and Body of Leviathan: A Thought Experiment On Executive Power' (Jul 18 2024) online: *The New Digest* <https://thenewdigest.substack.com/p/

the-head-and-body-of-leviathan?r=d9obe&utm_campaign=post&utm_medium=email&triedRedirect=true>.

'Universalism and Nationalism: Thesis and Hypothesis' (Dec 20 2024) online: *SSRN* <https://papers.ssrn.com/sol3/papers.cfm?abstract_id=5059515>.

'Someone Is Defying the Supreme Court, but It Isn't Trump' (Jul 31 2025) onhline: *New York Times* <www.nytimes.com/2025/07/31/opinion/supreme-court-trump-judges-defiance.html>.

Vermeule, Adrian, and Patrick Deneen, 'In Honor of Ryszard Legutko' (Jun 20 2022) online: *Postliberal Order* <www.postliberalorder.com/p/in-honor-of-ryszard-legutko>.

Walker, Peter, 'Badenoch Says Tories Open to Quitting More Treaties to Increase Deportations' (Oct 5 2025) online: *The Guardian* <www.theguardian.com/politics/2025/oct/05/badenoch-says-tories-could-quit-more-treaties-to-increase-deportations>.

Walsh, Daisy, 'What Happened When Israel Sent Its Refugees to Rwanda' (Jun 22 2022) online: *BBC* <www.bbc.com/news/world-61882542>.

Walsh, Peter William, 'Q&A: The UK's Former Policy to Send Asylum Seekers to Rwanda' (Jul 25 2024) online: *Migration Observatory* <https://migrationobservatory.ox.ac.uk/resources/commentaries/qa-the-uks-policy-to-send-asylum-seekers-to-rwanda/>.

Ward, Ian, 'JD Vance Could Lead the Post-Liberal Elite – An Interview with Patrick Deneen' (Jul 18 2024) online: *Politico* <www.politico.com/news/magazine/2024/07/18/jd-vance-world-view-sources-00168984>.

'The Seven Thinkers and Groups That Have Shaped JD Vance's Unusual Worldview' (Jul 18 2024) online: *Politico* <www.politico.com/news/magazine/2024/07/18/jd-vance-world-view-sources-00168984>.

'Welcome to the Carl Schmitt Gesellschaft e.V.' online: *Carl-Schmitt Gesellschaft e. V.* <www.carl-schmitt.de/en/>.

'What Is the Josias' online: *The Josias* <https://thejosias.com/about/>.

Wolfson, Lord David, 'Foreword' to Richard Ekins, 'Human Rights and the Rule of Law' (Apr 17 2024) online: *Policy Exchange* <https://policyexchange.org.uk/wp-content/uploads/Human-Rights-and-the-Rule-of-Law.pdf>.

'The Rule of Law: At Home, Abroad – and in Westminster' (Mar 25 2025) online: *Policy Exchange* <https://policyexchange.org.uk/events/the-rule-of-law-at-home-abroad-and-in-westminster/>.

Wright, Jeremy, 'The Importance of International Law for Government Lawyers' (Oct 15 2015) online: *Gov.UK* <www.gov.uk/government/speeches/the-importance-of-international-law-for-government-lawyers>.

Younge, Gary, 'Scapegoating the Immigrant' (Oct 17 2024) online: *New York Review of Books* <www.nybooks.com/articles/2024/10/17/scapegoating-the-immigrant-gary-younge/>.

INDEX

For EU product safety concerns, contact us at Calle de José Abascal, 56–1°, 28003 Madrid, Spain or eugpsr@cambridge.org.

www.ingramcontent.com/pod-product-compliance
Lightning Source LLC
LaVergne TN
LVHW011810200926
848484LV00005B/1129
* 9 7 8 1 0 0 9 8 6 4 4 7 3 *